The Mammoth Book of

Life Before
the Mast

Also available

The Mammoth Book of Ancient Wisdom
The Mammoth Book of Armchair Detectives & Screen Crimes
The Mammoth Book of Arthurian Legends
The Mammoth Book of Battles
The Mammoth Book of Best New Horror 11
The Mammoth Book of Best New Science Fiction 13
The Mammoth Book of Bridge
The Mammoth Book of British Kings & Queens
The Mammoth Book of Cats
The Mammoth Book of Chess
The Mammoth Book of Comic Fantasy
The Mammoth Book of Dogs
The Mammoth Book of Erotica
The Mammoth Book of Gay Erotica
The Mammoth Book of Heroic and Outrageous Women
The Mammoth Book of Historical Detectives
The Mammoth Book of Historical Erotica
The Mammoth Book of Historical Whodunnits
The Mammoth Book of How It Happened
The Mammoth Book of International Erotica
The Mammoth Book of Jack the Ripper
The Mammoth Book of Lesbian Erotica
The Mammoth Book of Lesbian Short Stories
The Mammoth Book of Men O'War
The Mammoth Book of Mindbending Puzzles
The Mammoth Book of Murder
The Mammoth Book of New Erotica
The Mammoth Book of New Sherlock Holmes Adventures
The Mammoth Book of Nostradamus and Other Prophets
The Mammoth Book of Oddballs and Eccentrics
The Mammoth Book of Private Lives
The Mammoth Book of Seriously Comic Fantasy
The Mammoth Book of Short Erotic Novels
The Mammoth Book of Sports & Games
The Mammoth Book of Sword & Honour
The Mammoth Book of Tasteless Lists
The Mammoth Book of the Third Reich at War
The Mammoth Book of True War Stories
The Mammoth Book of 20th Century Ghost Stories
The Mammoth Book of Unsolved Crimes
The Mammoth Book of War Diaries and Letters
The Mammoth Book of the Western
The Mammoth Book of the World's Greatest Chess Games

THE MAMMOTH BOOK OF

Life Before the Mast

An Anthology of Eye-Witness
Accounts from the Age of Fighting Sail

EDITED BY JON E. LEWIS

ROBINSON
London

Constable & Robinson Ltd
3 The Lanchesters
162 Fulham Palace Road
London W6 9ER
www.constablerobinson.com

First published in the UK by Robinson,
an imprint of Constable & Robinson Ltd 2001

A copy of the British Library Cataloguing in
Publication Data is available from the British Library.

ISBN 1–84119–175–2

Printed and bound in the EU

10 9 8 7 6 5 4 3 2

For my father, who also went down to the sea.
And, of course, for Penny, Freda and Tristram.

"Now, boys, pour it into them!"
Captain Isaac Hull

"We have only one great object in view,
that of annihilating our enemies . . ."
Admiral Lord Nelson

Contents

Introduction

"England expects that every man will do his duty".

So did Nelson famously signal his forces before the epochal naval battle of Trafalgar, October 21, 1805. Simultaneously a sure-fire igniter of patriotism, the message also contained a steely undercurrent of sea-war ruthlessness, caught in the words "every" and "duty". This Nelsonian combination of deft psychological touch and daring commitment to total war was almost unique in the later 18th and early 19th centuries, with an obvious exception – Napoleon Bonaparte. It is not too fanciful to see Horatio Nelson as the Napoleon of the ocean blue, and only too easy to see why the Nelsonian era of fighting sail grips the imagination of anybody even remotely touched by an interest in history or the sea.

Before the Mast presents a broadside of eye-witness accounts of naval warfare from the French Revolutionary War (1793–1802), the Napoleonic War (1803–1815) and the War of 1812 (1812–1815). Nelson himself is here of course, writing on the Nile campaign, but in general the voices heard are those of the lesser-known, junior officers and "tars" in the smokey, roaring thick of the action from the "Glorious First of June", 1794, through to the exploits of the USS *Hornet* in 1815. Many decisive engagements are "eye-witnessed", yet the purpose of the book is not a history in first-hand accounts of naval warfare in Nelson's time, more to paint a vivid but real picture of life in the "wooden world" in time of war, trawled from memoirs, journals, ship's logs and personal letters. It is perhaps curious that this said "true naval life" – beset by death, disease, brutal punishment, impressment, tempests (all of which feature large in the following pages) – could also be more romantic and full of derring-do than even fiction-master C.S. Forester could conjure, the exemplar being Thomas Cochrane and his dashing exploits on the sloop *Speedy*. For tragedy, meanwhile, few naval novelists would dare to pen as strange a tale as that of John Brown and his fellow deserters who, adrift on the high sea, turned cannibal. James Gardner's narrative of life as a midshipman is to be counted as one of the most colourful naval recollections ever committed to paper.

If the men of the British Royal Navy dominate the following pages, this is pardonable, for the years 1793 through 1815 were after all, when Nelson and Britannia ruled the waves, when the French and Spanish pretensions to naval mastery were scuppered for ever and the USA merely the newcomer on the watery block.

Much of the Royal Navy's mastery of the seas was, of course, due to Nelson's inspired leadership and tactics, but there were other and deeper causes too.

The Royal Naval had drastically bettered its fighting capability after the Revolutionary War against America, improving everything from signalling to the men's health (reducing the incidence of scurvy by use of lemon juice), and entered the French Revolutionary War in good order. The French, meanwhile, under the new guillotine-happy, anti-aristocratic revolutionary regime had beheaded (literally, in some cases) its naval officer class, with many ships left under no effective control. Although Napoleon tried to rebuild the French navy (see Appendix III for the relative battle-fleet tonnages of the combatant nations), the right officer stuff was oftentimes found wanting. The great gap in capability and experience between the Royal Navy and the French navy, together with its Spanish ally, was only proved at Trafalgar in 1805.

There was another, more prosaic reason for British superiority at sea. By the end of the 18th century Britain had begun the Industrial Revolution, creating an economic boom that allowed extraordinary levels of taxation and government borrowing. Despite the small size of the "sceptr'd isle" it was able to finance a world class navy; Napoleonic France, meanwhile, always creaked and strained in financing the war effort, and usually resorted to plundering its neighbours – and thus, in a vicious, self-defeating spiral, creating more enemies for itself.

The Napoleonic War at sea did not cease in 1805, but it certainly lessened in intensity and glory. Nelson was dead, and the French barely able to put up a force worth the fighting. It was, consequently, a somewhat complacent and self-satisfied Royal Navy that engaged the embryonic fleet of the United States in 1812, and found to its surprise that American frigates were not only superior in build but in crewing too, a lesson learned the hard way when the USS *Constitution* captured HMS *Guerriere* on 19 August 1812 (see pages 318–321 for Isaac Hull's account). Although the steam age was but a generation away, the spirited engagements of the War of 1812 at least ensured for armchair sailors everywhere that the great age of fighting sail went out with a bang not a whimper.

William Parker

The Glorious First of June

1794

The first major naval engagement of the War with Revolutionary France, the "Glorious First of June" was fought off Ushant in 1794, when Lord "Black Dick" Howe – in a piece of pure naval unorthodoxy – attacked the rear of a French fleet of similar size (26 vessels) but consisting of larger ships.

Twelve-year-old Midshipman William Parker aboard the Orion *penned a dramatic account of the action, and a subsequent drunken mutiny, in a letter to his father. Parker had entered the service a year before, as captain's "servant"; he left it as admiral.*

June 17, 1794

Lord Howe always likes to begin in the morning and let us have a whole day at it. The next morning [June 1st] early the signal was made to form the line of battle; we beat to quarters and got up sufficiently of powder and shot to engage the enemy. The enemy also formed their line to leeward. Upon our making observations on the enemy's fleet we found that one of their three-deck ships was missing, but counted twenty-eight sail-of-the-line, which was two more than they had on May 29. We supposed the Isle d'Aix squadron had joined them, and the ship that we had disabled on the 29th had bore up for Brest or sunk, and some thought the *Audacious* must have taken one of them, and took her away from the fleet, as she was missing May 30; but the best joke was that the French Commander-in-Chief had the impudence to say to those ships who joined him that he had thrashed us on the 29th completely, and that he only wanted to have another little dust with us before he should carry us all into Brest. Our fleet was formed, and we only waited to get near enough to the enemy to begin.

At eight the action began, and the firing from the enemy was very smart before we could engage the ship that came to our turn to engage, as every ship is to have one because our line is formed ahead, and theirs is formed also. Suppose their first or leading ship is a 100 guns and ours a 74, our ship must engage her. I believe we were the ninth or tenth ship; our lot fell to an 80-gun ship, so we would not waste our powder and shot by firing at other ships, though I am sorry to say they fired very smartly at us and unluckily killed two men before we fired a gun, which so exasperated our men that they kept singing out, "For God's sake, brave captain, let us fire! Consider, sir, two poor souls are slaughtered already." But Captain Duckworth would not let them fire till we came abreast of the ship we were to engage, when Captain Duckworth cried out,

"Fire, my boys, fire!" upon which our enraged boys gave them such an extraordinary warm reception that I really believe it struck the rascals with the panic. The French ever since the 29th (because we so much damaged one of their ships) called us the little devil and the little black ribband, as we have a black streak painted on our side. They made the signal for three or four of their ships to come down and sink us, and if we struck to them to give us no quarter; but all this did not in the least dishearten our ship's company, and we kept up a very smart fire when some of the enemy's masts and yards went over their side, which we gave credit for some of our doing.

The smoke was so thick that we could not at all times see the ships engaging ahead and astern. Our main-topmast and main-yard being carried away by the enemy's shot, the Frenchmen gave three cheers, upon which our ship's company, to show they did not mind it, returned them the three cheers, and after that gave them a furious broadside. About this time a musket ball came and struck Captain Duckworth between the bottom part of his thumb and finger, but very slightly, so that he only wrapped a hand-kerchief about it, and it is now almost quite well. But to proceed with my account: at about ten the *Queen* broke their line again, and we gave three cheers at our quarters; and now we engaged whichever ship we could best. A ship of 80 guns, which we had poured three or four broadsides into on May 29, we saw drawing ahead on our lee quarter to fire into us, which ship our ship's company had a great desire to have made strike to us on the 29th, and now quite rejoiced at having an opportunity of engaging her again, gave three cheers at their quarters, and began a very smart firing at their former antagonist.

Their firing was not very smart, though she contrived to send a red-hot shot into the captain's cabin where I am quartered, which kept rolling about and burning everybody, when gallant Mears, our first lieutenant, took it up in his speaking-trumpet and threw it overboard. At last being so very close to her we supposed her men had left their quarters, as Frenchmen do not like close quarters. She bore down to leeward of the fleet, being very much disabled. The French fleet then ran away like cowardly rascals and we made all the sail we could.

Lord Howe ordered our ships that were not very much disabled to take the prizes in tow, and our own dismasted ships, who were erecting jury masts as fast as possible. But I forgot to tell you that the ship which struck to us was so much disabled that she could not live much longer upon the water, but gave a dreadful reel and lay down on her broadside. We were afraid to send any boats to help them, because they would have sunk her by too many poor souls getting into her at once. You could plainly perceive the poor wretches climbing over to windward and crying most dreadfully. She then righted a little, and then her head went down gradually, and she sunk. She after that rose again a little and then sunk, so that no more was seen of her. Oh, my dear father! when you consider of five or six hundred souls destroyed in that shocking manner, it will make your very heart relent. Our own men even were a great many of them in tears and groaning, they said God bless them. Oh, that we had come into a thousand engagements sooner than so many poor souls should be at once destroyed in that shocking manner. I really think it would have rent the hardest of hearts . . .

Most of our brave boys have undone all the good they ever did. They contrived to smuggle a great deal of liquor into the ship, and with the joy of the victory, most of the ship's company got so drunk that they mutinied. They said that they would have liberty to go ashore. They released the English prisoners out of irons. Every officer belonging to the ship was sent for. The Captain almost broke his heart about it. Seven of the ringleaders were seized by the officers and twenty others, when they were put in irons; and the next morning, when they were told of their night's proceedings they all cried like children. They punished the twenty with two dozen lashes each, and the seven were kept in irons to be hung, if tried by a Court Martial; but Captain Duckworth came on board today and said that, as he was of a forgiving temper, he gave them into the hands of the ship's company, that he looked up to them with love for the services they had done him . . .

James Gardner

The Pimp, the Smuggler, and the Mutineers: The Extraordinary Voyages of the *Gorgon* and the *Hind*

1794-7

*The author of a classic collection of naval Recol-
lections, James Anthony Gardner had his name
entered on the books of various HM vessels at the
age of five. He was a midshipman at twelve, but was
unable to cast off this lowly rank for many long
years. And so it was that Gardner was still a
midshipman at twenty-four, when he joined the*
Gorgon *at San Fiorenzo in Corsica.*

In July 1794 I joined the *Gorgon*, Captain James
Wallis, at St Fiorenzo, and after considerable delay
sailed for Gibraltar with the convoy bound for England under Vice-Admiral P. Cosby, who had his flag

on board the *Alcide*, 74. The following men of war, to the best of my recollection, in company: *Alcide*, 74 (Vice-Admiral Cosby); *Commerce de Marseilles*, 136; *Gorgon*, 44; *Pearl*, 36; *Topaze*, 36; *St Fiorenzo*, 36; *Modeste*, 32.

At the time we left Corsica we had forty-seven French prisoners on board. One of them could play the violin remarkably well. One morning on the forecastle, this man was reading to some of his comrades, and having his violin with him, Mr Duncan (our late master in the *Berwick*) requested him to play *Ça Ira*, which he for some time refused, being fearful of giving offence. At last he struck up the Marseilles hymn accompanied by his voice, which was very good, and when he came to that part "*Aux armes, Citoyens, formez vos bataillons*," etc., he seemed inspired; he threw up his violin half way up the foremast, caught it again, pressed it to his breast, and sung out "*Bon, Ça Ira*," in which he was joined by his comrades.

> *Fired with the song the French grew vain,*
> *Fought all their battles o'er again,*
> *And thrice they routed all their foes; and thrice they*
> *   slew the slain;*

and seemed ready and willing for any mischief. But our soldiers were called up and the French were sent below, and not so many allowed to be on deck at a time.

On the passage we were frequently sent as a whipper-in among the convoy. On one occasion, a master of a merchantman was rather slack in obeying the signal and gave tongue when hailed; upon which Captain

Wallis sent the first lieutenant and myself to take charge of his vessel. It was in the evening, blowing fresh, with a heavy sea, and we had great difficulty in getting on board; our boat cut as many capers as a swing at a fair, and in returning got stove alongside. We remained all night on board and had to prick for the softest plank. When Edgar, the first lieutenant, awoke in the morning, it was laughable to hear him exclaim, "God bass 'e" (for he could not say "blast ye," and for this he was nicknamed little Bassey) "What's got hold of me?" The fact was the night was hot, and the pitch in the seams waxed warm, and when he attempted to rise, he found his hair fastened to the deck and his nankin trowsers also. He put me in mind of Gulliver when fastened to the ground by the Liliputians. Captain Wallis having sent for us, we took this chap in tow. It blew very fresh, and the wind being fair, we towed him, under double reefed topsails and foresail, nine knots through the water, so that his topsails were wet with the spray. The master would sometimes run forward and hail, saying, "I'll cut the hawser"; and Captain Wallis would reply, "If you do, I'm damned if I don't sink you, you skulking son of a bitch; I mean to tow you until I work some buckets of tar out of the hawser."

Our admiral (Cosby) was a glorious fellow for keeping the convoy in order, and if they did not immediately obey the signal, he would fire at them without further ceremony.

We had a very pleasant passage to Gibraltar, where we remained some time in the New Mole, and then started for Cadiz to take in money and to join the convoy assembling there for England. While lying at

Gibraltar a Portuguese frigate arrived, and one of our midshipmen (Jennings, a wag) was sent on board with a message from Captain Wallis. Having stayed a long time, the signal was made for the boat, and when she returned the captain asked Jennings what detained him. "Why, sir, to tell you the truth, saving your presence" (for Jennings was a shrewd Irishman), "the commanding officer of the frigate was so busy lousing himself on the hen-coop that I could not get an answer before."

On the passage we got on shore a few leagues to the southward of Cadiz, and had very near taken up our quarters on the shoals, and, what was remarkable, a frigate had been sent before us for the same purpose, but got on shore in this place, and was obliged to return, and we (being clever) after laughing at the circumstance, were sent to repair her errors and went bump on shore on the very spot.

When we arrived at Cadiz to join the convoy and to bring home dollars, the merchants used to smuggle the money off to the ship to avoid paying the duty; and for every hundred taken on board, they would give as a premium two dollars and sometimes two and a half. It was a dangerous traffic, but very tempting; and some of our officers while lying there made sixty and others eighty pounds. On one occasion, my old shipmate, Lieutenant Chantrell, fell down in the street with six hundred dollars at his back – a moderate load – and sung out to some of the Spaniards who were looking on, "Come here, you sons of ——, and help me up." Had they known what he had at his back they would have helped him up to some purpose; imprisonment and slavery would have been the punishment. The manner they carried the dollars was this. A double piece of canvas made to contain them in rows, fixed to the back inside the waistcoat, and tied before. It was to an English hotel where they were sent to be shipped. This house was kept by Mr, or rather Mrs, Young, an infernal vixen, who would make nothing of knocking her husband down with a leg of mutton or any other joint she had in the larder, and he fool enough to put up with it. She used to charge us very high for our entertainment, which is the case in all English houses abroad; and if you have a mind to be treated fairly you must go to a house kept by a native, who will never impose on you. Having got a load of dollars to take off, we found our boat had left the landing place; so we hired a shore boat, and it appeared their custom house officers had suspicions, for they gave chase, and it was by uncommon exertion that we escaped, as they were nearly up with us when we got alongside. And yet those very men who would have seized us used to smuggle. I saw one of them come alongside and throw into the lower-deck port a bag of dollars containing, as I understood, a thousand, with a label on the bag, and then shove off his boat to row guard and prevent smuggling!

At Cadiz there is a beautiful walk with trees, called the Alameda, much frequented, particularly on a Sunday. It has three walks for the different grades of people. I happened to be on shore with some of our officers on the above day, and taking a stroll through the Alameda, we observed several well-dressed women in a balcony of one of the large houses that overlooked the walks. When they caught sight of us, they beckoned, and we went, as we thought, into the house. On going up two pairs of stairs without seeing any one, we imagined it was a trick, when casting my eye to a door that was partly open, I saw a fellow with a drawn stilletto ready to make a stab; upon which I called to the rest to make their retreat as fast as possible. One of them (a Mr Crump) was deaf, and I was obliged to push him downstairs as I could not make him understand. This was a warning not lost upon us.

The *America*, 64, having arrived at Cadiz to take charge of the convoy, we were put under her orders, and having got on board the money, sailed with the convoy for Lisbon.

Farewell and adieu, ye fair Spanish Ladies,
Farewell and adieu, ye Ladies of Spain;
For we've received orders to sail for old England,
In hopes in short time for to see you again.
                                    – Old Song.

After a passage of near three weeks we arrived in the Tagus, fortunately the day before a tremendous hurricane, which blew dead upon the shore, came on and lasted a considerable time.

A droll circumstance happened while at Lisbon. A party of us had been to see the famous aqueduct over the valley of Alcantara, and on coming back, one of them (Tomlinson, of the *Berwick*) to show his dexterity jumped on the back of a donkey. He had on a round jacket and light nankin pantaloons; the latter he split from clue to earing, and was obliged to walk to the boat in that situation, and by way of helping a lame dog over a stile, we took the longest way, where we had to pass by several ladies, with his shirt sticking out and every one laughing at him. He declared to me it was the most miserable time he ever experienced in the whole course of his life.

We were one day accosted while walking in Black-Horse Square, by a genteel-looking young man who, in broken English, said he would be happy to show us about the city, which offer was accepted, though much against my will. As we were walking through the streets, I observed the people as they passed us to laugh and point to others and then at us. At last we met an officer belonging to our squadron, who asked if we knew the person we had in company, because, says he, "If you don't I'll tell you. He is the noted pimp of Lisbon, and makes a trade of showing, not only the city, but all the ladies of easy virtue from the lowest brothel in Bull Bay to the highest in the upper town." This was quite enough, and we told the fellow to be off, but he had the impudence to follow us to the boat for payment, and even got upon the gang board and was coming in, when Jennings, in his dry way, said to the bowman, "Don't you see the gentleman is dusty? Have you no way of rubbing it off?" winking at the time. Upon this the bowman without any ceremony pitched him overboard up to his neck and then shoved off. We met the fellow several times after, but he took good care to steer clear.

I went with Lieutenant Chantrell to dinner at an ordinary at Lisbon. Among the company were several Americans. One of the dishes at the bottom of the table occasioned a dispute that had nearly terminated in a battle. A Yankee from the head of the table came and snatched up a beef-steak pie that an English master of a transport (one of our convoy) was serving out, and carried it off to his companions; upon which the Englishman stood up and harangued his countrymen as follows: "I say, if you stand this you ought to be damned, and may as well take a purser's shirt out of the rigging.* Now, I move that all you that are Englishmen shall rise from the table and throw the Yankees out of the window." This speech had the same effect as that of Nestor's to the Greeks, and the Yankees would for a certainty have been thrown into the street, had not Lieutenant Chantrell requested them to forbear, observing that abuse was innocent where men were worthless. This had the desired effect; and the pie being restored to its place in rather a diminished state, and the Yankee who took it away saying he only meant it in Har-mo-ny, the war was put an end to, and the dinner ended in peace.

One of our men having deserted, I was sent with Ducker, the boatswain, and a couple of marines to hunt in Bull Bay, which is the Wapping of Lisbon, and after a long search we found him and were returning to the boat. In passing through one of their dirty streets, something which shall be nameless was hove out of a window and fell upon the shoulder of Ducker, about the size of a large epaulette. I wished him joy of his promotion and told him that he looked extremely well in his new uniform. A piece of the same material fell on his nose and stuck out like the horn of a rhinoceros. I never saw a fellow so vexed. He was going to break the windows, but I told him to consider, as Bull Bay was

---

* A shirt was the merchantman signal requesting a man-of-war boat to be dispatched.

not to be attacked too hastily. I had hardly made the observation when his foot slipped, and he fell back in the gutter, where he lay cursing the whole race of Portuguese. Then

Vigorous he rose; and from the effluvia strong
Imbibed new strength, and scoured and stunk
along.*

I thought I should have died a-laughing, while he was cursing every native he met with until he got to the boat.

We remained several weeks at Lisbon collecting the convoy. At last when everything was ready we got under way, I think the latter end of September, the following men of war in company: *America*, 64 (Hon. John Rodney, commodore, having charge of the convoy); *Gorgon*, 44 (Captain Wallis); *Pearl*, 36; *Topaze*, 36; *St. Fiorenzo*, 36 (Capt. Sir C. Hamilton (?)); *Modeste*, 32 (Captain [Byam Martin]); *Alert*, 18.

We had a most dreadful passage home, blowing a gale of wind the whole time with seldom more sail set than a close-reefed main topsail. The French squadron that captured the *Alexander*, 74, had been on the lookout for us. We had several French officers (emigrants) who had left Toulon at the evacuation. They were in the greatest tribulation all the passage for fear of being taken. We had also many invalids from the fleet, of very little service had we met with an enemy; and our effective complement I think mustered under a hundred, so that we should have stood but a poor chance

* *The Dunciad*, ii. 105.

had we met with the squadron. The forty-seven
French prisoners that we had with us were left at
Gibraltar, which was a great relief to the emigrants
we had on board, as they were in constant fear of their
taking the ship from us. Fortunately for them and for
us the Jacobin squadron got on the wrong scent.

I don't know how it happened, but some people kept
an odd kind of reckoning, and we had some idea of
making the banks of Newfoundland instead of the
British Channel. However, at last we got to the northward and westward of Scilly, with the wind at SW; but
it must be understood, to give the devil his due, that
we had not an observation for a long time, and our
dead reckoning was not to be trusted; but at last we
found out by instinct or soundings that we were not in
the right place. Now it so happened that we were lying
to on the larboard tack, the wind, as I have stated, at
SW, under a close-reefed main topsail and storm
staysails, when in a thundering squall it shifted to
NNW and took us slap aback. Over she went, with the
upper dead-eyes on the lower rigging in the water, and
we thought she never would right, but the old ship
came to herself again. She was a noble sea-boat; it
would have been worth any man's while to leave the
feast, the dance, or even his wife, to have been on
board this ship in a gale of wind to witness her glorious
qualities.

I must now speak of Jerry Hacker, the purser. He
was a man, take him all in all, ye ne'er will see his like
again. He messed by himself in the cockpit, and would
sit in his cabin in the dark with a long stick in his hand,
calling out to everyone that came down the cockpit
ladder, "What strange man is that?" He was in con-

stant fear of being robbed or cheated, and lived in the most miserable manner. I have known him to corn meat in his hand-basin and in something else. He was suspicious to a degree and always saying he should be ruined, though there was little fear of that, as Jerry took good care to trust no one; and what he was only charged two shillings a gallon for, he kindly offered to let me have for five shillings, paying ready money; but I was not to be taken in so easy. He could not bear the sight of a midshipman in the cockpit, and did every-thing in his power to annoy them, and before I joined the ship, he used to sing a verse of an old song reflecting on the midshipmen. One morning while I was in the cockpit, he was quarrelling with some of them, and then struck up his favourite air, not think-ing that any person knew the song but himself. How-ever, in this he was mistaken, and when he had finished the following verse, I struck up another that settled him.

Tune, The Black Joke.
Ye salt beef squires and quarter deck beaus,
Who formerly lived upon blacking of shoes:
* With your anchors a-weigh and your topsails*
*   a-trip.*
If they call us by name and we don't answer,
*   Sir!*
They start us about till not able to stir;
* A lusty one and lay it well on.*
If you spare them an inch you ought to be
*   damn'd;*
With your anchors a-weigh and your topsails
*   a-trip.*

Our b — of a purser, he is very handy,
He mixes the water along with the brandy;
* Your anchors a-weigh and your topsails a-trip*
The bloody old thief he is very cruel;
Instead of burgoo he gives us water gruel;
* A lusty one and lay it well on.*
If you spare him an inch you ought to be damn'd,
With your anchors a-weigh and your topsails
*   a-trip.*

After hearing the last verse Jerry's "heavenly voice was heard no more to sing," and he looked with an evil eye upon me ever after.

In the gale of wind near the Channel, when we were taken aback in the squall that I have mentioned, every article we had was broken with the exception of the cover of a very large mess teapot. This we handed round as a measure to one another with wine from a black jack. I remember being at supper soon after the squall, in the midship berth in the cockpit, the ship rolling gunwale under, when we heard a noise in the after-hold like the rush of many waters, and it struck everyone that a butt end had started and that we should founder in a few minutes. The alarm was given immediately. The sick and lame left their hammocks; the latter forgot his crutch, and leaped – not exulting – like the bounding roe. Down came the captain and a whole posse of officers and men. The gratings were instantly unshipped, and in rushed the carpenter and his crew, horror-struck, with hair standing on end, like quills on the fretful porcupine; when, behold, it was a large cask of peas that had the head knocked out, and the peas as the ship rolled rushed along with a noise exactly like that of water.

After looking at one another for some time the following ludicrous scene took place, which I was an eye-witness to: –

The captain shook his head, took snuff, and went upon deck.

Old Edgar, first lieutenant, followed, and said, "God bass 'e all."

Billy Chantrell gave a grin, and damn'd his eyes.

The parson exclaimed, "In the midst of life we are in death."

The carpenter said, "Damn and b—— the peas."

Old Jerry Hacker, the purser, swore he was ruined, as no allowance would be made him; and cursed the field the peas grew in; and the French emigrant captain (Dubosc) said, "it was as vel for him to stay at de Toulon and be guillotined, as to come to dis place and be drowned in de vater."

I never shall forget this scene as long as I live. I dined with Captain Wallis the next day, and he asked me, in a very knowing manner, if he should help me to some peas soup.

After standing to the southward for some time until we thought we had got into 49°30′ by our dead reckoning, which is the latitude of mid-channel, we then altered our course to SEbE½E. I had a presentiment that something bad was hanging over us, and I went on the fore topsail yard (I think about nine at night) to look out ahead, the ship scudding at the rate of eleven knots, which brought to my mind the following lines:

The fatal sisters on the surge before
Yoked their infernal horses to the prow. – Falconer.

But in this instance they were outwitted, for lo and behold, after running some time I saw a light right ahead, which I instantly knew to be Scilly light, and I called to Captain Wallis, who immediately hauled the ship off to the southward. If the weather had not cleared after the squall before mentioned we should certainly have made the port where Sir Clowdsiley Shovell took in his last moorings.

The gale separated the convoy, and in standing up Channel we had near run on the Bolt Head, but hauled off just in time. At last we arrived at Spithead, where a large fleet of men-of-war were assembled. Before we came to an anchor we had nearly run foul of several ships, and I remember the *Invincible*, 74, hailing us, saying, "You have cut my cable, sir." This was not all, for we shaved off the old *Royal William's* quarter gallery, which some shipwrights were repairing – who had barely time to save them-selves. We were not allowed to anchor at Spithead, but to proceed to the Motherbank to perform quarantine on December 4, 1794, after the most extraordinary voyage that ever took place since the expedition of the Argonauts. Here I left the *Gorgon* and joined the *Victory*, who I found to my astonishment at Spithead.

Before I quit the *Gorgon* I must relate a few things . . . As I have stated before, every ship has strange characters, and the *Gorgon* had her full share. I shall begin with the captain, who was a very good seaman and had many good qualities, but at times he appeared half mad. He once said to me, pointing to Ducker, the boatswain, on the forecastle, "I'll hang that fellow; and you go down directly and take an inventory of his

stores." I could hardly keep my countenance, but went
forward, and as the captain turned his back I said to
Ducker, "You are going to be hanged, and I am sent
for a piece of white line to tuck you up genteelly." On
my reporting progress, he seemed to have forgot that
he gave such an order, and, taking a pinch of snuff,
merely said, "Let the fellow go to hell, and say no
more about him."

The first lieutenant, Edgar, was another strange and
unaccountable being. He had sailed round the world
with Cook, and was master of the ship Captain Clerke
commanded. He was a good sailor and navigator, or
rather had been, for he drank very hard, so as to
entirely ruin his constitution. He and the captain often
quarrelled, particularly at night. I have heard the
captain say, "Edgar, I shall get another first lieutenant." The other would answer, "Ye-ye-ye-yes, sir,
another first lieutenant." The captain again, "Edgar,
you are drunk." "No, sir, bass me if I am." A day or
two before we left Corsica, the captain ordered the
sails to be bent and went on shore to St Fiorenzo. On
coming on board late at night he asked Edgar if the
sails were bent. This question Edgar could not answer,
his memory having failed him; and on the captain
asking him again, he said, "Bass me if I know, but
I'll look up," forgetting it was dark. "You need not do
that," says the other, "for damn me if you can see a
hole through a grating." Then taking a pinch of snuff,
part of which blew into Edgar's eye, he asked him
down to supper. This the other readily agreed to, but
said, Bass him, if he could see the way.

Our gunner was one of the drollest fellows I ever
met with – it was his delight to come on the forecastle

in the first watch and sing comic songs to amuse the midshipmen assembled there. "Arthur O'Bradley" was one that he used to sing with a great deal of humour. I believe it contained forty verses. "Bryan O'Lynn" was another which I shall relate, leaving out the lines that may not be liked by those endued with fine feelings.

> Bryan O'Lynn and his wife, and wife's mother,
> They all hid under a hedge together;
> But the rain came so fast they got wet to the skin —
> We shall catch a damned cold, says Bryan O'Lynn.
>
> Bryan O'Lynn and his wife, and wife's mother,
> They went in a boat to catch sprats together;
> A butt end got stove and the water rushed in —
> We're drowned, by the holy, says Bryan O'Lynn.
>
> Bryan O'Lynn and his wife, and wife's mother,
> They all went on a bridge together;
> The bridge it broke and they all fell in —
> Strike out and be damned, says Bryan O'Lynn.
>
> Bryan O'Lynn and his wife, and wife's mother,
> They all went out to chapel together;
> The door it was shut and they could not get in —
> It's a hell of a misfortune, says Bryan O'Lynn.
>
> Bryan O'Lynn and his wife, and wife's mother,
> They went with the priest to a wake together,
> Where they all got drunk and thought it no sin —
> It keeps out the cold, says Bryan O'Lynn.

Bryan O'Lynn and his wife, and wife's mother,
They went to the grave with the corpse together;
The earth being loose they all fell in –
Bear a hand and jump out, says Bryan O'Lynn.

Bryan O'Lynn and his wife, and wife's mother,
When the berring was over went home together;
In crossing a bog they got up to the chin –
I'm damned but we're smothered, says Bryan
O'Lynn.

Bryan O'Lynn and his wife, and wife's mother,
By good luck got out of the bog together;
They went to confess to Father O'Flinn –
We're damnation sinners, says Brian O'Lynn.

Bryan O'Lynn and his wife, and wife's mother,
Resolved to lead a new life together;
And from that day to this have committed no sin –
In the calendar stands Saint Bryan O'Lynn.

I have left out four verses as being rather out of order. I have heard the old gunner sing this when the sea has been beating over the forecastle and the ship rolling gunwale under. We used to get a tarpaulin in the weather fore rigging as a screen, and many a pleasant hour have I passed under its lee, with a glass of grog and hearing long-winded stories. Alas! how dead are times now. Captain Wallis behaved very kindly to me. I used to dine with him two or three times a week. He had, as I have stated, strange whims and few men are without them, but his many good qualities threw them in the background, and I have with grateful remembrance and respect for his memory, to be thankful for his kindness, and particularly for the certificate he gave me on leaving the ship.

Madame Trogoff, the French admiral's widow, came to England and was a passenger in his cabin. She was a very agreeable woman. We had several French officers (emigrants) who had left Toulon at the evacuation. They were in the greatest tribulation all the passage for fear of being taken. We had also many invalids from the fleet, of very little service had we met with an enemy; and our effective complement I think mustered under a hundred, so that we should have stood but a poor chance had we met with the squadron that I have already mentioned. The forty-seven French prisoners that we had with us were left at Gibraltar, which was a great relief to the emigrants we had on board, as they were in constant fear of their taking the ship from us.

In January 1795 Gardner was finally promoted, being appointed second lieutenant aboard HMS Hind.

After being sworn in at the Admiralty* I left London to join the *Hind*, 28, Captain Richard Lee, at Sheerness, in January, 1795. The Medway and Thames being frozen over, there was no communication with the men-of-war. I proceeded on my journey by coach as far as Sittingbourne, and then walked most of the

---

* Before the repeal of the Test Act in 1828 it was required that "all persons holding any office of profit or trust, civil or military, under the crown, take the oath of allegiance and supremacy, receive the Sacrament of the Lord's Supper according to the rites of the Church of England, and subscribe to the declaration against transubstantiation".

way through deep snow to the King's ferry, which was also frozen over. At this time my health was very bad, and coming from a fine climate to one noted for gloomy skies, fog, rain, bitter cold and everything else that was damnable, I had nearly sunk under it, and I have to acknowledge how much I was obliged to Mr Poulden, an officer in the Navy, and brother to Captain Poulden, RN, for his kind attention. He was a fellow traveller going also to join his ship at Sheerness. The snow was several feet deep, and the cold dreadful, and it was with the greatest difficulty and fatigue that we reached the public house near the ferry without being frost-bitten.

You who are not too young (for it's difficult now to find an old person), must remember the cruel winter the latter end of 1794 and beginning of 1795. To my surprise I met at the public house an old messmate of mine (a Mr Simmonds) formerly of the *Panther*, and going also to join his ship. We were half-starved and waited a considerable time for our host to bring in the dinner, which he did at last. To our horror and amazement, it consisted of a leg of pork of enormous size, without a bit of lean, and coarse white cabbage boiled with it, and as greasy as the devil. I shall never forget the consternation we were in; nothing else could be had, and what made it more vexatious was the praises the great fat fool of a John Bull landlord was passing on it. We were obliged to swallow this greasy morsel from downright hunger, and from its rancid taste in danger of cholera morbus.

The passage being frozen, we had no other resource than to cross the ice on foot, which we did at great hazard, it cracking and bending all the way. I had a small portmanteau, for which I paid a soldier to carry, as he was going the same way; but when we had crossed, his heart failed him and he refused to follow (for we passed over one by one), and it was a long time before we could prevail on him to make the attempt; but by promising him a shilling or two more he took courage until he got half way over, when he imagined the ice was giving way, and there he stood panic-struck. We really felt for the poor fellow, but at last he made a desperate effort and got safe over though dreadfully frightened. After a dismal walk we got to Sheerness, emphatically styled by the late Captain Gunter, RN, "the – hole of the world."

I found Captain Lee in lodgings; he seemed much surprised at seeing me as he had no communication with the Admiralty for a long time. He seemed astonished at my walking across the ferry, which he considered a very hazardous undertaking. After waiting a few days we forced a passage through the ice and got on board; and soon after, followed his worship, old Stamp, the Mayor of Queenborough, as pilot, and well known as a most respectable boroughmonger of large property and powerful interest, and would be a pilot merely because he liked it. We soon got under way, and in a few hours anchored in the Downs, where we found the *Leopard*, 50 (the flagship), and several men of war. We remained but a short time and then proceeded to Spithead with a convoy.

We were on this service up and down Channel, and to Ireland, for several months without anything material happening, until being off Waterford, after seeing the convoy safe, we saw a suspicious lugger, which we gave chase to and, after a run of forty leagues, had the good fortune to capture – the *Speedwell*, smuggling lugger, pierced for eighteen guns which she had thrown overboard, as we counted the carriages that were disposed of soon after the guns. Her cargo consisted of spirits, tobacco, tea, nankins, etc., with thirty-nine gigantic smugglers; one we supposed was killed, as the muster roll had forty. We pressed the crew and took the vessel to Belfast, where her cargo was sold. Captain Lee, who was a good calculator, offered the first lieutenant, Hickey, and myself £58 15s. apiece for our prize-money, which after some consideration we accepted; but when the prize-money was paid, the share of a lieutenant was only £50, so that he lost by the spec. £17 10s., besides losing with the marine officer. We kept the crew as part of our ship's company, but they contrived to desert at different times with the exception of four.

I well remember while lying in Dublin Bay, and being at breakfast with Captain Lee, in course of conversation he observed that the four remaining smugglers were the best men in the ship and that he was very proud of them. He had hardly made the observation when the officer of the watch reported that the jolly boat was missing; the hands were immediately turned up to muster, when it was found that the four worthies had set off in the boat, when or where nobody could tell. The captain looked at us, and we at him, but no one could keep countenance. It could not be proved in whose watch the boat was taken. We found her at Dunleary, but never heard of the deserters.

While at Carrickfergus the assizes were held and we had an invitation to dine with the grand jury. We passed a very pleasant day; upwards of two hundred were present, and several excellent songs were sung by one of the counsellors, who was considered equal to Braham or Incledon. Having proceeded to Plymouth with a convoy we remained some time in the Sound, when the *Medusa*, 50, Captain James Norman, arrived with the West India convoy, part of which had been captured by the enemy's cruisers and we were put under his orders to proceed with the convoy to the Downs.

It is well remembered by those who are not too young that the latter end of 1795 was a very tempestuous season, and it was a long time before an opportunity offered to sail; we once made the attempt and had nearly got on shore near the Mewstone. In working out, our main topsail yard was carried away in a squall, and we were obliged to anchor; but the gale increasing, the cable was cut, and we again anchored in the Sound. On 3rd November, the wind being favourable, the commodore made the signal to get under way, and we were ordered to lead up Channel. On the night of the 5th (it being light winds the whole of the time from our leaving the Sound), between Beachy Head and Dungeness it came on to blow a complete hurricane, with heavy rain at south; and on the morning of the 6th, it blew, if possible, harder, and our situation on a lee shore dreadfully alarming, in Rye Bay, with only storm staysails, which at last blew out of the bolt rope; the main topsail also split to pieces from the fourth reef, leaving not a wreck behind, and we expected the ship would upset under bare poles.

As second lieutenant, I was stationed on the forecastle, and seeing a light right ahead I pointed it out to Tim Coghlan, our master, who swore it was Dungeness light and that we were all lost; at the same time asking me for the key of the case, as he was going to step down for a lunch, being infernally hungry and thirsty. I asked Captain Lee, who was on deck all night – for he was an officer that never flinched, and where there was danger he was always to be seen cool and intrepid – to take some refreshment. "Why," says, he, "I don't know what to say about the eating part of the business, but I think we shall get plenty to drink, and that presently."

Had the gale continued at south, nothing could have saved us. With a tremendous sea, and breakers at no great distance, there was no chance of reaching the Downs as we could not get round Dungeness; when in a dreadful squall of thunder, lightning, hail and rain, the wind shifted to north or NNW, which is off the land, and blew with the utmost violence. But towards daylight it got more moderate and we stood for the Downs, where we anchored with part of the convoy in a shattered condition, the remainder coming in soon after. Two of them were lost on the French coast when the wind shifted to the northward.

Captain Lee soon after left the ship, with the good wishes of every officer and man on board. He was a brave, generous, and meritorious officer, an excellent sailor and skilful pilot for the British, as well as Irish Channels, and well deserving of the honours he now enjoys. He was succeeded by Captain John Bazely, who was one of the best officers in the Navy for skill, activity, and high sense of honour, well read and possessing an excellent under-standing, and his death will long be lamented as a loss to the service and to society.

19th November, another tremendous gale came on at SSW, which lasted the whole of the day and most of the night. This was the gale that Admiral Christian's fleet suffered so much in. We expected every minute to part and about the last quarter flood we began to drive; but before we could let go our sheet anchor she brought up. The *Glebb*, 74, the flagship of the Russian admiral (Henikoff) lying abreast of us,* parted and brought up with her last anchor within half a mile of the Break. The *Montagu*, 74, under jury masts, from the westward, anchored in our wake, and ran her cable out to the clinch before she brought up. Had she parted, God knows what would have become of us, as it was the height of the gale, with thick weather, and nothing could have prevented her being on board of us, as all her sails were blown from the yards. Had the gale lasted much longer it would been of serious consequence to the ships in the Downs.

Sailed with a convoy to the westward, which service we were employed on, cruising occasionally in the Channel and Bay, for several months. In May, 1796, coming into Plymouth Sound from a cruise, and blowing hard, we anchored astern of the *Alfred*, 74, who had driven without our being aware of it, so that we found ourselves in an awkward berth without room to moor. We then attempted to get under way, but the gale increasing from the SW, we were unable to weather Mount Batten and came to again. We soon after parted, and let go another anchor and brought up between two rocks in a perilous situation, with two anchors ahead; but fortunately it got more moderate, and, observing there was an undertow, so that when she pitched there appeared no strain upon the cables,

---

* After the Anglo-Russian alliance of 1795 a squadron of twelve ships was sent to cruise in the North Sea and Channel.

we thought there was no occasion to cut away our masts; and our opinion was right, notwithstanding the wish of the knowing ones who came down by hundreds and chalked in large letters on the rocks – "Cut away your masts." This was dictating with a vengeance by a set of vagabond landsmen, fellows that could rob a house easier than knot a rope yarn, and be damned to them. A lighter with an anchor and cable came out soon after; and the wind shifting, we got under way and anchored in a safe berth.

Sailed to the westward and cruised in the Bay, and on our return to the Sound received orders to proceed to Spithead and fit for foreign service, and about the latter end of August sailed with a small convoy for Quebec. Nothing particular happened until we got on the Banks of Newfoundland, when we fell in with a French squadron under Admiral Richery. It was in the forenoon watch, blowing very hard, the wind WNW with a heavy sea, under a close-reefed main topsail and foresail, when we observed a ship of the line to windward with her head to the SW, under the same sail. Made the private signal, which was not answered. Most of our convoy had parted company in the gale. Bore up and made sail. The enemy also bore up and made all sail in chase until sunset, when he gave over chase and hauled his wind to the northward. We hauled our wind also, and stood to the southward. Separated from the remainder of the convoy during the night, it blowing strong with thick weather. There was great exultation at our outsailing the enemy, and some on board were wishing to have another trial, and their wishes were not disappointed; for in three days after, about six in the morning, two line-of-battle ships were observed astern about two leagues off.

The private signal was made, but not answered. We were under close-reefed topsails and foresail, steering WSW, the wind NW. The enemy made sail and stood after us. We immediately let two reefs out of the topsails, set topgallant sails and hauled the maintack on board, with jib a third in and spanker. It was neck or nothing, and those who wished for another chase looked rather glum and had not quite so good an opinion of our sailing on a wind as they had when before it. For my part I expected we should upset, and it was with uncommon alacrity in making and shortening sail between the squalls that we escaped upsetting or being taken. The enemy knew well what he was about, for he kept rather on our lee quarter with his fore topmast studding sail boom run out, and the sail ready for setting in case we had kept away. At one time his weather main-topsail sheet gave way and he was only ten minutes in setting the sail again; his jib also split, which he unbent and had another set in twenty minutes, which did him great credit. Luckily for us the sea was nearly abeam; had we been on the other tack we must have been taken, as we should then have bowed [i.e. bows on to] the sea. I remember heaving the log and she was going ten knots. But notwithstanding our good sailing the enemy gained on us fast, and we should have been captured for a certainty if the Frenchman had possessed more patience.

And so it happened; for a little before six, when he was within gunshot, the greedy fellow let another reef out of his topsails, and just as he had them hoisted, away went his foreyard, jib-boom, fore topmast and main-topgallant mast. The other line-of-battle ship was hull down astern. The chase lasted twelve hours, during which time we ran near forty leagues. Shortened sail and wore ship, and as we passed to windward, we counted fifteen ports of a side on his lower deck.

Nothing further happened, except losing a poor fellow overboard in the Gulf of St Lawrence, until we got to Quebec. The convoy also escaped and came in soon after; one of them was chased, but by fixing a pole on a tub with a lantern on the top, and steering another course in the night, escaped. We remained at Quebec until the latter end of November, and then sailed with a couple of fur ships for England under convoy. We left Quebec in the evening. I had the first watch, and I never shall forget the cold as long as I live.

Nothing remarkable happened until we got to the southward of Cape Clear, which bore north according to our dead reckoning, and if I remember correctly on the 23rd December, 1796, about eight in the evening we saw a squadron of men-of-war, one of them with a top light, standing to the northward, the wind about west, and at no great distance. We immediately hauled off to the southward, put out all our lights and hailed the two vessels under our charge to do the same. After standing to the southward some time, we altered our course and saw no more of them. The wind soon after shifted to the eastward and blew a heavy gale. Lost sight of our convoy and after buffeting about for some days we were obliged, for want of fuel, to put into Cork, where we found several men-of-war preparing to sail in consequence of the French being off Bantry Bay. All the carriages and horses that could be found were put in requisition to take the troops to that quarter, and when we had completed our stores and water we sailed with a squadron of frigates under Captain Jon Faulknor to the southward in quest of the enemy, but they had left Bantry, where Lord Bridport was off with the grand fleet, who we joined with our squadron. I believe this was the time that General Grouchy with eight thousand men (before the arrival of our fleet) anchored in the bay; but from fear, or some other cause, thought it safer to set off than to land; and at Bantry, as well as at Waterloo, showed great want of judgment.*

We were attached to the grand fleet as a repeating frigate; and in January, 1797, we chased by signal and captured the French privateer *La Favorite*, of eight guns and sixty men, out but a short time from Brest and had taken nothing. After removing the chief part of the prisoners, I was put on board as prize master with two midshipmen and twelve men, with orders to stay by the fleet; but on examining her defects I found her in a very bad condition, upon which I separated from the fleet in the evening and stood for the Channel (being then in the Bay). We had nearly been run down by a three-decker – I believe the *Prince George*, commanded by the late Sir Joseph Yorke – in the rear of the fleet, and the night being as black as Erebus we had a narrow escape. Portsmouth being the place of rendezvous, we stood up Channel with the wind at SW

* An expedition under General Hoche with Grouchy as second-in-command reached Bantry Bay on 21 December, but was prevented from landing by a severe snowstorm. The Channel Fleet under Lord Bridport did not reach the spot until 9 January, by which time the French had returned to port. Faulknor commanded one of the six frigates of the Irish guard.

the day after leaving the fleet, blowing a gale, under a close-reefed main topsail and foresail.

We had not an observation for several days before we parted from the grand fleet, and in running up Channel we got into Portland Race. I have been in many noted places, but this infernal race was worse than all, and I expected every moment we should founder. The privateer being deep-waisted, I ordered her ports to be knocked out so as to let the sea have a clear passage through; our hatches were battened down, but we were in danger of being washed overboard. The sea appeared like a pot boiling, and the spray beat over our topsail yards. Hauled off to the southward, and fortunately got safe out of one of the most damnable places I ever was in. The Frenchmen were in the utmost terror and cursed the hour they ever left Brest. By our account we were half-way between the Start and Portland, which was very fair considering everything. During the night it fell calm and towards morning the wind freshened at SE with thick weather; at daylight, stood in and sounded fifteen fathoms near St Alban's Head, and, it clearing away, bore up and made sail for Plymouth. When near the Start we hoisted the Union Jack over the French at the gaff end; but the Jack blowing away, and the halliards getting foul, we could not for some time haul down the French colours, which frightened a brig that was near, and a frigate coming from Torbay under jury masts fired (I believe) at us but at too great a distance to take effect. However, we got our colours to rights and I hailed the brig, who seemed very much alarmed until I informed him we came from the grand fleet, a prize to the *Hind*.

In the evening we anchored in Cawsand Bay, and next morning I waited on Sir Richard King, the port admiral, who behaved in the kindest manner, and on my explaining my reasons for leaving the fleet he said I did what was very proper.

As no dispatches had arrived, I was ordered by Sir Richard to write an account of what happened in the fleet from the day we joined Lord Bridport until I left with the prize, and also to give an account of our proceedings from the time we fell in with Richery's squadron until our arrival at Cork. I was put into a room and desired to take my seat at a table with a quire of foolscap placed before me; and like a fool I looked, for it was a long time before I knew what to write, or how to begin. At last I took courage, and filled three or four sheets; bad grammar, no doubt. Sir Richard read the whole and said it would do very well – many thanks to him. He laughed heartily when I told him I got into Portland Race and what a panic the prisoners were in.

I had sent a pilot off to take the brig into Hamoaze and walked down with Sir Richard to Mutton Cove, as he wished to see her as she passed. He told me he was once put prize master when a lieutenant, on board of such another and had left the fleet as I had done and for the same reason. This made me easy and quieted my fears. Captain Bazely's father was port admiral in the Downs, and I wrote to him stating our arrival and received an answer thanking me for the information respecting his son. We had not been long at Plymouth before the *Hind* left the fleet and put into Portsmouth, and not finding me there supposed we were lost, until Captain Bazely received a letter from his father saying he had heard from me, and that we were all well and safe at Plymouth, and in a few days I received the following letter from Captain Bazely:

Hind, Portsmouth, February, 1797.

"Gardner, my good fellow, I am truly happy to find you are in the land of the living, and that it was through necessity you put into Plymouth. We are ordered to Sheerness to dock, where I shall be devilish glad to see you; so get on board some vessel bound to the Downs with your party, and be sure to call on my father, who will be very glad to see you and will send some craft to take you to the Nore. We are all well. – Believe me to remain, with best wishes,

Yours most faithfully,
John Bazely, Junr."

After clearing the prize and delivering her up to Mr Hemmings, the master attendant at Plymouth and agent for Lord Bridport (who I have every reason to thank for his great civility while I remained in Hamoaze, in the many invitations I had to dine at his house, where he made a point to introduce me to the captains who visited there). I was put on board the *Medusa*, 50, commanded by my old messmate Jack Eaton, who was to take us as far as Portsmouth. On our arrival at Spithead we were put on board the *Weasel*, commanded by Captain Lewis, and sailed for the Nore, where we soon arrived and joined our ship at Sheerness, and I was well received by the captain and my messmates. Went into dock and when refitted proceeded to Portsmouth, where we remained but a short time and sailed with a convoy for Oporto. We had a very pleasant passage and took out Captain A. Ball on his way to join his ship, who left us off Oporto. On our return we recaptured a brig in the Bay of Biscay, and I was put on board as prize master; but from ill-health I went back to my ship and the first lieutenant took charge of the prize in my room.

On our arrival at Spithead, the latter end of April, 1797, we found the fleet in a high state of mutiny.* We had orders to fit for foreign service, and I had directions to go with a party of seamen and marines to the dockyard for new cables and stores. The mutiny, which in some measure had been suppressed, broke out afresh on board the *London*, 98, Vice-Admiral Colpoys, and some of the mutineers were killed; but the officers were overpowered and the admiral's flag struck by the scoundrels, and the bloody flag of defiance hoisted in its room. I went with my party to the yard in the morning and began to get off the stores, when a marine said he would not assist in rousing [heaving] the cable into the lighter and advised the others to knock off; upon which I told him if he did not immediately take hold of the cable with the rest I would cut him down (which was my intention). This had the effect and he went to work with the others. When I got on board our men were in a state of mutiny, and every ship at Spithead and St Helen's the same. I had the first watch that night, and the master relieved me at twelve, and everything seemed

* The Mutiny at Spithead broke out on 17 April, the far more dangerous outbreak at the Nore occurring on 12 May – "Parker's Floating Republic". Gardner's experience was typical of most of the officers involved, though some were treated more harshly and one or two were flogged by the mutineers.

quiet; but about three bells in the morning watch I was
sent for by the captain, and on my coming on deck I
found the ship's company assembled there and the
captain, in the most impressive manner, requesting
them to return to their duty, but all to no purpose. Had
we been the only ship, we should soon have driven the
scoundrels to the devil; but as we were situated,
surrounded by line-of-battle ships acting in the same
disgraceful manner, it would have been of little use to
resist. About six a paper was handed up to the captain
with the following order in writing:

"It is the unanimous opinion of the ship's company
that Captain Bazely, Lieutenants Hickey and Gardner, Mr White, the purser, and Messrs Kineer and
Allen, midshipmen, are to quit the ship by six, or
violent measures will be taken to enforce the order."

Soon after six the barge was manned and armed;
every vagabond had a cutlass, and our trunks were
handed in, with orders from the delegates not to carry
them anywhere for us. I had a brace of pistols with a
double charge which I put in my great-coat pockets in
case I should want their assistance. It was blowing a
gale of wind at NE when we left the ship, and near ten
o'clock before we landed on Point beach; our things
were handed out, and I desired the bowman and one or
two more, who I knew to be great scoundrels, to take
them to Turner's (living on the beach, and only a step
from the boat) showing them at the same time my
pistols and saying, "You understand me." They then
most reluctantly took our things to the place I directed. This was all I wanted, as I heard some of the
ringleaders say as we were quitting the ship "that if
any of the boat's crew assisted in taking our things to

any place after landing they should be severely ducked on their return"; and they were as good as their word; for those fellows got a fine ducking the moment they got on board, the others having reported them.

We left the *Hind* in May, 1797, but before I close my account I must relate a few anecdotes as they come to my recollection. I shall begin with the surgeon, who was a very worthy fellow and much respected, but was strange, so that we thought him half cracked, and he had the name of Benjamin Bullock the Madman (a character in some work that I forget). I was one morning walking the deck with him when the postman came on board and presented a letter directed to "Robert Anderson, Esq., or Benjamin Bullock, Esq., Surgeon of H.M. ship *Hind*. With speed." The letter ran thus: "Take care when you are going on shore, and do not on any account pass the Devil's Point where Bullocks are put to death daily for the use of the fleet. So no more at present from yours to command. J. Talgol, Slaughter House, Devil's Point."

He accused me of writing the letter, but he was mistaken, and from that day to this I know nothing of the author. He was greatly enraged and vowed vengeance against me and my friend Harley the purser, who was the person that gave him the name of Ben Bullock. It happened some time after that Harley and myself were going on shore and Anderson said he would take a passage with us. When near the Devil's Point, which we had to pass, I gave orders to the boat's crew to pull with all their might, "Give way, my lads, give way until we pass this place." Anderson looked at me and said, "What the hell are you afraid of now? You are always croaking about some damned thing or other." "My good fellow," says I, "it is on your account that I am so anxious. Don't you remember the friendly letter you had warning you to beware of the Devil's Point? It is on this account that I want to pass it in such a hurry, as you may be taken out and cut up for fresh beef." And what made things worse, on our landing the first object that drew our attention was a large board over a warehouse, with "Bullock and Anderson" on it in gilt letters of immense size, to his astonishment and vexation.

At another time, when we had a large party on board I was sitting at the bottom of the table and Anderson at the head as caterer. I happened to be in conversation with Harley, who in the heat of argument was energetically moving his hand up and down; which Anderson observed, and leaving the head of the table with a knife in each hand he placed himself between me and Harley, and holding a knife against our breasts says he: "That's for thee, and that's for thou; I know well what you meant by moving your hand up and down like a cleaver cutting up bullocks for the fleet, and be damned to you both. Now do it again if you dare." After some difficulty we persuaded him to go to the head of the table again; but those who were strangers to his whims looked on him with an evil eye.

Our master (Coghlan) was a very droll fellow and fond of carrying sail in a boat. Being sent from the Sound to the dockyard on duty, it came on to blow a heavy gale of wind, and we struck yards and topmasts. In the first watch about six bells I was walking the deck with Captain Lee, who observed how glad he was our boat was safe, as he had no doubt Mr Coghlan had gone on board the flagship in the harbour. He had not long made the observation, when I thought (it being moonlight) I saw something in the direction of Drake's Island and pointed it out to Captain Lee, who said it could not be a boat, as nobody would be mad enough to risk his life on such a night. By this time the object drew near, when to our astonishment we were hailed by Coghlan to throw a rope, and in a moment he flew alongside. We got the yard and stay tackles over instantly, got the men in, and ran the boat up in safety although a heavy sea was running. When Coghlan came upon deck, the captain asked if he was not ashamed of himself in risking the lives of the people in the wanton manner he had done. Tim with the greatest simplicity said "Sir, if you had seen her (meaning the boat) fly from the top of one sea to another without stopping between, you would really have admired her. She darted through the breakers when crossing the Bridge (a dangerous reef of rocks between Drake's Island and Mount Edgcumbe) like a race horse. I never was in such a boat in my life." Captain Lee, vexed as he was, could not help smiling, at the same time telling Tim if he did so again strange things would take place. Coghlan's name was John, but someone had written to Steele saying his name was Timothy and it was put so on the list.* Coghlan on this wrote to say it was not his name and requested Steele, to alter it; but the same wag who had written before did so again, and when the list was printed his name stood as John Timothy Coghlan, and remained so, and we always called him Tim. He has gone to his long

* Steele's list of naval officers was published between 1779 and 1814. It became the model for the later official Navy List.

home and has left behind the character of an honest and worthy fellow. He left the *Hind* to be master of the *Trent*, 36, going to the West Indies. I dined with him a short time before he sailed, and he was pointing out the different members of the mess, saying that none of them could live in such a climate. Poor fellow, he little thought while making that remark that they all returned and he the only one that sunk the victim of all-conquering death.

At the time we had nearly got on shore and lost an anchor near the Mewstone, when working out with the convoy, I was sent the next morning to acquaint Commissioner Fanshawe of the circumstance, and to request he would order a lighter with a new cable and to weight the anchor we had lost. I recollect he was dressed in an old blue coat with a red handkerchief about his neck, and in a very crabbed humour. After staring at me for some time he roared out, "I shall do not such thing. What brought you there? Go and tell your captain if he gets into a hole he must get out of it again. I shall give him no assistance and you may be off and tell him so." I told him that we were out of the hole and that I only delivered my orders as I was directed. At the same time I would thank him to write down the words he had just made use of, as verbal messages were uncertain. "Be off, sir," says he, "and if your memory is good enough to recollect what your captain said you cannot forget what I have stated; so no more palaver"; and grinning at me with a horrid set of teeth; he concluded by saying, "I have other things to think of than bothering my brains about people who get into a lubberly situation and don't know how to get out." I looked at him without making any reply, when turning on his heel, he said, "Aye, you may look."

As I am not fond of making mischief, I thought it best to say nothing to Captain Lee but merely state he refused to send the lighter. This put the captain in a terrible rage, but the lighter being sent off the next morning, the matter ended. Commissioner Fanshawe was one of the first seamen in the Navy, and also one of the bravest officers that ever did honour to the service, a rigid disciplinarian, and to sum up all, a tight hand of the watch, as the saying is.

Coming from the westward to the Downs and when round the Foreland, the captain ordered the colours to be hoisted, when up went a swaggering French ensign and jack, which at first was not taken notice of, but was soon observed by the captain, who ran forward calling out to me, "Look at the French jack, sir; haul it down directly." "Sir," said I, "the French ensign is at the mizen peak." This he had not seen, and I thought he would have gone jumping mad. However, they were hauled down; but as if the devil would have it, instead of our own, up went Dutch colours. Nobody could keep their countenance, and a general laugh went through the ship and also in the men-of-war lying in the Downs who had observed the transaction.

While at Carrickfergus we were on very friendly terms with the officers of the Irish militia and dined often at the different messes. I remember on a rejoicing day calling with some more on the officers of the Cavan militia. On going upstairs to their messroom, we found several seated round the fire with a half barrel of gunpowder busily employed making fireworks for the evening amusement. Our visit was not of long duration, and I can truly say for myself that I

only made one step downstairs and was off like a shot –
Nor cast one longing, lingering look behind.

When in Hamoaze our boatswain was tried by a
court martial for repeated drunkenness and dismissed
the service. At the trial the captain of the *Tremendous*,
74, was unable to attend from indisposition, and the
surgeon being sent for to attend the court and give in
his report, he happened to make some remarks that the
court considered disrespectful; upon which he was
given in charge of Lieutenant Richards, first of the
Cambridge, 84, on board of which ship the trial took
place, until the court should determine. He was not
long kept in suspense, for on the court opening he was
sentenced to three months' imprisonment in the Mar-
shalsea for contempt of court, and sent off that day.
People should be careful.

On the passage to Quebec, after parting from our
convoy, about eight in the evening, with little wind
and going two knots, and nothing in sight, a voice was
heard astern hailing, "On board the *Hind*, ahoy!" I
must confess I was a little staggered, and some curious
remarks were made by the seamen. One fellow said,
"I'll be damned if we were off the Cape but I should
think it was the Flying Dutchman." "As to that," says
another, "he has got a roving commission and may
cruise where he likes." "Bad luck to me," says a
marine, "if it's not a mermaid." "And to sum up,"
says old Macarthy, the quartermaster, "it may be the
poor fellow that fell overboard the other day." However, the voice hailed again, saying, "Bear a hand and
send the boat, for I'm damned if I can keep up much
longer." The jolly boat was immediately lowered
down from the stern and sent in the direction of the

voice; and will it be believed that the fellows were afraid to take into the boat one of the maintopmen (who had fallen overboard out of the main chains, being half asleep) until he had told his name and answered several ridiculous questions?

Gardner finally retired the service with the rank of commander.

Admiral Sir Horatio Nelson

The Nile Campaign

1798

The Nile campaign was the making of Nelson. It made him a world figure; it also won him the adoration of Lady Hamilton, soon to become his mistress and mother of his illegitimate daughter Horatia.

Nelson hoisted his flag as Rear-Admiral of the Blue in HMS Vanguard at 8 p.m. 29 March. Three months later he was entrusted with the command – over two senior officers, Sir William Parker and Sir John Orde – of a squadron of twelve Sail of the Line and ordered to seek out the French "Armament", Admiral De Bruey's Toulon fleet conveying the French army to Egypt.

To Lady Nelson   Lisbon, *1st May, 1798*

I joined the Fleet yesterday, and found Lord St. Vincent everything I wished him; and his friends in England have done me justice for my zeal and affection towards him. I have my fears that he will not be much longer in this Command, for I believe he has written to be superseded, which I am sincerely sorry for. It will considerably take from my pleasure in serving here; but I will hope for the best. The Dons have, I find, long expected my return with Bomb-vessels, Gunboats, and every proper implement for the destruction of Cadiz and their Fleet. They have prepared three floating batteries to lie outside their walls, to prevent the fancied attack; and, lo, the mountain has brought forth a mouse: – I am arrived with a single Ship, and without the means of annoying them. The Admiral probably is going to detach me with a small Squadron; not on any fighting expedition, therefore do not be surprised if it should be some little time before you hear from me again. I direct this to our Cottage,* where I hope you will fix yourself in comfort and I pray that it may very soon please God to give us Peace. England will not be invaded this summer. Buonaparte is gone back to Italy, where 80,000 men are embarking for some expedition. With every kind wish that a fond heart can frame, believe me, as ever, your most affectionate husband.

HORATIO NELSON

To the Captains of the *Orion, Alexander* and *Vanguard*

Gibraltar Bay, *7th May, 1798*

It being of the very greatest importance that the Squadron should not be separated, it is my

* Before Nelson left England, he obtained the object he had so long desired by purchasing a "cottage" and a few acres of land, called "Round-Wood", near Ipswich.

positive orders that no temptation is to induce a Line-of-Battle Ship to separate from me, except the almost certainty of bringing a Line-of-Battle Ship of the Enemy to Action; but in common chaces, if the weather is such as to risk separation, or the approach of night, it is my directions you leave off the chace, and rejoin me, even without waiting the signal of Recall, unless I make the signal to continue the pursuit, by No. 104, page 30, S.B.

HORATIO NELSON

To Lord St Vincent.
Vanguard, off Cape Sicie, *May 17th, 1798*

My Lord,
    This morning, the *Terpsichore* captured a small French Corvette, of six guns and sixty-five men, which came out of Toulon at 11 o'clock, last night. From the general report of Vessels spoke, you will observe the uniformity of the reports – viz., that an expedition is preparing to sail from Toulon. We have separately examined the crew of this Corvette, and, from the whole, I believe the following may be depended on as near the truth – that Buonaparte arrived at Toulon last Friday and has examined the troops which are daily embarking in the numerous Transports; that Vessels with troops frequently arrive from Marseilles; it is not generally believed that Buonaparte is to embark, but no one knows to what place the Armament is destined. Fifteen Sail of

the Line are apparently ready for sea, but nineteen are in the harbour, and yet it is said only six Sail of the Line are to sail with the Transports now ready; that about 12,000 men are embarked; their cavalry arrived at Toulon, but I cannot learn that any are yet embarked. Reports say they are to sail in a few days, and others that they will not sail for a fortnight. This Corvette was bound to the westward, I believe, with dispatches, but the Commander denies it.

The Admiral Brueys has his Flag in *L'Orient*, 120 guns; *Le Formidable* and *Spartanade*, of 80 guns, are also Flag-ships. The Venetian Ships are considered as very bad in every respect, but I do not learn that the Fleet is deficient in either men or stores. All this information is but little more than you knew when I left you, but, still, knowing that late information of the state of the Enemy's Fleet is desirable, I send an intelligent young man, Mr Charles Harford, who has just served his Time, with this letter, and I beg leave to recommend him to your notice. You may rely, my Lord, that I shall act as occasions may offer, to the best of my abilities, in following up your ideas for the honour of His Majesty's Arms, and the advantage of our Country, and believe me, your Lordship's obedient Servant,

HORATIO NELSON

I saw three French Frigates this afternoon, but as they did not see the Squadron, I am in hopes of getting near them. The Squadron is as I wish them.

Vanguard, Island of St Peter's, in Sardinia,
May 24th, 1798

My dearest Fanny*,

I ought not to call what has happened to the *Vanguard* by the cold name of accident: I believe firmly, that it was the Almighty's goodness, to check my consummate vanity. I hope it has made me a better Officer, as I feel confident it has made me a better Man. I kiss with all humility the rod.

Figure to yourself a vain man, on Sunday evening at sun-set, walking in his cabin with a Squadron about him, who looked up to their Chief to lead them to glory, and in whom this Chief placed the firmest reliance, that the proudest Ships, in equal numbers belonging to France, would have bowed their Flags; and with a very rich Prize lying by him. Figure to yourself this proud, conceited man, when the sun rose on Monday morning, his Ship dismasted, his Fleet dispersed, and himself in such distress, that the meanest Frigate out of France would have been a very unwelcome guest. But it has pleased Almighty God to bring us into a safe Port, where, although we are refused the rights of humanity, yet the *Vanguard* will in two days get to sea again, as an English Man-of-War.

The exertions of Sir James Saumarez, in the *Orion*, and Captain A. Ball, in the *Alexander*, have been wonderful; if the Ship had been in England, months would have been taken to send

---

* His wife, Lady Francis.

her to sea: here, my operations will not be delayed four days, and I shall join the rest of my Fleet on the rendezvous.

If this letter gets to you, be so good as to write a line to Lord Spencer, telling him that the *Vanguard* is fitted tolerably for sea, and that what has happened will not retard my operations. We are all health and good humour: tell Lady Saumarez Sir James never was in better health. With kind love to my Father, believe me ever your affectionate husband,

HORATIO NELSON

I have wrote to Lord S. by another, but I still wish you to write a line to say we are all well, for yours may arrive and his Lordship's miscarry.

P.S. Mr Thomas Meek, who was recommended by Mr Hussey and my brother Suckling, was killed, and several seamen were wounded.

To Lord St Vincent
Vanguard, Island of St. Peter's, in Sardinia,
May 24th, 1798

My Lord,

I am sorry to be obliged to inform you of the accidents which have happened to the *Vanguard*. On Saturday, May the 19th, it blew strong from the NW. On Sunday it moderated so much, as to enable us to get our top-gallant masts and yards aloft. After dark it began to blow strong; but as the

Ship was prepared for a gale, my mind was easy. At half-past one AM on Monday, the main-top-mast went over the side, as did soon afterwards the mizen-mast. As it was impossible for any night-signal to be seen, I had hopes we should be quiet till day-light, when I determined to wear, and scud before the gale; but about half-past three the fore-mast went in three pieces, and the bowsprit was found to be sprung in three places. When the day broke, we were fortunately enabled to wear the Ship with a remnant of the spirit-sail. The *Orion*, *Alexander*, and *Emerald* wore with us; but the *Terpsichore*, *Bonne Citoyenne*, and a French Smyrna ship, continued to lay to under bare poles. Our situation was 25 leagues south of the Islands of Hieres; and as we were laying with our head to the NB, had we not wore, which was hardly to be expected, the Ship must have drifted to Corsica. The gale blew very hard all the day, and the ship laboured most exceedingly. In the evening, being in latitude 40° 50′ N, I determined to steer for Oristan Bay, in the Island of Sardinia: during the night, the *Emerald* parted company, for what reason I am at present unacquainted with. Being unable to get into Oristan, the *Alexander* took us in tow, and by Captain Ball's unremitting attention to our distress, and by Sir James Saumarez's exertions and ability in finding out the Island of St Peter's, and the proper anchorage, the *Vanguard* was, on May the 23rd, at noon, brought safely to an anchor into the harbour of St Peter's.

I have the honour to be, &c.

HORATIO NELSON

To the Viceroy of Sardinia
His Britannic Majesty's Ship *Vanguard*,
At Anchor, off the Island of St Peter's,
26th May, 1798

Sir,

Having, by a gale of wind sustained some trifling damage, I anchored a small part of his Majesty's Fleet, under my orders, off this Island, and was surprised to hear, by an Officer sent by the Governor, that admittance was to be refused to the Flag of his Britannic Majesty into this Port. When I reflect that my most gracious Sovereign is the oldest, (I believe,) and certainly the most faithful, Ally which his Majesty of Sardinia ever had, I could feel the sorrow which it must have been to his Majesty to have given such an order, and also for your Excellency, who has to direct its execution. I cannot but look at Africa's shore, where the followers of Mahomet are performing the part of the good Samaritan, which I look for in vain at St Peter's, where it is said the Christian Religion is professed. May I request the favour of your Excellency to forward one Letter for his Britannic Majesty's Minister at Turin, and the other for his Britannic Majesty's Consul at Leghorn. May God Almighty bless your Excellency is the sincere wish of your most obedient servant,

HORATIO NELSON

To Lord St. Vincent
31st May, 1798

My dear Lord,
     My pride was too great for man; but I trust my
friends will think that I bore my chastisement like
a man. It has pleased God to assist us with his
favour, and here I am again off Toulon. I am, &c.
                    HORATIO NELSON

*A week later Captain Troubridge brought the following
Orders to Nelson from Lord St Vincent: "In pursuance
of instructions I have received from the Lords Commissioners of the Admiralty, to employ a squadron of his
Majesty's Ships within the Mediteranean, under the
command of a discreet Officer, (copies of which are
enclosed and of papers necessary for your guidance) in
conformity thereto, I do hereby authorize and require
You, on being joined by the Ships named in the margin*
(Culloden, Goliath, Minotaur, Defence, Bellerophon,
Majestic, Audacious, Zealous, Swiftsure, Theseus) *to
take them and their Captains under your command, in
addition to those already with you, and to proceed with
them in quest of the Armament preparing by the Enemy
at Toulon and Genoa . . . On falling in with said
Armament, or any part thereof, you are to use your
utmost endeavours to* take, sink, burn or destroy it . . ."

To Lord St Vincent   *June 11th*

     The *Mutine*, Captain Hardy, joined me on the
5th, at day-light, with the flattering account of
the honour you intended me of commanding such

a Fleet. *Mutine* fell in with *Alcmene,* off Barcelona on the 2nd. Hope had taken all my Frigates off the rendezvous, on the presumption that the *Vanguard,* from her disabled state, must return to an Arsenal. I joined dear Troubridge with the reinforcement of ten Sail of the Line, and the *Leander* on the 7th in the evening: it has been nearly calm ever since, which grieves me sorely. The French have a long start but I hope they will rendezvous in Tclamon bay, for the 12,000 men from Genoa in 100 Sail of Vessels, escorted by a Frigate, had not put to sea on the 2nd, nor were all the troops embarked. You may be assured I will fight them the moment I can reach their Fleet, be they at anchor, or under sail, I am, &c.

HORATIO NELSON

To Lord St Vincent   *12th of June, 1798*

As I see no immediate prospect of a Letter, I shall continue my private one in form of a Diary, which may not be unpleasant to rcfer to: therefore to begin. Being so close to the Enemy, I take the liberty of keeping *Orion* for a few days. Owing to want of wind, I did not pass Cape Corse until this morning; at four we were becalmed. The moment we had passed, I sent the *Mutine* to look into Telamon Bay, which, as all the French troops had not left Genoa on the 6th, I thought a probable place for the rendezvous of a large Fleet; and went with the Squadron between Monte Christi, and Giulio, keeping the Continent close on board.

13th of June. – *Mutine* joined; nothing in Telamon Bay. I then ran the Fleet between Plenosa and Elba, and Monte Christi; and on the 14th at noon, am now off Civita Vecchia; spoke a Tunisian cruiser, who reported he had spoke a Greek, on the 10th, who told him, that on the 4th, he had passed through the French Fleet, of about 200 Sail, as he thought, off the NW end of Sicily, steering to the eastward. Am in anxious expectation of meeting with Dispatch-boats, Neapolitan cruisers, &c., with letters for me from Naples giving me information.

15th of June. – Off the Ponza Islands; my hopes of information were vain. Not finding a Cruiser, I shall send Troubridge into Naples, in the *Mutine*, to talk with Sir William Hamilton and General Acton. Troubridge possesses my full confidence, and has been my honoured acquaintance of twenty-five years' standing. I only beg that your Lordship will believe, I shall endeavour to prove myself worthy of your selection of me for this highly honourable Command. Not a moment shall be lost in pursuing the Enemy. I am, &c.

HORATIO NELSON

To Earl Spencer
Vanguard, off the Island of Ponza,
15th June, 1798

My Lord,
Not having received orders from my Com-

mander-in-Chief to correspond with the Secretary of the Admiralty, I do not feel myself at perfect liberty to do it, unless on extraordinary occasions, when I shall send copies of my Letters to Lord St Vincent; but as your Lordships must be anxious to hear of us, I take the liberty of acquainting you that Captain Troubridge joined on the 7th, but it was the 12th before we passed Cape Corse. The last account I had of the French Fleet, was from a Tunisian Cruiser, who saw them on the 4th, off Trapani, in Sicily, steering to the eastward. If they pass Sicily, I shall believe they are going on their scheme of possessing Alexandria, and getting troops to India – a plan concerted with Tippoo Saib, by no means so difficult as might at first view be imagined; but be they bound to the Antipodes, your Lordship may rely that I will not lose a moment in bringing them to Action, and endeavour to destroy their Transports. I shall send Captain Troubridge on shore to talk with General Acton, and I hope the King of Naples will send me some Frigates; for mine parted company on the 20th of May, and have not joined me since. The whole Squadron is remarkably healthy, and perfectly equal to meet the French Fleet. As I send this before I receive accounts from Naples, it is not in my power to say anything more of the Enemy, for I shall make sail and pass the Faro of Messina the moment Captain Troubridge returns.

Highly honoured as I feel with this very important command, I beg you will believe that I

shall endeavour to approve myself worthy of it,
and that I am, with the highest respect,
    Your Lordship's most obedient servant,
                    HORATIO NELSON

I have taken the liberty of enclosing a letter
for Lady Nelson, which I beg your Lordship
will have the goodness to order to be sent to her.

To Lord St Vincent
            Vanguard, off the Islands of Ponza,
                        June 15th, 1798

My Lord,
    I have the honour to acquaint you of my
arrival here with the whole Line-of-Battle Ships,
the Fifty, and Brig, all in the most perfect
health. I am sending Captain Troubridge in
the *Mutine* to see Sir William Hamilton* and
General Acton, and to get accounts of the
French Fleet. I shall lay with the Squadron
off Ischia till Captain Troubridge's return, when
not a moment shall be lost in pursuing the
Enemy, and bringing them to Action. With
the highest respect, believe me, your Lordship's
most obedient servant,
                    HORATIO NELSON

* Sir William Hamilton, British ambassador to Naples, husband
of Emma Hamilton.

To Sir William Hamilton
Vanguard, off the Faro of Messina,
June 20th, 1798

My dear Sir,
   I have thought so much, and heard so much, of
the French, since I left Naples, that I should feel
culpable, was I for a moment to delay expressing
my sentiments on the present situation of the
Kingdom of the Two Sicilies. I trust it will be
received as I mean it – as proof of the lively
interest I take in the fate of their Sicilian Majesties. I shall begin by supposing myself commanding a Fleet attending an Army which is to invade
Sicily. If the General asked if Malta would not be
a most useful place for the depot of stores, &c.,
&c., my answer would be, if you can take Malta, it
secures the safety of the Fleet, Transports, stores,
&c., and insures your safe retreat should that be
necessary; for if even a superior Fleet of the
Enemy should arrive, before one week passes,
they will be blown to leeward, and you may pass
with safety. This would be my opinion. There
can be no doubt but the French know as well as
you and I do, that their Sicilian Majesties called
for our help to save them, (even this is crime
enough with the French). Here we are, and are
ready, and will shed our blood in preventing the
French from ill-treating them. On the arrival of
the King's Fleet I find plenty of good will towards us, with every hatred towards the French;
but no assistance for us – no hostility to the
French. On the contrary, the French Minister

is allowed to send off Vessels to inform the Fleet of my arrival, force, and destination, that instead of my surprising them, they may be prepared for resistance. But this being past, I shall endeavour briefly to state what in my opinion is now best to be done, and what Naples ought to do, if it is earnestly wished to save Sicily. I shall suppose the French not advanced since the last accounts, but still on Gozo and Comino, the Fleet anchored between them. By the communication from Naples, they will be formed in the strongest position, with Batteries and Gun-boats to flank them. We shall doubtless injure them, but our loss must be great; and I do not expect to force them from the anchorage, without Fire-ships, Bomb-vessels, and Gun-boats when one hour would either destroy or drive them out. If our Fleet is crippled, the blockade ends; if not, it will be continued, by attention, and sending two Ships at a time to Sicily to get refreshments, for the summer, at least; but whenever this Fleet may be drawn away, and the Ministry find what has passed at Naples – *no co-operation*, although we are come to their assistance – who can say that the Fleet will be kept in these seas? I have said and repeat it, *Malta is the direct road to Sicily*. It has been, and may be yet in the King of Naples' power, by giving me help of every kind, directly to destroy this Armament, and force the Army to unconditional submission. Naples must soon find us masts, yards, stores, ammunition, &c., &c., Will not this be a declaration of War against the French? – therefore why delay sending help, if it is only six Gun-boats at a time. But not a moment must be lost – it can never be regained. I recollect General Acton, in his letter to you calling for our help, says, "Will the King and Ministry wish to see these fine Countries in the hands of the French?" the answer is, No; and we have sent the means of preventing it. It may now be asked – will the Ministry of their Sicilian Majesties permit these fine Countries to fall into the hands of the French? This will assuredly happen if they do not co-operate with us. If I have wrote my mind too freely, I trust it will be excused. The importance of the subject called for my opinion. I have given it like an honest man, and shall wish to stand or fall with it.

I am, dear Sir, with the highest respect, &c.
HORATIO NELSON

To George Baldwin, Consul at Alexandria
Vanguard, at Sea, *26th June, 1798*

Sir,

The French having possessed themselves of Malta, on Friday, the 15th of this month, the next day, the whole Fleet, consisting of sixteen Sail of the Line, Frigates, Bomb-vessels, &c. and near three hundred Transports, left the Island. I only heard this unpleasant news on the 22nd, off Cape Passaro. As Sicily was not their object, and the wind blew fresh from the westward, from the time they sailed, it was clear that their destination was to the eastward; and I think their object is, to possess themselves of some Port in Egypt, and to fix themselves at the head of the Red Sea, in order to get a formidable Army into India; and, in concert with Tippoo Saib, to drive us, if possible, from India. But I have reason to believe, from not seeing a Vessel, that they have heard of my coming up the Mediterranean, and are got safe into Corfu. But still I am most exceedingly anxious to know from you if any reports or preparations have been made in Egypt for them; or any Vessels prepared in the Red Sea, to carry them to India, where, from the prevailing winds at this season, they would soon arrive; or any other information you would be good enough to give me, I shall hold myself much obliged.

I am, Sir, &c.
HORATIO NELSON

To Sir William Hamilton
Vanguard, Syracuse, *July 20th, 1798*

My dear Sir,

It is an old saying, "the Devil's children have the Devil's luck." I cannot find, or to this moment learn, beyond vague conjecture where the French Fleet are gone to. All my ill fortune, hitherto, has proceeded from want of Frigates. Off Cape Passaro, on the 22nd of June, at daylight, I saw two Frigates, which were supposed to be French, and it has been said since that a Line of Battle Ship was to leeward of them, with the riches of Malta on board, but it was the destruc-

tion of the Enemy, not riches for myself, that I
was seeking. These would have fallen to me if I
had had Frigates, but except the Ship of the Line,
I regard not all the riches in this world. From
every information off Malta I believed they were
gone to Egypt. Therefore, on the 28th, I was
communicating with Alexandria in Egypt, where
I found the Turks preparing to resist them, but
know nothing beyond report. From thence I
stretched over the Coast of Caramania, where
not meeting a Vessel that could give me information, I became distressed for the Kingdom of the
Two Sicilies, and having gone a round of 600
leagues at this season of the year (with a single
Ship) with an expedition incredible, here I am as
ignorant of the situation of the Enemy as I was
twenty-seven days ago. I sincerely hope, that the
Dispatches which I understand are at Cape Passaro, will give me full information. I shall be able
for nine or ten weeks longer to keep the Fleet on
active service, when we shall want provisions and
stores. I send a paper on that subject herewith.
Mr Littledale is, I suppose, sent up by the Admiral to victual us, and I hope he will do it
cheaper than any other person; but if I find
out that he charges more than the fair price,
and has not the provisions of the very best qual-
ity, I will not take them; for, as no Fleet has more
fag than this, nothing but the best food and
greatest attention can keep them healthy. At this
moment, we have not one sick man in the Fleet.
In about six days I shall sail from hence, and if I
hear nothing more from the French, I shall go to

the Archipelago where if they are gone towards Constantinople I shall hear of them. I shall go to Cyprus, and if they are gone to Alexandretta, or any other part of Syria or Egypt, I shall get information. You will, I am sure, and so will our Country, easily conceive what has passed in my anxious mind, but I have this comfort, that I have no fault to accuse myself of. This bears me up, and this only. I send you a Paper, in which a letter is fixed for different places, which I may leave at any place, and except those who have the key, none can tell where I am gone to.

July 21st. – The Messenger has returned from Cape Passaro, and says, that your letters for me are returned to Naples. What a situation am I placed in! As yet, I can learn nothing of the Enemy; therefore I have no conjecture but that they are gone to Syria, and at Cyprus I hope to hear of them. If they were gone westward, I reply that every place in Sicily would have information for us, for it is news too important to leave me one moment in doubt about. I have no Frigate, nor a sign of one. The masts, yards, &c., for the *Vanguard* will, I hope, be prepared directly; for should the French be so strongly secured in Port that I cannot get at them, I shall immediately shift my Flag into some other Ship, and send the *Vanguard* to Naples to be refitted; for hardly any other person but myself would have continued on service so long in such a wretched state. I want to send a great number of Papers to Lord St Vincent, but I dare not trust any person here to carry them even to Naples. Pray send a copy of my letter to Lord Spencer. He must be very anxious to hear of this Fleet. I have taken the liberty to trouble your Excellency with a letter for Lady Nelson. Pray forward it for me, and believe me, with the greatest respect, your most obedient Servant,

HORATIO NELSON

To Lady Nelson   Syracuse, *July 20th, 1798*

I have not been able to find the French Fleet, to my great mortification, or the event I can scarcely doubt. We have been off Malta, to Alexandria in Egypt, Syria, into Asia, and are returned here without success: however, no person will say that it has been for want of activity. I yet live in hopes of meeting these fellows; but it would have been my delight to have tried Buonaparte on a wind, for he commands the Fleet, as well as the Army. Glory is my object, and that alone. God Almighty bless you.

HORATIO NELSON

To the Commanders of any of His Majesty's Ships

Vanguard, Syracuse, *22nd July, 1798*

Sir,
Resting with the greatest confidence that had the French Fleet proceeded to the westward from Malta, that his Majesty's Minister at Naples

would have taken care to have lodged information for me in every Port in Sicily, knowing I was gone to the eastward, I now acquaint you that I shall steer direct for the Island of Cyprus, and hope in Syria to find the French Fleet. I am, &c.

HORATIO NELSON

Having received some vague information of the Enemy, I shall steer to the north of Candia, and probably send a Ship to Milo, and if the Enemy are not in those seas, I shall pass on for Cyprus, Syria, and Egypt.

At 4 p.m. on the afternoon of 1 August 1798, HMS Zealous *made the signal for the French fleet, sixteen Sail of the Line, anchored in Aboukir Bay. The battle commenced two and half hours later, after nightfall.*

To Lord St Vincent
Vanguard, off the Mouth of the Nile,
3rd August, 1798

My Lord,
Almighty God has blessed his Majesty's Arms in the late Battle, by a great Victory over the Fleet of the Enemy, who I attacked at sunset on the 1st of August, off the Mouth of the Nile. The Enemy were moored in a strong Line of Battle for defending the entrance of the Bay, (of Shoals,) flanked by numerous Gun-boats, four Frigates, and a Battery of Guns and Mortars on an Island in their Van; but nothing could withstand the Squadron your Lordship did me the honour to

place under my command. Their high state of discipline is well known to you, and with the judgment of the Captains, together with their valour, and that of the Officers and Men of every description, it was absolutely irresistible. Could anything from my pen add to the character of the Captains, I would write it with pleasure, but that is impossible.

I have to regret the loss of Captain Westcott of the *Majestic*, who was killed early in the Action; but the Ship was continued to be so well fought by her First Lieutenant, Mr Cuthbert, that I have given him an order to command her till your Lordship's pleasure is known.

The Ships of the Enemy, all but their two rear Ships, are nearly dismasted: and those two, with two Frigates, I am sorry to say, made their escape; nor was it, I assure you, in my power to prevent them. Captain Hood most handsomely endeavoured to do it, but I had no Ship in a condition to support the *Zealous*, and I was obliged to call her in.

The support and assistance I have received from Captain Berry cannot be sufficiently expressed. I was wounded in the head, and obliged to be carried off the deck; but the service suffered no loss by that event; Captain Berry was fully equal to the important service then going on, and to him I must beg leave to refer you for every information relative to this Victory. He will present you with the Flag of the Second in Command, that of the Commander-in-Chief being burnt in *L'Orient*.

Herewith I transmit you Lists of the Killed and

Wounded, and the Lines of Battle of ourselves and the French. I have the honour to be, my Lord, your Lordship's most obedient Servant,

HORATIO NELSON

To the Respective Captains of the Squadron
Vanguard, off the Mouth of the Nile,
2nd August, 1798

Almighty God having blessed His Majesty's Arms with Victory, the Admiral intends returning Public Thanksgiving for the same at two o'clock this day; and he recommends every Ship doing the same as soon as convenient.

HORATIO NELSON

To the Captains of the Ships of the Squadron
Vanguard, off the Mouth of the Nile,
2nd day of August, 1798

The Admiral most heartily congratulates the Captains, Officers, Seamen, and Marines of the Squadron he has the honour to command, on the event of the late Action; and he desires they will accept his most sincere and cordial Thanks for their very gallant behaviour in this glorious Battle. It must strike forcibly every British Seaman, how superior their conduct is, when in discipline and good order, to the riotous behaviour of the lawless Frenchmen.

The Squadron may be assured the Admiral will not fail, with his Dispatches, to represent their truly meritorious conduct in the strongest terms to the Commander-in-Chief.

HORATIO NELSON

On 3rd August, the Captains of the Squadron met on board the Orion, *Captain Sir James Saumarez, the senior Captain, and second in command.*

"The Captains of the Squadron under the Orders of Rear-Admiral Sir Horatio Nelson, K.B., desirous of testifying the high sense they entertain of his prompt decision and intrepid conduct in the Attack of the French Fleet, in Bequier Road, off the Nile, the 1st of August, 1798, request his acceptance of a Sword; and, as a further proof of their esteem and regard, hope that he will permit his Portrait to be taken, and hung up in the Room belonging to the Egyptian Club, now established in commemoration of that glorious day.

"Dated on board of His Majesty's Ship, Orion *this 3rd of August, 1798.*

Jas. Saumarez	*D. Gould*
T. Troubridge	*Th. Foley*
H. D. Darby	*R. Willett Miller*
Tho. Louis	*Ben. Hallowell*
John Peyton	*E. Barry*
Alex. John Ball	*T. M. Hardy*
Sam. Hood."	

To the Captains of His Majesty's Ships off the Nile

Vanguard, August 3rd, 1798

Gentlemen,
    I feel most sensibly the very distinguished hon-

our you have conferred upon me by your Address of this day. My prompt decision was the natural consequence of having such Captains under my command, and I thank God I can say, that in the Battle the conduct of every Officer was equal. I accept, as a particular mark of your esteem, the Sword you have done me the honour to offer, and will direct my Picture to be painted the first opportunity, for the purpose you mention.

I have the honour to be, Gentlemen,
With the highest respect, your most obliged,
HORATIO NELSON

The Rt. Hon. Lord Nelson, K.B.

My Lord,
Herewith I send you a Coffin made of part of *L'Orient*'s Main mast, that when you are tired of this Life you may be buried in one of your own Trophies – but may that period be far distant, is the sincere wish of your obedient and much obliged servant,
Ben Hallowell
"Swiftsure, May 23rd, 1799"

Nelson much appreciated the macabre gift, and was later buried in it.

To the Lord Mayor of London
Vanguard, Mouth of the Nile,
8th August, 1798

My Lord,
Having the honour of being a Freeman of the

City of London, I take the liberty of sending to your Lordship, the Sword of the Commanding French Admiral, Monsieur Blanquet, who survived after the Battle of the first, off the Nile; and request, that the City of London will honour me by the acceptance of it, as a remembrance, that Britannia still rules the Waves, which, that She may for ever do, is the fervent prayer of your Lordship's most obedient Servant,

HORATIO NELSON

To Earl Spencer, First Lord of the Admiralty
Mouth of the Nile, *9th August, 1798*

My Lord,
    Was I to die this moment, "Want of Frigates" would be found stamped on my heart. No words of mine can express what I have, and not be left without Ships, for each Prize takes a Ship of the Line to man her, and attend to her wants. This you will believe, when I tell you that only two masts are standing, out of nine Sail of the Line. *L'Orient* certainly struck her colours, and did not fire a shot for a quarter of an hour before, unfortunately for us, she took fire; but although we suffer, our Country is equally benefited. She had on board near six hundred thousand pounds sterling; so says the Adjutant-General of the Fleet, who was saved out of her, and although he does not say she struck her colours, yet he allows that all resistance on her part was in vain. Admiral Brueys was killed early in the battle, and

from the commencement of the fight, declared all was lost. They moored in a strong position in a Line of Battle, with Gun-boats, Bomb-Vessels, Frigates, and a gun and mortar Battery on an Island in their Van, but my band of friends was irresistible. The French Army is in possession of Alexandria, Aboukir, Rosetta, Damietta, and Cairo; and Buonaparte writes that he is sending a detachment to take possession of Suez and Fayoum.

By the intercepted letters from the Army (for we took the Vessel with Buonaparte's courier) they are grievously disappointed, the Country between their Posts completely hostile. I have little doubt but that Army will be destroyed by plague, pestilence, and famine, and battle and murder, which that it may soon be, God grant. The Turks will soon send an Army into Syria, and as for the present, we block them up by sea, they must soon experience great distress. I hope to find, on my arrival at Naples, that the Emperor and many other Powers are at war with the French, for until they are reduced there can be no peace in this world. The Admiral having sent up Mr Littledale, the victualling of the Fleet does not rest with me.

September 7th

I feel so much recovered, that it is probable I shall not go home at present. The Turks have seized all French Ships in the Levant, in consequence of the taking a Turkish sixty-gun Ship at Alexandria, and seizing all Turkish property. This was done on the 14th of August. I shall always receive pleasure in hearing from you, both as a public and private man; and believe me, dear Sir, &c.

HORATIO NELSON

To Earl Spencer
Vanguard, 7th September, 1798

My Lord,
   On the 15th August, I received Earl St Vincent's most secret Orders and Letters. As not a moment was to be lost, I determined to destroy the three Prizes (*Guerrier, Heureux,* and *Mercure,*) which had not sailed with Sir James Saumarez, and they were set on fire on the 18th. I rest assured that they will be paid for, and have held out that assurance to the Squadron; for if an Admiral is, after a victory, only to look after the captured ships, and not distressing the Enemy, very dearly indeed does the Nation pay for the Prizes, and I trust that £60,000 will be deemed a very moderate sum; and I am bold to say, when the services, time, and men, with the expense of fitting those three Ships for a voyage to England is valued, that Government will save nearly as much as they are valued at. I rejoice, in the present instance, that a particular regard for my own interest cannot be supposed to actuate me, for if the moderate sum of £60,000 is paid, my share can only be £625, while if it is not paid, I have defrauded the Commander-in-Chief and the other Classes, of the sums set off against them—

Commander-in-Chief	£3,750	0	0
Junior Admirals, each	625	0	0
Captains, each	1,000	0	0
Lieutenants' Class, each	75	0	0
Warrant Officers, each	50	0	0
Petty Officers, each	11	0	0
Seamen and Marines, each	2	4	1

Your Lordship will do me the justice to say, that pay for Prizes, in many instances, (it is not a new idea of mine,) would be not only an amazing saving to the State, without taking into calculation what the Nation loses by the attention of Admirals to the property of the Captors, an attention absolutely necessary as a recommence for the exertions of the Officers and men. An Admiral may be amply rewarded by his feelings and the approbation of his superiors, but what reward have the inferior Officers and men but the value of the Prizes? If an Admiral takes that from them, on any consideration, he cannot expect to be well supported. However, I trust, as in all other instances, if, to serve the State, any persons or bodies of men suffer losses, it is amply made up to them; and in this I rest confident my brave associates will not be disappointed. I have the honour to be, &c.

HORATIO NELSON

DISPOSITION OF THE FLEET UNDER MY COMMAND

Vanguard, 13th September, 1798

Vanguard – Wants new masts and bowsprit, but

shall defer getting them till I know the situation of [:]

Culloden – To be careened at Naples.

Alexander – When her masts are reduced and secured, to be sent down the Mediterranean, unless particularly wanted for a month or six weeks.

Goliath – Ordered to be sent from Alexandria the moment the *Lion* arrives. Main-mast bad.

Zealous	
Swiftsure	
Emerald	Ordered to cruise off Alexandria
Alcmene	as long as they
Seahorse	can with propriety.
La Fortune	

Thalia – Joined me this morning.

Terpsichore – Sent by Captain Dixon to Naples, and from thence to join the Commander-in-Chief. (Parted company 20th May).

Transfer – Never joined. Reported to be gone to Cyprus.

Lion – Joined Captain Hood off Alexandria, the 25th August.

Mutine – Going down with Dispatches.

Bonne Citoyenne – Gone to Naples.

Earl St. Vincent – With Captain Retalick, to join the Portuguese Squadron.

Portuguese Squadron – Returning from Alexandria, and requested to block up Malta.

Minotaur	Ordered, when Sir James
	Saumarez gets between Sardinia
Audacious	and Minorca, to join me at Naples.

Orion
Defence
Bellerophon } On their passage to Gibraltar
Theseus   with the Prizes.
Majestic
Flora, Cutter – Gone to Alexandria.

HORATIO NELSON

Began at Sea,
September 16th, 1798

My dearest Fanny,

It is hardly possible for me to know where to begin. My head is almost turned by letters already and what am I not to expect when I get on shore. Noise enough to distract me. My head is healed and I am better.

The Kingdom of the two Sicilies are mad with joy from the throne to the peasant all are alike. From Lady Hamilton's letter the situation of the Queen was truly pitiable. I only hope I shall not have to be witness to a renewal of it. I give you Lady Hamilton's words. "How shall I describe the transports of the Queen? Tis not possible. She fainted, cried, kissed her husband, her children, walked frantic about the room, cried, kissed and embraced every person near here exclaiming Oh, brave Nelson; Oh God bless and protect our brave deliverer! Oh Nelson, Nelson, what do we not owe you! Oh victor, saviour of Italy! Oh that my swollen heart could not tell him personally what we owe to him.'" You may judge of the rest, but my head will not allow to tell you half. So much for that.

My fag without success would have had no effect. But blessed be God for his goodness to me. I have your letters of May 22nd, June 11th and July 16th. The box you were so good as to send me with places, seal etc. if sent by *L'Aigle* is lost but never mind that, I feel equally your kindness. Do not send any more. What is likely to go on here time only can shew. I am sure I cannot guess, but as the French have only one regular ship of the line, tis not likely I shall see any more fighting. As to Round Wood if the place or neighbourhood is not to your satisfaction, I hope the country will put me in a situation of choosing another, but my dear Fanny unless you can game, and talk scandal, that is lies, most probably your company will never be coveted by country town tabbies. Young people have more goodness than old cats. I put Hoste into a sloop of war. I hope Lord St Vincent will allow him to remain in her. His father is under no obligation to me. If he writes stuff tell him so. All must go to Earl St Vincent I have not power to make a cook. The Queen of Naples has given Hoste a very elegant ring value at least £500 sterling. So much for being a messenger of good news. Sir James Saumarez is on his passage home, so that Lady Saumarez will have the pleasure of his company this winter. Had his wound been very little deeper it would have done his business but as it is, he is not the worse. Josiah is in the *Bonne Citoyenne*. I see no prospect of his being made post. I wish he was as great a favourite of Lord St Vincent's as I wish him, but that is not my fault. However, I hope he will do well in time. He is young and will not endeavour to make him agreeable for his interest or comfort.

September 25th. – The poor wretched *Vanguard* arrived here on the 22nd. I must endeavour to convey to you something of what passed, but if it was so affecting to those only who are united in bonds of friendship what must it be to my dearest wife. My friends say everything which is most dear to me in this world. Sir William and Lady Hamilton came out to sea attended by numerous boats with emblems etc. My most respectable friends had really been laid up and seriously ill, first from anxiety and then from joy. It was imprudently told Lady Hamilton in a moment. The effect was a shot. She fell apparently dead and is not yet perfectly recovered from severe bruises. Alongside my honoured friends came, the scene in the boat appeared terribly affecting. Up flew her ladyship and exclaiming: "Oh God is it possible," fell into my arms more dead than alive. Tears however soon set matters to rights, when alongside came the King. The scene was in its way affecting. He took me by the hand, calling me his deliverer and preserver, with every other expression of kindness. In short all Naples calls me "Nostra Liberatore" for the scene with the lower classes was truly affecting. I hope one day to have the pleasure of introducing you to Lady Hamilton. She is one of the very best women in this world. How few could have made the turn

she has. She is an honour to her sex and a proof
that even reputation may be regained, but I own
it requires a great soul*. Her kindness with Sir
William to me is more than I can express. I am in
their house, and I may now tell you it required all
the kindness of my friends to set me up. Her
ladyship, if Josiah was to stay, would make something of him and with all his bluntness I am sure
he likes Lady Hamilton more than any female.
She would fashion him in 6 months in spite of
himself. I believe Lady Hamilton intends writing
you.

May God Almighty bless you, my dearest
Fanny, and give us in due time a happy meeting.
Should the King give me a peerage I believe I
scarcely need state the propriety of your going to
court. Don't mind the expense. Money is trash.
Again God Almighty bless you.

Ever your most affectionate
HORATIO NELSON

You cannot write to Naples by common post.
The Admiralty or Secretary of State is the only way.

To Earl Spencer
Naples, *September 25th, 1798*

My Lord,
Culloden and *Alexander* arrived here the 16th.
The former is at Castel-à-Mare, where every

* Emma Hamilton was a former street-walker and concubine.

assistance is afforded her. *Alexander* is fitting for two months' service, when from her battered state she must go down the Mediterranean. Captain Ball is so anxious to get at the *Guillaume Tell*, that she will soon be ready. He is emulous to give the final blow to the French Navy in the Mediterranean (for I reckon, nor do the Enemy, the Venetian Ships as anything). I wish my friend Ball was fairly alongside of her: our Country need not fear the event. His activity and zeal are eminently conspicuous even amongst the Band of Brothers – each, as I may have occasion to mention them, must call forth my gratitude and admiration. On the 22nd, the wreck of *Vanguard* arrived in the Bay of Naples. His Sicilian Majesty came out three leagues to meet me, and directly came on board. His Majesty took me by the hand and said such things of our Royal Master, our Country, and myself, that no words I could use would in any degree convey what so apparently came from the Royal heart. From his Majesty, his Ministers, and every class, I am honoured by the appellation of "Nostro Liberatore."

You will not, my Lord, I trust, think that one spark of vanity induces me to mention the most distinguished reception that ever, I believe, fell to the lot of a human being, but that it is a measure of justice due to his Sicilian Majesty and the Nation. If God knows my heart, it is amongst the most humble of the creation, full of thankfulness and gratitude! I send your Lordship a correct statement of the loss of the Enemy in the Battle of the Nile. The hand of God was visible from the first to the last. The fate of *Généreux* and miserable condition of *Guillaume Tell* are farther proofs of it. All glory be to Him! Amen!

With my sincerest respects to Lady Spencer, the Dowager Lady Spencer, Lady Lucan, and those of your Lordship's family who have honoured me by their notice, and I beg you will allow me to assure you with what respect I am,

Your most faithful Servant,
HORATIO NELSON

I have this moment Letters from Mr Wyndham at Florence, telling me, that three of the Venetian Ships (64s) with eleven Transports, are ready to sail from Toulon. I hope Naples is on the eve of declaring: also, *I hope* – but it is a distant one – that the Portuguese are off Malta, when all is right.

For his leadership in the Battle of the Nile, Nelson was raised to the peerage as Baron Nelson of the Nile and parliament voted him a pension of £2,000 per annum. The King of Naples conferred on him the title Duke of Bronte.

John Brown

"So Mad a Scheme": The Suffering of a Deserter Turned Cannibal

1799

The perilous escapades of six deserters from the artillery garrison on the Island of St Helena occasioned a Court of Enquiry on 12 December 1801, at which one of the survivors, John Brown, delivered the "Singular and Affecting Narrative upon Oath".

In June 1799, I belonged to the first company of Artillery in the service of this garrison, and on the 10th of that month, about an hour before parade time, M'Kinnon, gunner and orderly of the 2nd company, asked me if I was willing to go with him on board an American ship called the *Columbr[i]a*, Capt. Henry Lelar (the only ship then in the roads); after some conversation I agreed, and met him about seven o'clock at the plathouse, where I found one M'Quinn, of Major Seale's company, another man called Brighouse, another called Parr, and the sixth Matthew Conway.

Parr was a good seaman and said he would take us to the Island of Ascension, or lay off the harbour till said *Columbr[i]a* could weigh anchor and come out. We went down about eight o'clock to the West Rocks, where the American boat was waiting for us, manned with three of the American seamen, which took us alongside the *Columbr[i]a*. We went on board – Parr down to the cabin, and we changed our clothes after having been on board half an hour.

Brighouse and Conway proposed to cut a whale boat from out of the harbour to prevent the *Columbria* from being suspected, which they effected, having therein a coil of rope and five oars, with a large stone she was moored by – this happened about eleven at night.

We observed lanthorns passing on the line towards the Sea Gate, and hearing a great noise, thought we were missed and searched for. We immediately embarked in the whale boat, with about 25 pounds of bread in a bag, and a small keg of water, supposed to contain about 13 gallons, one compass and one quadrant, given to us by the Commanding Officer of the *Columbria*; but in our hurry the quadrant was either left behind or dropped overboard.

When we left the ship, pulling with two oars only to get ahead of her, the boat was half full of water and nothing to bale her out; in this condition we rowed out to sea, and lay off the island, a great distance, expecting the American ship hourly.

About twelve o'clock the second day, no ship appearing, by Parr's advice we bore away, steering N by W and then NNW for the Island of Ascension, using our hankerchiefs as substitutes for sails. We met a gale of wind which continued for two days, the weather then become very fine, and we supposed we had run about ten miles an hour. M'Kinnon kept a reckoning with pen, ink and paper supplied by the *Columbria*, as also charts and maps.

We continued our course till about the 18th in the morning, when we saw a number of birds but no land. About twelve that day Parr said we must be past the island, accounting it to be 800 miles from St Helena. We then each of us took our shirt and with them made a small sprit sail, and laced our jackets and trowsers together at the waistband to keep us warm, and then altered our course to W by N thinking to make Rio de Janeiro, on the American coast. Provisions running very short, we allowed ourselves only one ounce of bread every 24 hours and two mouthfulls of water.

We continued until the 26th, when all our provisions were expended. On the 23rd M'Quinn took a piece of bamboo in his mouth to chew, and we all followed his example. On that night, it being my turn to steer the boat, and remembering to have read of persons in our situation eating their shoes, I cut a piece off one of mine; but it being soaked in sea water, I was obliged to spit it out, and take the inside sole, which I eat part of, and distributed to the rest, but we found no benefit from it.

On the 1st of July, Parr caught a dolphin with a gaff that had been left in the boat. We all fell on our knees, and thanked God for his goodness to us. We tore up the fish and hung it to dry; about four we eat part of it, which agreed with us pretty well. On this fish we subsisted till the 4th, about eleven o'clock, when finding the whole expended, bones and all, Parr, myself, Brighouse and Conway, proposed to scuttle the boat, and let her go down, to put us out of our misery: the other two objected, observing that God, who had made man, always found him something to eat.

On the 5th, about eleven, M'Kinnon proposed *that it would be better to cut lots for one of us to die, in order to save the rest*; to which we consented. The lots were made. William Parr being sick two days before with the spotted fever, was exclude. He wrote the numbers out, and put them in a hat, which we drew out blind-fold and put them in our pockets. Parr then asked whose lot it was to die; none of us knowing what number we had in our pocket, each one praying to God that it might be his lot. It was agreed that No.5 should die; and that the lots being unfolded, M'Kinnon's was No.5.

We had agreed that that whose lot it was should *bleed himself to death*; for which purpose we had provided ourselves with nails sharpened, which we got from the boat. M'Kinnon with one of them cut himself in three places, in his foot, hand and wrist: and praying God to forgive him, died in about a quarter of an hour.

Before he was quite cold, Brighouse, with one of those nails, cut a piece of flesh off his thigh and hung it up, leaving his body in the boat. About three hours after we all eat of it – only a very small bit. This piece

lasted us until the 7th. We dipped the body every two
hours in the sea to preserve it. Parr having found a
piece of slate in the bottom of the boat, he sharpened it
on the other large stone, and with it cut another piece
off the thigh, which lasted us until the 8th when it
being my watch, and observing the water, about break
of day, to change colour, I called the rest, thinking we
were near shore, but saw no land, it not being quite
daylight.

As soon as day appeared, we discovered land right
ahead, and steered towards it. About eight in the
morning we were close to the shore; there being a
very heavy surf, we endeavoured to turn the boat's
head to it, but being very weak we were unable;
soon after the boat upset! Myself, Conway and Parr
got on shore. M'Quinn and Brighouse were
drowned!

We discovered a small hut on the beach, in which
were an Indian and his mother, who spoke Portuguese,
and I, understanding the language, learnt that there
was a village, about three miles distance, called Bel-
mont; this Indian went to the village and gave information that the French had landed, and in about two
hours the Governor of the village, (a clergyman), with
several armed men, took Conway and Parr prisoners,
tying them by their hands and feet, and slinging them
on a bamboo stick, and in this manner took them to the
village. I being very weak, remained in the hut some
time, but was afterwards taken.

On our telling them we were English, we were
immediately released and three hammocks provided;
we were taken in then to the Governor's house, who let
us lay on his own bed, and gave us milk and rice to eat;

but not having eaten anything for a considerable time, we were lock-jaw'd, and continued so until the 23rd, during which time the Governor wrote to the Governor at St Salvador, who sent a small schooner to a place called Porto Seguro, to take us to San Salvador. We were conducted to Porto Seguro on horseback, passing through Santa Croix, where we remained about ten days; afterwards we embarked, and on our arrival at St Salvador, Parr, on being questioned by the Governor, answered, that our ship had foundered at sea, and that we had saved ourselves in the boat; that the ship's name was the *Sally*, of Liverpool, and belonged to his father, and was last at Cape Coast Castle, on the coast of Africa, to touch at Ascension for turtle, and then bound for Jamaica. Parr said he was the Captain.

We continued at St Salvador about 13 days, during which time the inhabitants made up a subscription of 200 pounds each man. We then embarked in the *Maria*, a Portuguese ship, for Lisbon; Parr as mate, Conway, boatswain's mate, myself, being sickly, as passenger. In 13 days we arrived at Rio de Janeiro. Parr and Conway sailed for Lisbon and I was left in hospital; in about three months, Captain Elphinstone, of the *Diomede*, pressed me into his Majesty's service, giving me the choice of remaining on that station or to proceed to the Admiral at the Cape. I chose the latter, and was put with seven suspected deserters on board the *Ann*, a Botany Bay ship, in irons, with the convicts. When I arrived at the Cape I was put on board the *Lancaster*, 64. I never entered. I at length received my discharge, since which I engaged in the *Duke of Clarence* as a seaman; I was determined to give myself up at the first opportunity, in order to relate my sufferings to the men of this garrison, to deter them from attempting so mad a scheme again.

Thomas Cochrane

The Cruise of the *Speedy*

1800–1

Captain Lord Cochrane entered the Navy in 1793 as midshipman on Gardner's old ship, the Hind *before serving on HMS* Barfleur. *After bringing Nelson's prize the* Généreux *safely to port in 1800, Cochrane received his own command, the sloop* Speedy *and so began the fighting exploits which would make him the very model for dashing naval commanders in historical fiction.*

The *Speedy* was little more than a burlesque on a vessel of war, even sixty years ago. She was about the size of an average coasting brig, her burden being 158 tons. She was crowded, rather than manned, with a crew of eighty-four men and six officers, myself included. Her armament consisted of fourteen 4-*pounders!*, a species of gun little larger than a blunderbuss, and formerly known in the service under the name of "miñion", an appellation which it certainly merited.

Being dissatisfied with her armament, I applied for

and obtained a couple of 12-pounders, intending them
as bow and stern chasers, but was compelled to return
them to the ordnance wharf, there not being room on
deck to work them; besides which, the timbers of the
little craft were found on trial to be too weak to
withstand the concussion of anything heavier than
the guns with which she was previously armed.

With her rig I was more fortunate. Having carried
away her mainyard, it became necessary to apply for
another to the senior officer, who, examining the list of
spare spars, ordered the *foretopgallant-yard* of the
Généreux to be hauled out *as a mainyard for the
Speedy!*

The spar was accordingly sent on board and rigged,
but even this appearing too large for the vessel, an
order was issued to cut off the yard-arms and thus
reduce it to its proper dimensions. This order was
neutralized by getting down and planing the yard-
arms as though they had been cut, an evasion which,
with some alteration in the rigging, passed undetected
on its being again swayed up; and thus a greater spread
of canvas was secured. The fact of the foretopgallant-
yard of a second-rate ship being considered too large
for the mainyard of my "man-of-war" will give a
tolerable idea of her insignificance.

Despite her unformidable character and the personal discomfort to which all on board were subjected, I
was very proud of my little vessel, caring nothing for
her want of accommodation, though in this respect
her cabin merits passing notice. It had not so much as
room for a chair, the floor being entirely occupied by
a small table surrounded with lockers, answering the
double purpose of storechests and seats. The diffi-

culty was to get seated, the ceiling being only five feet
high, so that the object could only be accomplished
by rolling on the locker, a movement sometimes
attended with unpleasant failure. The most singular
discomfort, however, was that my only practicable
mode of shaving consisted in removing the skylight
and putting my head through to make a toilet-table of
the quarterdeck.

In the following enumeration of the various cruises
in which the *Speedy* was engaged, the boarding and
searching innumerable neutral vessels will be passed
over, and the narrative will be strictly confined – as in
most cases throughout this work – to log extracts,
where captures were made, or other occurrences took
place worthy of record.

May 10. – Sailed from Cagliari, from which
port we had been ordered to convoy fourteen sail
of merchantmen to Leghorn. At 9 a.m. observed
a strange sail take possession of a Danish brig
under our escort. At 11:30 a.m. rescued the brig
and captured the assailant. This prize – my first
piece of luck – was the *Intrépide*, French privateer
of six guns and forty-eight men.

May 14. – Saw five armed boats pulling towards us from Monte Cristo. Out sweeps to
protect convoy. At 4 p.m. the boats boarded
and took possession of the two sternmost ships.
A light breeze springing up, made all sail towards
the captured vessels, ordering the remainder of
the convoy to make the best of their way to
Longona. The breeze freshening we came up
with and recaptured the vessels with the prize

crews on board, but during the operation the armed boats escaped.

May 21. – At anchor in Leghorn Roads. Convoy all safe. 25. – Off Genoa. Joined Lord Keith's squadron of five sail of the line, four frigates and a brig.

26, 27, 28. – Ordered by his lordship to cruise in the offing, to intercept supplies destined for the French army under Massena, then in possession of Genoa.

29. – At Genoa some of the gun-boats bombarded the town for two hours.

30. – All the gun-boats bombarded the town. A partial bombardment had been going on for an hour a day, during the past fortnight, Lord Keith humanely refraining from continued bombardment, out of consideration for the inhabitants, who were in a state of absolute famine.

This was one of the *crises* of the war. The French, about a month previous, had defeated the Austrians with great slaughter in an attempt, on the part of the latter, to retake Genoa; but the Austrians, being in possession of Savona, were nevertheless able to intercept provisions on the land side, whilst the vigilance of Lord Keith rendered it impossible to obtain supplies by sea.

It having come to Lord Keith's knowledge that the French in Genoa had consumed their last horses and dogs, whilst the Genoese themselves were perishing by famine, and on the eve of revolt against the usurping force – in order to save the carnage which would ensue, his lordship caused it to be intimated to Massena that a defence so heroic would command honourable terms of capitulation. Massena was said to have replied that if the word "capitulation" were mentioned his army should perish with the city; but, as he could no longer defend himself, he had no objection to "treat". Lord Keith, therefore, proposed a treaty, viz, that the army might return to France, but that Massena himself must remain a prisoner in his hands. To this the French general demurred; but Lord Keith insisting – with the complimentary observation to Massena that "he was worth 20,000 men" – the latter reluctantly gave in, and on the 4th of June, 1800, a definite treaty to the above effect was agreed upon, and ratified on the 5th, when the Austrians took possession of the city, and Lord Keith of the harbour, the squadron anchoring within the mole.

This affair being ended, his lordship ordered the *Speedy* to cruise off the Spanish coast, and on the 14th of June we parted company with the squadron.

June 16. – Captured a tartan off Elba. Sent her to Leghorn, in the charge of an officer and four men.

22. – Off Bastia. Chased a French privateer with a prize in tow. The Frenchman abandoned the prize, a Sardinian vessel laden with oil and wool, and we took possession. Made all sail in chase of the privateer; but on our commencing to fire she ran under the fort of Caprea, where we did not think proper to pursue her. Took prize in tow, and on the following day left her at Leghorn, where we found Lord Nelson, and several ships at anchor.

25. – Quitted Leghorn, and on the 26th were
again off Bastia, in chase of a ship which ran for
that place, and anchored under a fort three miles
to the southward. Made at and brought her away.
Proved to be the Spanish letter of marque *Assun-
cion*, of ten guns and thirty-three men, bound
from Tunis to Barcelona. On taking possession,
five gun-boats left Bastia in chase of us; took the
prize in tow, and kept up a running fight with the
gun-boats till after midnight, when they left us.

29. – Cast off the prize in chase of a French
privateer off Sardinia. On commencing our fire
she set all sail and ran off. Returned and took the
prize in tow; and the 4th of July anchored with
her in Port Mahon.

July 9. – Off Cape Sebastian. Gave chase to
two Spanish ships standing along shore. They
anchored under the protection of the forts. Saw
another vessel lying just within range of the forts;
– out boats and cut her out, the forts firing on the
boats without inflicting damage.

July 19. – Off Caprea. Several French privateers in sight. Chased, and on the following
morning captured one, the *Constitution*, of one
gun and nineteen men. Whilst we were securing
the privateer, a prize which she had taken made
sail in the direction of Gorgona and escaped.

27. – Off Planosa, in chase of a privateer. On
the following morning saw three others lying in a
small creek. On making preparations to cut them
out, a military force made its appearance, and
commenced a heavy fire of musketry, to which it
would have answered no purpose to reply. Fired

several broadsides at one of the privateers, and sunk her.

31. – Off Porto Ferraio in chase of a French privateer, with a prize in tow. The Frenchman abandoned his prize, of which we took possession, and whilst so doing the privateer got away.

August 3. – Anchored with our prizes in Leghorn Roads, where we found Lord Keith in the *Minotaur*.

Lord Keith received me very kindly, and directed the *Speedy* to run down the Spanish coast, pointing out the importance of harassing the enemy there as much as possible, but cautioning me against engaging anything beyond our capacity. During our stay at Leghorn, his lordship frequently invited me ashore to participate in the gaieties of the place.

Having filled up with provisions and water, we sailed on the 16th of August, and on the 21st captured a French privateer bound from Corsica to Toulon. Shortly afterwards we fell in with HMS *Mutine* and *Salamine*, which, to suit their convenience, gave into our charge a number of French prisoners, with whom and our prize we consequently returned to Leghorn.

On the 14th of September we again put to sea, the interval being occupied by a thorough overhaul of the sloop. On the 22nd, when off Caprea, fell in with a Neapolitan vessel having a French prize crew on board. Recaptured the vessel, and took the crew prisoners.

On the 5th of October, the *Speedy* anchored in Port Mahon, where information was received that the Spaniards had several armed vessels on the look-out for us, should we again appear on their coast. I therefore applied to the authorities to exchange our 4-pounders for 6-pounders, but the latter being too large for the *Speedy*'s ports, we were again compelled to forego the change as impracticable.

October 12. – Sailed from Port Mahon, cruising for some time off Cape Sebastian, Villa Nova, Oropesa, and Barcelona; occasionally visiting the enemy's coast for water, of which the *Speedy* carried only ten tons. Nothing material occurred till November 18th, when we narrowly escaped being swamped in a gale of wind, the sea breaking over our quarter, and clearing our deck, spars, &c., otherwise inflicting such damage as to compel our return to Port Mahon, where we were detained till the 12th of December.

December 15. – Off Majorca. Several strange vessels being in sight, singled out the largest and made sail in chase; shortly after which a French bombard bore up, hoisting the national colours. We now cleared for action, altering our course to meet her, when she bore up between Dragon Island and the Main. Commenced firing at the bombard, which returned our fire; but shortly afterwards getting closer in shore she drove on the rocks. Three other vessels being in the passage, we left her, and captured one of them, the *La Liza* of ten guns and thirty-three men, bound from Alicant to Marseilles. Took nineteen of our prisoners on board the *Speedy*. As it was evident that the bombard would become a wreck, we paid no further attention to her, but made all sail after the others.

December 18. – Suspecting the passage between Dragon Island and the Main to be a lurking-place for privateers, we ran in again, but found nothing. Seeing a number of troops lining the beach, we opened fire and dispersed them, afterwards engaging a tower, which fired upon us. The prisoners we had taken proving an incumbrance, we put them on shore.

December 19. – Stood off and on the harbour of Palamos, where we saw several vessels at anchor. Hoisted Danish colours and made the signal for a pilot. Our real character being evidently known, none came off, and we did not think it prudent to venture in.

It has been said that the *Speedy* had become the marked object of the Spanish naval authorities. Not that there was much danger of being caught, for they confined their search to the coast only, and that in the daytime, when we were usually away in the offing; it being our practice to keep out of sight during the day, and run in before dawn on the next morning.

On the 21st, however, when off Plane Island, we were very near "catching a Tartar." Seeing a large ship in shore, having all the appearance of a well-laden merchantman, we forthwith gave chase. On nearing her she raised her ports, which had been closed to deceive us, the act discovering a heavy broadside, a clear demonstration that we had fallen into the jaws of a formidable Spanish frigate, now crowded with men, who had before remained concealed below.

That the frigate was in search of us there could be no doubt, from the deception practised. To have encountered her with our insignificant armament would have been exceedingly imprudent, whilst escape was out of the question, for she would have outsailed us, and could have run us down by her mere weight. There was, therefore, nothing left but to try the effect of a *ruse*, prepared beforehand for such an emergency. After receiving at Mahon information that unusual measures were about to be taken by the Spaniards for our capture, I had the *Speedy* painted in imitation of the Danish brig *Clomer*; the appearance of this vessel being well known on the Spanish coast. We also shipped a Danish quartermaster, taking the further precaution of providing him with the uniform of an officer of that nation.

On discovering the real character of our neighbour, the *Speedy* hoisted Danish colours, and spoke her. At first this failed to satisfy the Spaniard, who sent a boat to board us. It was now time to bring the Danish quartermaster into play in his officer's uniform; and to add force to his explanations, we ran the quarantine flag up to the fore, calculating on the Spanish horror of the plague, then prevalent along the Barbary coast.

On the boat coming within hail – for the yellow flag effectually repressed the enemy's desire to board us – our mock officer informed the Spaniards that we were two days from Algiers, where at the time the plague was violently raging. This was enough. The boat returned to the frigate, which, wishing us a good voyage, filled, and made sail, whilst we did the same.

I have noted this circumstance more minutely than it merits, because it has been misrepresented. By some of my officers blame was cast on me for not attacking the frigate after she had been put off her guard by our false colours, as her hands – being then employed at their ordinary avocations in the rigging and elsewhere – presented a prominent mark for our shot. There is no doubt but that we might have poured in a murderous fire before the crew could have recovered from their confusion, and perhaps have taken her, but feeling averse to so cruel a destruction of human life, I chose to refrain from an attack, which might not, even with that advantage in our favour, have been successful.

It has been stated by some naval writers that this frigate was the *Gamo*, which we subsequently captured. To the best of my knowledge this is an error.

December 24. – Off Carthagena. At daylight fell in with a convoy in charge of two Spanish privateers, which came up and fired at us; but being to windward we ran for the convoy, and singling out two, captured the nearest, laden with wine. The other ran in shore under the fort of Port Genoese, where we left her.

25. – Stood for Cape St Martin, in hope of intercepting the privateers. At 8 a.m. saw a privateer and one of the convoy under Cape Lanar. Made sail in chase. They parted company; when, on our singling out the nearest privateer, she took refuge under a battery, on which we left off pursuit.

30. – Off Cape Oropesa. Seeing some vessels in shore, out boats in chase. At noon they returned pursued by two Spanish gunboats, which kept up a smart fire on them. Made sail to intercept the gun-boats, on which they ran in under the batteries.

January 10, 1801. – Anchored in Port Mahon, and having refitted, sailed again on the 12th.

16. – Off Barcelona. Just before daylight chased two vessels standing towards that port. Seeing themselves pursued, they made for the battery at the entrance. Bore up and set steering sails in chase. The wind falling calm, one of the chase drifted in shore and took the ground under Castel De Ferro. On commencing our fire, the crew abandoned her, and we sent boats with anchors and hawsers to warp her off, in which they succeeded. She proved to be the Genoese ship *Ns. Señora de Gratia*, of ten guns.

22. – Before daylight, stood in again for Barcelona. Saw several sail close in with the land. Out boats and boarded one, which turned out a Dane. Cruising off the port till 3 a.m., we saw two strange vessels coming from the westward. Made sail to cut them off. At 6 p.m. one of them hoisted Spanish colours and the other French. At 9 p.m. came up with them, when after an engagement of half an hour both struck. The Spaniard was the *Ecce Homo*, of eight guns and nineteen men, the Frenchman, *L'Amitié*, of one gun and thirty-one men. Took all the prisoners on board the *Speedy*.

23. – Still off Barcelona. Having sent most of our crew to man the prizes, the number of prisoners on board the *Speedy* became dangerous; we therefore put twenty-five of the Frenchmen into one of their own launches and told them to make the best of their way to Barcelona. As the prizes were a good deal cut up about the rigging, repaired their damages and made sail for Port

Mahon, where we arrived on the 24th, with our convoy in company.

28th. – Quitted Port Mahon for Malta, not being able to procure at Minorca various things of which we stood in need; and on the 1st of February, came to an anchor at Valetta, where we obtained anchors and sweeps.

An absurd affair took place during our short stay at Malta, which would not have been worthy of notice, had it not been made the subject of comment.

The officers of a French royalist regiment, then at Malta, patronized a fancy ball, for which I amongst others purchased a ticket. The dress chosen was that of a sailor – in fact, my costume was a tolerable imitation of that of my worthy friend, Jack Larmour; in one of his relaxing moods, and personated in my estimation as honourable a character as were Greek, Turkish, or other kinds of Oriental disguises in vogue at such reunions. My costume was, however, too much to the life to please French royalist taste, not even the marlinspike and the lump of grease in the hat being omitted.

On entering the ball-room, further passage was immediately barred, with an intimation that my presence could not be permitted in such a dress. Good-humouredly expostulating that, as the choice of costume was left to the wearer, my own taste – which was decidedly nautical – had selected that of a British seaman, a character which, though by no means imaginary, was quite as picturesque as were the habiliments of an Arcadian shepherd; further insisting that as no rule had been infringed, I must be permitted to exercise my discretion. Expostulation being of no avail, a brusque answer was returned that such a dress was not admissible, whereupon I as brusquely replied that having purchased my ticket, and chosen my own costume in accordance with the regulations, no one had any right to prevent me from sustaining the character assumed.

Upon this a French officer, who appeared to act as master of the ceremonies, came up, and without waiting for further explanation, rudely seized me by the collar with the intention of putting me out; in return for which insult he received a substantial mark of British indignation, and at the same time an uncomplimentary remark in his own language. In an instant all was uproar; a French picket was called, which in a short time overpowered and carried me off to the guard-house of the regiment.

I was, however, promptly freed from detention on announcing my name, but the officer who had collared me demanded an apology for the portion of the *fracas* concerning him personally. This being of course refused, a challenge was the consequence; and on the following morning we met behind the ramparts and exchanged shots, my ball passing through the poor fellow's thigh, and dropping him. My escape, too, was a narrow one – his ball perforating my coat, waistcoat, and shirt, and bruising my side. Seeing my adversary fall, I stepped up to him – imagining his wound to be serious – and expressed a hope that he had not been hit in a vital part. His reply – uttered with all the politeness of his nation – was, that "he was not materially hurt." I, however, was not at ease, for it was impossible not to regret this, to him, serious *dénouement* of a

trumpery affair, though arising from his own intem-
perate conduct. It was a lesson to me in future never to
do anything in frolic which might give even uninten-
tional offence.

On the 3rd of February we sailed under orders for
Tripoli, to make arrangements for fresh provisions for
the fleet. This being effected, the *Speedy* returned to
Malta, and on the 20th again left port in charge of a
convoy for Tunis.

24th. – At the entrance of Tunis Bay we gave chase
to a strange sail, which wore and stood in towards the
town, anchoring at about the distance of three miles.
Suspecting some reason for this movement, I dispatched an officer to examine her, when the suspicion
was confirmed by his ascertaining her to be *La Belle
Caroline*, French brig of four guns, bound for Alexandria with field-pieces, ammunition, and wine for the
use of the French army in Egypt.

Our position was one of delicacy, the vessel being in
a neutral port, where, if we remained to watch her, she
might prolong our stay for an indefinite period or
escape in the night; whilst, from the warlike nature
of the cargo, it was an object of national importance to
effect her capture. The latter appearing the most
beneficial course under all circumstances, we neared
her so as to prevent escape, and soon after midnight
boarded her, and having weighed her anchor, brought
her close to the *Speedy*, before she had an opportunity
of holding any communication with the shore.

The following day was employed in examining her
stores, a portion of her ammunition being transferred
to our magazine, to replace some damaged by leakage.
Her crew, now on board the *Speedy* as prisoners,

becoming clamorous at what they considered an illegal
seizure, and being, moreover, in our way, an expedient
was adopted to get rid of them, by purposely leaving
their own launch within reach during the following
night, with a caution to the watch not to prevent their
desertion should they attempt it. The hint was taken,
for before daylight on the 27th they seized the boat,
and pulled out of the bay without molestation, not
venturing to go to Tunis lest they should be retaken.
We thus got rid of the prisoners, and at the same time
of what might have turned out their reasonable complaint to the Tunisian authorities, for that we had
exceeded the bounds of neutrality there could be no
doubt.

On the 28th we weighed anchor, and proceeded to
sea with our prize. After cruising for some days off
Cape Bon, we made sail for Cagliari, where we arrived
on the 8th of March, and put to sea on the 11th with
the prize in tow. On the 16th, anchored in Port
Mahon.

On the 18th we again put to sea, and towards
evening observed a large frigate in chase of us. As
she did not answer the private signal, it was evident
that the stranger was one of our Spanish friends on the
look-out. To cope with a vessel of her size and armament would have been folly, so we made all sail away
from her, but she gave instant chase, and evidently
gained upon us. To add to our embarrassment, the
Speedy sprung her main-topgallant-yard, and lost
ground whilst fishing it.

At daylight the following morning the strange frigate was still in chase, though by crowding all sail
during the night we had gained a little upon her; but

during the day she again recovered her advantage, the more so, as the breeze freshening, we were compelled to take in our royals, whilst she was still carrying on with everything set. After dark, we lowered a tub overboard with a light in it, and altering our course thus fortunately evaded her. On the 1st of April we returned to Port Mahon, and again put to sea on the 6th.

April 11. – Observing a vessel near the shoal of Tortosa, gave chase. On the following morning her crew deserted her, and we took possession. In the evening anchored under the land.

13. – Saw three vessels at anchor in a bay to the westward of Oropesa. Made sail up to them and anchored on the flank of a tengun fort. Whilst the firing was going on, the boats were sent in to board and bring out the vessels, which immediately weighed and got under the fort. At 5:30 p.m. the boats returned with one of them; the other two being hauled close in shore, we did not make any further attempt to capture them. As the prize, the *Ave Maria*, of four guns, was in ballast, we took the sails and spars out of her, and set her on fire.

On the following morning at daybreak, several vessels appeared to the eastward. Made all sail to intercept them, but before we could come up, they succeeded in anchoring under a fort. On standing towards them, they turned out to be Spanish gun-boats, which commenced firing at us. At 10 a.m. anchored within musket-shot, so as to keep an angle of the tower on our beam, thus

neutralising its effect. Commenced firing broadsides alternately at the tower and the gunboats,
with visible advantage. Shortly before noon made
preparation to cut out the gun-boats, but a fresh
breeze setting in dead on shore, rendered it impossible to get at them without placing ourselves
in peril. We thereupon worked out of the bay.

15. – Two strange sail in sight. Gave chase, and
in a couple of hours came up with and captured
them. Made sail after a convoy in the offing, but
the wind falling light at dusk, lost sight of them.

On the 26th we anchored in Mahon, remaining
a week to refit and procure fresh hands, many
having been sent away in prizes. On the 2nd of
May put to sea with a reduced crew, some of
whom had to be taken out of HM's prison.

We again ran along the Spanish coast, and on the
4th of May were off Barcelona, where the *Speedy*
captured a vessel which reported herself as Ragusan,
though in reality a Spanish four-gun tartan. Soon
after detaining her we heard firing in the WN-W and
steering for that quarter fell in with a Spanish privateer, which we also captured, the *San Carlos*, of
seven guns. On this a swarm of gun-boats came out of
Barcelona, seven of them giving chase to us and the
prizes, with which we made off shore, the gun-boats
returning to Barcelona.

On the following morning the prizes were sent to Port
Mahon, and keeping out of sight for the rest of the day,
the *Speedy* returned at midnight off Barcelona, where we
found the gun-boats on the watch; but on our approach
they ran in shore, firing at us occasionally. Suspecting

that the object was to decoy us within reach of some larger vessel, we singled out one of them and made at her, the others, however, supporting her so well that some of our rigging being shot away, we made off shore to repair, the gun-boats following. Having thus got them to some distance, and repaired damages, we set all sail, and again ran in shore, in the hope of getting between them and the land, so as to cut off some of their number. Perceiving our intention, they all made for the port as before, keeping up a smart fight, in which our foretopgallant-yard was so much injured, that we had to shift it, and were thus left astern. The remainder of the day was employed in repairing damages, and the gun-boats not venturing out again, at 9 p.m. we again made off shore.

Convinced that something more than ordinary had actuated the gun-boats to decoy us – just before daylight on the 6th we again ran in for Barcelona, when the trap manifested itself in the form of a large ship, running under the land, and bearing ES-E. On hauling towards her, she changed her course in chase of us, and was shortly made out to be a Spanish xebec frigate.

As some of my officers had expressed dissatisfaction at not having been permitted to attack the frigate fallen in with on the 21st of December, after her suspicions had been lulled by our device of hoisting Danish colours, &c., I told them they should now have a fair fight, notwithstanding that, by manning the two prizes sent to Mahon, our numbers had been reduced to fifty-four, officers and boys included. Orders were then given to pipe all hands, and prepare for action.

Accordingly we made towards the frigate, which was now coming down under steering sails. At 9:30 a.m., she fired a gun and hoisted Spanish colours, which the

Speedy acknowledged by hoisting American colours, our object being, as we were now exposed to her full broadside, to puzzle her, till we got on the other tack, when we ran up the English ensign, and immediately afterwards encountered her broadside without damage.

Shortly afterwards she gave us another broadside, also without effect. My orders were not to fire a gun till we were close to her; when, running under her lee, we locked our yards amongst her rigging, and in this position returned our broadside, such as it was.

To have fired our popgun 4-pounders at a distance would have been to throw away the ammunition; but the guns being doubly, and, as I afterwards learned, trebly, shotted, and being elevated, they told admirably upon her main deck; the first discharge, as was subsequently ascertained, killing the Spanish captain and the boatswain.

My reason for locking our small craft in the enemy's rigging was the one upon which I mainly relied for victory, viz that from the height of the frigate out of the water, the whole of her shot must necessarily go over our heads, whilst our guns, being elevated, would blow up her main-deck.

The Spaniards speedily found out the disadvantage under which they were fighting, and gave the order to board the *Speedy*; but as this order was as distinctly heard by us as by them, we avoided it at the moment of execution by sheering off sufficiently to prevent the movement, giving them a volley of musketry and a broadside before they could recover themselves.

Twice was this manoeuvre repeated, and twice thus averted. The Spaniards finding that they were only punishing themselves, gave up further attempts to board and stood to their guns, which were cutting up our rigging from stem to stern, but doing little farther damage; for after the lapse of an hour the loss to the *Speedy* was only two men killed and four wounded.

This kind of combat, however, could not last. Our rigging being cut up and the *Speedy*'s sails riddled with shot, I told the men that they must either take the frigate or be themselves taken, in which case the Spaniards would give no quarter – whilst a few minutes energetically employed on their part would decide the matter in their own favour.

The doctor, Mr Guthrie, who, I am happy to say, is still living to peruse this record of his gallantry, volunteered to take the helm; leaving him therefore for the time both commander and crew of the *Speedy*, the order was given to board, and in a few seconds every man was on the enemy's deck – a feat rendered the more easy as the doctor placed the *Speedy* close alongside with admirable skill.

For a moment the Spaniards seemed taken by surprise, as though unwilling to believe that so small a crew would have the audacity to board them; but soon recovering themselves, they made a rush to the waist of the frigate, where the fight was for some minutes gallantly carried on. Observing the enemy's colours still flying, I directed one of our men immediately to haul them down, when the Spanish crew, without pausing to consider by whose orders the colours had been struck, and naturally believing it the act of their own officers, gave in, and we were in possession of the *Gamo* frigate, of thirty-two heavy guns and 319 men, who an hour and a half before had looked upon us as a certain if not an easy prey.

Our loss in boarding was Lieutenant Parker, severely wounded in several places, one seaman killed and three wounded, which with those previously killed and wounded gave a total of three seamen killed, and one officer and seventeen men wounded.

The *Gamo*'s loss was Captain de Torres – the boatswain – and thirteen seamen killed, together with forty-one wounded; her casualties thus exceeding the whole number of officers and crew on board the *Speedy*.

Some time after the surrender of the *Gamo*, and when we were in quiet possession, the officer who had succeeded the deceased Captain Don Francisco de Torres, not in command, but in rank, applied to me for a certificate that he had done his duty during the action; whereupon he received from me a certificate that he had "conducted himself like a true Spaniard", with which document he appeared highly gratified, and I had afterwards the satisfaction of learning that it procured him further promotion in the Spanish service.

Shortly before boarding, an incident occurred which, by those who have never been placed in similar circumstances, may be thought too absurd for notice. Knowing that the final struggle would be a desperate one, and calculating on the superstitious wonder which forms an element in the Spanish character, a portion of our crew were ordered to blacken their faces, and what with this and the excitement of combat, more ferocious looking objects could scarcely be imagined. The fellows thus disguised were directed to board by the head, and the effect produced was precisely that calculated on. The greater portion of the Spaniard's crew was prepared to repel boarders in that direction, but stood for a few moments as it were transfixed to the deck by the apparition of so many diabolical looking figures emerging from the white smoke of the bow guns; whilst our other men, who boarded by the waist, rushed on them from behind, before they could recover from their surprise at the unexpected phenomenon.

In difficult or doubtful attacks by sea – and the odds of 50 men to 320 comes within this description – no device can be too minute, even if apparently absurd, provided it have the effect of diverting the enemy's attention whilst you are concentrating your own. In this, and other successes against odds, I have no hesitation in saying that success in no slight degree depended on out-of-the-way devices, which the enemy not suspecting, were in some measure thrown off their guard.

The subjoined tabular view of the respective force of the two vessels will best show the nature of the contest.

Gamo	Speedy
Main-deck guns. – Twenty-two long 12-pounders.	Fourteen 4-pounders.
Quarter-deck. – Eight long S-pounders, and two 24-pounder carronades.	None.
No. of crew, 319.	No. of crew, 54.
Broadside weight of shot, 190 lbs.	Broadside weight of shot, 28 lbs.
Tonnage, 600 and upwards.	Tonnage, 158.

It became a puzzle what to do with 263 unhurt prisoners now we had taken them, the *Speedy* having only

forty-two men left. Promptness was however necessary; so driving the prisoners into the hold, with guns
pointing down the hatchway, and leaving thirty of our
men on board the prize – which was placed under the
command of my brother, the Hon. Archibald Cochrane, then a midshipman – we shaped our course
to Port Mahon – not Gibraltar, as has been recorded –
and arrived there in safety; the Barcelona gun-boats,
though spectators of the action, not venturing to
rescue the frigate. Had they made the attempt, we
should have had some difficulty in evading them and
securing the prize, the prisoners manifesting every
disposition to rescue themselves, and only being de-
terred by their own main deck guns loaded with
cannister, and pointing down the hatchways, whilst
our men stood over them with lighted matches.

Our success hitherto had procured us some prize-
money, notwithstanding the peculations of the Mediterranean Admiralty Courts, by which the greater
portion of our captures was absorbed.

Despite this drawback, which generally disinclined
officers and crews from making extraordinary exertions, my own share of the twelvemonth's zealous
endeavours in our little sloop was considerable, and
even the crew were in receipt of larger sums than those
constituting the ordinary pay of officers; a result
chiefly owing to our nocturnal mode of warfare, together with our refraining from meddling with vessels
ascertained to be loading in the Spanish ports, and
then lying in wait for them as they proceeded on their
voyage.

One effect of our success was no slight amount of ill-
concealed jealousy on the part of officers senior to

myself, though there were some amongst these who, being in command of small squadrons instead of single vessels, might, had they adopted the same means, have effected far more than the *Speedy*, with an armament so insignificant, was calculated to accomplish.

After remaining some days at Port Mahon to refit, we prepared to return to our cruising ground, where, from private information, we knew that other prizes were at hand. In place of being permitted so to do, the *Speedy* received an order to proceed to Algiers, for the purpose of representing to the Dey the illegality of his cruisers having taken a British vessel in retaliation for an Algerine captured whilst violating the law of block-ade.

The mission was a singular one to be entrusted to the captain of one of the smallest and worst-armed vessels in the British service. Remonstrance, to be effectual with a piratical government, ought to have been committed to an officer armed with sufficient force at least to induce respect. There was, however, no alternative but to obey, and a short time saw us at anchor off the mole of the predatory potentate.

The request for an interview with his highness occasioned no little dissatisfaction amongst his ministers, if those who were quite as much his masters as his subordinates could be so termed. After some consultation the interview was, however, granted, and a day was appointed to deliver my message.

The invariable Moslem preliminary of taking coffee having been gone through, I was ushered through a series of galleries lined with men, each bearing on his shoulder a formidable-looking axe, and eyeing me with an insolent scowl, evidently meant to convey the satisfaction with which they would apply its edge to my vertebræ should the caprice of their chief so will.

On reaching the presence of the Dey – a dignified-looking and gorgeously-attired person, seated cross-legged on an elevated couch in one corner of the gallery, and surrounded by armed people of most unprepossessing appearance – I was marched up between two janizaries, and ordered to make three salaams to his highness.

This formality being complied with, he rudely demanded, through the medium of an interpreter, "What brought me there?" The reply was that "I was the commander of an English vessel of war in the roads, and had been deputed, on behalf of my Government, respectfully to remonstrate with his highness concerning a vessel which his cruisers had taken contrary to the laws of nations." On this being interpreted, the ferocious scowls of the bystanders were exchanged for expressions of injured innocence; but the Dey got in a great passion, and told the interpreter to inform me that "remonstrance came with an ill grace from us, the British vessels being the greatest pirates in the world, and mine one of the worst amongst them", which complimentary statement was acknowledged by me with a formal bow.

"If I did right", continued the Dey, through his interpreter, "I should put you and your crew in prison till" (naming a captured Algerine vessel) "she was restored; and but for my great respect for the English Government, and my impression that her seizure was unauthorized, you should go there. However, you may go, with a demand from me that the vessel unjustly taken from us shall be immediately restored."

This decision appeared to be anything but satisfactory to the oligarchy of which his court was composed, as savouring of a clemency to which they were little inclined. From the boisterous conversation which ensued, they were evidently desirous of prolonging my stay to an indefinite period, or perhaps of terminating it summarily through the instrumentality of the axe-men who lined the galleries, as a few years afterwards they terminated the existence of the Dey himself.

To confess the truth, there was some room for self-congratulation on quitting the presence of such barbarians, to whom I was not fairly accredited for such a mission. However, the remonstrance confided to me being duly delivered, we returned to Minorca to report progress, though not without being chased by an Algerine cruiser on our way. As the *Speedy* outsailed her, and as there was no beneficial object to be gained by interfering with her, we stood on without further notice.

On arriving at our former cruising ground we encountered a Spanish privateer of six guns, which was captured. This vessel was fitted out at my own private expense, and my brother appointed to command her, as a tender to the *Speedy*, several enemy's vessels having previously escaped for want of such aid.

In a few days after this we fell in with the *Kangaroo*, Captain Pulling, who, being senior to me, was therefore my commanding officer. Running down the coast in company, we attacked the fort of Almanara, and after silencing it, brought off a Spanish privateer of seven guns.

On the 8th of June the *Speedy* ran into Oropesa,

where, on the 13th and 14th of April, we had fought an action with the fort and gunboats. Perceiving several vessels at anchor under the fort, it was deemed advisable to make offshore, with the intention of running in again at midnight and cutting some of them out.

We had not proceeded far before we again fell in with the *Kangaroo*, when informing Captain Pulling of what we had seen, he declined the night attack, preferring to postpone operations till the following day. Accordingly, at noon on the 9th, we went in, and made out a twenty-gun xebec and three gunboats, with ten sail of merchantmen under three convoy. It was determined to attack them as they lay; the *Kangaroo* anchoring well up to and engaging the fort, whilst the *Speedy* and her tender under my brother's orders encountered the xebec and the gunboats – the *Speedy* anchoring in a line between those vessels and the *Kangaroo*.

For some hours an incessant cannonade was kept up on both sides, the *Kangaroo*'s fire flanking the fort, whilst the slackened fire of the Spanish vessels showed that our shot had told. At this juncture, a twelve-gun felucca and two more gunboats having arrived from Valentia to their assistance, the Spaniards took heart, and the action became nearly as brisk as before.

The felucca and the newly-arrived gunboats were, however, for a time beat off, and after an hour's additional firing the xebec, two gunboats, and some of the convoy were sunk, the remaining gunboats shortly afterwards sharing the same fate.

The action had now continued for upwards of nine hours, during which the *Speedy* had expended nearly all her ammunition – namely, fourteen hundred shot –

and the *Kangaroo* was much in the same predicament. As the felucca and gunboats had again come up, it was necessary to effect something decisive. Captain Pulling, therefore, slipping his cable, shifted close to the fort, which was soon afterwards abandoned, and the *Speedy* closed with the felucca and her consorts, which forthwith fled. Had they remained, we had not half a dozen rounds left to continue the action.

Both vessels now hoisted out boats and made for the merchantmen. Three of these had been sunk, and four others driven on shore; we, however, brought away the three still afloat. By this time a number of Spanish troops lined the beach for the protection of the vessels ashore, and as we had scarcely a shot left, it was impracticable to reply to the musketry, within range of which the boats must necessarily have been placed had the attempt been made. We therefore relinquished the endeavour to get off the stranded vessels.

It may be useful here to remark that on board the *Kangaroo* were some guns fitted on the non-recoil principle, and that during the action these broke from their breechings, one, if not more, endangering the vessel by bounding down the hatchways into the hold.

On our return to Port Mahon with the prizes, the *Gamo* had not been purchased by the Government; but, to my regret, this useful cruiser had been sold for a trifle to the Algerines, whilst I was condemned to continue in the pigmy and now battered craft by which she had been taken. To have obtained command of the *Gamo*, even as a means of deception on the enemy's coast, I would scarcely have changed place with an admiral.

But a more cruel thing still was in store for me. The

commandant lived in the house of a Spanish merchant who had a contract for carrying the mails to Gibraltar. The vessel employed for this purpose was a notoriously bad sailer, and when the *Speedy* was ready for sea, instead of being permitted to return to our cruising ground, she was ordered to convoy this tub of a packet to Gibraltar, with further instructions to take the letter-bag on board the *Speedy*, protect the packet, put the mail on board her as soon as we arrived off the Rock, and return without holding any communication with the shore! – the evident object of the last injunction being that the service which had been thrust upon us should not become known!

The expectation of the packet-master, doubtless, was that we should put to sea out of privateer reach. In place of this, we ran along the Spanish coast, our superior sailing enabling us, without delay, to scrutinize every creek as we passed. Nothing, however, occurred till we were close in with a bay, or rather indentation of the shore, near Alicant, where, seeing some vessels at anchor, we made towards them, on which they weighed and deliberately ran ashore. To have stopped to get them off would have been in excess of our instructions. To set fire to them was not; and as one was laden with oil, and the night following very dark, the result was a blaze which illumined the sky for many miles round.

Unluckily for us, three French line-of-battle ships, which afterwards turned out to be the *Indomitable*, the *Dessaix*, and the *Formidable*, were in the vicinity, and being attracted by the light of the burning vessels, ran inshore to see what was the matter.

At daybreak on the morning of July 3rd these large

ships were observed in the distance, calling up to our imaginations visions of Spanish galleons from South America, and accordingly the *Speedy* prepared for chase. It was not till day dawned that we found out our mistake, the vessels between us and the offing being clearly line-of-battle ships, forbidding all reasonable hope of escape.

It was about four o'clock in the morning when we made out the French ships, which immediately on discovering us gave chase. Being to windward, we endeavoured to escape by making all sail, and, as the wind fell light, by using our sweeps. This proving unavailing, we threw the guns overboard, and put the brig before the wind; but notwithstanding every effort, the enemy gained fast upon us, and, in order to prevent our slipping past, separated on different tacks, so as to keep us constantly within reach of one or the other; the *Dessaix*, being nearest, firing broadsides at us as she passed when tacking, at other times firing from her bow-chasers and cutting up our rigging.

For upwards of three hours we were thus within gunshot of the *Dessaix*, when, finding it impossible to escape by the wind, I ordered all the stores to be thrown overboard, in the hope of being able, when thus further lightened, to run the gauntlet between the ships, which continued to gain upon us.

Watching an opportunity when the nearest line-of-battle ship was before our beam, we bore up, set the studding-sails, and attempted to run between them, the French honouring us with a broadside for this unexpected movement. The *Dessaix*, however, immediately tacked in pursuit, and in less than an hour got within musket-shot. At this short distance she let fly at us a complete broadside of round and grape, the object evidently being to sink us at a blow, in retaliation for thus attempting to slip past, though almost without hope of escape.

Fortunately for us, in yawing to bring her broadside to bear, the rapidity with which she answered her helm carried her a little too far, and her round shot plunged in the water under our bows, or the discharge must have sunk us; the scattered grape, however, took effect in the rigging, cutting up a great part of it, riddling the sails, and doing material damage to the masts and yards, though not a man was hurt. To have delayed for another broadside would have been to expose all on board to certain destruction, and as further effort to escape was impotent, the *Speedy*'s colours were hauled down.

On going aboard the *Dessaix* and presenting my sword to the captain, Christie Pallière, he politely declined taking it, with the complimentary remark that "he would not accept the sword of an officer who had for so many hours struggled against impossibility," at the same time paying me the further compliment of requesting that "I would continue to wear my sword, though a prisoner" – a request with which I complied; Captain Pallière at the same time good-naturedly expressing his satisfaction at having terminated our exploits in the cruising line, they having, in fact, special instructions to look out for us. After this reception it is scarcely necessary to add that I was treated with great kindness by my captors.

Thus ended the thirteen months' cruise of the *Speedy*, during which we had taken and retaken upwards of fifty vessels, one hundred and twenty-two guns, and five hundred and thirty-four prisoners.

After the capture of the *Speedy* the French line-of-battle ships stood along the coast, and proceeded with her and the unlucky packet which had been the primary cause of the disaster to Algeciras. During this passage I had ample opportunity of observing the superior manner in which the sails of the *Dessaix* were cut, and the consequent flat surface exposed to the wind, this contrasting strongly with the bag reefs, bellying sails, and breadbag canvas of English ships of war at that period.

As there was no force at Gibraltar adequate to an attack of the French squadron, the authorities lost no time in transmitting intelligence of their arrival to Sir James Saumarez, then blockading the Spanish squadron in Cadiz. The French meanwhile proceeded to water and refit, evidently with the intention of passing the Straits with the first fair wind.

Quitting Cadiz, Sir James Saumarez immediately sailed for Algeciras with his squadron, consisting of the *Cæsar*, *Venerable*, *Audacious*, *Hannibal*, *Superb*, *Pompée*, *Spencer*, *Calpe*, and *Thames*, these reaching the bay on the 6th of July.

At the time of their first appearance I was conversing with Captain Pallière in his cabin, when a lieutenant reported a British flag over Cabritta Point, and soon afterwards the topgallant masts and pendants of a British squadron became visible. We at once adjourned to the poop, when the surprise of the French at the sight of a more numerous squadron became not unreasonably apparent. Captain Pallière asked me "if I thought an attack would be made, or whether the

British force would anchor off Gibraltar?" My reply was "that an attack would certainly be made, and that before night both British and French ships would be at Gibraltar", at the same time adding that when there, it would give me great pleasure to make him and his officers a return for the kindness I had experienced on board the Dessaix!

The French admiral, however, determined that his ships should not be carried across the bay if he could help it. Before the British squadron had rounded the point the French out boats, with kedges and stream anchors, for the purpose of warping inshore, so as to prevent the approaching squadron from cutting them out; but the order was so hurriedly executed that all three ships were hauled aground, with their sterns presented to the approaching British force – a position which could not have been taken by choice, for nothing could apparently be more easy than to destroy the French ships, which, lying aground stern on, could only use their stern-chasers.

To employ their consequently useless hands to some purpose, the French landed a considerable portion of their crews to man the Spanish batteries on the island, as the ships' guns could not be brought to bear. Two of the British ships anchored, and opened upon the French ships aground; but being exposed to the fire of some of the newly-manned forts higher up the bay, the heavy guns of which were admirably handled by the French seamen, both the British vessels slipped their cables, and, together with the remainder of the squadron, which did not anchor at all, backed their maintop-sails for the purpose of maintaining their position. The wind, however, blowing from the westward, with a rapid current sweeping round the bay, thwarted this intention, and the British squadron quickly drifted past the enemy, firing as they went.

Perhaps I ought previously to have mentioned an incident demonstrative of the *sang froid* of my captor. After having satisfied himself that an action with a superior force was inevitable, Captain Pallière remarked "that it should not spoil our breakfast", in which he had invited me to join him. Before the meal was ended a round shot crashed through the stern of the *Dessaix*, driving before it a shower of broken glass, the *débris* of a wine bin under the sofa.

We forthwith jumped up from table and went on the quarter-deck; but a raking shot from Sir James Saumarez's ship sweeping a file of marines from the poop not far from me, I considered further exposure on my part unnecessary, and went below to a position whence I could nevertheless at times see what was going on.

The *Hannibal*, having with the others forged past the enemy, gallantly filled and tacked with a view to get between the French ships and the shore being evidently unaware of their having been hauled aground. The consequence was that she ran upon a shoal, and remained fast, nearly bow on to the broadsides of the French line-of-battle ships, which, with the shore batteries and several gunboats, opened upon her a concentrated fire. This, from her position, she was unable to return. The result was that her guns were speedily dismounted, her rigging shot away, and a third of her crew killed or wounded; Captain Ferris, who commanded her, having now no alternative but to strike his colours – though not before he had displayed an amount of endurance which excited the admiration of the enemy.

A circumstance now occurred which is entitled to rank amongst the curiosities of war. On the French taking possession of the *Hannibal* they had neglected to provide themselves with their national ensign, and, either from necessity or bravado, rehoisted the English flag upside down. This being a well-known signal of distress, was so understood by the authorities at Gibraltar, who, manning all government and other boats with dockyard artificers and seamen, sent them, as it was mistakenly considered, to the assistance of the *Hannibal*.

On the approach of the launches I was summoned on deck by the captain of the *Dessaix*, who seemed doubtful what measures to adopt as regarded the boats now approaching to board the *Hannibal*, and asked my opinion as to whether they would attempt to retake the ship. As there could be no doubt in my mind about the nature of their mission or its result, it was evident that if they were allowed to board nothing could prevent the seizure of the whole. My advice, therefore, to Captain Pallière was to warn them off by a shot, hoping they would thereby be driven back and saved from capture. Captain Pallière seemed at first inclined to take the advice, but on reflection – either doubting its sincerity, or seeing the real state of the case – he decided to capture the whole by permitting them to board unmolested. Thus boat by boat was captured, until all the artificers necessary for the repair of the British squadron, and nearly all the sailors at that time in Gibraltar, were taken prisoners!

In this action the French and Spaniards suffered

severely both as regarded ships and men, their masts
and hulls being much knocked about, whilst several
Spanish gunboats were sunk. The wonder to me was
that the British squadron did not anchor; for the
French ships being aground, stern on, could have
offered little resistance, and must have been destroyed. It is true that the batteries on shore were
admirably served, and thus constituted a formidable
obstacle; but had not the squadron drifted past the
French ships, the latter might have been interposed
between the batteries and the British force, when the
fire of the former would have been neutralized, and the
enemy's ships aground destroyed with comparatively
little loss. It is not, however, my purpose or province
to criticize the action, but simply to give the details, as
personally witnessed from that extraordinary place for
a British officer, the deck of a French ship!

Neither the imprisonment of the captured crews nor
my own was of long duration. The day after the action
Sir James Saumarez sent Captain Brenton into Algeciras Bay with a flag of truce, to endeavour to effect an
exchange of the gallant Captain Ferris, his officers,
and crew. At that time there was no regulated system
of exchange between the belligerent powers, but Captain Brenton succeeded in procuring the release of the
crew of the *Hannibal* and the entrapped artificers,
together with the officers and men of the *Speedy*.
Admiral Linois would not at first give me up, but
on further consideration allowed me to go with the
other officers to Gibraltar on *parole*. My complete
release was eventually effected for the second captain
of the *San Antonio*, taken shortly afterwards.

The French ships having lost no time in communicating with the Spanish admiral at Cadiz, he promptly appeared off Algeciras with a reinforcement of six ships of the line, several frigates, and gunboats. The enemy having by this time warped off their grounded ships, as well as the *Hannibal*, and having by the 12th got them in seagoing order, the whole sailed from Algeciras, followed by the British squadron, which, by great exertions, had been got in readiness for pursuit.

Of the action which subsequently took place I have no personal knowledge, other than that of a scene witnessed by myself from the garden of the commissioner's house, in which I was staying.

The enemy were overtaken at dusk, soon after leaving the bay, and when it had become dark Captain Keats, in the *Superb*, gallantly dashed in between the two sternmost ships, firing right and left, and passed on. Of course I do not assert myself to have been personally cognizant of the way in which the attack was made, the firing only being visible from the Rock, but that this is the correct version of the affair rests upon indisputable authority. The movement was so rapidly executed that the *Superb* shot ahead before the smoke cleared away, and the Spanish ships, the *Real Carlos* (112) and the *San Hermenegildo* (112), mistaking each other for the aggressor, began a mutual attack, resulting in the *Real Carlos* losing her foretop-mast, the sails of which, falling over her own guns, caught fire. While in this condition the *Hermenegildo* – still engaging the *Real Carlos* as an enemy – in the confusion fell on board her, and caught fire also. Both ships burned till they blew up, and nearly all on board perished, a few survivors only escaping on board the

Superb, as Captain Keats was taking possession of a *third* Spanish line-of-battle ship, the *San Antonio* – for whose second captain, as has been said, I was exchanged.

In 1809 Cochrane led the celebrated fireship attack at Aix Roads (see pp 243), but fell foul of the Admiralty for publiclly criticizing his lacklustre commander, Admiral Gambier. Cochrane then compounded his misfortunes by becoming embroiled in a financial scam, at which he departed Britain to take command of, successively, the navies of Chile, Brazil, and Greece. In 1831 he succeeded to the earldom of Dundonald and was granted a free pardon for past misdeeds. He was also restored to the Royal Navy as a rear-admiral.

George Vernon Jackson

The Perilous Adventures and Vicissitudes of a Midshipman

1801–4

The eldest son of a Royal Navy purser, George Jackson was followed down to the sea by all his four brothers. Three of them were killed on active service.

At the age of fourteen, in the year 1801, I entered the Royal Navy. My name, according to a practice sometimes observed in those days with respect to youngsters destined for the service, had been successively borne since 1795 upon the books of the *Trident*, *Minerva*, *Princess Augusta*, and *Maidstone*. A cadetship for me had now been obtained by my father from an old schoolfellow of his, named Sir Edward Hamilton, commanding the *Trent*, 36 guns. And so, at the period mentioned, I left home in the charge of my father for Portsmouth, where, with a £2 note in my pocket, I embarked in a cutter *en route* to join the *Trent*, then lying off St Malo watching the movements of two French frigates. From the cutter I was shifted several times to other vessels, and after twelve days' cruising about found myself safely deposited at last on board the good ship *Trent*.

I was quite an "unlicked cub" in every sense of the term, and had all my troubles before me. When I went to sea there were few of the advantages that a boy enjoys now* on entering the profession of a sailor. He then had to encounter vicissitudes no longer known, and fight his way upwards through many a weary and disheartening struggle.

The appearance of the big ship awed and astonished me. Like all novices, I felt awkward and nervous in my new position among so many strange things and strange faces; but a Midshipman† is never left long alone to moralise over first impressions, and I was soon introduced, after a fashion, to my fellow-messmates, and initiated into the mysteries of a Midshipman's berth. Here I enjoyed the usual entertainment bestowed upon fresh arrivals, and formed in consequence anything but an encouraging opinion of the career before me.

Being a stranger, I was invited to dine with the Captain, whom, from stories already related to me, I began to regard as something preternaturally awful. Just before I joined, a Midshipman had been flogged and turned out of the ship, and this fact gave my

* *I.e.*, 1865.
† He was entered in the Ship's Muster Roll, not as a Midshipman, but as a Boy, 1st Class.

associates a capital foundation for enlarging upon the Captain's character. The memory of the dinner haunts me still after the lapse of sixty and odd years.

At the proper time I repaired to my chest to get rigged out for the occasion, accompanied by such of the Midshipmen who were not on duty, all anxious to lend a hand in overhauling the possessions of a new-comer. Their assistance was a questionable advantage, and served only to retard and bewilder me. With characteristic activity and zeal, they soon displayed the contents of my chest, and handed me the articles in requisition with such critical remarks upon each as their judgment prompted.

Every one knows the economy with which a young boy's naval outfit is regulated, and the providence of my tailor was no exception to the rule; my uniform would have suited a shape twice my dimensions. We wore knee-breeches then, and I can laugh now at the absurd picture I presented in a pair that nearly eclipsed me. Do what I would, there was no help for it; the upper part of the abominable things were close under my arms, and the legs hung dangling about within a few inches of my heels. My appearance seemed to afford my companions unqualified pleasure, who, when they had duly supplied me with a coat and vest to correspond, declared with one accord that I was perfect. "You must take your dirk", said one, "And this", said another, and so on until I became so confused that I was quite at a loss what to do. By nature I was much below the average height of boys of my age, and, moreover, had a pale face and by no means robust aspect, which defects considerably in-creased my ungainliness under the circumstances.

My toilet finished, I joined the Second Lieutenant, who had also been invited, on his way to the Captain's cabin. On entering the same we were met by Sir Edward Hamilton, who in no wise reassured my failing nerves by exclaiming as his eyes fell upon my person, "Why, what the devil have we got here? He looks as if he had been swallowed and thrown up again." This complimentary idea expressed, we were ordered to take our seats. My miseries had only commenced; the ordeal of dinner was to be gone through, and how I was to act or what to do I couldn't for the life of me determine. The bare thought of sitting at the same table with such an ogre was enough to stupify one with terror.

Whilst the covers were being removed, Sir Edward turned sharply towards me and said, "Take a glass of wine, sir." "No, sir, thank you", I replied timidly, but was electrified by his shouting out savagely, "What, sir. Devil take it! Take one directly." I mechanically filled a glass and gulped down the contents, which might have been physic for all I knew at the moment. "Now, sir," rejoined my tormentor, "do you ever drink grog?" "No, sir, never," I gasped out faintly, expecting an order forthwith to drink a hogshead on the spot; but I was spared so much by his adding, "Then I shall give orders that you are to have some every day; you look as if you needed it." I did not dare to make a worse exhibition of myself, but would have given a great deal to enjoy a jolly good cry.

The sight of the dessert cheered me; at last dinner was coming to a close. I scarcely recollect how I managed to get thus far through the meal, but can easily call to mind being sensibly moved by the presence of a small bottle full of delicious green "plums" that stood in front of my plate. To every child, ignorant of the nature of olives, they offer an enticing prospect, and I resolved to make them compensate for my previous abstinence. It struck me as rather odd that they were not touched for some time, and much as I longed to be at them, I could not summon up courage enough to begin the attack. When the bottle was on the move I was again surprised at observing that no one took more than one, or two at the outside. I was not so moderate, but when my turn came boldly sent five or six rolling on to my plate. "Put all those back again, sir, but one," thundered our host, "and if you like that you shall have all the rest." I believe that I replaced them with my fingers, but I will not be certain, and then put the remaining one in my mouth, only to find myself in a ridiculous predicament, with every one at the table enjoying the joke. As all things have an end, so had my memorable dinner with the Captain of the *Trent*, and right glad I was when dismissed. Sir Edward would not let me depart in peace. Ere I had gained the cabin door he cried, "Look ye here, sir, go at once to the ship's tailor and have a fathom cut off those internal tails of yours."

When thrown together within the narrow compass of a ship's sides people soon become tolerably well acquainted with each other, and it was not long before I learnt the characters and dispositions of my messmates. There were six or seven of us, two only of whose names I can remember, one being a kindhearted and gentlemanly youth, and the other as much the reverse as he could possibly be. I will call the latter Wiggins for the sake of his descendants, who would not be proud of his history. He was cock of the walk, and a disagreeable tyrannical fellow; hated, but feared by all in the Midshipmen's mess. Had it not been from a dread of coming across the Captain, we should have got to blows much sooner than we did. The men were cleaning the steerage one morning, and I wished to go to my chest, but I was forbidden to do so by Wiggins. I persisted, and was about to accomplish my purpose when he ran up as I was stooping to raise the lid and brutally inflicted a kick upon my face. This was a *casus belli* with a vengeance, and without one instant's consideration I sprang upon him with the ferocity of a young tiger. He was not prepared for the assault, never dreaming that one so inferior to him in size would show fight. He was mistaken – the sequel proved his worth, and stamped him always afterwards as a coward. He was overpowered in a few seconds, and went forth from the affray with a sound drubbing and with a very conspicuous eye. The fight was hardly over when I repented my rashness, and positively trembled in my shoes lest it should reach the ears of the Captain. My alarm redoubled as Wiggins's eye grew blacker, and a council was held to debate what was best to be done. The Midshipmen were on my side, and a solemn promise was ultimately extorted from Wiggins that the cause of his disfigurement should be kept a secret, and some plausible story invented to account for it. Unfortunately for my peace of mind Wiggins had the afternoon watch with me, and when the Captain went on deck it would be next to impossible to avoid discovery.

Sir Edward was one of those men who allow nothing to escape them. He could see through a plank a little farther than most of his fellow-creatures, and seeing, would follow up his observations with a pertinacity that defied interruption. Despite the agreement between us, I knew that Wiggins was not to be trusted; he had pledged himself under compulsion, and, like all vanquished bullies, had done so with a very bad grace. There was a surly hang-dog look about that damaged eye that promised mischief, and I prepared myself to guard against treachery. Our watch had begun, and with it my new troubles, for Wiggins lost no opportunity of making the object of his grievance apparent to everybody. Many were the dodges and shifts to which I resorted in order to get between him and the dangerous side of the quarter-deck, but without avail. The Lieutenant of the watch soon remarked it, and called out, "Halloa, Mr Wiggins, where did you get that black eye?" "Mr Jackson gave it to me, sir." "Well, I must say you have begun early, youngster", rejoined the Lieutenant, whilst Wiggins, with a triumphant leer, rolled the discoloured orb towards me. I stood aghast, not knowing what was about to happen, looking first at the Lieutenant and then at the paltry fellow at my side. At this juncture the Captain appeared, and the Lieutenant left us. Wiggins gave an avenging grin, and seemed vastly to relish my discomfiture. But his malice was frustrated this time, for the Lieutenant, I have reason to think, was my friend. Wiggins gained no profit by his breach of faith, and no more notice was taken of the occurrence.

This contretemps was of use to me, as it secured me during the remainder of my stay on board from fresh disturbance, and effectually reduced Wiggins to his proper level.

I should be loth to say what my opinion of Sir Edward Hamilton might have become had I stopped much longer in the *Trent*. As each day passed, so did I conceive new terrors of this man. A more uncompromising disciplinarian did not exist, or one less scrupulous in exacting the due fulfilment of his orders, whatever they were. To give a notion of what he could say in a comparatively sober moment, I will relate part of a conversation which I overheard between him and a Lieutenant as they paced the deck together one afternoon. The Lieutenant remarked in a quiet tone of voice, in reply to some expression from the Captain, "You are mistaken, sir, I assure you; I had not the slightest intention to offend you." "Offend me, sir!" cried Sir Edward, stopping short and confronting him, "offend me, sir! By God, if I suspected such a thing, I would go down to my cabin and fetch a sword and cut you down to the deck!" That sort of conduct might have been tolerated in Sir Edward's days, but would not quite suit the present times. As it happened, even then, when a man in such power seldom put much restraint upon himself, Sir Edward went too far, and was subsequently relieved of all future command because of his excessive severity.

The *Trent*, I must admit, was in excellent order; indeed, as regards discipline and the general efficiency of her company, she was equal, if not superior, to any other frigate afloat; but these qualities had all been promoted at no small sacrifice of humanity. No sailor was allowed to walk from one place to another on deck, and woe betide the unfortunate fellow who halted in his run aloft, unless expressly bidden to do so for some particular purpose. The "cat" was incessantly at work.

The man who approached at a walk when called by a Midshipman, instead of running for his life, the penalty he paid for this offence was a "starting" at the hands of the Boatswain's mate.

After I had been some time in the *Trent*, Sir Edward declared himself incapable of fulfilling his promise to my father of giving me a permanent rating in his ship, and I was therefore handed over without much more ado to Captain Rotheram of the *Lapwing*, 28 guns, to which vessel I was transferred – not at all sorry for the exchange – and rated accordingly.

I wish it was possible for a Midshipman of 1865 to serve for a few weeks under the old régime of the period upon which I am now engaged. The comparison between the two systems would be sufficiently odious to reconcile him heartily to any imaginary hardships complained of under existing regulations. On board the *Lapwing* I found nothing in the shape of mess traps in the Midshipmen's berth but a large wooden bowl. Like the plan adopted at the thieves' ordinary, the food was placed on the table, and the means for its consumption left entirely to the resources of the consumers. Clasp-knives prevailed at meal times, and such other aids to dissection as the Midshipmen might have at hand.

Being minus such property, but gifted with an excellent appetite, I dispensed with ceremony of every kind, and made a grab at the contents of the bowl. This proceeding, however, was summarily denounced by the others, who declared such conduct unbecoming to the society of gentlemen, and they threatened to chalk my fingers if I repeated it. In this state I was patronised by the Sergeant of Marines, who charitably lent me a knife and spoon until I could supply myself with similar conveniences, taking care at the same time to keep them always in sight and reclaim them when done with, a precaution he excused himself for taking by referring to the propensities of the boy who attended our mess.

After remaining inactive for some weeks, the *Lapwing* was ordered to Plymouth, and as the Captain's wife was living there, strange to say the order was obeyed with alacrity. We started in almost a gale of wind, in which we could only just lay our course. The Captain must have had a very pleasant lady for his wife; and despite the weather he carried a very heavy press of sail. In this trip we were struck by one of those extraordinary seas for which there is no accounting, and against which it is impossible to guard. They seem to be caused by the waves meeting in opposite directions, and are very ugly things to come across.

The shock we sustained fairly started five bolts of our main chains, and strained several of the planks. The sail was shortened in a trice, and a large hawser passed over one of the tops, and made fast on either side, to keep the masts from going overboard.

At Plymouth my real adventures may be said to have begun. The jolly-boat was sent ashore with a hospital party, and as I had asked leave to do so, I accompanied it. When the men were landed I volunteered to remain and look after the boat. Permission was readily accorded, but before the Doctor's mate left, he fumbled about in his pocket, and then inquired of me whether I had brought any money from the ship. I showed him my two-pound note, which he directly "borrowed" and then disappeared. I was delighted to have a boat all to myself, and began to pole about, never dreaming of the tide, which soon went out and deposited me helpless upon the mud. There I remained until it came in again, and the Doctor's mate and boat's crew returned. It was getting dark when we shoved off for the ship, and a squall was springing up. As it freshened we found it difficult to make any way, and the waves dashed in volumes over the boat. I began to feel nervous, the more so because the Doctor's mate did not look as if he was pleased with our position. I must have revealed my fears in my face, as the Coxwain called out, "Don't you be afraid, Mr Jackson; I'll look after you." As it was impossible to get on with safety through the squall, we determined to make for the shore again.

As we neared it, I stood up to be ready to disembark, and the Doctor's mate did likewise; but in his anxiety to get first made a rush forward, and as he passed shoved me right over the gunwale into the water. Daniels, the Coxwain, saw the accident, and as the water was deep, he was after me in a moment, and despite the height and roughness of the waves, he secured me and brought me on land. I had some minutes in the water, and felt half-drowned when rescued; but they carried me up to a small inn, where I was quickly put into a warm bed and my clothes laid out to dry. In the morning I was found curled up like a dog under the sheets in the middle of the bed fast asleep, and none the worse for my ducking. I was soon roused and dressed, and set off to the boat with the Doctor's mate, who on the way patronisingly informed me that after paying for my night's lodging and giving Daniels something in the way of a reward for having saved my life, there was nothing left of the two pounds. Young and green as I was, I took all he said for gospel, and agreed not to mention that he had kindly saved me the trouble of laying out the money, should I be asked any questions on the ship. With great forethought he enumerated a list of various articles in the purchase of which I could always account for the absence of my money, without the slightest necessity for revealing his share in the transaction. He spoke so fast in order to settle the matter before we reached the boat that I quite forgot the fictitious list, and only remembered the item "apples", upon which he had laid some stress as being a source of attraction most fatal to the purses of seafaring youths.

As luck would have it, not long after the event the Captain asked me what money I had on board.

"None, sir," I replied, feeling somewhat warm about the cheeks, and conscious of the duty I owed to the Doctor's mate.

"None?" said he. "Did you not bring any with you to the ship?"

"Yes, sir."

"How much?"

"Two pounds."

"And pray what have you done with that sum already?"

"I – I bought some apples, sir," said I, getting very confused.

"Two pounds' worth of apples! Nonsense, boy; impossible. Now go below and make out a list of all you have bought with the money."

I started off to obey him, but deuce a bit would anything come into my noddle but "apples", so I went

to my friend the Doctor's mate and acquainted him of
the fix I was in. I must admit he looked rather blank at
the news, especially when I told him how fickle my
memory had been, and that "apples" had alone survived the wreck. I forget now what he called me, but
whatever it was, he instantly relented and made me out
an appropriate account of my one night's expenditure.
Apples naturally predominated, and to a most unwholesome extent, so much so, that the Captain on reading
the list declined still to credit it, and became more
inquisitive than ever. He let me off at last with a
caution, expressing also a suspicion that there had
been more hands than one concerned in the mysterious disappearance of the two pounds.

We had some queer characters in the *Lapwing*, but
amongst any body of men so promiscuously collected
as may be a ship's company, you are certain to find odd
specimens of human nature. Our Boatswain was one.
A better warrant officer never existed – when he was
sober, – nor a man more generally liked; but his bane
was the grog-bottle.

On leaving Plymouth we took to cruising off
Guernsey, and were riding out a gale soon after
our arrival there when the *Spitfire*, Captain Robert
Keen, another man-of-war similar to ourselves,
dragged her anchor and drifted alongside of us. We
were in such close quarters that the muzzles of our
guns got into her ports, and as we rose and she fell
they were almost rent from their carriages. Everything was in dire confusion, and all hands alive save
the Boatswain, who, in a fit of drunkenness, had taken
up his position under the break of the quarter-deck,
and in the presence of the Captain was roaring out,

"There she goes, grind away! Look at the ——, there she goes." Captain Rotheram was in no humour to be trifled with, and had scarcely let go the flood-gates of his wrath upon the drunken Boatswain and got clear of the *Spitfire*, when, to the astonishment of everybody, a stentorian voice from the ship commenced to hail the Captain of the other vessel. "Captain Keen, sir," shouted he, "Captain Keen", repeated the voice again and again, the individual addressed replying each time with fresh vigour. "Aren't you ashamed of yourself, sir?" it continued; "call yourself a sailor, sir." Captain Rotheram's amazement may be imagined as he ran from one place to another in vain trying to discover the offender, shouting as he did so, "I am not hailing you, Captain Keen. It's some damned blackguard who I'll catch presently." After the lapse of a few minutes the culprit was brought to light, and turned out to be the Captain's own servant, who, following the Boatswain's example, had been taking a drop too much, and was amusing himself at his master's expense by hailing the *Spitfire* from the quarter-gallery of the Captain's cabin. When called upon to answer his absurd misconduct, he began to howl most piteously and beseeched the Captain, as he loved him, to give him "a dozen." "Flog me, sir; do, sir – I'm a scoundrel, sir. Please give me a dozen, sir." He, like the Boatswain, was also a good and valuable man when sober, and as this was his first serious shortcoming, the Captain ordered him to be tied to the rigging, instead of granting his request. I could not help thinking what his fate would have been under Sir Edward Hamilton.

As the Prince of Wales was recruiting himself at

Brighton we were instructed to proceed there, and lay off to be in attendance on his Royal Highness. Proceeding thither we passed a sunken ship with her topgallant masts visible out of the water. On consequent inquiry we were informed that a boy had been saved out of the wreck by some fishermen not long before, whose testimony afterwards went to prove that the ship had been scuttled to gain the insurance, but not in sufficiently deep water. As events showed, the Captain had forgotten to insure his own neck also against the possible consequences of his villainy, for he was convicted of the crime and hanged.

It is my opinion that many men would find themselves longer in their coffins if they did not take better precautions than did this less cunning individual, and use the lead freely before putting in the auger.

When relieved from duty at Brighton, and during a Sunday's cruise off Beachy Head, we ran aground upon the Sovereign Shoal – an accident that was generally attributed by the sailors to a sermon which had been preached on board by a clergyman passenger. With considerable hard work and the exertion of many ingenious contrivances, we managed to float her again, not, however, without springing a dangerous leak through which it was calculated the water came in at the rate of nine feet an hour. By unremitting labour at the pumps, we kept her up long enough to reach Sheerness, when the vessel went immediately into dock and was paid off. Whilst occupied in getting the ship off the Shoal, it was amusing to see how some women – forty or fifty in number – who were on board exerted themselves at the ropes. The rules of the service were not always so stringently enforced as they are now, and Jack often smuggled his sweetheart on board for a short cruise.

1802 TO JUNE 1804

Mr Coffin, the Commissioner at Sheerness, was an awful character in the eyes of most youngsters in the Navy to whom he was known personally or by repute, and no one cared to go before him twice. It was my turn to wait upon him, and I came in for a treat at once. "Sir, you have come into my presence without a cocked-hat in opposition to the rules of the Lords Commissioners of the Admiralty. I therefore decline to give you your pay." Captain Rotheram, who was present, took hold of my arm and led me up to another Midshipman who sported the article in requisition and transferred it, *pro tem*, from his head to mine, and thus supplied the omission. The Midshipman had a head as big again as mine, and the hat nearly proved an extinguisher; but it suited the purpose so far, and I returned to the Commissioner. Despite the cocked-hat I was still in his clutches. He demanded my journal – about the last thing in the world I should have cared to put into the hands of such a tyrant. My handwriting was of the vilest possible description; moreover, I had thoughtlessly beguiled many an idle hour by scribbling all sorts of nonsense in its pages – adding frequently such remarks on general topics as a volatile mind might suggest to me, who was not particularly versed in polite language. I am not sure that the monotony of writing was not occasionally broken by attempts at a higher order of art. Where an uncertainty existed, in some places, about the spelling of a word, I had adopted a method of my own, and the whole thing

was as unfitted as could be for the inspection of such a
man. Luckily for me, the style of writing discouraged
him from examining the subject-matter too minutely.
One glance at the first few leaves sufficed. "If ever you
come before me again, sir, with such a book as this, I'll
withhold your pay and report you directly." The great
man looked terrific, and I got farther into the cocked-
hat for refuge, determining, as I quitted his presence,
to exercise my talents for composition in a more
private direction in future, and try to improve my
"fist".

Mr Coffin must have been to Naval men what I have
heard the Proctors described as being to undergrad-
uates at the Universities. He was always turning up
when least expected, and asking unpleasant questions.
If he caught an Officer in mufti, it was "Your name
and ship, sir?" and the offender was invariably despatched back on board under arrest. No excuse was
ever allowed – go back he must. With old hands the
difficulty was easily disposed of; they went to their
ships and said nothing about the arrest; and to do the
Commissioner what little justice even "the old gentleman himself" may claim, he seldom followed up his
game unless in a more than usually sour frame of
mind.

One story told of this person will exhibit a feature of
his coarse and eccentric nature. A youngster of very
good family waited on Mr Coffin, bearing from an
aunt a letter of introduction in which she mildly
solicited Mr Coffin's interest with the Admiralty for
her nephew. "Tell your aunt, sir," he cried, "with my
compliments, that I am no more to the Lords Commissioners than a louse on an elephant's back!"

He was a great friend of Admiral Earl St Vincent, who perhaps from a somewhat similar temperament not only cultivated his intimacy, but permitted him to indulge his eccentricities without restraint. Once on a visit to the Admiral, he astonished his Lordship's valet one morning by letting himself out of a window, and walking off with a huge brown-paper parcel under his arm. The valet reported the circumstance at breakfast. "Oh, let him alone," replied the Earl, "he'll be back to dinner"; and so he was, though he made no apology for his absence during the day, nor for his strange method of exit from the house. He found his match at last. In a weak moment he married, and was shortly afterwards turned adrift by his wife and her mother for insisting on cooking his own meals in the kitchen of his mother-in-law's house, and his wife never returned to him.

The *Carysfort* was the next ship I joined (Captain Robert Fanshawe), and once more, "ere we parted for ever", Mr Coffin and I came into collision. He went on board to make an advance of pay to the officers and men. "Your journal, sir?" he remarked the moment I stood before him. I handed it over and was immediately refused my share of the advance, and the Captain was admonished on the spot to withhold all allowances until my handwriting had considerably improved. This deprivation put me *hors de combat* with the Mess. My subscription was owing, and the caterer inflexible. Get money I must, anyhow, and he advised me to borrow from the Captain. My greenness was not yet all rubbed off, and taking him at his word I applied without delay. "By God, sir," said the Captain, "but you have some brass. I am instructed to retain your pay as a punishment, and you have the impu-

dence to ask me to hand you some money." Seeing me
rather shut up at this attack, he ceased ringing the
changes upon my audacity, and on learning my motive
for applying, kindly accommodated me, and increased
his kindness by making me always write my journal in
his cabin, where I could be overlooked and instructed.

When the war broke out again in 1803, we were at
Shields with other men-of-war, engaged in the impressment of men for the service. Our instructions
were to spare no effort in procuring fresh hands, and
we succeeded beyond our hopes. From Shields we
went to Shetland, and I daresay there are people living
there yet to whom a remembrance of our visit still
clings. We carried off every able-bodied male we could
lay our hands upon. I think the number we captured in
Shetland alone amounted to seventy* fine young fellows. When the ship was on the point of leaving, it was
a melancholy sight; for boatloads of women – wives,
mothers, and sisters – came alongside to take leave of
their kidnapped relatives. Being young at the business
I was not always proof against some of the trials I
encountered ashore, and often repented having made a
capture when I witnessed the misery it occasioned in
homes hitherto happy and undisturbed. Our gang was
a most effective, energetic party, and few escaped its
vigilance. On one occasion, whilst prowling about in
the execution of our duty, I espied a tall handsome lad
coming into our vicinity unawares. On catching sight
of me he fled like a deer. I was young and active too,
and started off in pursuit; the race was becoming mine
when he made for a house and dashed through the

* The actual number was sixty-five.

open doorway. I was on his heels directly, but found myself arrested by a poor, respectable-looking woman who fell upon her knees, and beseeched me, with clasped hands and tears streaming down her face, to spare her boy. Her entreaties were joined by several young girls present, all of whom were exhibiting the same tearful propensity. I gave in at once and left the spot with a queer sensation in the throat, and grumbling an incoherent anathema against the whole sex. These were strange times when a youngster of my age could lay violent hands upon almost any man he came across and lead him into bondage; but such was the law, and to resist it was dangerous and sometimes productive of even greater evils. There is a fine touching old song which was composed about this period, illustrating the cruelties of impressment. It became a universal favourite with the poorer classes. Such an influence did this song exercise upon the people that it was forbidden to be sung in public. I forget the name of it, but the commencing line was: "The voyage is passed; on England's shore."

Tyrannical and opposed as it was to the English character and ideals, impressment of men for service in the Navy was at the time a necessary evil. By fair means or foul we were compelled to procure men, and without these forcible procedures we never could have manned our famous "old wooden walls," or done that execution on the broad seas for which our Navy is so justly celebrated.

One fact deserves notice: I frequently captured men who, though inclined to be violent at first, soon resigned themselves to their fate, and became voluntary members of the pressgang, to which they became very valuable auxiliaries.

Our man-catching occupations at an end, we returned to Portsmouth to fit out for the West Indies. Here the excellency of our crew was first displayed. We went into dock on a Wednesday, and were to leave the harbour behind us the following Saturday. Considering the work there was to be done, such expedition was remarkable, and almost unprecedented.

We were indebted to our late efforts at impressment for as fine a body of men as ever sailed in a ship. We took their average height, and it was a trifle under six feet. Captain Fanshawe was a host in himself as an executive officer, though not twenty-one years of age. In addition to his abilities as a Commander, he possessed all the attributes of a gentleman, and was deservedly esteemed. As regards the ship herself, we were also specially favoured, as she was believed to be the handsomest frigate yet built by English hands.

On the eve of our departure a painful incident occurred amongst the crew. There was a man distinguished from the rest by an unusually handsome person and address, and by his evident superiority of education. It was easy to see that at some former period of his life he had filled a position very different from the one which he at present occupied. No one, however, could draw from him anything of his past history – he became an object of interesting mystery to all hands. During the last four hours of his leave on shore he had engaged with another sailor, for a small wager, to drink a greater quantity of spirits in a given time than his comrade. Gin was the liquor selected; and he won the stake, returning to the ship apparently none the worse for his insane contention. His "lady-love" had gone on board to take leave of him, and he lay down upon the deck with his head resting upon her lap, and dropped off, as she thought, asleep. Presently she tried to rouse him and failed. One of his messmates passing, stopped and shook him, but to no purpose. Thinking that he was feigning they handled him more roughly, but the unfortunate creature never moved again; he was stone dead.

The first port we stopped at was Cork, where we met the *Apollo*, Captain Dixon, and collected a convoy bound for Madeira. We proceeded with strong westerly winds prevailing. Eight days later we boarded a Portugese stranger, from whom we learnt that she had only lost sight of land that morning. This news astonished us not a little, and the Captain increased his sail, whilst the breeze sprang up into a gale drawing round to the south. Concluding that the Commodore with the convoy would be on the other tack, we wore round at midnight, knowing that he could not be far from the land. At daylight one of the merchantmen spoke to us, and said that she had touched ground. Another soon afterwards gave us intelligence of having seen several vessels ashore, escaping shipwreck herself by a miracle. Captain Fanshawe thereupon drew as many of the fleet together as he could find, and we continued our voyage. On arriving at Madeira all the Captains came on board, each telling his own story about the disasters of the storm which had separated us, and confirming our worst anxieties. The *Apollo* had been wrecked, and out of sixty-nine vessels which had composed the convoy when we started from Cork harbour, only thirty-nine reached their destination. Chronometers were then hardly invented, and when we compared the various reckonings of the Captains, it was startling to observe the discrepancies they exhibited. One thing they conclusively established, that all the ships had been driven out of their course by one cause, and I sometimes ask myself the question whether strong north-west winds could divert any portion of the Gulf Stream to the south-east, as I found the same deviation to occur at a subsequent period when taking the *Serapis* out to Jamaica. None of the Captains, though many of them experienced navigators, could explain the cause of the misreckoning, which appeared to them to be unaccountable.

We stayed at Madeira several days in the hope that some of the missing vessels would appear, but as none did so, we pursued our journey with such vessels as were ready to go. At Barbados, our next rendezvous, we took a short spell, and were honoured by a visit from "Lady Rodney". Intimation had been given us of her Ladyship's intention, and all the necessary preparations were made for her reception. I was one of those deputed to meet our illustrious visitor, and enjoyed the privilege of handing her up the vessel's side. On reaching the deck, I remember well, she sat upon one of the carronade's sides, and received the officers presented to her with a dignity and grace becoming her station in life. The Second Lieutenant, a fine dashing fellow, was particularly favoured by her Ladyship, who selected his arm in descending to the gunroom, where all the dirty linen was made up into bundles for her to take ashore.

"Lady Rodney" was a sable washerwoman, and enjoyed a monopoly amongst the ships of war at Barbados. As black as a coal, and overflowing with her own importance, her visits on board, irrespective of their professional value, were always anticipated with no small degree of entertainment by the officers, who vied with each other in showing her that deference she never failed to exact from her clients. Her pseudonym had been acquired, I believe, from a trifling act of gallantry once paid her in former days by a noble sailor, whose name and title she thereupon assumed, and kept until the day of her death. In most tropical ports you are sure to find one or more noted characters of the same description. The votaries of the washing-tub comprise an important class, and have ready access to the ships in harbour, where they do not hesitate to make themselves quite at home, and strike up a lasting, and I wish I might add always platonic, friendship with their employers. They are desperately jealous of any rival, and it is an unpardonable crime in their eyes to be deprived of any share of their accustomed privileges. As a general rule they are scrupulously honest if you happen to be friends; and who would not be on amicable terms with his washerwoman under such circumstances? In some other parts of the world this class of person is rather to be dreaded than trusted.

Apropos of their honesty, I may relate an event that happened to a brother officer of mine a few years later which will tend to illustrate it. We were at Gibraltar awaiting orders, and Parker, one of the Lieutenants, thought it a good opportunity to go in for a general cleansing of his wardrobe. He was a great dandy in his way, and morbidly addicted to superfine shirts with any quantity of pearl buttons down the bosoms, considered rather a luxury in those days. He never ventured into public assemblies without making a public display of this conceit, and naturally was celebrated for it. During a run of gaiety on shore these precious shirts had become exhausted, and were sadly in need of a "Lady Rodney's" good services. He therefore entrusted them to the care of an accommodating handmaid, who undertook the responsible charge and promised to be extra punctual. A day or two later we received our orders to start at a few hours' notice, and Parker's consternation may be imagined. A summons was despatched to the washerwoman, but no answer was returned. The anchor was tripped – the sails bent – Parker distracted. At the very last moment a boat pushed alongside and a parcel was handed on board. Parker rushed forward to secure the treasure, and in the joy of the moment tendered a coin in excess of the expense incurred, and liberally declined any change. We sailed, and everything went smoothly with Parker until his watch was over and he repaired to his cabin to put away his shirts. His face was a picture when he appeared on deck, uttering the most terrible maledictions against the woman who had betrayed him. The shirts were safe, and washed almost to a fault, but the *buttons* – "devil a one has that imp of Satan left on the whole lot!" shouted poor Parker. The careful washerwoman, wise in her generation, and appreciating the value of pearl buttons, had made the most of a bargain that might never fall to her lot again. As for Parker, unfortunate man, the joke was too good not to be enjoyed, and every one laughed at his mishap, nor did he hear the last of it for many a long day.

The convoy was abandoned at Barbados, and we went cruising off Martinique, where I made my first acquaintance with an enemy's cannon-balls. We were standing in towards the harbour, when the Captain, who was spying ashore, suddenly exclaimed, "They're going to fire!" and as he spoke a shot came whizzing over our foremast followed by others, all well directed but much too high to do us any harm. One only gave us the least concern; it passed between our main and foremast, about two or three feet above the hammock nettings. This was the occasion of a bit of pleasantry at the expense of a Midshipman that we youngsters did not forget in a hurry. He was standing at the moment close under the spot where the shot passed, and instinctively bent down his head as it flew over. The Captain perceiving what he did, said, smiling, whilst he imitated the gesture with his finger, "That won't save you, Jerry, that won't save you." Alas for Jerry, he had been a big man amongst us, but his day was gone. Every one of us took up the Captain's example, and on the slightest provocation, would perform the same action and cry, "That won't save you, Jerry, that won't save you."

As nothing was to be gained by offering ourselves as a passing target for our friends on dry land, we wore off to a more agreeable distance. Near Martinique is a place called Diamond Rock, in possession of the English and occupied by a Commander, two Lieutenants, and some men. One of the Lieutenants at the Rock insisted on trying to make me a disciple of the "fragrant weed", and failed most disastrously in his kind intentions. I became so horribly ill, and took such a dislike to him, and tobacco, and the place in consequence, that I never think of them without a qualm. Perhaps I lacked energy to persevere and conquer, but

I have never touched tobacco since, and perhaps am all the better for it. From being considered a filthy indulgence, it has reached the character of a gentlemanly habit, so I must not abuse "what all the world approves". A long way off, and in the open air; I do not mind it much, and even this is a great admission to make. There are some young fellows I know who, when they come to see me, are sure to have a stale pipe somewhere in their pockets, and I can scent them afar off; but they assure me the more beastly a pipe looks and smells, the nicer it is to smoke. So much for taste, but all this is a digression; but for the matter of that it is not likely to be the last I shall make on the way.

Others had received permission to land on Diamond Rock as well as myself, and at the appointed hour a boat was sent from the ship to take us back. At starting the sea was washing in pretty freely, and the Midshipman in charge of the boat was cautioned to keep farther from the cliff; but like all boys, he knew his duty as well as anybody else, and did not require to be told. The caution soon proved a necessary one, for a huge sea running into the shore curled up the cliff with the speed of thought, and falling far outwards, struck the water with prodigious force not half an oar's length from our bows. A little nearer and we should have been successfully swamped or had the bottom of the boat knocked out. No other warning was needed, and we quickly adopted the first suggestion. We experienced some excitement after leaving Diamond Rock by running the frigate aground, and incurred serious damage thereby. The *Cyane* being in sight, we signalled her to keep us company as soon as we got off, and made directly to English Harbour, Antigua. Next

morning the Carpenter ran on deck from the store-
room, and gave the alarm that the ship was sinking by
the head. The Captain ordered the guns overboard
without delay. The *Cyane*, observing our confusion,
ran alongside just as the Carpenter made a second
appearance declaring the alarm to be false and un-
founded. Two of our guns were already gone, and two
of our anchors. We then entered English Harbour and
set to work stripping the ship, which labour was soon
accomplished. The weather here was frightfully hot,
and it is deserving of notice how careful Captain
Fanshawe was of his crew: running up awnings wherever he could, and taking every possible means of
protecting the men from the sun's scorching rays.
His attention to this matter led the Commissioner
to remark that he had done more for his ship's company than any other Captain he had known. No precaution, however, availed to ensure their safety. That
terrible epidemic "yellow fever" broke out among
them, and thirteen persons were attacked, including
the Captain, Surgeon (Robert Skelly), Second Lieutenant, a Midshipman named Campbell, and myself.
But of that number only Campbell and myself left the
hospital alive.* I cannot say how long we were in
durance vile, but we were prisoners in the wards for
several weeks, and even when quite convalescent our
legs would hardly support our bodies. Campbell suffered more than I did, indeed the doctors had almost
given him up. During the progress of the disease he
had begun to exhibit its worst features, and in one part
of his body mortification had commenced. The flesh

* Actually there were forty-seven deaths among the officers and
men of the *Carysfort* during this brief epidemic.

was attacked, gradually sloughing away. Next to con-
fluent smallpox, I should imagine yellow fever to be
the most malignant and incurable of the epidemic
diseases. Its real nature can be conceived only by those
who have witnessed its horrors. The Spaniards call it
"vomits" from the black vomit that nearly always
ensues, after which there is little or no hope of the
patient's recovery. When attacked by this accursed
retching, the sufferer frequently springs up in his bed
and expels the dark thick fluid from his mouth several
feet beyond him in a moment of intense agony; and at
times the patient is suddenly seized with such violent
convulsions that the force of several powerful men is
hardly sufficient to hold him down. This singular
malady is so deceptive that the patient will sink at
intervals into a calm and apparently refreshing sleep,
as still as a child's slumber, and start suddenly thence
without the slightest warning into one of those terrible
fits. Before my attack I had been constantly to the
hospital in charge of the sick, and the sights I there
witnessed no doubt made an injurious impression
upon me and accelerated my illness. On the last
occasion I was greatly affected and depressed by a
scene in the wards. One unfortunate creature lay in the
throes of death. From every orifice in his body a thin
bloody serum was oozing, and the natural colour of his
skin was changed to a ghastly muddy yellow. To add to
the hideousness of the spectacle, his person was literally swarming with minute white ants, called by the
natives, I believe, "walky-walky ants"; and where the
secretion exuded these detestable insects were collected thickest, gathered round the margin of the fluid,
and feasting upon their odious banquet. Wherever a

dead body is they are certain to congregate, but in this instance they were too eager to wait until death had finished his work. I called the Doctor's attention to the case, and he declared it impossible to remedy the evil. The legs of the bed were standing in pans of water, but no other resources were equal to the emergency, and the wretched victim lingered on under the additional affliction to his appointed hour. On quitting the ward I became gradually sensible of an approaching illness – a feeling of oppression crept over me, attended by a slight pain in the back. I returned to the hospital and consulted the Doctor, who spoke cheerfully and recommended me to turn in at once and submit to his treatment. This advice I declined to follow, preferring to go to the ship, or rather to the capstan-house, into which the Officers had been temporarily transferred. I reached the spot with difficulty – I was weary and giddy, and gladly lay down upon my cot. The next day I was ordered to the hospital whether I would or no. The fever was coming on, and made me restless and fretful. On entering the hospital I flatly refused to take the room allotted to me, and asked to be put into the one at the other end of the building. The Doctor kindly humoured me. Then I objected to the bed; there was an ugly stain upon the pillow. "I will not go there," I cried, "a man has died in that bed!" "Give him another bed", said the Doctor, and after a few more objections had been satisfied, I gave myself up entirely to the faculty and prepared to meet the enemy. What occurred during the next fortnight I do not recollect, but as soon as the virulence of the malady had subsided, I began to realise the mistake I had made in the choice of a room. The window next to my bed, and from which I could easily look, commanded an uninterrupted view of the dead-house outside, so that I could plainly see the bodies being carried there from the hospital.

On approaching convalescence, Campbell and I, hearing of each other's recovery and eager for companionship, soon found opportunities of indulging the wish, and when the nurses were absent would exchange visits, often at the expense of our equilibrium, being scarcely capable of standing upright for a minute at a time. We were discovered in the act one morning by the Doctor, who, being the best of good fellows, promised to put us both into a room by ourselves if we engaged to wait a day or two longer. He kept his word, and we were overjoyed to be together again without fear of disturbance.

As our health improved, our appetites revived, and we were put upon full rations with the privilege of naming occasionally any particular food we might fancy. We took advantage of this liberty directly and called for roast pork, which was supplied to us. The sight of it made us ravenous, me especially, and an attack on the dish was made the moment it appeared. But alas for poor Campbell's judgment – the sight of the savoury meat, such as his soul loved, was enough for him. His knife and fork dropped from his grasp, and he fell back satisfied and sickened. Not so with me! each mouthful of the dainty meal provoked a fresh relish, and before the matron's return I had devoured my own share and Campbell's too. She, kind soul, remarking how matters stood, brought him a large bowl of sago and left it beside him. This proved as unavailing as the pork, and he pushed it with loathing over to me, where it quickly followed after the pork. For a short time I felt contented and happy, but my stomach was not prepared to be taxed with such an unusual burden and began to rebel. The result was that in a few hours I was suffering all the tortures of a greedy surfeit, which completely threw me back and retarded my recovery. Before this unlucky feast I had been by far the stronger of the two. Now Campbell took the lead, and kept it until we were discharged from the hospital.

Jackson's perils did not end here. Five years later he was made a prisoner of war, following a spirited action off Guadalope in which his ship, the Junon, *sustained sixty killed and wounded. In April 1812 Jackson made a dramatic escape from confinement in France, "liberating" a fishing boat and sailing single-handed to the Isle of Wight.*

"Till We Are Crowned with Victory": The Battle of Copenhagen

1801

In 1800 Prussia, Russia, Sweden and Denmark formed the Armed Neutrality of the North to resist the British design of preventing trade between neutral countries and France. The Danish fleet posed a particularly dangerous threat and in a piece of classic frigate diplomacy, Britain dispatched Admiral Sir Hyde Parker, Horatio Nelson, and twenty-six ships of the line to Copenhagen with the demand that the Danes leased their fleet to His Majesty. The ultimatum was rejected, and the British responded with all cannon blazing. One of the most storied actions in naval history, the Battle of Copenhagen witnessed the Royal Navy at its most audacious, down to Nelson's pretended blindness to Parker's signal for withdrawal and the sailing of some of Nelson's ships to the landward of the anchored enemy vessels to make a surprise attack. It also saw the Royal Navy at its most doggedly determined. The typical, "no frills" account of the action from the log of the Defiance *is accompanied by a vivid letter from the ship's commander, Rear-Admiral Thomas Graves.*

April 1st.

P.M. – Half-past three, weighed and made sail, the fleet in company. ½ past 5, came to with the best bower in 7 fathoms, veered to a cable. Copenhagen NW by N 7 or 8 miles. At ½ past 6, unbent the sheet cable, got it out of the starboard gun-room port and bent it to the spare anchor. At 8, the enemy firing shells at our ships. At 12, answered night signal 19 [want boats to tow].

April 2nd.

A.M. – At 4, do. weather. At 7, hoisted out the flat-bottomed boat. At 9, weighed and stood in abreast of Copenhagen town in company with the *Elephant*, Vice-Admiral Nelson; *Edgar, Monarch, Ganges, Russell, Bellona, Isis, Glatton, Polyphemus, Blanche, Amazon* and *Arrow*. 17 past 11, a general action took place between our ships and the Danish vessels and batteries. Let go our stern anchors with a spring on do. abreast of the Crown Battery, which wounded our main and mizen masts and bowsprit the first broadside. At noon, moderate weather.

P.M. – Moderate and fair. The action was continued warm on both sides. 14 past 3, the enemy ceased firing. We found that 13 of their vessels had struck. Cut the spring and stern cable and made sail. ½ past 3, our ship took the ground. Run out the stream anchor and cable, which we hove home. At 7, a gun-brig came to assist us, which carried out our small bower-anchor, the cable from the stern port. Hove with both capstans and ditto. Found it necessary to lighten the ship. Started 30 butts of water. Hove overboard a quantity of purser's wood.

April 3rd.

A.M. – Ditto weather. Hove the ship off. Employed warping into the anchorage with the assistance of the *Jamaica* and *Acorn*. Slipped the small bower and stream owing to their being out of the stern port, and in shoal water abreast of the Crown Battery. Five sail of the line struck, twelve razees and prams also struck. Small vessels employed towing them out. One ship of the line blew up and some of the razees. Mustered the ship's company, and found Lieut. Gray and 25 men killed, 56 men wounded.

LETTER FROM REAR-ADMIRAL THOMAS GRAVES.

Defiance, off the town of Copenhagen, April 3rd, 1801.

Dear Brother, – Yesterday an awful day for the town of Copenhagen. Eleven sail of our ships under the command of Lord Nelson, under whom I served that day, attacked the floating batteries, ships, gun-vessels, and their works on shore, which lasted five hours, with as many hard blows and as much obstinacy as has been ever known, and with great loss on both sides, but finally ended in the complete overthrow of their outer defence. We have now eleven sail of their vessels in our possession. Two ran on shore, one sank, and one was blown up in the action. It was, certainly, a most gallant defence, and words cannot speak too high of the boldness of the attack, considering all the difficulties we had to struggle with, and their great superiority in number and weight of guns. I think we were playing a losing game in attacking stone walls, and I fear we shall not have much to boast of when it is known what our ships suffered, and the little impression we made on their navy. Lord Nelson tells me I shall be made a Baronet, but I shall only ask for justice being done to my two brothers. Lord Nelson was appointed to command this attack, and he asked for me to serve with him; if not, you might depend on my not staying behind when anything was to be done. I think yesterday must prove that the enterprise of the British is invincible. Our loss in killed and wounded was only *ninety*. Lord Nelson's ship not thirty, but the *Monarch* that was next to us in the attack, and not so much exposed to the great Crown Battery, lost between two and three hundred men killed and wounded. Boys escaped unhurt. *I am told* the battle of the Nile was nothing to this. I am happy that my flag was not a month hoisted before I got into action, and into the hottest one that has happened the whole of the war. Considering the disadvantages of navigation, the approach to the enemy, their vast number of guns and mortars on both land and sea, I do not think there ever was a bolder attack. Some of our ships did not get into action, which made those who did feel it the hotter. In short, it was worthy of our gallant and enterprising little Hero of the Nile. Nothing can exceed his spirit.

Sir Hyde made the signal to discontinue the action before we had been at it two hours, supposing that our ships would all be destroyed. But our little Hero gloriously said, "I will not move till we are crowned with victory, or that the Commander-in-Chief sends an officer to order me away." And he was right, for if we had discontinued the action before the enemy struck, we should have all got aground and have been destroyed. As it was, both Lord Nelson's ship and the *Defiance* got aground in coming off. Lord Nelson sent for me at the close of the action, and it was beautiful to see how the shot beat the water all round us in the boat. Give my love to my dear daughter. She has ever the most ardent prayers for her happiness. The destruction amongst the enemy is dreadful. One of the ships that was towed into the fleet yesterday had between two and three hundred dead on her decks, besides what they had thrown overboard.

My dear Brother,
Your most affectionate friend,
THOS. GRAVES.
To John Graves, Esq.,
Barley House, Exeter.

R.F. Roberts

Trafalgar:
The Midshipman's View

1805

The most famous of English sea battles was fought off Cadiz on Monday, 21 October 1805. After rousing the patriotic hearts of his men with the signal "England expects every man will do his duty", Nelson daringly struck at the rear of the Combined (French and Spanish) Fleet whilst cutting off its van. The annihilation of Villeneuve was complete; of the French admiral's 33 ships, 18 were captured immediately, 4 surrendered later, and 11 reached Cadiz but never ventured to sea again. French and Spanish pretentions to naval power were shattered to driftwood for ever.

Midshipman Roberts fought in the battle aboard Nelson's flagship, HMS Victory.

"Victory," at Sea
Off Trafalgar, 22nd Oct., 1805.

Dear Parents,

I have just time and opportunity to tell you that we had a desperate engagement with the enemy, and, thank God, I have so far escaped unhurt. The Combined Fleet came out of Cadiz on Saturday morning with a determination to engage and blow us up (as the prisoners say) out of the water, but they are much – very much – mistaken. I can't tell you how many we have taken and destroyed, they say fifteen, but it is quite uncertain. *I* don't think it is so many; but none of us know at present, but amongst the taken is a fourdecker which struck to the *Neptune*. We engaged her for some time and then she fell astern of us.

I am sorry – very sorry – to tell you that amongst the slain is Lord Nelson, his secretary Mr Scott, and Mr Whipple, Captain Hardy's clerk, whom you know. Out of four marine officers two were wounded and the Captain killed. It was as hard an action, as allowed by all on board this ship, as ever was fought. There were but three left alive on the Quarterdeck, the enemy fired so much grape and small shot from the rigging, there was one ship so close to us that we could not run out our guns their proper length. Only conceive how much we must have smashed her, every gun was trebly shotted for her.

We have a great many killed and wounded – dangerously wounded – 21 amputations. I am happy to say Captain Hardy escaped unhurt, but we have one Lieutenant killed and two wounded, and one midshipman killed and three wounded. We had no less than ten ships on ours.

I forgot to tell you that we engaged them on Monday, we began at 12 o'clock and continued till ½ past 4. The enemy consisted of 35 sail of the Line, 4 frigates, 2 brigs; and our fleet of 27 sail of the line, 4 frigates and a schooner and sloop. Unluckily for us Admiral Lewes had been sent a little time before with 5 sail of the line up the Gut.

This morning the enemy are out of sight and we have the prizes in tow, going I believe for Gibraltar. We have several ships fit for the enemy now, and if they should come to attack us we should be able to give them a warm reception, they have most of them had enough of it; there are several lame ducks gone off. The rascals have shot away our mizen mast and we are very much afraid of our main and foremasts. The *Royal Sovereign* has not a stick standing – a total wreck. It was she that began the action in a noble manner, engaging four of them at the same time. Admiral Collingwood had shifted his flag on board of her a few days before. Two of the enemy blew up and one sank. You can have no conception whatsoever what an action between two fleets is; it was a grand but an awful sight indeed; thank God we are all so well over it.

Admiral Nelson was shot early in the action by a musket ball from the enemy's top, which struck him a little below the shoulder, touched the rib and lodged near his heart. He lived about 2 ½ hours after; then died without a groan. Every ship that struck, our fellows ceased firing and gave three cheers like Noble Britons. The Spaniards fought very well indeed, as did the Frenchmen. Scarcely any prizes have a stick standing. One that we had possession of, and struck to us, had 75 killed in her middle deck, and many more in her lower deck. Capt. Duff (I believe he commands the *Colossus*) is killed, but I have not heard of any more captains being killed. I will give you all the particulars in my next, but you must excuse me now as really we are in such confusion that I can't tell how I have written this. I thought you would be uneasy if you did not hear of me by the first ship, so I have as my duty requires written to you.

Remember me to all that ask for me, and believe me

Your dutiful son

R. F. Roberts.

P.S. – We have 40 men wounded, 9 officers, and (I think) as many killed. It was a much harder action than the Nile, several in our ship say so. The carpenter whom you saw at Mr Jacob's was there, and has been in several other actions with Lord Nelson, and he says it is the hardest action he was ever in. There were a thousand shot on each deck, and the middle deck in the action was obliged to be supplied with more. One poor fellow lost both his legs in the action, and is since dead of his wounds.

Lord Nelson's last request was that his body might be taken to England. This ship will not be able to come home with him yet, so I suppose he will be sent by some other. We expect to come to England as soon as we can get a jury mast rigged and a little repaired . . .

Sam

Trafalgar: The View from the Lower-Deck

1805

A view of Trafalgar from the lower-deck of the Royal Sovereign.

"Royal Sovereign."

Honoured Father,

This comes to tell you I am alive and hearty except three fingers; but that's not much, it might have been my head. I told brother Tom I should like to see a greadly battle, and I have seen one, and we have peppered the Combined rarely; and for the matter of that, they fought us pretty tightish for French and Spanish. Three of our mess are killed, and four more of us winged. But to tell you the truth of it, when the game began, I wished myself at Warnborough with my plough again; but when they had given us one duster, and I found myself snug and tight, I set to in good earnest, and thought no more about being killed than if

I were at Murrell Green Fair, and I was presently as busy and as black as a collier. How my fingers got knocked overboard I don't know, but off they are, and I never missed them till I wanted them. You see, by my writing, it was my left hand, so I can write to you and fight for my King yet. We have taken a rare parcel of ships, but the wind is so rough we cannot bring them home, else I should roll in money, so we are busy smashing 'em, and blowing 'em up wholesale.

Our dear Admiral Nelson is killed! so we have paid pretty sharply for licking 'em. I never sat eyes on him, for which I am both sorry and glad; for, to be sure, I should like to have seen him – but then, all the men in our ship who have seen him are such soft toads, they have done nothing but blast their eyes, and cry, ever since he was killed. God bless you! chaps that fought like the devil, sit down and cry like a wench. I am still in the *Royal Sovereign*, but the Admiral [Collingwood] has left her, for she is like a horse without a bridle, so he is in a frigate that he may be here and there and everywhere, for he's as *cute* as here and there one, and as bold as a lion, for all he can cry! – I saw his tears with my own eyes, when the boat hailed and said my lord was dead. So no more at present from your dutiful son,

SAM.

William Beatty

The Death of Nelson

1805

Adorned with his gleaming awards and medals on the Victory's *quarterdeck, Admiral Lord Horatio Nelson made a conspicuous target for French sharpshooters at Trafalgar. William Beatty was the* Victory's *surgeon.*

About half an hour before the enemy opened their fire, the memorable telegraphic signal was made, that "ENGLAND EXPECTS EVERY MAN WILL DO HIS DUTY," which was spread and received throughout the fleet with enthusiasm. It is impossible adequately to describe by any language the lively emotions excited in the crew of the *Victory* when this propitious communication was made known to them: confidence and resolution were strongly portrayed in the countenance of all; and the sentiment generally expressed to each other was that they would prove to their country that day how well British seamen *could* "do their duty" when led to battle by their revered admiral.

The signal was afterwards made to "prepare to anchor after the close of the day;" and Union Jacks were hoisted at the foretop mast and topgallant stays of each ship, to serve as a distinction from the enemy's, in conformity with orders previously issued by the commander in chief. By his Lordship's directions also, the different divisions of the fleet hoisted the St George's or White Ensign, being the colours of the commander in chief: this was done to prevent confusion from occurring during the battle, through a variety of national flags.

The *Royal Sovereign* now made the signal by telegraph, that "the enemy's commander in chief was in a frigate." This mistake arose from one of their frigates making many signals.

Lord Nelson ordered his line to be steered about two points more to the northward than that of his second in command, for the purpose of cutting off the retreat of the enemy's van to the port of Cadiz; which was the reason of the three leading ships of Admiral Collingwood's line being engaged with the enemy previously to those of the commander in chief's line.

The enemy began to fire on the *Royal Sovereign* at thirty minutes past eleven o'clock; in ten minutes after which, she got under the stern of the *St. Anna*, and commenced a fire on her. Lieutenant Pasco, signal officer of the *Victory*, was heard to say while looking through his glass, "There is a topgallant yard gone." His Lordship eagerly asked, "Whose topgallant yard is that gone? Is it the *Royal Sovereign*'s?" and on being answered by Lieutenant Pasco in the negative, and that it was the enemy's, he smiled, and said: "Collingwood is doing well."

At fifty minutes past eleven, the enemy opened their fire on the commander in chief. They shewed great coolness in the commencement of the battle; for as the *Victory* approached their line, their ships lying immediately ahead of her and across her bows fired only one gun at a time, to ascertain whether she was yet within their range. This was frequently repeated by eight or nine of their ships, till at length a shot passed through the *Victory*'s main topgallant sail; the hole in which being discovered by the enemy, they immediately opened their broadsides, supporting an awful and tremendous fire.

In a very short time afterwards, Mr Scott, public secretary to the commander in chief, was killed by a cannon shot while in conversation with Captain Hardy. Lord Nelson being then near them; Captain Adair of the marines, with the assistance of a seaman, endeavoured to remove the body from his Lordship's sight: but he had already observed the fall of his secretary; and now said with anxiety, "Is that poor Scott that is gone?" and on being answered in the affirmative by Captain Adair, he replied, "Poor fellow!"

Lord Nelson and Captain Hardy walked the quarter deck in conversation for some time after this, while the enemy kept up an incessant raking fire.

A double-headed shot struck one of the parties of marines drawn up on the poop, and killed eight of them; when his Lordship, perceiving this, ordered Captain Adair to disperse his men round the ship, that they might not suffer so much from being together.

In a few minutes afterwards a shot struck the fore

brace bits on the quarter deck, and passed between Lord Nelson and Captain Hardy; a splinter from the bits bruising Captain Hardy's foot, and tearing the buckle from his shoe. They both instantly stopped; and were observed by the officers on deck to survey each other with inquiring looks, each supposing the other to be wounded. His Lordship then smiled, and said: "This is too warm work, Hardy, to last long"; and declared that "through all the battles he had been in, he had never witnessed more cool courage than was displayed by the *Victory*'s crew on this occasion."

The *Victory* by this time, having approached close to the enemy's van, had suffered very severely without firing a single gun: she had lost about twenty men killed, and had about thirty wounded. Her mizzen topmast, and all her studding sails and their booms on both sides were shot away; the enemy's fire being chiefly directed at her rigging, with a view to disable her before she could close with them.

At four minutes past twelve o'clock, she opened her fire, from both sides of her decks, upon the enemy; when Captain Hardy represented to his Lordship, that "it appeared impracticable to pass through the enemy's line without going on board some one of their ships."

Lord Nelson answered, "I cannot help it: it does not signify which we run on board of; go on board which you please; take your choice."

At twenty minutes past twelve, the tiller ropes being shot away: Mr Atkinson, the master, was ordered below to get the helm put to port; which being done, the *Victory* was soon run on board the *Redoubtable* of seventy-four guns.

On coming alongside and nearly on board of her, that ship fired her broadside into the *Victory*, and immediately let down her lower deck ports; which, as has been since learnt, was done to prevent her from being boarded through them by the *Victory*'s crew. She never fired a great gun after this single broadside.

A few minutes after this, the *Téméraire* fell likewise on board of the *Redoubtable*, on the side opposite to the *Victory*; having also an enemy's ship, said to be *La Fougueux*, on board of *her* on her other side: so that the extraordinary and unprecedented circumstance occurred here, of *four* ships of the line being *on board of each other* in the heat of battle; forming as compact a tier as if they had been moored together, their heads lying all the same way. The *Téméraire*, as was just before mentioned, was between the *Redoubtable* and *La Fougueux*.

The *Redoubtable* commenced a heavy fire of musketry from the tops, which was continued for a considerable time with destructive effect to the *Victory*'s crew: her great guns however being silent, it was supposed at different times that she had surrendered; and in consequence of this opinion, the *Victory* twice ceased firing upon her by orders transmitted from the quarter deck.

At this period, scarcely a person in the *Victory* escaped unhurt who was exposed to the enemy's musketry; but there were frequent huzzas and cheers heard from between the decks, in token of the surrender of different of the enemy's ships. An incessant fire was kept up from both sides of the *Victory*: her larboard guns played upon the *Santissima Trinidada* and the *Bucentaur*; and the starboard guns of the middle and lower decks were depressed, and fired with a diminished charge of powder, and three shot each, into the *Redoubtable*. This mode of firing was adopted by Lieutenants Williams, King, Yule, and Brown, to obviate the danger of the *Téméraire*'s suffering from the *Victory*'s shot passing through the *Redoubtable*; which must have been the case if the usual quantity of powder, and the common elevation, had been given to the guns.

A circumstance occurred in this situation which showed in a most striking manner the cool intrepidity of the officers and men stationed on the lower deck of the *Victory*. When the guns on this deck were run out, their muzzles came into contact with the *Redoubtable*'s side; and consequently at every discharge there was reason to fear that the enemy would take fire, and both the *Victory* and the *Téméraire* be involved in her flames. Here then was seen the astonishing spectacle of the fireman of each gun standing ready with a bucket full of water, which as soon as his gun was discharged he dashed into the enemy through the holes made in her side by the shot.

It was from this ship (the *Redoubtable*) that Lord Nelson received his mortal wound. About fifteen minutes past one o'clock, which was in the heat of the engagement, he was walking the middle of the quarter deck with Captain Hardy, and in the act of turning near the hatchway with his face towards the stern of the *Victory*, when the fatal ball was fired from the enemy's mizzen top; which, from the situation of the two ships (lying on board of each other), was brought just abaft, and rather below, the *Victory*'s main yard, and of course not more than fifteen yards

distant from that part of the deck where his Lordship
stood. The ball struck the epaulette on his left
shoulder, and penetrated his chest. He fell with his
face on the deck. Captain Hardy, who was on his right
(the side furthest from the enemy) and [had] advanced
some steps before his Lordship, on turning round, saw
the serjeant major (Secker) of Marines with two seamen raising him from the deck; where he had fallen on
the same spot on which, a little before, his secretary
had breathed his last, with whose blood his Lordship's
clothes were much soiled.

Captain Hardy expressed a hope that he was not
severely wounded; to which the gallant chief replied:
"They have done for me at last, Hardy."

"I hope not," answered Captain Hardy.

"Yes," replied his Lordship;" my backbone is shot
through."

Captain Hardy ordered the seamen to carry the
admiral to the cockpit; and now two incidents occurred strikingly characteristic of this great man,
and strongly marking that energy and reflection which
in his heroic mind rose superior even to the immediate
consideration of his present awful condition. While
the men were carrying him down the ladder from the
middle deck, his Lordship observed that the tiller
ropes were not yet replaced; and desired one of the
midshipmen stationed there to go upon the quarter
deck and remind Captain Hardy of that circumstance,
and request that new ones should be immediately rove.
Having delivered this order, he took his handkerchief
from his pocket and covered his face with it, that he
might be conveyed to the cockpit at this crisis unnoticed by the crew.

Several wounded officers, and about forty men, were likewise carried to the surgeon for assistance just at this time; and some others had breathed their last during their conveyance below. Among the latter were Lieutenant William Andrew Ram, and Mr Whipple, captain's clerk. The surgeon had just examined these two officers, and found that they were dead; when his attention was arrested by several of the wounded calling to him, "Mr Beatty, Lord Nelson is here: Mr Beatty, the admiral is wounded."

The surgeon now, on looking round, saw the handkerchief fall from his Lordship's face; when the stars on his coat, which also had been covered by it, appeared. Mr Burke the purser, and the surgeon, ran immediately to the assistance of his Lordship; and took him from the arms of the seamen who had carried him below. In conveying him to one of the midshipmen's berths, they stumbled; but recovered themselves without falling. Lord Nelson then inquired who were supporting him; and when the surgeon informed him, his Lordship replied, "Ah, Mr Beatty! you can do nothing for me. I have but a short time to live: my back is shot through."

The surgeon said, "he hoped the wound was not so dangerous as his Lordship imagined, and that he might still survive long to enjoy his glorious victory."

The Rev. Dr Scott, who had been absent in another part of the cockpit administering lemonade to the wounded, now came instantly to his Lordship; and in the anguish of grief wrung his hands, and said: "Alas, Beatty, how prophetic you were!" alluding to the apprehensions expressed by the surgeon for his Lordship's safety previous to the battle.

His Lordship was laid upon a bed, stripped of his clothes, and covered with a sheet. While this was effecting, he said to Dr Scott, "Doctor, I told you so. Doctor, I am gone;" and after a short pause he added in a low voice, "I have to leave Lady Hamilton, and my adopted daughter Horatia, as a legacy to my country."

The surgeon then examined the wound, assuring his Lordship that he would not put him to much pain in endeavouring to discover the course of the ball; which he soon found had penetrated deep into the chest, and had probably lodged in the spine. This being explained to his Lordship; he replied, "he was confident his back was shot through." The back was then examined externally, but without any injury being perceived; on which his Lordship was requested by the surgeon to make him acquainted with all his sensations. He replied, that "he felt a gush of blood every minute within his breast: that he had no feeling in the lower part of his body: and that his breathing was difficult, and attended with very severe pain about that part of the spine where he was confident that the ball had struck; for," said he, "I felt it break my back."

These symptoms, but more particularly the gush of blood which his Lordship complained of, together with the state of his pulse, indicated to the surgeon the hopeless situation of the case; but till after the victory was ascertained and announced to his Lordship, the true nature of his wound was concealed by the surgeon from all on board except only Captain Hardy, Dr Scott, Mr Burke, and Messrs. Smith and Westemburg the assistant surgeons.

The *Victory*'s crew cheered whenever they observed

an enemy's ship surrender. On one of these occasions, Lord Nelson anxiously inquired what was the cause of it; when Lieutenant Pasco, who lay wounded at some distance from his Lordship, raised himself up, and told him that another ship had struck, which appeared to give him much satisfaction.

He now felt an ardent thirst; and frequently called for drink, and to be fanned with paper, making use of these words: "Fan, fan!" and "Drink, drink!" This he continued to repeat, when he wished for drink or the refreshment of cool air, till a very few minutes before he expired. Lemonade, and wine and water, were given to him occasionally. He evinced great solicitude for the event of the battle, and fears for the safety of his friend Captain Hardy. Dr Scott and Mr Burke used every argument they could suggest, to relieve his anxiety.

Mr Burke told him "the enemy were decisively defeated, and that he hoped his Lordship would still live to be himself the bearer of the joyful tidings to his country."

He replied, "It is nonsense, Mr Burke, to suppose I can live: my sufferings are great, but they will all be soon over."

Dr Scott entreated his Lordship "not to despair of living," and said "he trusted that Divine Providence would restore him once more to his dear country and friends."

"Ah, Doctor!" replied his Lordship, "it is all over; it is all over!"

Many messages were sent to Captain Hardy by the surgeon, requesting his attendance on his Lordship; who became impatient to see him, and often exclaimed: "Will no one bring Hardy to me? He must be killed: he is surely destroyed."

The Captain's aide de camp, Mr Bulkley, now came below, and stated that "circumstances respecting the fleet required Captain Hardy's presence on deck; but that he would avail himself of the first favourable moment to visit his Lordship."

On hearing him deliver this message to the surgeon, his Lordship inquired who had brought it.

Mr Burke answered, "It is Mr Bulkley, my Lord."

"It is his voice", replied his Lordship: he then said to the young gentleman, "Remember me to your father."

An hour and ten minutes however, elapsed from the time of his Lordship's being wounded, before Captain Hardy's first subsequent interview with him; the particulars of which are nearly as follow.

They shook hands affectionately, and Lord Nelson said: "Well, Hardy, how goes the battle? How goes the day with us?"

"Very well, my Lord," replied Captain Hardy: "we have got twelve or fourteen of the enemy's ships in our possession; but five of their van have tacked and shew an intention of bearing down upon the *Victory*. I have therefore called two or three of our fresh ships round us, and have no doubt of giving them a drubbing."

"I hope," said his Lordship, "none of *our* ships have struck, Hardy."

"No, my Lord," replied Captain Hardy; "there is no fear of that."

Lord Nelson then said: "I am a dead man, Hardy. I am going fast: it will be all over with me soon. Come

nearer to me. Pray let my dear Lady Hamilton have
my hair, and all other things belonging to me." Mr
Burke was about to withdraw at the commencement of
this conversation; but his Lordship, perceiving his
intention, desired he would remain.

Captain Hardy observed, that "he hoped Mr Beatty
could yet hold out some prospect of life."

"Oh! no," answered his Lordship; "it is impossible.
My back is shot through. Beatty will tell you so."

Captain Hardy then returned on deck, and at parting shook hands again with his revered friend and
commander.

His Lordship now requested the surgeon, who had
been previously absent a short time attending Mr
Rivers, to return to the wounded; and give his assistance to such of them as he could be useful to; "for,"
said he, "you can do nothing for me." The surgeon
assured him that the assistant surgeons were doing
everything that could be effected for those unfortunate
men; but on his Lordship's several times repeating his
injunctions to that purpose, he left him surrounded by
Dr Scott, Mr Burke, and two of his Lordship's do-
mestics.

After the surgeon had been absent a few minutes
attending Lieutenants Peake and Reeves of the marines, who were wounded; he was called by Dr Scott to
his Lordship, who said: "Ah, Mr Beatty! I have sent
for you to say what I forgot to tell you before, that all
power of motion and feeling below my breast are gone;
and *you*," continued he, "very well *know* I can live but
a short time." The emphatic manner in which he
pronounced these last words, left no doubt in the
surgeon's mind, that he adverted to the case of a

man who had, some months before, received a mortal injury of the spine on board the *Victory*, and had laboured under similar privations of sense and muscular motion. The case had made a great impression on Lord Nelson: he was anxious to know the cause of such symptoms, which was accordingly explained to him; and he now appeared to apply the situation and fate of this man to himself.

The surgeon answered, "My Lord, you told me so before", but he now examined the extremities, to ascertain the fact; when his Lordship said, "Ah, Beatty! I am too certain of it: Scott and Burke have tried it already. *You know* I am gone."

The surgeon replied: "My Lord, unhappily for our country, nothing can be done for you", and having made this declaration he was so much affected, that he turned round and withdrew a few steps to conceal his emotions.

His Lordship said: "I know it. I feel something rising in my breast," putting his hand on his left side, "which tells me I am gone." Drink was recommended liberally, and Dr Scott and Mr Burke fanned him with paper.

He often exclaimed, "God be praised, I have done my duty", and upon the surgeon's inquiring whether his pain was still very great, he declared, "it continued so very severe, that he wished he was dead. Yet," said he in a lower voice, "one would like to live a little longer, too"; and after a pause of a few minutes, he added in the same tone, "What would become of poor Lady Hamilton, if she knew my situation?"

The surgeon, finding it impossible to render his Lordship any further assistance, left him to attend

Lieutenant Bligh, Messrs. Smith and Westphall, mid-shipmen, and some seamen, recently wounded.

Captain Hardy now came to the cockpit to see his Lordship a second time, which was after an interval of about fifty minutes from the conclusion of his first visit. Before he quitted the deck, he sent Lieutenant Hills to acquaint Admiral Collingwood with the lamentable circumstance of Lord Nelson's being wounded.

Lord Nelson and Captain Hardy shook hands again: and while the captain retained his Lordship's hand, he congratulated him even in the arms of Death on his brilliant victory; "which," he said, "was complete; though he did not know how many of the enemy were captured, as it was impossible to perceive every ship distinctly. He was certain however of fourteen or fifteen having surrendered."

His Lordship answered, "That is well, but I bargained for twenty": and then emphatically exclaimed, "*Anchor*, Hardy, *anchor!*"

To this the captain replied: "I suppose, my Lord, Admiral Collingwood will now take upon himself the direction of affairs."

"Not while I live, I hope, Hardy!" cried the dying chief; and at that moment endeavoured ineffectually to raise himself from the bed.

"No," added he; "do *you* anchor, Hardy."

Captain Hardy then said: "Shall *we* make the signal, Sir?"

"Yes," answered his Lordship; "for if I live, I'll anchor." The energetic manner in which he uttered these his last orders to Captain Hardy, accompanied with his efforts to raise himself, evinced his determination never to resign the command while he retained the exercise of his transcendent faculties, and that he expected Captain Hardy still to carry into effect the suggestions of his exalted mind; a sense of his duty overcoming the pains of death.

He then told Captain Hardy, "he felt that in a few minutes he should be no more", adding in a low tone, "Don't throw me overboard, Hardy."

The captain answered: "Oh! no, certainly not."

"Then," replied his Lordship, "you know what to do: and," continued he, "take care of my dear Lady Hamilton, Hardy; take care of poor Lady Hamilton. Kiss me, Hardy."

The captain now knelt down, and kissed his cheek; when his Lordship said, "Now I am satisfied. Thank God, I have done my duty."

Captain Hardy stood for a minute or two in silent contemplation: he then knelt down again and kissed his Lordship's forehead.

His Lordship said: "Who is that?"

The captain answered: "It is Hardy" to which his Lordship replied, "God bless you, Hardy!"

After this affecting scene Captain Hardy withdrew, and returned to the quarter deck; having spent about eight minutes in this his last interview with his dying friend.

Lord Nelson now desired Mr Chevalier, his steward, to turn him upon his right side; which being effected, his Lordship said: "I wish I had not left the deck, for I shall soon be gone." He afterwards became very low; his breathing was oppressed, and his voice faint.

He said to Dr Scott, "Doctor, I have *not* been a *great* sinner"; and after a short pause, "*Remember*, that I leave Lady Hamilton and my daughter Horatia as a legacy to my country: and," added he, "never forget Horatia."

His thirst now increased; and he called for "Drink, drink", "Fan, fan!" and "Rub, rub!" addressing himself in the last case to Dr Scott, who had been rubbing his Lordship's breast with his hand, from which he found some relief. These words he spoke in a very rapid manner, which rendered his articulation difficult: but he every now and then, with evident increase of pain, made a greater effort with his vocal powers, and pronounced distinctly these last words: "Thank God, I have done my duty"; and this great sentiment he continued to repeat as long as he was able to give it utterance.

His Lordship became speechless in about fifteen minutes after Captain Hardy left him. Dr Scott and Mr Burke, who had all along sustained the bed under his shoulders (which raised him in nearly a semi-recumbent posture, the only one that was supportable to him), forbore to disturb him by speaking to him; and when he had remained speechless about five minutes, his Lordship's steward went to the surgeon, who had been a short time occupied with the wounded in another part of the cockpit, and stated his apprehensions that his Lordship was dying.

The surgeon immediately repaired to him, and found him on the verge of dissolution. He knelt down by his side, and took up his hand; which was cold, and the pulse gone from the wrist.

On the surgeon's feeling his forehead, which was

likewise cold, his Lordship opened his eyes, looked up, and shut them again.

The surgeon again left him, and returned to the wounded who required his assistance; but was not absent five minutes before the steward announced to him that "he believed his Lordship had expired." The surgeon returned, and found that the report was but too well founded: his Lordship had breathed his last, at thirty minutes past four o'clock; at which period Dr Scott was in the act of rubbing his Lordship's breast, and Mr Burke supporting the bed under his shoulders.

Thus died this matchless hero, after performing in a short but brilliant and well filled life, a series of naval exploits unexampled in any age of the world. None of the sons of fame ever possessed greater zeal to promote the honour and interest of his king and country; none ever served them with more devotedness and glory, or with more successful and important results. His character will for ever cast a lustre over the annals of this nation, to whose enemies his very name was a terror. In the battle off Cape St Vincent, though then in the subordinate station of a captain, his unprecedented personal prowess will long be recorded with admiration among his profession. The shores of Aboukir and Copenhagen subsequently witnessed those stupendous achievements which struck the whole civilized world with astonishment. Still these were only preludes to the Battle of Trafalgar: in which he shone with a majesty of dignity as far surpassing even his own former renown, as that renown had already exceeded every thing else to be found in the pages of naval history; the transcendently brightest star in a galaxy of heroes. His splendid example will operate as an everlasting impulse to the enterprising genius of the British Navy.

From the time of his Lordship's being wounded till his death, a period of about two hours and forty-five minutes elapsed; but a knowledge of the decisive victory which was gained, he acquired of Captain Hardy within the first hour and a quarter of this period. A partial cannonade, however, was still maintained, in consequence of the enemy's running ships passing the British at different points; and the last distant guns which were fired at their van ships that were making off, were heard a minute or two before his Lordship expired.

A steady and continued fire was kept up by the *Victory*'s starboard guns on the *Redoubtable*, for about fifteen minutes after Lord Nelson was wounded: in which short period Captain Adair and about eighteen seamen and marines were killed; and Lieutenant Bligh, Mr Palmer midshipman, and twenty seamen and marines, wounded, by the enemy's musketry alone.

The *Redoubtable* had been on fire twice, in her fore chains and on her forecastle: she had likewise succeeded in throwing a few hand grenades into the *Victory*, which set fire to some ropes and canvas on the booms. The cry of "Fire!" was now circulated throughout the ship, and even reached the cockpit, without producing the degree of sensation which might be expected on such an awful occasion: the crew soon extinguished the fire on the booms, and then immediately turned their attention to that on board the enemy; which they likewise put out by throwing buckets of water from the gangway into the enemy's chains and forecastle, thus furnishing another admirable instance of deliberate intrepidity.

At thirty minutes past one o'clock, the *Redoubtable*'s musketry having ceased, and her colours being struck; the *Victory*'s men endeavoured to get on board her: but this was found impracticable; for though the two ships were still in contact, yet the top sides or upper works of both fell in so much on their upper decks, that there was a great space (perhaps fourteen feet or more) between their gangways; and the enemy's ports being down, she could not be boarded from the *Victory*'s lower nor middle deck. Several seamen volunteered their services to Lieutenant Quilliam, to jump overboard, swim under the *Redoubtable*'s bows, and endeavour to get up there; but Captain Hardy refused to permit this. The prize, however, and the *Victory*, fell off from each other; and their separation was believed to be the effect of the concussion produced by the *Victory's* fire, assisted by the helm of the latter being put to starboard.

Messrs Ogilvie and Collingwood, midshipmen of the *Victory*, were sent in a small boat to take charge of the prize; which they effected. After this, the ships of the enemy's van, that had shown a disposition to attack the *Victory*, passed to windward; and fired their broadsides not only into her and the *Téméraire*, but also into the French and Spanish captured ships indiscriminately: and they were seen to back or shiver their topsails for the purpose of doing this with more precision.

The two midshipmen of the *Victory* had just boarded the *Redoubtable*, and got their men out of the boat; when a shot from the enemy's van ships that were making off cut the boat adrift. About ten minutes after taking possession of her, a midshipman came to her from the *Téméraire*; and had hardly ascended the poop, when a shot from one of those ships took off his leg. The French officers, seeing the firing continued on the prize by their own countrymen, entreated the English midshipmen to quit the deck, and accompany them below. The unfortunate midshipman of the *Téméraire* was carried to the French surgeon, who was ordered to give his immediate attendance to him in preference to his own wounded: his leg was amputated, but he died the same night.

The *Redoubtable* suffered so much from shot received between wind and water, that she sank while in tow of the *Swiftsure* on the following evening, when the gale came on; and out of a crew originally consisting of more than eight hundred men, only about a hundred and thirty were saved: but she had lost above three hundred in the battle.

It is by no means certain, though highly probable, that Lord Nelson was particularly aimed at by the enemy. There were only two Frenchmen left alive in the mizzen top of the *Redoubtable* at the time of his Lordship's being wounded, and by the hands of one of these he fell. These men continued firing at captains Hardy and Adair, Lieutenant Rotely of the marines, and some of the midshipmen on the *Victory*'s poop, for some time afterwards. At length one of them was killed by a musket ball: and on the other's then attempting to make his escape from the top down the rigging, Mr

Pollard (midshipman) fired his musket at him, and shot him in the back; when he fell dead from the shrouds, on the *Redoubtable*'s poop.

The writer of this will not attempt to depict the heartrending sorrow and melancholy gloom, which pervaded the breast and the countenance of every individual on board the *Victory* when his Lordship's death became generally known. The anguish felt by all for such a loss, rendered doubly heavy to *them*, is more easy to be conceived than described: by his lamented fall they were at once deprived of their adored commander, and their friend and patron.

The battle was fought in soundings about sixteen miles to the westward of Cape Trafalgar; and if fortunately there had been more wind in the beginning of the action, it is very probable that Lord Nelson would still have been saved to his country, and that every ship of the line composing the Combined fleets would have been either captured or destroyed: for had the *Victory* been going fast through the water, she must have dismasted the *Redoubtable*, and would of course have passed on to attack another ship; consequently his Lordship would not have been so long nor so much exposed to the enemy's musketry. From the same circumstance of there being but little wind, several of the enemy's ships made off before the rear and bad sailing ships of the British lines could come up to secure them.

The *Victory* had no musketry in her tops: as his Lordship had a strong aversion to small arms being placed there, from the danger of their setting fire to the sails; which was exemplified by the destruction of the

French ship *L'Achille* in this battle. It is a species of warfare by which individuals may suffer, and now and then a commander be picked off: but it never can decide the fate of a general engagement; and a circumstance in many respects similar to that of the *Victory*'s running on board of the *Redoubtable*, may not occur again in the course of centuries.

The loss sustained by the *Victory* amounted to fifty-five killed, and a hundred and two wounded; and it is highly honourable to the discipline and established regulations of the ship, that not one casualty from accident occurred on board during the engagement.

Nelson's body was brought back to a sorrowing nation and accorded a place of rest in St Paul's Cathedral. On every anniversary of Trafalgar, all Royal Navy messes still toast "the Immortal Memory".

James R. Durand

The Mutiny on the *Constitution*

1805–6

James R. Durand entered the US Navy in 1804, after throwing over an apprenticeship as a farmer. He served initially on board the John Adams *before being drafted to the US man-of-war* Constitution *in the Mediterranean.*

The United States Man-of-War Constitution
To my dissatisfaction, I found very different treatment on board her than that which I had experienced on the *John Adams*. The *Constitution* was commanded by Commodore Rodgers and his first lieutenant, Mr Blake, I am sorry to say but I must keep up the truth of my narrative, was cashiered out of the English service.

By coming to the United States this Mr Blake initiated himself into the American service by throwing around a little money and a few high-sounding words. Accordingly he had been entered on board as First Lieutenant. He thought to cut as many capers and exercise as much power as his tyrannical disposition could suggest to him.

The old rat, however, was soon caught in his own tricks. His treatment of the crew was so ill, that it is with the greatest delicacy I attempt to detail a few of his outrages. First of all, as soon as I went on board, I was mustered and stationed in the foretop of the starboard watch. The ship was much larger than the one I was accustomed to, therefore I did not know where my station was.

Lieutenant Blake ordered the boatswain's mate to apply the lash to me. Then, thinking the man did not strike me hard enough to satisfy his own hellish disposition, the Lieutenant must needs fall to himself and flog me until he was weary. That was his practice on all occasions.

Soon after, the sailors found out the history of this run-a-way British villain and we made a general protest before the Captain, saying that we would not serve under him any longer and petitioning the Captain to give us another officer.

I was now pretty smart and active and was accordingly made boatswain over the ship's boys. The custom is this: one boy is master over all the rest and when any boy is to be flogged, the master does it, instead of the boatswain's mate of the ship, who flogs the crew. I do not mention my appointment by way of boasting, because it is the most disagreeable duty that I was ever called upon to perform.

I shall here mention a circumstance that happened while I was on duty as boatswain. One morning this

Mr Blake came on deck and saw one of the boy's trowsers lying there. The boy had gone below to get a brush to scrub them.

"Get the cat", ordered this renagado lieutenant. When I fetched it, he told me to give the poor boy five dozen lashes.

Then, because he thought I did not strike hard enough, he snatched the cat out of my hand and struck me as hard as possible and then flogged the boy most cruelly.

Our blockading fleet consisted of nine sail besides nine gunboats. Our fleet was:

Constitution, 44 guns; *Essex*, 44 guns; *John Adams*, 36 guns; *Congress*, 38 guns; brigs *Siren*, 18 guns; *Argus*, 18 guns; *Vixen*, 12 guns; Schooners *Enterprise*, 12 guns and *Nautilus*, 12 guns; Total, 9 sail.

Negotiations now took place between our commander and the Tunisians. After the Tripolitans had made peace, the Tunisians thought themselves smart in making a disturbance, but we quickly brought them to terms as I have stated. Once a brig attempted to run by us into the port, trailed by our brig *Vixen*, but out of reach of the *Vixen*'s guns.

Commodore Rodgers ordered us to clear and to get ready two brass pieces which we had captured from the Turks and which would throw shot a great distance. We hastily mounted them on the fore-castle of the *Constitution* and brought one of them to bear on the brig. So we brought her to very quick.

Nothing in particular took place that is worth mentioning, except a court martial which we held on the *Constitution*. They tried John Graves, captain of the main-top of the ship, for desertion. He was sentenced to receive three hundred lashes along side of the ships or be "whipped through the fleet" as they call it.

We now sailed for Malta and then to Sadacroix, where we stripped the *Constitution* of her sail and rigging and built a gig boat. For three months we tarried there, doing various kinds of work in the navy yard. I was five times innoculated for the small pox but as often it failed to have the desired effect.

At length, we sailed to Palermo, where an English fleet was lying at anchor. Here I saw some members of their crews flogged through the fleet, as had been done with the captain of our main-top. They were followed by musicians as they were taken from ship to ship. At the end of this punishment they were put under hospital treatment until they were again capable of duty, if indeed they survived the flogging, which they seldom did.

We went to Algiers. Here the Dey gave us a feast. There was nothing these Turks would not do for us, since we had bottled up the ports at Tunis and Tripoli. The feast consisted of beef, mutton and various fresh meats and vegetables, enough for all our crew of 450 men and with an abundance left over. The Dey came on board us, to make his compliments to Commodore Rodgers. He brought his retinue of attendants with him and was very splendidly entertained by our commander for four or five hours.

When he approached alongside, a salute was fired, every yard was manned and every one of the crew was dressed all in white. When he returned to shore, another salute was fired and our commander accompanied him.

Nothing else transpired here, except a ludicrous

accident which befell me alone. One day when I was on shore, I chanced to meet a Turkish woman, dressed in black with a white muffler on. Nothing could be seen but her eyes. The novelty of her dress, coupled with the strange appearance of the streets which are covered overhead, threw me into a strange surprise. So that I, although I was a stouthearted tar, ran all the way back to the place where I had left the boat's crew. Then I fully informed myself about their customs of dress.

Learning is at a low ebb in this country. Some of the governors are unable to write their own names. The people have manners like the Egyptians. They subsist by piracy. They are bold and enterprising in their attacks and will fight desperately to obtain a prize at sea. However, they are much inferior to Europeans in the construction and management of their ships.

I shall conclude the subject of Algerian customs by making some remarks about their treatment of Christian captives. They are wholly destitute of humanity and when any Christian has fallen into their power, he is taken to a market and sold to the highest bidder. Then too, he is often bastinadoed by his captors, to make him tell the condition of his property in his native land, for the Algerians love to make their captives buy their liberty by paying a ransom. Few captives survive the hardships imposed upon them for any length of time.

After three weeks in Algiers, there came on board a Turkish ambassador and we carried him to Sardinia, where we landed him. There, in the harbor of Calleroy, I saw an excellent row galley, with a keel 162 feet long. These gallies never carry any sail but are propelled by ninety to a hundred oars or sweeps. These are exercised or pulled by Christian captives. The captives are chained to the oars and their taskmasters apply supple jack to their naked bodies at every failure or inability to obey orders. They suffer everything that man can suggest to render them more miserable. Their pitiable condition I shall remember as long as my memory lives.

After cruising about, we came to Cadiz, where the whole Spanish and French fleet lay. At the mouth of the harbor Lord Nelson was lying with 27 English sail of the line. The French and Spanish fleet consisted of 33 sail.

The British, seeing us make for the harbor, made sail after us. But our old *Constitution* showed them her stern. We entered the harbor and came to anchor. I belonged to the first lieutenant's boat and so had an opportunity to go aboard several French men-of-war as he went about the fleet. At length, our officers went to a ball upon a French 74, called the *Neptune*.

An Exchange of Officers
On the 19th day of October, 1805, we put to sea, but having little wind, did not get far from land. At day light, we found ourselves close in to the British fleet. Signals were given from the Admiral's ship to give us chase and soon one of their sail came within hail.

"What ship are you?"

"U.S. frigate *Constitution*."

"Where from?"

"Cadiz."

"Then," came the reply, "I'll send my boat on board."

So their captain came on board and, after holding some conversation with Commander Rodgers, sailed directly back to the British admiral. The admiral immediately made signal for the whole fleet to close and to stand a little out to sea.

On the 21st the combined fleets really got out of the harbor to attack the English. We supposed that the action started about 9 o'clock, when we were ten miles off. We could not see them long, but their cannon made a tremendous thunder. We proceeded on to Gibraltar, where we gave the information that the combined fleets were really engaging the English fleet. After a visit to Sadacroix and Malta, we returned to Gibraltar.

Commodore Rodgers went on board the frigate *Essex*, and the tyrannical lieutenant Mr Blake, before mentioned, was exchanged for a first lieutenant named Ludlow, who had belonged to the *Essex*. Captain Campbell took command of the *Constitution* to my great satisfaction.

Under orders from our government, the *Essex* now sailed for home. The gun boats accompanied her to America. I had been in the U. States' service for one year and ten months and had only two months more service to make up the term of my enlistment. Had I been permitted to return on the *Essex*, that term would have expired by the time I reached New York. Instead of this, I was obliged to stay on the *Constitution* and made a second round of the straits. We sailed up the straits to Algiers, Malta and Tunis. At this last port, we stayed some time, as our Captain had considerable business to transact for the government. I nearly lost my life there, when a heavy sea washed me overboard.

However I caught a rope, when twenty-feet astern and made it fast around my middle. I was hauled out but the rope was so small that it cut me and I could not return to duty for some time.

On our passage to Malta, we experienced a heavy gale of wind. We came out of Tunis in very agreeable weather, with every sail set, but the ship was struck by what we call a Levant wind, which almost upset her. We had just time to take in our studding sails and royals, and attempted to get down our top-gallant yards. But it was all in vain. The gale was so violent that it was impossible.

Sailing Master Baggot came forward with two bottles of rum which he offered to any man who would go to the mast head and cut the top gallant yards away. Many of the sailors wished for the rum, but no one dared attempt it. We hauled our mainsail up to the yard, but could not hand it. It blew all to pieces. It was five o'clock in the afternoon and the gale continued until nine in the morning.

Our main sail was sprung astern three times, the length of the ship. We repaired our ship in Malta. The damages in cost amounted to 500 $.

At Sadacroix, we remained some time. The officers took their pleasure on shore while the men stayed hard at work on board, greatly abused and hindered by the younger officers.

The Mutiny on the Constitution

One Sunday, all hands were called to go into the water to wash. One of the men swam as far as the ship's buoy. A lieutenant called to him to return, but the noise of the water prevented the sailor hearing the command. The lieutenant then ordered someone to swim out and tell him to come aboard, which he did immediately he heard the order.

"Strip", ordered the lieutenant, as soon as he came on deck.

Having nothing on but a thin cotton shirt, the man refused.

At which Lieutenant Burroughs seized a hand-spike and struck at him with all his might. The sailor dexterously avoided the blow, which would have caused his death. This produced an alarm among us, for we said that the man should not be punished.

Mr Burroughs then went up on the quarter deck and ordered the marines to fire upon us, but they refused. So the officers got their swords and pistols and stood guard on us themselves. They now piped down the hammocks and ordered every man to bed. We obeyed them.

Then they sent for the Captain who was at Cutania, a town seven miles away from the ship. He came up the side of the ship in great haste, but being a man of noble mind, proceeded to inquire into the matter with great regularity. In spite of the fact that he had heard only the officers' side of the matter in their message, he looked hard at the lieutenant when he found him in arms on the deck.

"Follow me to my cabin," he ordered, "I fear me there is some misconduct among the officers as well as among the crew."

After a short stay in his cabin, he caused the purser to come up into his quarters and to make out a ship's list of every man in service; those whose enlistments had expired in one roll and those who still owed service in another roll. This was done according to order. The next morning at 8 o'clock, the captain called all hands to the quarter deck and directed those whose times were out to remain.

"Now," said the Captain, "state your grievances."

So the armorer of the ship, whose name was Shoemaker, related every circumstance of abuse we had suffered during the Captain's absence, stating that men had been flogged six months after their time of service had expired. They informed him that they would be happy to proceed to America quietly under his command, if he would give the order to sail at once. Otherwise they would take command of the ship themselves and conduct her thither.

"Well," said the Captain, "if you have a mind to take the ship, you may. But if you will wait until I can settle my business, I will sail for America and make the voyage as quick as possible and from now on, no man shall be punished unless he deserves it."

At this time, there were three men in irons. They were the man who was ordered to pull off his shirt to be flogged, the boatswain's mate who refused to flog him and another man who said he should not be flogged. They were kept in irons until we reached America, where, as I have since heard, they recovered some hundred dollars damages.

The Captain hurried to despatch his business. We came to Messina. As the Captain was about to go on shore, he ordered the top-gallant-yards to be sent down. The men would not obey, saying that they were homeward bound and that home they would go. So the Captain did his business without making them comply.

Six days later, we came to Naples. There are said to be not less than 300 lawyers in Naples. At first I thought this a great exaggeration, but according to the best information I could obtain, it was the case.

From Naples, we went to Leghorn where we took on board some marble, which was to be used for erecting a monument to the illustrious Washington. We stopped at Salamanca where bull fights are exhibited for three days in the public square in the month of June, each year. The officers had a ball here.

At Malaga we heard of the action between the United States frigate *Chesapeake* and the British 50 gun ship *Leopard*. In consequence of this and of spreading rumors, our Captain supposed that war had taken place between the two countries.

Homeward Bound

We had then only 44 guns mounted. Our Captain called all hands on deck and asked us if we would fight our way to America, if he mounted four more guns. We answered him in the affirmative with three hearty cheers. Accordingly we went to work, mounted four more guns and got ready for sea after eight days in port.

Because of the supposed war with England, our Captain ran past the port of Gibraltar and into the harbor of Algeziras. Then he sent a boat into Gibraltar to get information about the war. The boat crew found that in Gibraltar they knew nothing about it.

On the same day, the American sloop of war, *Wasp*, came in through the gut of Gibraltar. Our Captain made signal for her to anchor alongside, which she did. She had orders for us to proceed to America as soon as possible. We sent the *Wasp* to Malaga for provisions and water. She returned in two days.

So we now set sail for Boston, after being up the Mediterranean two years and nine months. We had a tolerable good passage and in 45 days arrived off Boston light house, on the 5th of December 1806.

We lay in Boston for twelve days and then received orders to go to New York to be paid off. During this time I belonged to the boat party, but I cannot say I thought myself under actual hire as my enlistment had long since expired. But I hoped to receive my pay for past services, over and above the term of my enlistment also I was not willing to be counted in any way disorderly or mutinous. So I continued to do duty.

One evening our officers went ashore to a ball. I belonged to the boat that took them thither. We were under the command of a midshipman who had orders to wait for the party until a certain hour in the evening. Since the officers did not arrive at that hour, we thought to go back on the frigate, but the midshipman said he would stay as long as he thought proper.

It was very cold and, as the boat was along side the wharf, we asked permission to go up on the wharf and exercise to make ourselves warm. The midshipman granted this.

The officers not returning, the midshipman called to us to come in the boat and take him on board. I did not hear his first call and for this reason exasperated him greatly. As soon as we were on board the frigate, the midshipman made complaint to the Master of the *Constitution* who was his brother.

The Master, without asking or hearing my defense,

give me twelve stripes as hard as he could strike with a three inch rope, which sorely bruised me.

I considered myself my own man, as the term of my enlistment had been up these eight or nine months. Therefore I put on what clothing I could wear that belonged to me and quitted the ship. I have not seen the officers since nor as yet received any pay for my services up the Mediterranean, which pay amounts to more than 350 $.

I must here ask the reader the propriety of making small boys, 10 to 12 years of age, officers and giving them full authority to flog and abuse the men, when they are as yet unacquainted with the actual duty belonging to a ship. I have known them to give orders which were executed according to their command, but which proved wrong, when reviewed by an older officer. Then I have heard the midshipmen deny having given the order in question and the men who obeyed them faithfully were flogged for it.

Durand was later pressed into Royal Navy service and, to his bitter despair, forced to fight his native country when the War of 1812 broke out.

William Dillon

The Prize

1807–8

*A veteran of "The Glorious First", William Dillon
served on the West Indies station before being taken
prisoner off Holland by the French in 1803. Finally
released in 1807, he returned to Britain anxious to
resume his war, but with little track record all he
could find to command was a distinctly inferior
brigantine by the name of* Childers.

My first duty was to present myself to the port
admiral, Thomas Wells, Esq. This was the officer
under whom I had served in the *Defence*. Consequently I was well received by him. After the etiquette
usual on such occasions, he insisted upon my immediately putting to sea. However, when he heard of my
having nothing ready, and that I had quitted London
the day of my appointment, he agreed to allow me two
days, that indulgence being obtained with great difficulty: but I was obliged to act accordingly. He invited
me to dine, then sent for Mrs Wells and his daughters,

to whom he presented me. They recognized me although we had not met for fourteen years. They were extremely affable, and I was astonished that those fine girls still remained without husbands.

I next – it being the 19th – proceeded off to the *Childers*, where Capt Innes was waiting to receive me. My commission having been read to the crew and all the officers introduced to me, I became installed in the command of the brig. I agreed to take many articles from Capt Innes which I thought would answer my purpose until I reached Leith, where I had directed all my luggage to be sent from London. Capt Innes then went on shore, where we were to meet to settle other matters. I then bent my steps round the vessel, and was surprised at her diminutive dimensions. There was only one lieutenant, although she was allowed two: in fact, there was no cabin fitted for a second. My inspection was not of a nature to be pleasing, but I made no remarks, not wishing anyone to suppose that I was disappointed. However, I was most seriously annoyed at all I saw. When I entered the cabin, I met the youth who was there in attendance, to whom I put some questions. This lad, anxious to please his new captain, let out a number of things that had better never have been mentioned. The cabin was very small and not very clean, which made me make some remarks on that score. "Very true, sir", said the youth. "We have been labouring heart and soul these two days to put the vessel to rights to please you." The more I saw the more I had reason to regret having accepted the command. When the officers felt themselves at liberty to offer their remarks, I found them all discontented. They could not help alluding to the throwing of the guns overboard. I made no replies, but listened patiently to all they said. After remaining on board two or three hours to ascertain the exact condition of the brig, I went on shore. In my conversations with Capt Innes, I tried to discover the real cause of his giving up the command. He did not appear inclined to say much on the subject. He had been in the brig some time, and had made £15,000 prize money. He thought he was entitled to a larger vessel. However he assured me that, with proper management, I should take prizes, as the Norwegians and Danes had constant communications by sea, and a good look out would ensure success.

On the following day I mustered the brig's crew and exercised them at the guns – carronades, I should say. She mounted 14 of them, 12 lbers, with a crew of 63 men and boys, her proper complement being 86. The carronades, being new, were sealed, and I did all I could to inspire confidence in the men I had under command. The weather was cold, and we were visited with snow storms – not a pleasant season of the year to put to sea with an unknown crew, as it was probable that many of my regulations differed from those of the late captain. However, I had undertaken the task: therefore perseverance was my motto. I met several acquaintances among the captains. One of them, with whom I sailed in the *Prince George*, Baker, commanded a fine sloop of war. I had some long interesting conversations with him. He assured me that I should not be able to keep up the respectability of my station under £500 a year. "Why," said I, "I have already spent that sum in my outfit!" "Very true," he replied. "It's what we all do. And if you have not

something beyond your pay the case is desperate."
That literally was mine; but I did not like to tell him
so. The *Childers'* pay was about £250 per annum, out
of which there were many deductions, such as the
agent's charges and the income tax. I confess I pondered a good deal over the position I was placed in.
However, hopes of good luck buoyed me up. I met
here a Capt Sturt, in command of a fine brig of war.
This officer made himself known shortly afterwards
by carrying off a nun from one of the convents at
Madeira. This was a regular sailor's frolic.

My hours were counted, and I found there would be
no peace for me until I left Sheerness. I had taken with
me a fine youth of the name of Parker as a naval cadet:
also a mate, Mr Knight, whom I appointed as an
acting lieutenant. I was exerting myself to the utmost
to make the best of a bad bargain. I had only one day
more to remain at anchor, and I devoted it entirely to
the brig. I had her thoroughly washed below, cleaned
and smoked. While this operation was proceeding, I
saw the smoke coming out of the seams, which indicated her crazy state. The officers pointed to many
parts of the vessel, proving that she was worn out: in
short, I began to be seriously impressed with the
awkward situation in which I found myself. The
Childers was in fact an inferior command to the gun-
brigs under lieutenants, which mounted 18 heavier
guns than those on board my craft. Turning all these
matters over in my mind, being alone in my cabin
whilst the crew were at dinner, I was suddenly seized
with a fit of despair, and I thought it my duty to let
Lord Gambier know all the difficulties I had exposed
myself to in taking command of such a rotten vessel. I

wrote my letter accordingly, and requested his Lordship to have me removed to a better one. I have often thought of that act since. It was, probably, lucky that I had not written the letter on shore, as if I had it would have been instantly sent to the post office. What the result would have been no one knows. But, on board the brig, I waited until the boat's crew had dined, and in the meantime I reflected upon the contents of my letter to the leading naval Lord of the Admiralty. He had acknowledged to me that he expected I would refuse the command: consequently he might be prepared for receiving my letter. However, upon more mature reflection I tore it up. I treated all the difficulties made by the officers with contempt, and finally made up my mind to brave every danger. I had not been accustomed to the management of a brig, but my own conscience led me to believe that I should succeed in my undertaking. I had not much confidence in the first lieutenant – he was very young and had not much experience – but I had a better opinion of the crew. There were some stout fellows amongst them, and my knowledge of that class of man inclined me to place reliance upon their exertions. Therefore the die was cast. I had come to the conclusion that it was more manly to trust to my fate than to make difficulties. Under these feelings my future conduct was regulated.

On the 22nd, being ready for sea, I took leave of Ad. Wells and his family. I had lent the young ladies some caricatures, which were returned: then, off to the *Childers*, and removed from the Little Nore further out. My whole thoughts were now taken up with my official duties. I had two pilots for the North Sea: they were very uncouth fellows. I slept on board for the first time. The following day, at half past two, the brig was under sail; but I cannot pass unnoticed what appeared to me an unpardonable neglect on the part of the late captain. The capstan bars were so long that they overlaid the tiller. I was all astonishment to perceive that this tiller was lashed on one side to make room for the bars to go round. Consequently, the instant the anchor was out of the ground the brig lost the use of her helm. Upon my mentioning this bad contrivance to the first lieutenant and the master, they said that they always had managed in that way. "It is a very lubberly act," I replied, "and it shall be instantly remedied." So soon as the sails were trimmed I sent for the carpenter, and ordered him to shorten the capstan bars so many inches; next, to curtail the tiller, that it might be used free of the bars. These orders were instantly executed, and everybody appeared to wonder why such a measure had not been thought of before. The safety of a vessel depends upon the motion of the rudder. So long as it remains unmanageable no one can tell what accidents may occur. This improvement for the better caused some remarks, which I could not help overhearing. It was thought that the captain knew what he was about.

In passing the *Namur*, the flag ship, at the Great Nore I received nine seamen for a passage to Yarmouth. In the evening, a fog coming on, I was obliged to anchor. The next day, Sunday, I read the Articles of War to the crew. I then acquainted them that, in so small a vessel, every precaution was necessary to prevent surprise; in consequence where of the brig's company were never to quit the deck all together, but one watch was to be constantly on deck, and to be armed. That regulation was instantly put in force, and a number of others, the details of which I shall not dwell upon, were adopted. But I gave the crew to understand that I did not mean to be captured without a sharp defence, and every soul on board was to practice, as often as circumstances would allow, the broadsword exercise. The Marines I ordered up, inspected all their muskets, and saw them put into order fit for use. They had scarcely reported them as such when a vessel was seen nearing us. She was instantly hailed, but as the answer was not satisfactory a volley of musketry was discharged at her by the Marines of the watch – a very lucky warning, as, if the stranger had not been alarmed, he would probably have run on board of us in the fog. The vessel was an English fishing craft, and the chief received a jobation from me for not keeping a better look out. That act of mine proved to my crew that I was in earnest.

On the following afternoon the fog cleared and, the wind being fair, the brig was soon under way with studdingsails set. The crew were exercised at the guns. At dinner time one watch remained on deck till relieved by the other, having had theirs. At nightfall I was again obliged to anchor with a fog, but the next morning a fresh breeze sent it off, and by daylight we were making the best of our way towards Yarmouth. At night Lowestoft lights were seen. Shortly afterwards a lugger closed upon us. A shot was instantly fired at her, and repeated till she brought to. I sent a boat to board her. She was from Rochester bound to Yarmouth. On the afternoon of the 26th we anchored in Yarmouth Roads.

I lost no time in presenting my respects to the

admiral, B. Douglas. His son, who was still at Verdun, had written to him about me, and I was most courteously received. The supernumeraries were sent to the *Amelia*, and by 10 o'clock the next day the *Childers* was under sail, bound to Leith. At night the weather had a threatening appearance, and as we were now more out to sea I issued night orders. The officer of the watch was astonished that I did not hand the square mainsail. He came to me to request that I would do so. It had, he said, always been done before. "Then," said I, "that custom will be changed. Should a gale of wind come on, you may furl it, but not before. If we can't fight we must be prepared to make sail." That order, and others, were very different from those they had been used to act under. One of the most unpleasant duties of a captain is to train the crew of a vessel which has been disciplined by another commander. If his regulations differ from what they have previously been used to, it occasions unpleasant occurrences, murmurs, and sometimes even mutiny. In this case, however, luckily for me, every one became aware that my orders were based upon good principles, not upon whims, and the officers and crew soon began to understand my ways.

I was anxious to be acquainted with the qualities of the *Childers*. The little experience I had of her led me to believe that she was over-masted, as she appeared to sail better, and be more easy, under reduced canvas. I made many enquiries relating to her guns being thrown overboard, and concluded that it was all through bad management. She was lying to in a gale of wind, with the helm lashed alee. That old system, by which many of our ships had been injured by getting sternway, I thought had been abandoned. But it was not so in the *Childers*, for it was while she had sternway that the sea came in and nearly swamped her. Therefore, to prevent her going down, away went the guns. If I recollect rightly, those which had just been shipped were of a lighter calibre than those thrown away, and no doubt the brig had not so much stability on the water as formerly. Turning the officers' statements to account, I sent for all of them and pointed out the evil consequences of lashing the helm to leeward, and forbad its being done again. I next had the seamen and quarter masters aft, explaining to them that, in future, the brig was to be constantly kept under command of the helm – that is, to have headway. I threatened the steersmen with punishment if it ever came to my knowledge that the helm was lashed to leeward. I ordered a card to be stuck on the binnacle with written instructions on it directing the helm to be kept amidships during stormy weather. This plan, on being followed out, proved that I was right: for, instead of laying the vessel to in a gale of wind, I kept her under the storm staysails, always forging ahead and under control of the helm. The change for the better became evident to all on board. The gunner, who had been nine years in the brig, and who had charge of a watch at sea, was the first to notice the improvement in the ease of her motions. There was no sudden jerking, but the vessel yielded gradually to the pressure of the wind and, with the assistance of the storm staysails, went slowly through the water, to the astonishment of all the seamen who wondered that no other officer had thought of such a system before. The gunner, who proved to be a thorough good seaman, repeated over and again his regrets that this plan had not been put in practice sooner, as it would have prevented many a sail being blown away and eased the wear of the hull. All my orders, I now observed, were attended to with alacrity: it was evident the crew had confidence in their captain.

When the officers knew I had been so long detained at Verdun, they inquired if Mr Temple was an acquaintance. When they heard my reports of that gentleman's proceedings, they were astonished, as they had formed the highest opinion of him. They had received him on board as a passenger when in the Baltic. He had, after his escape from France, visited Russia and, luckily finding his way on board the *Childers*, came to England in her. He had by his lively disposition and other attractive qualities completely captivated their good feelings towards him. However, I requested them not to bring his name again under my notice.

We were 13 days getting to Leith, during which we encountered a great deal of stormy weather. It had been my object to keep near the land, expecting by so doing to make better progress. I was right in my judgment, but the unruly pilots lost by night what I had gained by day. So soon as they knew that I was in bed, they would shape the brig's course out into the middle of the ocean. Consequently we encountered tremendously high seas: the vessel laboured woefully and shipped immense quantities of water, the leeside being constantly submerged. All this rolling about woke me, and, inquiring of the officer of the watch, I was informed that the pilot had stood away from the land. I finally put a stop to these whims. One night I went on deck to see what was going on. The vessel was rolling to an alarming extent. I was suddenly jerked from one side to the other, and fell on the cap of one of the carronade screws. The pilot who witnessed this accident, a stout lusty fellow, never came to my assistance: nor did anyone till I called out for help. I thought one of my ribs was broken, as the pain was intense. I could not keep my body upright for a long while afterwards. The crew were seized with colds and coughs: in short, the whole of us were laid up by the mismanagement of the pilots. The master was a young officer, and only acting. I therefore found myself obliged to interfere and take upon myself a responsibility not usual in such cases. The pilots kept out to sea at nights because they felt no uneasiness when at a distance from the land. But when it was near they were fidgety. The consequence of all this was that the rigging became so slack from the labouring of the vessel that I was obliged to run into Berwick Bay to set it up. Putting to sea the next day, we found the fore-topmast sprung, and I had to shift it for a sound one. Finding my arguments had no effect on these obstinate pilots, I assumed the charge myself, and gave written orders at night for the management of the brig. We soon benefited by the change. By keeping at a moderate distance from the shore we had smoother water, and gained ground rapidly. On our way we boarded only two vessels – English ones – nothing like an enemy being seen.

On the 9th of February we anchored in Leith Roads. Never in my life did I feel greater relief from anxiety, as every soul on board was a martyr to coughs, hoarseness and alarming colds, so severe had been the weather. When I reported my arrival to Ad. Vashon, who held the naval command, and represented to him the state of the *Childers'* crew, he expressed a very proper feeling in their behalf. It was not only their case which required consideration, but also my own: I was completely knocked up. He assured me that time would be given for rest, etc., and that he should not think of ordering the vessel to sea till the crew had recovered from their fatigues. He also expressed his astonishment at such a useless vessel being kept in the Service. So far I had reason to be satisfied, as I now knew for certain that I should have time to fit out my brig; and I hoped to make all on board comfortable, as far as circumstances would allow. Our arrival made the fourth brig of war stationed here to cruize against the enemy. The admiral had his flag on board the *Texel*, a 64. There was a sort of depot at Leith for naval stores, but nothing in the shape of a dock yard.

Having now time to look about me, my first object was to make my cabin more comfortable. There was only room for the half of a round table in it, which was placed against the fore bulkhead. This arrangement would only admit of three, but I was determined somehow or other to find space for four. There was a stove against the after bulkhead, which I could not well do without in the winter: but it was much in the way. At last I contrived to cut away the bulkhead, making a grove to receive it. By that means I gained nearly 24 inches in length, which enabled me to fit up a small round table, with four chairs conveniently placed. I could now invite a friend or two to dine with me. I had to set all my wits to work to turn to the best account a cabin scarcely deserving the name of

one. The officers were astonished at my perseverance
and ingenuity in overcoming obstacles that no other
captain had hitherto attempted. The other brigs on the
station could easily have hoisted mine in, so much
superior were they in size and dimensions. They were
armed with sixteen 32 lb carronades and two long
nines, with a crew of 120 men. The names of their
commanders were G. Andrews, F. Baugh and my old
shipmate of the *Alcide*, Sanders. My again meeting
him was a rencontre for which I was not prepared.
However, on our acquaintance being renewed, he
conducted himself very properly, and a friendly intercourse was established. The four of us formed a mess
at the principal inn, on the pier of Leith. There was a
naval club which met occasionally in Edinburgh,
which I attended once or twice. I there made the
acquaintance of several naval officers of distinction,
among the number Capt George Hope, who at that
time was Captain of the North Sea fleet under Ad. Sir
James Saumarez, and who afterwards, when a Lord of
the Admiralty, became a useful friend.

As the crew were recovering from their complaints,
I employed them in making such improvements as I
thought necessary: but the more I examined the contents of the vessel under my command, the more I had
reason to despond. The stores were in a most neglected state, and, after weighing all these defects in
my mind, I thought it my duty to lay the case before
the admiral. He gave strong symptoms of displeasure
at having such a vessel under his flag. He ordered the
master of the *Texel* to take a survey of the brig's
condition. That officer in the performance of his duty
gave the strongest signs of dissatisfaction – even of

disgust – at all he saw, and he did not hesitate to declare that he thought the *Childers* unfit for sea service. He accordingly made his report to the admiral verbally, upon which I was directed to apply for a survey of the vessel's capabilities. I was not prepared for such a proceeding, but as the commander in chief seemed determined that something of the kind should be done, there appeared to me no backing out of the position in which I unexpectedly found myself. I thought the requesting of a survey of a vessel to which I had just been appointed might offend the Admiralty. Consequently, in my official letter, which, in the first instance was addressed to the admiral, I began by saying, "Acting under your directions, I have to report the defective state of the sloop under my command." Admiral Vashon noticed its commencement, and appeared inclined to disapprove of the sentence: but, without allowing me time to make my reply, he said, "Very well. I don't mind. I shall send it." I was considerably annoyed. The brig, everybody knew, was a worn-out craft, but I should have taken my chance in her. When I thought it my duty to represent her inefficient condition, I had not contemplated the consequences. I thought the admiral would order a supply of better stores, and direct the other defects to be made good on the spot. But when the case took the turn mentioned, I felt myself justified in placing the principal responsibility on the admiral. He was an odd-tempered man, and a stranger to me; and I felt embarrassed in my early dealings with him. However, I thought it prudent to write to Lord Gambier and explain all that had passed between the admiral and self.

Whilst employed in improving my cabin I could get no assistance from the naval depot. I was consequently obliged to buy plank and other things. The first lieutenant of the flag ship, Mr Peake, had been my shipmate in the *Alcide*. When he heard that I had been buying the articles mentioned, he hastened to the naval yard, and in strong terms pointed out to the authorities there the impropriety of making an officer in my situation purchase deal boards for his cabin. His representation produced its effect, and one of the clerks from the office came and requested me to send my bill to him. He also made a sort of apology for what had happened. I could not help reminding him that my application for a supply of the articles had been refused. I shall here state that I was obliged to buy log lines, as there were none in store, and the admiral carried his ideas of economy to such a pitch that he would not allow any to be purchased. Therefore the brig's speed through the water was reckoned at my expense.

It took three days to convey a letter from Leith to London. On the seventh day an order arrived from the Admiralty, directing that the *Childers* should be examined, whether sound or not. In the meantime all my traps had arrived from London, and I had the means of making my preparations. The admiral did not invite us often to his house. His son commanded the flag ship. Mrs Vashon appeared an amiable person, but as there was not much sociability I was left a great deal to my own resources. Capt Sanders resided at a different inn from mine, but he came to us to dine. He had nicknamed my brig "the Half-Moon Battery", and was not backward in passing severe strictures upon her inefficiency, as the brig that he commanded – the *Bellette* – was one of the most powerful in our Navy. At one of our mess dinners he proposed that the whole of us should share prize money together: but nothing was decided. The *Childers'* defective sails were sent to the *Texel* to be repaired, and the officers from the yard were employed in examining our timbers, but as the vessel was afloat the survey could only be partial.

As time passed on, I invited my brother officers to come and dine with me. The tray which I depended on so much had not yet been used, but now was the time for displaying it. We were all seated in my cabin waiting the appearance of dinner, when my steward announced that the passage leading into it was so narrow that the tray could not be brought in. Here was a disappointment! The dishes were handed in separately. The casualty did not interfere much with our dinner, which proved a very sociable one, and Sanders was so anxious to see the tray that it was produced. He was so much pleased with the construction of it that he purchased it. In a few days he became my constant companion, and would not let me rest until I wrote a letter to Lord Mulgrave in his behalf, reminding his Lordship of a promise that he had made to Lord Chatham to promote him. Hitherto I knew nothing of Sanders. At times he gave himself consequential airs, wishing it to be understood that he possessed considerable influence. He assumed importance from the circumstance of his commanding so fine a vessel. However, not having much faith in this gentleman's assertions, I demanded explanations, which proved him to be the son of a surgeon who had for many years been attached to Lord Chatham's household. Thereat Mr Sanders did not rise much in my estimation. His authoritative bearing, with other freaks, were not suited to his connexions. I had supposed him, by his sayings and doings, to be a member of some high aristocratic family. He was fond of the bottle, and during our rambles he had frequently indulged in that failing. It fell to my lot to carry him home one night in a hack carriage, but he never refunded to me my expenses therefore, or even thanked me for my care of him. Therefore, instead of an agreeable companion, I found him a regular bore.

The builders, having terminated their examination of the *Childers'* timbers, declared them to be sound – a result no one expected. However, so it was, and I, her captain, lost no time in completing all that was required. I fitted a boarding netting to the brig, and had the boats, such as they were – a cutter and jolly boat – well repaired for cutting out work. The first orders I received were to take charge of a convoy for Gothenburg. When the merchants heard that the *Childers* had been appointed to perform that duty, they protested against placing their property under the care of such an inefficient vessel of war, and they remonstrated. Consequently a sloop, the *Snake*, with 32 lber carronades, was ordered round from Sheerness to relieve me of my charge. This was no great compliment to my brig!

In a short time all the provisions were on board, a few volunteers came from the *Rendezvous*, and I was anxious to try my fate on the briny waves. I hove up one anchor to be ready to start at a moment's notice. The admiral had arranged that the four brigs should put to sea at the same time, and we, the commanders, agreed to have a parting dinner at the inn. Here the proposal was renewed to share prize money together. Sanders made use of some very ill-timed expressions relating to my brig, remarking that she would be taken by the smallest enemy privateer: and that, the others' vessels being so much superior to mine, the risk was not a fair one. I retorted upon Sanders, stating that, as he had been the first to moot the question of sharing, he ought to be the last to make such out-of-the-way observations. "If I am attacked," I said, "I shall not be so easily captured as you imagine. Therefore, to close the bargain with you, I will agree to share prize money with you for three months, or not at all. It is now for you to decide." In conclusion no agreement was made. The party broke up, and we repaired on board our separate vessels. I had received a clerk recommended by Mrs V., also a steward who had been employed in her establishment. When Ad. Vashon gave me my sailing instructions, he authorized me to seek shelter against stormy weather wherever I might find it convenient, and not to expose my crew to chances of sickness. I was to cruize off Gothenburg to annoy the enemy to the best of my power. Having settled everything satisfactorily, I took my leave.

On the 10th of March, by 11 o'clock in the morning, the *Childers* was under sail, favoured with a good breeze and fine weather. So soon as we were clear of the land I exercised the seamen at the guns and the sword exercise. The boats were also put into good order, with a certain number of men fixed upon ready for boarding ships at anchor. I explained to the crew my determination to be constantly ready for action, by night or by day, directing them to keep their cutlasses and pistols in fighting condition. The next day I boarded a whaler bound to Davis Straits, but nothing of consequence occurred till the 14th when we made the land, and I saw the coast of Norway, of stupendous height, for the first time. I had suited my dress for sea service in a small vessel – a round jacket, etc. When exercising the seamen at the guns and the Marines with muskets, I appeared on deck with my sabre drawn and pistols in my belt. This proceeding seemed to be approved of by all under my command, as I noticed cheerful countenances in every direction. My orders were obeyed with alacrity and apparent good will. All these indications gave me confidence, which led me to rely on their support in the event of meeting an enemy.

It was about 1 o'clock of this day that a vessel was seen from the mast head. Sail was instantly made in chace of her. The stranger closed in with the land, by which means we lost sight of her. My dinner hour was ½ past 2 p.m. By ½ past 4 we had closed this mountainous coast and again got sight of the chace. We were now in smoother water, but the stranger disappeared among the rocks. Not thinking it prudent to stand too near to this high land, I hoisted out the cutter. Volunteers offered themselves with an animated spirit that was truly gratifying. A certain number having been selected, I gave the command of her to the master, Mr Wilson, directing him to proceed inshore and bring out the vessel. He had no sooner left the brig when more volunteers came forward, anxious to assist the cutter. Not wishing to thwart their bold intentions, I had the jolly boat lowered and soon manned, the purser requesting to lead her. He evinced such determination that I complied with his wishes. All this time my dinner remained on the table. I had been so often interrupted during the chace that I had not finished the necessary meal. The two boats that had gone away contained twenty-four of my best men. They were soon out of sight, and the *Childers* lay to, waiting the result of their exertions.

More than an hour elapsed, and no boats were to be seen. I became anxious, as the day was closing: and this feeling was considerably increased when the man aloft on the look-out, shouted in a loud voice, "A large vessel coming towards us from under the land!" All our attentions were instantly directed to the object. Opposite to that part of the coast where I had hove to, the land trended to the north east. A long inlet extending to some distance was discerned, which the pilots informed me led to the port of Hitteroe. It was from thence that this stranger was approaching under topgallant sails. The two lusty pilots gave symptoms of extreme alarm, declaring that the enemy's vessel was a very powerful one, and that I should either be taken or sunk. I desired them to keep silence and attend to my orders: but they became so refractory that I was obliged to order them below, as their sayings made a strong impression upon the seamen. I then called the crew to their guns and prepared for action.

As the stranger drew out from his apparently confined inclosure, he was still end on, and I could not see his rig. But the size of his bows indicated a vessel of some dimensions. Then, as he shaped his course towards the *Childers*, we saw the length of his hull: he was a large brig,* mounting nine long heavy guns

---

* The *Lügum* (20), from Denmark.

upon his broadside. This was not a very agreeable visitor, and I now found myself in a most awkward position. The boats had not yet hove in sight from the NW – that is, on my right – and I was, I confess, almost at a loss how to act. If I attempted to draw further off from the land, I exposed my boats to capture. Therefore, after a few seconds of meditation, I determined to bring my opponent to action. He continued to near me, and when he was about a mile off upon my starboard bow, I fired a shot at him. At the same time up went the colours of Old England. My firing obliged him to alter his course: therefore, instead of closing nearer, he hauled off. This was a most critical moment for me. When he changed his plan, which at first seemed to be one of attack, he hoisted the Danish ensign and kept aloof, whereby the advantage instantly turned in my favour: which had its effect on my crew. Fortunately for me, I had now time to make my arrangements.

But before I could make sail, to bring the enemy to action, my boats hove in sight, coming from a deep creek on our left, with a galliot in tow, under sail. Its crew, not being armed, had been unable to resist the attack of my boats, but had fled on shore, where they hurled down from the rocks huge stones. But fortunately no one had been injured by them. My crew were firing their muskets, and a similar fire was noticed from the prize, which circumstance led me to believe that my men were still contending with the Danes. However, the firing soon ceased, and the boats neared us rapidly. Yet notwithstanding these favourable appearances I was still in a very embarrassed position, because it lay in the power of the enemy to capture my boats and retake the galliot. Why the Dane did not make that exertion is no affair of mine. By his not doing so, my boats finally rejoined me, my opponent looking quietly on all the while. I now gave directions for the security of the prize, placing an officer in command of her. The boats were hoisted in, and I made sail to attack the Dane.

The day had just closed. I had therefore to beat to windward to reach him. He kept so close to the land that I could not get inshore of him. My broadsides were directed only as often as they could bear, I was obliged to shorten sail, and I could only aim at him as the flash of his guns indicated his position. Darkness now came on, which for a short while interrupted our fire. Many broadsides had been exchanged, but as yet the *Childers* had not received any injury of consequence. There was only a light air so close to the high land, and the water was as smooth as a millpond. Under these circumstances all the advantages lay with the enemy. He could see us as we were outside, but we could not see him. I therefore ceased cannonading till the moon enabled us to see what we were about. It was during this interval that we heard sounds very similar to the rowing of boats, and an impression naturally arose that the enemy was receiving men from the shore. Our quietness did not last long, for the Dane, profiting by his position, opened his fire in slow succession. One of his shots went clean through both sides of the *Childers* just above the line of flotation. Another shot lodged in the lower deck. It weighed 22 lbs English, so that I was led to believe that he had long 18 lbers – overwhelming odds against 12 lb carronades. The moon at last, being at its full, shone

forth in all imaginable splendour. Being now enabled
to ascertain my exact position, I thought myself rather
too near the land, upon an hostile coast. Judging it
imprudent to expose my vessel to such unusual dangers, I directed the pilots to widen our distance, and,
having placed her about three miles from the shore, I
again hove to, waiting the proceedings of the Dane.

The heavens were cloudless; the stars and planets
were seen in all their brilliancy. The enemy set his
square mainsail, and, shaping a diagonal course, gradually increasing his distance from the land, he neared
us. I was on the watch for a favourable moment to tack.
I now ascertained that all the captains of the guns were
on board the prize, which, in a certain way, was a loss.
At about 11 o'clock I thought I had obtained the object
I had been endeavouring to realise. I instantly set the
courses and tacked the *Childers*. When round, I had
the enemy on the lee bow. I then made a short speech
to my crew, telling them that I meant to lay him on
board on the weather bow and that they were all to
follow me. They instantly armed themselves and patiently waited for orders. My clerk attended me carrying my sword. We were favoured with one of the finest
nights I ever beheld. Every object could be seen as
plainly as by daylight.

We stood on towards our opponent, and for a time
all my plans bore the appearance of success. But, at the
critical moment of weathering the Dane, the wind
headed us two or three points. He, taking advantage
of that circumstance, luffed up as close as he could,
and my expectations were foiled. Instead of gaining
the wind I was obliged to bear up to prevent the jib
booms of the two vessels coming in contact with each

other, and pass along to leeward, as near as it could be done without touching the enemy, myself directing the motions of the man at the helm.

When the two jib booms were clear of each other, I ran forward to ascertain that the steersman was acting properly. Then we poured a broadside of round and grape shot into the enemy's deck. His vessel leaning over into the wind, not one of the shot, I imagine, failed of doing mischief, and the groans of his men were distinctly heard. Then, coming aft and still directing the man at the helm, I had reached the lee side of the capstan when I was hurled down by it with such violence that I felt as if life had departed. My left arm was jammed against the edge of the lee carronade slide and my body smothered underneath the capstan. I lay in that position a few seconds till the smoke cleared away, when, my person being missed by the first lieutenant, he set to work to ascertain what had become of me. When he discovered my helpless position, with the assistance of some of the seamen he lugged me out from under the capstan, and as they were raising me from the deck my senses returned. The first words I heard were, "The captain is killed!", repeated several times. Moving my arms and opening my eyes contradicted that assertion. My clerk had received a shot in the body which killed him outright, and I was covered with his gore. Altogether I was in a shocking plight, suffering great pain in both my legs and left arm. Having been removed to the weather side, I was seated on one of the carronade slides. At that moment the Dane fired two stern guns, but they missed us. I now ordered the first lieutenant to tack and lay the enemy on board on the weather quarter, but whilst he was preparing to do so the gunner called out from below that the magazine was afloat and the brig sinking. This report was confirmed by the carpenter. Consequently, renewing the action was out of the question. The enemy widened his distance by keeping on the opposite tack, and all that I could do was to close with the prize to save my crew. The enemy's last broadside killed two and wounded nine, including myself, severely. When the surgeon, Mr Allen, came to my relief, I desired him to dress the wounded men first of all, then return to me. In the meantime he sent me some wine and water. When we got near the galliot we hove to. The pumps were at work and the dead were committed to the deep. Meanwhile, the Dane, standing on on the same tack, closed in with the land and we soon lost sight of him. This brought on 2 o'clock of the morning. The jolly boat was lowered, to communicate with the prize and then to examine the damages sustained by the enemy's fire. There were eight shot between wind and water on the starboard side, seven of which penetrated the hull.

The surgeon, having dressed all the wounded, repaired to me again. I was taken down to my cabin, which I found in a wretched condition. My steward had not removed a single article from the table on which my dinner had been laid. Most of them had been smashed to atoms. I had not returned to my cabin from the moment I left it to direct the motions of the *Childers*, about 4 o'clock in the afternoon. It was afloat, and the prospect was anything but agreeable. The Surgeon found my left leg most severely contused. The right one was cut open from the knee, down the bone to the ankle, by a splinter. Had it penetrated the thickness of a wafer deeper, the bone would have been broken to pieces. My left wrist was bleeding freely and the arm below the shoulder in acute pain. Whilst he was dressing me, the first lieutenant came to report that one of the pumps was choked and the brig sinking. "Well," said I, "if that is the case I cannot help you. We must all go down together. Give me your hand, and God bless you. I have done my duty and am resigned to my fate." Whether the cool and determined manner in which I delivered these words had any effect upon the lieutenant, I know not. But he hastened on deck and in the course of a quarter of an hour returned to acquaint me that the pump had been set to rights and that there was a chance of saving the *Childers*. At that moment the water in my cabin was about six inches deep, and as clear as the sea without. The surgeon quitted me, and I attempted to get some sleep.

After a few hours the surgeon renewed his visit, and reported favourably. He expected from the severity of the contusions that an inflammation would ensue. Fortunately for me that was not the case, but he entreated me to remain quiet. The report of the injuries we had received in the action was now laid before me. Both the lower masts were struck by shot, also the bowsprit. The rigging and sails were very much cut, and several shots had struck the hull. However, by the afternoon of the 15th the damages were repaired, and the shot holes under water stopped, so that we were able to shape a course for Leith Roads. The action had lasted, with intervals, upwards of seven hours against an enemy of vastly superior force. Twenty guns were counted plainly on his deck – that is, twenty on the sides and two in the stern. When I reflected upon the conduct of the enemy, he appeared, during the whole proceeding, to have been deficient in energy, as I always attacked him. He had the advantage of the weather gage, and might at his convenience have closed upon me. But instead of doing so he allowed me to bring him to action, waiting very quietly the result. Had he, when I attempted to cross his bow from the leeward, borne down upon me, the consequences might have been most fatal to the *Childers*. I have often thought of it. His vessel, being of considerably more burden than mine, when coming in contact would probably have overpowered her, and she would have gone down. After I had poured my last broadside into him, he never altered his course, but permitted me to close with the prize and make all my arrangements without annoyance. Consequently, I beat off an enemy after a very severe contest of long duration, and bore away in triumph the vessel which he evidently intended to recapture.

In the afternoon I directed the galliot to be taken in tow. She was called the *Christina*, and had only a part of her cargo in – 45 casks of fish, some iron and other materials. She did not sail well: she was accordingly taken under our stern. The damages inflicted upon my property were very serious. Three trunks containing my wearing apparel were shot through; my writing case – a very handsome one – shattered to pieces. A small pocket book containing £25 in bank notes was never recovered, but my purse with 11 guineas in it was brought to me, as well a diamond pin. Altogether my losses by the engagement could not easily be replaced. The next day I was carried on deck to breathe some fresh air. As we were proceeding towards the coast of Scotland, we passed the convoy which I had taken charge of at Leith but afterwards delivered over to the *Snake*. We exchanged the private signal with that ship. Her captain would not be liable to any annoyance from the Dane that I had engaged.

On the 18th we anchored in Leith Roads. I had dictated to the purser my official report of the action as I was in too much pain to write. When he had completed it, I sent for the officers that they might hear the statement of our proceedings. They appeared not satisfied with it, saying that I had not done myself justice, as the action was one of the hardest fought of the war, the odds being immense and that I had not sufficiently explained the enemy's vast superiority. The officers and crew repeated over and over again that the late captain never would have done anything of the kind. He would not have gone so close inshore. My only reply was that I preferred underrating the action to making a boasting report. The truth would soon be known and our exertions would be appreciated accordingly.

Not long after the *Childers* had anchored, in the forenoon, I was carried on shore and took up my quarters at the Britannia Inn on the pier of Leith, on the second floor, that I might be out of the way of all interruption. On my leaving the *Childers*, the crew gave me three hearty cheers.

My principal anxiety, now, was to learn what light my action would be viewed in by the Admiralty. The next was to recover the use of my limbs. I could not walk without crutches and my left arm was nearly useless. The following day the admiral called to see me. As I was in acute pain, he did not stay long, merely asking a few questions as to the state of the weather and the number of hours the action lasted. He then withdrew. So soon as the public became acquainted with the particulars of this engagement, all sorts of reports were in circulation – among others that the vessel I had fought was not a man-of-war but a privateer. Many officers of the Navy called. One in particular passed some very appropriate compliments upon my exertions, assuring me that I should receive promotion. "You command," said he, "the very worst craft in the Navy, and you have fought a vessel of vastly superior force, bringing away a prize. You are entitled to reward, and I am sure the Admiralty will place that construction upon your conduct. Promotion will be the result." I differed with him on that part relating to my advancement, as I had not captured the enemy, and told him so. "Well," he replied, "recollect what I tell you. You have performed wonders under the circumstances, and you will be noticed accordingly."

The reports to which I here allude no doubt made some impression upon Ad. Vashon as in two or three days he called again, and appeared in very ill temper. He overloaded me with questions and found fault with my report of the injury done to the rigging: in short, seemed inclined not to believe any of my statements, and refused to approve of my demand for the proper quantities of rope to replace those which had been shot away, unless I altered it. This was one of the most unpleasant official interviews I ever had in my life. I submitted patiently to all he said. I was in pain, suffering from the wounds, and therefore allowed him, without making any replies, to settle the fate of the *Childers* as he thought proper. Among other questions, he demanded in peremptory tones, "How do you know that your enemy had long 18 lbers? The prize you have taken is not worth two pence." I told him that I saw, and very nearly touched, the guns, that the shot on board weighed 22 lbs English, and that I would send him one. After he took his leave, I directed that one of them should be sent to his house.

On the 24th, in the morning, the surgeon had dressed my wounded limbs, it being about eight in the morning. He retired, and I set to with my razors. In the course of five minutes he returned. "What has brought you back again, Doctor?" I demanded. "I merely called to inquire whether you had received your letters from London", said he. "Not yet", was my answer. He kept pacing the room behind my chair, which made me look round, and I noticed an expression on his countenance that gave rise to an opinion of something having happened. "Will you have the goodness, Capt Dillon," said he, "to lay your razor down?" I did so. He instantly caught hold of my right hand with considerable energy, saying,

"I wish you joy, sir. You are a post captain!"

William Dillon was knighted in in 1835, and retired the service as Rear-Admiral of the Red.

William Dawson

The Fortune of War

1808

For two years, 1806–8, the French frigate Piedmontaise *(46) cruised the Indian Ocean wreaking
havoc with British shipping, until chased and cor-
nered by His Majesty's ship* St. Fiorenzo.

His Majesty's Ship St. FIORENZO, at Sea,
6th March 1808.

Sir,
It is with great regret I have to inform you of the death
of Capt. Hardinge, late of His Majesty's ship *St.
Fiorenzo*, who fell gloriously in the early part of an
action on the 8th instant, between his Majesty's ship
St. Fiorenzo, and the French national frigate *La
Piedmontaise*.

The *St. Fiorenzo* sailed from Point de Galle on Friday
the 4th inst. at half past eleven A.M.. On the 6th, at
seven A.M. passed three Indiamen, and shortly after,

saw a frigate bearing N.E.. We immediately hauled our wind in chase, and made all sail, being at that time in lat. 7 deg. 32 min. long 77 deg. 58 min. We made the private signal, which was not answered; and at five showed our colours, which the enemy took no notice of. At forty minutes past eleven P.M. we ranged alongside of him on the larboard tack, and received his broadside. Alter engaging till fifty minutes past eleven P.M. within a cable's length, the enemy made sail ahead, out of the range of our shot; we ceased firing, and made all sail after him; continuing to come up with him till daylight, when finding he could not avoid an action, he wore, as did we also. At twenty-five minutes past six recommenced the action, at the distance of half a mile, gradually closing with him to a quarter of a mile. The fire was constant and well-directed on both sides, though that of the enemy slackened towards the later part of the action. At a quarter past eight P.M. the enemy made all sail away. Our main-topsail-yard being shot through, the main-royal-mast, and both main-topmast-stays, the main-spring-stay, and most of the standing and running rigging, and all our sails shot to pieces, and most of our cartridges fired away (as our guns were directed at his hull he was not much disabled about his rigging), we ceased firing, and employed all hands in repairing the damage sustained, and fitting the ship again for action. From the great injury our masts, yards and sails had received, I am sorry to observe that it was not in our power to chase to renew the action immediately; We however, succeeded in keeping sight of him during the night; and at nine A.M. on the 8th. the ship being perfectly prepared for action, we bore down upon the enemy under all sail; he did not endeavour to avoid us till we hauled athwart his stern, for the purpose of gaining the weather gage, and bringing him to close fight, when he hauled up also, and made all sail; but perceiving that we came fast up with him, and that an action was inevitable, he tacked, and at three we passed each other on opposite tacks, and recommenced action within a quarter of a cable's length. With grief, I have to observe that our brave captain was killed by a grape-shot the second broadside. When the enemy was abaft our beam he wore, and, after an hour and twenty minutes close action, struck their colours, and waved their hats for a boat to be sent them. She proved to be *La Piedmontais*, commanded by Mons. Epron, Capi-taine de Vaisseaux; she mounted 50 guns, long 18-pounders on her main-deck, and 36-pounder carro-nades on her quarter-deck. She had 366 Frenchmen on board, and nearly 200 Lascars, who worked their sails, She sailed from the Isle of France on the 30th December. In the action she had 48 killed and 112 wounded. The *St. Fiorenzo* has 13 killed and 25 wounded; and most of the latter are in a most promis-ing way. A list of them I have the honour to inclose for your information. The enemy was cut to pieces in his masts, bowsprit, and rigging; and they all went by the board during the night.

It is now a pleasing part of my duty to recommend to your particular notice the cool, steady, and gallant conduct of Lieutenants Edward Davies and Henry George Moysey; the latter, I am sorry to add, was severely wounded about ten minutes before the enemy struck. I also experienced very great assistance from

Mr Donovan, the master, by the judicious and sea-manlike manner in which he laid us close alongside the enemy. To Lieutenant Samuel Ashmore, of the royal marines, I am much indebted for the cool and deter-mined courage evinced by him through the whole action. Indeed, every officer, petty officer, seaman, and marine in the ship behaved in the most brave and gallant manner, and nobly maintained the prominence of the British flag. In the first boat from the prize came Mr W.F. Black, assistant surgeon of his Majesty's 86th regiment, captured by the *Piedmontaise* on his passage to Madras, who rendered the surgeon great assistance.

I am also much indebted to the officers of the army, and the captains and officers of the country ships, who were prisoners on board the enemy, for the great assistance they afforded us with their lascars in erect-ing jury masts, and working the ship into port, as from our weak state, and the great number of prisoners on board us, we could spare but few hands from our own ship to send on board the prize.

I have the honour to be, &c.
WILLIAM DAWSON.

To Sir Edward Pellew, Bart. Rear-admiral
of the Red, and Commander in Chief of
all his Majesty's ships and vessels in the East
Indies.

List of Officers, Seamen, and Marines killed and wounded on board his Majestey's Ship *St. Fiorenzo*,

in Action with La. *Piedmontaise* French National
Frigate, on the 6th, 7th, and 8th March, 1808.

Wounded on the 6th.
William Pitt, seaman, slightly; John Treacy, super-
numerary seaman, ditto; William Miller, seaman, ditto.

Killed on the 7th.
Thomas Martin, seaman; Charles Smallwood, ditto;
Robert Currell, ditto; John Middleton, ditto; William
Mcad, supernumary seaman; William Martin, marine;
John Luff, ditto; Joseph Litchfield, ditto.

Wounded on the 7th.
John Meadows, seaman, dangerously, since dead;
William Baldwin, seaman, lost a leg, since dead;
George Byng, seaman, severely; John Finch, seaman,
ditto; Francis Jackman, seaman, ditto; Walter Boze
seaman, ditto; William Long, seaman, ditto; John
Acton, seaman, lost two arms; Philip Ulrick, seaman,
severely; William Wakefield, seaman, lost an arm;
Richard Lock, seaman, slightly; William John Brown,
quartermaster, ditto; John Collier, seaman, ditto; Benjamin Pool, marine ditto.

Killed on the 8th.
George Nicholas Hardinge, Esq. captain; John Beer,
seaman; John Burn, ditto; Evan Jones, marine.

Wounded on the 8th.
Henry George Moysey, lieutenant, severely; Thomas
Gadsby, carpenter's mate, ditto; Thomas Clerk, sea-

man, dangerously; John M'Ewen, corporal of marines, ditto; Charles Richards, marine, lost an arm; Wm. Pope, marine, dangerously, since dead; Henry Thorn, boatswain's mate, slightly; William Davis, seaman, ditto; George Auger, seaman, ditto.

W. DAWSON
(Acting in command of His Majesty's ship *St. Fiorenzo*)

William Richardson

Aix Roads

1808–9

William Richardson was impressed into the Royal Navy in 1793. In the passage below he recounts the blockade of the French fleet in the Aix and Basque roadsteads, culminating in Cochrane's famous fire-ship attack on 11 April 1809.

On October 30, 1808, the *Caesar* got under way, and we joined the Channel fleet off Ushant, now under the command of Lord Gambier, consisting of: *Caledonia* (Lord Gambier, Capt William Bedford), 120 guns; *Royal George*, 100; *St George*, 98; *Dreadnought*, 98; *Téméraire*, 98; *Caesar* (Capt Charles Richardson), 80; *Achilles* (Sir Richard King), 74; *Triumph*, 74; *Dragon*, 74.

NOVEMBER 15TH. – A strong gale of wind came on from the westward, which caused us all to bear up for Torbay, and while lying there our crew got afflicted with ophthalmia; it began at the right eye and went out at the left, and continued near a week and then left us.

27TH. – The wind having come to the north-east, we got under way with fleet and got off Ushant again, but next day shifted to the westward, blew a storm, and drove us back to Torbay again.

DECEMBER 8. – The wind got to the north-east again; got under way and got off Ushant, but the wind increasing and continuing for several days drove the fleet a long way to the westward.

On the 22nd our signal was made to proceed to Rochefort and relieve the *Gibraltar*. It blew so hard that we bore away and scudded under our foresail. Next day, in setting the close-reefed maintopsail, it still blowing hard, rain and hail, it blew to pieces; sounded frequently in eighty fathoms. A grampus has been following the ship these last twenty-four hours.

DECEMBER 25. – Saw Sables d'Olonne lighthouse on the French coast, and, in working up along the shore towards Rochefort, the next day at noon we saw eight sail of the enemy's merchant vessels coming down along the shore before the wind, and we put our ships about to cut them off; and now followed a specimen of our captain's abilities.

As we stood in, with the weather moderate, we fired a great many shot, which caused six of them to bring to; but the other two ran on shore among the breakers and soon went to pieces. We now lowered down the quarter and stern boats to take possession of the remaining six, but in the hurry and confusion the captain hurried them away without any arms or ammunition to defend themselves. As the ship was near the land, we wore her round with her head to the offing and maintopsail aback; as she increased her distance gradually, which a ship will do although her maintopsail be aback, the enemy perceived it, and one of them being armed with about fifty soldiers on board took her station so as to prevent our boats from boarding the others. What was to be done? Our people had no arms or ammunition, so they adopted the wisest plan, and that was to return to the ship for some. The enemy, seeing this, bore away before the wind, and off they ran, and before our boats had reached the ship they had run so far to leeward that any idea of following them was given up, and they made their escape like birds getting free from the fowler.

I never in all my life saw such confusion as was in our ship at the time: the captain was driving the people about from one place to another; one of my crew, named Andrew Gilman, in firing one of the guns, was so flurried that he did not observe a samson post up behind him; the gun recoiled and killed him against it.

During the time of wearing the ship a boat had been hoisted up off the booms to be got out, but was left hanging in the stay tackles and cut a fine caper during the time, swinging about from one side to the other, until some of the people lowered her down of their own accord: had Sir Richard Strachan been in the ship at the time he certainly would have gone mad. And thus ended as lubberly a piece of business as ever was heard of, and to have six merchantmen almost under the muzzle of our guns and then let them all escape, beats everything!

Next day we ran into Basque Roads, but our ships were not there; saw the French squadron lying at the Ile d'Aix; as usual they fired a great many guns, but whether they were exercising their crews, or for some victory by land, we could not tell. So we sailed out again, and met the *Aigle* frigate, who informed us that our squadron was cruising forty miles to the north-west of this place.

On the first day of this important year [1809] we joined them, consisting of the *Defiance* (Captain Hotham senior officer), with the *Donegal* and *Gibraltar*, and soon after ran into Basque Roads and there came to anchor; the *Gibraltar* shared out her provisions among us and then sailed for England. The French ships continue to fire many guns, and we suppose they are exercising their people to fire well.

JANUARY 7. – This morning we saw a square-rigged vessel at sea and coming in before the wind right toward us. The *Donegal* lay inside, the *Defiance* in the centre, and ours the outside ship, and we made sure of taking a prize. Our captain (I suppose to make up for his late bad conduct) ordered me to get three of the main-deck guns shotted and pointed as far ahead as possible, and then go into the magazine and be ready to supply him with powder, all which was readily done, as if something extraordinary was to be performed; but he soon made as great a blunder as before, for before the vessel got within gunshot he began to fire, and the captain of the vessel, judging from this that we were enemies, altered his course and ran her on shore near the town of St Marie's.

The boats of the squadron, manned and armed,

immediately went after her; but by the time they got near, the beach was covered with troops and they had to return without performing anything. Thus we lost another prize; and she must have been of some value, as we heard afterwards that she was a West-Indiaman. Well might the *Defiance*'s people ask ours, when alongside in a boat soon afterwards, if we were friends to the French!

19TH. – Foggy weather. Observed a chasse-marée near to us; hoisted French colours and decoyed her alongside, to the utter surprise of the poor Frenchmen. Thus we got a prize at last, though of little value. In the evening saw a brig coming in, and the boats of our squadron went in pursuit of her. She ran on shore, and our people boarded, but could not get her off. Several shot were fired at them from the shore, but no harm done.

22ND. – Strong wind at south, and rain. Saw another French brig coming in, who, on discovering us, made off. In the afternoon another came in, and in passing fired three shot at her, and brought her to. She hoisted cartel colours, and proved to be the *Elizabeth* of London, with a hundred and forty of Junot's soldiers on board from Lisbon. Let her go to proceed to Rochefort, according to the Articles of Capitulation. They reported to us that the English had obtained a great victory in Spain.*

27TH. – Got under way with the squadron, stood out to sea, then rounded Baleines Lighthouse and came to

* Corunna, 16 January 1809.

anchor in the Breton Passage in 16 ½ fathoms. Next morning got under way and stood out to sea, where we met the *Indefatigable* frigate with dispatches, and were informed that Rear-Admiral Stopford was coming out to take the command, and would hoist his flag on board the *Caesar*. This news pleased us much, as we wanted a commander of such gallant abilities and knowledge.

29TH AND 30TH. – Met a convoy of victuallers, but the weather was so stormy these two days that we could get nothing out of them.

FEBRUARY 1. – Ran into Basque Roads, and there came to anchor. Five of the victuallers came in, and we got two of them alongside and cleared them of 119 tons of water. Then arrived more victuallers, and next day the *Naiad* frigate drove a brig on shore near St Marie's laden with brandy; but the surf soon destroyed her, and our boats chased a sloop on shore laden with prunes near the Breton batteries.

The enemy's squadron fired a great many guns to-day, and had their shops dressed with colours – the English ensign undermost, and the Union downwards. What daring fellows!

15TH. – This morning we saw two men hung at the yardarm of two of the enemy's line-of-battle ships.

The *Calcutta*, formerly a British 50-gun ship, had the English ensign hung Union downwards under her bowsprit, we supposed to insult us; yet they durst not venture to meet us, although they were superior in force. However, we paid them well for their auda-

ciousness soon after. In the evening Rear-Admiral
Stopford arrived in the *Amethyst* frigate.

Next morning the rear-admiral came on board and
hoisted his flag on board the *Caesar*, bringing with
him two lieutenants, a captain of marines, a chaplain, a
secretary and his clerk, two master's mates, nine
midshipmen, his coxswain and a band, and two live
bullocks, which were very acceptable, as we have not
tasted fresh beef this long time.

19TH. – Being Sabbath day, a church was rigged out
and divine service performed on board the *Caesar* for
the first time since I had belonged to her. The Rev Mr
Jones, the chaplain, preached an excellent sermon.
The ship's crew were very devout and attentive.
The rear-admiral was on his knees at prayer time;
but it was funny enough to see our captain, how
fidgety he was: he neither sat nor stood, and was as
unsteady as a weathercock. Some of our nobs thought
that a man could not be a good seaman without
swearing, but the admiral let them know the contrary.
In the afternoon we saw some chasse-marées stealing
along shore, and sent the boats of the squadron after
them; they captured two, one laden with rye and the
other with sardinian, a fish like dried herrings. The
whole was shared out to the squadron and the vessels
broken up for firewood, as their condemnation in
England would have cost more than they were worth.

21ST. – The wind having come from the east, we got
under way, and anchored outside of Baleines Lighthouse for fear the Brest fleet should slip out and come
this way, and which they actually did, as will be seen

presently. Among some prisoners taken a young man named Bordo (son of our French pilot of that name) was brought on board, and great was their joy in meeting each other again; but it did not last long, for in the evening they got drunk and fighting with each other, and the cause was that the father had married an Englishwoman. We had two more French pilots on board (both of them emigrants), one named Le Cam and the other Cameron, and although they had emigrated together they could never agree, and had separate messes. Cameron messed with me at first, but finding him a two-faced fellow I turned him off.

23RD. – Arrived the *Emerald* frigate from England with five live bullocks for the squadron, and exercised great guns and small arms at ten in the evening. Observed the *Amazon*, which was looking out in the north-west direction, letting off rockets, so we got the squadron under way to get near her; on meeting they told us they had seen nine sail of large ships coming along shore from the eastward, and steering for Basque Roads; we ordered her astern to inform the *Defiance* and *Donegal* of it, and to tell them to join us with all speed, and then prepared our ship for battle.

We had previously heard of a French squadron of frigates full of stores and ready to slip out of L'Orient for the West Indies, but they were blockaded by four sail of the line under Commodore Beresford; however, we thought they might have stolen out, and were coming this way to join the Rochefort squadron – we therefore crowded all sail to cut them off, and at midnight got sight of them.

It then fortunately for us fell a calm, which made us

uneasy lest they should escape; but at dawn a breeze sprang up, and we steered right for them. But judge of our surprise as the daylight appeared to find they were the Brest fleet, eight sail of the line, and one of them a three-decker of 120 guns, and two of them flagships, with two frigates accompanying them! They were going to Basque Roads thinking to catch us there, but thanks to Heaven they were too late, as we were on different tacks. We continued our course and fetched into their wake, then put about and followed them; if they had begun to chase us we must have been obliged to run, for what could our three sail of the line do against such a force? But strange to say they never seemed to interrupt us; perhaps they thought we were not the ships that had been in Basque Roads this winter and were hastening along to catch them.

We made a signal to the *Naiad*, one of our frigates, to proceed with all haste to our Channel fleet and inform Lord Gambier of the French fleet being here; but before she got hull down she made the signal that another squadron of the enemy was in sight, and coming toward us, which made some on board think we were now caught at last. However, although we had the Brest fleet, the Rochefort squadron, and the others moving down on us, thus being nearly surrounded by them, yet we kept up our spirits, being determined to fight to the last rather than be taken.

As our admiral knew we could not cope with the Brest fleet, we altered our course to meet those that were coming, and as we drew near found them to be three large French frigates followed by the *Amelia* English frigate and *Dotterel* brig. We got so near that I thought it impossible for them to escape our clutches, and they, seeing their danger, ran in under the batteries of Sables d'Olonne, and there let go their anchors and prepared for battle.

As the wind was now blowing towards the land Rear-Admiral Stopford thought it very improper to come to anchor on a lee shore to fight, but made the signal to prepare to do it with springs on the cables; but the *Defiance*, mistaking the signal, ran in and came to anchor. As she swung round the frigates and batteries cut her severely, so that she was soon obliged to cut her cable and come out again.

Her fore-topsail yard was shot away, her sails and rigging much cut up, and two men killed and twenty-five wounded; however, all the time she was in she behaved gallantly. Hundreds of French people were seen standing on the quays looking at us as we went in, but as soon as we opened our fire they dispersed in an instant. We and the *Donegal* kept under way and as close in shore as the water would admit, and in passing on each tack fired at the frigates, and soon sent them to the bottom; we had not a man hurt, thank God, but were hit by shot from them several times; one went into the bowsprit and another through the jibboom. The *Donegal* had one killed and six wounded.

At four in the afternoon we left and went after the Brest ships, who had been in sight all this time from our mast-heads, and followed them until they came to anchor in Basque Roads; but we kept our squadron under way near the entrance, as we saw some large ships in the offing, and coming toward us. Our noble admiral is as cool and steady as if no enemy was near, and well might a good Christian know no fear.

One of our frigates – I don't know which it was, as

they were changed so frequently – was stationed between us and the enemy to look out; and the latter had one of theirs for the same purpose, so they had frequently to pass each other on different tacks. British courage was severely tried, and the captain of our frigate asked permission by signal for liberty to engage the enemy; but our admiral for wise reasons would not grant it.

Next day, the ships we had seen in the offing joined us, and proved to be the squadron under the command of Commodore Beresford, consisting of the *Theseus* (Sir J. Beresford), 74 guns; *Valiant* (Capt John Bligh), 74; *Triumph*, 74; *Revenge* (Capt Car, or Ker), 74. They were a welcome addition to our little squadron, making us now seven sail of the line, and Sir John informed us that when the Brest fleet drove them away from blockading L'Orient, they ran close in and furled their sails, but when it came dark they set sail again, having never let go their anchors. This was a scheme to make Sir John believe they were going to remain there all night, in order to get a night's start of him, and catch us in Basque Roads before he could come to our assistance. They succeeded so far as getting the night run and no farther, and when Sir John missed them in the morning he came immediately to our assistance.

Although the enemy have now, in conjunction with the Rochefort squadron, eleven sail of the line and a 50, yet they do not think themselves safe. So they got under way to get under shelter of the batteries on the Ile d'Aix; but one of them carrying a broad pennant and named the *Jean Bart* (of 74 guns) got aground on the Palais shoal; soon after she heeled over, then filled, and became a wreck. During this time we had sent the

WILLIAM RICHARDSON

Indefatigable frigate to see into the state of the three frigates we had sunk at Sables d'Olonne, and she brought us information that they were wrecks and the French were getting all the stores out of them they could get at. Their names were the *Italien, Calypso,* and *Sybille,* each of 40 guns.

Rear-Admiral Stopford's letter to the Admiralty was as follows:

H.M.S. "CAESAR."
February 27, 1809
AT ANCHOR BALEINE LIGHTHOUSE N.E. TO N. 4 MILES
AND CHASSERON S.S.E. 10 MILES.
Sir,
You will be pleased to acquaint my Lords Commissioners of the Admiralty that on the 23rd instant, being at anchor NW of Chasseron Lighthouse, with the Caesar, Donegal *and* Defiance, Naiad *and* Emerald *frigates, the* Amazon *looking out to the NW, wind easterly, about 10 p.m. I observed several rockets in the NW quarter, which induced me to get under way and stand towards them; at 11 observed sails to the eastward and to which I gave chase with our squadron until daylight next morning, at which time the strange ships were standing into the Portuis Antioc (the passage to Rochefort) consisting of eight sail of the line, one of them a three-decker, and two frigates; they hoisted French colours, and conceiving them to be the squadron from Brest, I immediately dispatched the* Naiad *by signal to acquaint Lord Gambier.*

The Naiad *having stood a few miles to the NW, made signal for three sail appearing suspicious. I immediately chased them with the squadron under my command, leaving the* Emerald *and* Amethyst *to watch the enemy.*

I soon discovered them to be three French frigates stand-ing in for the Sables d'Olonne. I was at the same time joined by the Amelia *and* Dotterel.

The French frigates having anchored in a situation I thought attackable, I stood in with the Caesar, Donegal, Defiance, *and* Amelia, *and opened our fire in passing as near as the depth of water would permit the* Caesar *and* Donegal *to go into. The* Defiance, *being of much less draught of water, anchored within half a mile of them, and in which situation, so judiciously chosen by Captain Hotham, the fire of the* Defiance *and other ships obliged two of the frigates to cut their cables and run on shore.*

The ebb tide making and the water falling fast, obliged the Defiance *to get under sail and all the ships to stand out, leaving all the frigates on shore. Two of them heeling much, they have been noticed closely by Captain Rodd, and by whose report of yesterday afternoon, they ap-peared with all their topmasts down, sails unbent and main-yards rigged for getting their guns out, and several boats clearing them. I fancy they will endeavour to get over the bar into a small pier, but I am informed by the pilots that it is scarcely practicable.*

The batteries protecting these frigates are strong and numerous; the Caesar *has her bowsprit cut and rigging; the* Defiance *all her masts badly wounded, two men killed and twenty-five wounded; the* Donegal *one killed and six wounded. These French frigates had been out from L'Orient but two days, and by Captain Irby's report appear to be the* Italien, Furieuse, *and* Calypso.

I am very confident they will never go to sea again. My chief object in attacking them so near a superior force of the enemy was to endeavour to draw them out and give our squadrons more time to assemble, but in this I was disappointed. I returned to Chasseron at sunset, and observed the enemy anchored in Basque Roads, and on the 25th I was joined by Captain Beresford in the Theseus, *with the* Triumph, Valiant, *and* Revenge *and* Indefatigable *frigate. I therefore resumed the block-ade of the enemy's ships in Basque Roads and shall continue it until further orders. The enemy's forces consist of eleven sail of the line and* Calcutta, 50, *and four frigates; the force under my command are eleven sail of the line and five frigates.*

I have the honour to be, etc.,
ROBERT STOPFORD.

Here was a noble turn off for Captain Hotham's mistake in anchoring by saying his ship drew less water than the others; so did the *Amelia* but did not anchor. But what seemed strange was that he did not mention any assistance from Captain Richardson, captain of the *Caesar*; the reason was, in my opinion, that he did not like him.

26TH. – Sent the *Dotterel* in chase, which took a French sloop laden with wine and brandy; the French-man was much surprised in finding us here, as he had been told their fleet had cleared the coast of the English. In the night a French boat came secretly alongside from the shore, with a French general and his wife in her; he told us he had fled in consequence of a duel with a French officer, whom he shot; we sent them to England in the *Dotterel*.

28TH. – Sent in the *Donegal* and *Emerald* to recon-noitre the enemy's ships more closely, and they on their return reported that the *Jean Bart*'s masts were all gone and the ship full of water, with a lighter alongside to get out what they could save. Report says that Bonaparte has had the captain, whose name is Lebozec, tried and shot. Here the *King George* cutter arrived from England, to inform us that the Brest fleet had got out, and they were very much surprised to find that we were blockading them here. We got our squadron under way, went into Basque Roads, and anchored nearer the enemy.

MARCH 2. – Examined several galliards laden with brandy under licence to carry to our good citizens of London; they informed us that Austria had again declared war against France.

7TH. – Arrived and took command in chief, Admiral Lord Gambier in the *Caledonia*, with the *Tonnant*, *Bellona*, *Illustrious*, and several other smaller vessels, all from England; and next day arrived the *Mediator*, with a number of victuallers, and sent the *Defiance* to England to refit.

17TH. – This day we all shifted our anchorage and moored the ships in the form of an obtuse angle, reaching from one side the channel to the other, to stop the enemy's ships from getting in or out in the night-time. The *Caledonia* lay in the centre, the *Caesar* at one end and *Tonnant* at the other; the frigates and brigs lay in front, between us and the enemy, and the victuallers outside of all; two boats from each ship, manned and armed, rowed guard at night. We soon captured several chasse-marées, but gave the prisoners their liberty, and for which they were very thankful.

19TH. – Performed divine service, and when done a letter containing the thanks of the Lords Commissioners of the Admiralty to Rear-Admiral Stopford, the captains, officers and ships' companies of the squadron under his command was read, for their judicious and gallant conduct in destroying three of the enemy's frigates and afterwards blockading their fleet with an inferior force.

APRIL 1ST. – Observed the enemy very busy at low water on a rocky shoal named the Boyard, a long mile distant and abreast of the Ile d'Aix; and, supposing they intended to erect a battery there, the *Amelia* frigate and *Conflict* brig were sent in to annoy them; when they got as near as their depth of water would allow, they opened their fire and soon drove the enemy away in their boats; they then out boats, landed on the shoal, and upset the triangles the enemy had erected; the French fleet fired many shot at them during this gallant operation without hurting any one. Our boats (in number four) on their return saw five boats of the enemy coming after them and tossed up their oars to let them come near, but Monsieur soon altered his mind, and returned to his ships again without firing a shot.

3RD. – Arrived from England, in the *Impérieuse*, Lord Cochrane to command the fire-ships which the Lords of the Admiralty have proposed to be sent in among the enemy's ships; and a letter to that purport was posted up on board each line of battle ship for volunteers to man them. Numbers offered themselves on board the *Caesar*, but Mr Jones, our flag-lieutenant, Mr Winthorpe, acting lieutenant, and eight seamen were selected; no one was compelled to go, as the enemy by the laws of war can put any one to death who is taken belonging to a fire-ship.

5TH. – In consequence of some reproachful words uttered by Rear-Admiral Harvey against Lord Gambier, because his lordship could not grant him the command of leading in the fire-ships (as Lord Cochrane was sent here expressly by the Admiralty for that purpose), Rear Admiral Harvey was ordered to England, and there he was tried by a court-martial which dismissed him the service. He was, however, after some time reinstated.

Having got the victuallers cleared of the provisions and water, twelve of them were selected for fire-ships, and the *Mediator*, 36-gun frigate, was to be fitted for another, in order to go in ahead of the others and clear away all obstacles; eight others were expected from England, making in all twenty-one, and besides we fitted up three explosion vessels, to lead in the fire-ships and blow up first, to throw the enemy in consternation: all these ('twas thought) were sufficient to destroy the enemy's fleet. We got alongside one of the victuallers, a brig of 350 tons named the *Thomas*, and belonging to a Mr Cowey of North Shields, and immediately began to fit her up for a fire-ship; we made narrow troughs and laid them fore and aft on the 'tween-decks and then others to cross them, and on these were laid trains of quickmatch; in the square

openings of these troughs we put barrels full of com-
bustible matter, tarred canvas hung over them fastened to the beams, and tarred shavings made out of
brooms, and we cut four port-holes on each side for
fire to blaze out and a rope of twisted oakum well
tarred led up from each of these ports to the standing
rigging and up to the mastheads; nothing could be
more complete for the purpose.

We had captured lately several chasse-marées laden
with resin and turpentine, which answered our purpose well, and which probably had been intended by
the enemy for the same purpose against us. We placed
Congreve's rockets at the yard-arms, but this was an
unwise proceeding, as they were as likely to fly into
our boats when escaping, after being set on fire, as into
the enemy's. Having got all ready, she was hauled off
and anchored near us.

My next job was to fit up a chasse-marée (lately
taken) for an explosion vessel; but she rolled so much
alongside as to endanger her masts being carried away
against our rigging, so she was dropped astern, and
hung on by a rope, and then continued to roll as much
as ever; so that I had to change first one and then
another of the carpenter's crew who were on board
cutting the fuses, they being seasick. We stowed
thirty-six barrels of gunpowder (90 lb each) in her
hold upright and heads out, on each was placed a 10
inch bomb-shell, with a short fuse in order to burst
quickly.

A canvas hose well filled with prime powder was laid
for a train from the barrels to a small hole cut in her
quarter for the purpose, and the train was led through
it to her outside, which was well fastened – a port fire

which would burn twelve or fifteen minutes so as to give the people alongside in the boat who set it on fire sufficient time to escape before she exploded.

She, with two others fitted up by some of our other ships, was to go in a little before the fire-ships, run under the batteries, and then blow up, in order to put the enemy into such confusion that they might not attempt to board any of the fire-ships as they were running in. When this vessel was ready, I returned on board, it then being four in the afternoon, not having broke my fast the whole day – I had been so busily employed, and the business being so urgent, as she was expected to go in this night.

Lieutenant Davies took charge of her with the jolly-boat and crew; he and Mr Jones, who went in with the fire-vessel, got made commanders for this business, and well they deserved it; but I, who had the sole charge of fitting them up, the most trouble, and my clothes spoiled by the stuff, did not so much as get a higher rate, which I applied for, and which from my services I thought myself entitled to: such is the encouragement that warrant officers meet with in the Navy! If an action is fought, though they have the principal duty to do in it, they are seldom mentioned in the captain's letter; whilst the purser, doctor, and boys of midshipmen are greatly applauded, though some of them were no more use in the ship at the time than old women!

The following orders were issued:

All launches and other boats of the fleet to assemble alongside of the *Caesar* and act under the orders of Rear-Admiral Stopford; ships and other vessels to be stationed as follows:

The *Pallas*, *Aigle* and *Unicorn* to lie near the Boyard shoal and receive the boats as they return from the fire-ships.

The *Whiting* schooner, *King George* and *Nimrod* cutters, at the Boyard to throw Congreve's rockets; the *Indefatigable* and *Foxhound* to lie near Aix to protect the *Etna* while she threw her shells into that place; the *Emerald*, *Dotterel*, *Beagle*, *Insolent*, *Conflict* and *Growler* to make a diversion on the east side of Aix; the *Lyra* to lie with lights near the Boyard side, and the *Redpole* with lights on the Aix side, a mile and a quarter from the enemy, as a direction for the explosion and fire-ships to pass between.

Lord Cochrane in the *Impérieuse* was to act as circumstances would permit, he having superintendence of the explosion and fire vessels.

The French ships of the line lay in two tiers across the passage, rather outside of Aix, as they had not room enough to lie in our [*one*] line; the frigates lay to the eastward and a great number of gunboats to the westward across the passage, and without (where the line of battle ships lay), they had moored a large boom, well secured with chains and anchors, to stop any vessel from entering in. Admiral Willaumez, who commanded the squadron, that we chased in the West Indies in 1806 (which was separated from us in the hurricane), and who commanded the Brest fleet that we had followed in here, has been superseded by a mighty man, if many names can make him so: he is called "Lachaire Jacques Theodore Allemand". This would have disgusted old Mr Clark, master of the *Tromp* when I was in her: when mustering any of the people who came to join the ship, if they had two

Christian names he would say, "Au, mon, I suppose you have come from some 'great family,'" then turning aside and giving a grin, would say again, "I dinna ken how these people come by twa names – it was as much as my poor father and mother could do to get me christened David."

On April 11, at half-past eight in the evening, it being very dark, and a strong tide setting with blowing weather right towards the enemy's ships, the explosion vessels set off, followed by the *Mediator* and other fire-ships. The former soon blew up with a dreadful explosion. The *Mediator* carried away the boom laid across by the enemy, and the other fire-ships followed her in, and the elements were soon in a blaze by their burning. Shells and rockets were flying about in all directions, which made a grand and most awful appearance. All hands were up that were able on board all our fleet, to behold this spectacle, and the blazing light all around gave us a good view of the enemy, and we really thought we saw some of their ships on fire. But it seems they had been prepared for this business, for as the fire-ships closed on them, they slipped or cut their cables and ran their ships on shore; and the fire-ships, after being abandoned by our people, drove with the wind and tide up mid-channel, and passed them; but we were informed by some of the prisoners taken that the *Ocean* lost near two hundred men in extricating a fire-vessel from her, and that she cut and anchored three different times.

At daybreak the following morning we saw all the enemy's ships, except two, on shore on the Palais shoal. The *Ocean* was lying with her stern on the top of the bank and her bows in the water; but next high water she, with two others, by throwing their guns and heavy stores overboard, got afloat again and ran towards Rochefort, until they stuck on the bar, and there remained until they could get more lightened.

At 2 p.m. the *Impérieuse* and some others of a light draught of water which were inside of our fleet, ran into Aix Roads and opened their fire on the *Calcutta*, and soon made her strike her colours. They then set her on fire, as she was fast aground, but it was thought she might have been got off by lightening her. The two line of battle ships that had not been on shore now cut their cables and ran towards Rochefort, until the bar brought them up.

The *Revenge*, *Valiant*, and *Etna* bomb were soon after ordered in, and began firing on the other enemy's ships that lay aground, and at five in the evening the *Varsovie*, *Aquilon*, and *Tonnère* surrendered, and three more fire-vessels were ordered to be got ready with all dispatch. We got the *Sisters* transport alongside for one of them, and soon fitted her up in a temporary manner for the purpose, and this same afternoon, between five and six o'clock, we got the *Caesar* under way, and with the *Theseus* and three fire-vessels ran into Aix Roads.

N.B. – In passing the Aix batteries, where our French pilots had said there were as many guns as days in the year, we could not find above thirteen guns that could be directed against us in passing; and these we thought so little of that we did not return their fire, although they fired pretty smartly at us too with shot and shells, which made the water splash against the ship's side; yet (thank God) they never hit, though the passage here is only about a mile wide. Captain Beresford of the *Theseus* had his cow put into the ship's head to be out of the way of the guns; a shot from the enemy killed it, which was the only loss received.

About seven o'clock, just as we were getting nearly out of the range of their guns, our ship took the ground and stuck fast nearly close to the Boyard. The shot and shells were flying about us at the time from Aix and Oleron, but it soon came dark, and they left off, and we had the prudence to still keep all the sails set to make them believe we were running on. However, after dark we took them all in, and as the tide fell the ship heeled much, so we started thirty tons of water overboard to help to lighten her, and ran the after guns forward to bring her more on an even keel. During this business a light was seen by the enemy through one of our port-holes, and we soon had a shot whistling across our quarterdeck. The light was quickly extinguished, and they fired no more. But this shows what a predicament we should have been in had it been daylight.

At eleven at night, with the rise of the tide, she floated again, and we got her into deeper water, where we anchored her more clear from their shot and more clear from the *Calcutta*, which had been all in a blaze only a short distance from us; the latter when she blew up made a most dreadful explosion, having a great quantity of gunpowder on board and other stores which were intended for Martinique, had we not prevented her. It was said she was worth half a million sterling.

Fortunately none of her fiery timbers fell on board our ship: everything went upwards, with such a field of red fire as illuminated the whole elements. One of our French pilots was so frightened that he dropped down on the deck, and said afterwards that if anybody had told him that the English had done such things, and he had not seen them, he would say it was "one tam lie."

In the course of this eventful night Captain [*John*] Bligh of the *Valiant* was sent in with the boats manned and armed to reconnoitre the enemy more closely, and on his return informed us that they had got three lines of boats manned and armed to keep off any more fire-ships, and, it beginning to blow strong at the time, the attempt was given up. So we set fire to the *Varsovie*, a new 90-gun ship (for she carried that number), and to the *Aquilon* (74 guns), as they were waterlogged. They burnt to the water's edge, and then blew up. As for the *Tonnère* (74 guns), the enemy set fire to her them-selves, and then escaped in their boats.

In the place where we now had anchored we found our ships to ground at low water. And early in the morning, the wind having become favourable, we got under way with the other line of battle ships, and left this place, which may be compared to Portsmouth Harbour, and soon after anchored among our other ships in Basque Roads, which may be compared to Spithead. The enemy fired at us from Aix in passing their line, but, thanks to Providence, not a man was hurt.

The frigates and small craft we left inside, but the enemy had got their ships lightened so much, and into shoal water, that the shot from our frigates could not reach them.

Our loss on this occasion was as follows:

When our fire-ship had got near the enemy an

explosion vessel (which they did not see) blew up, and a piece of one of the shells, which had burst, struck the boat alongside of the fire-ship which Mr Winthorpe and his four men had to escape in, and stove in her quarter (they were light four-oared gigs, and selected for the purpose), and wounded the boat-keeper in the hand. When they left the fire-ship, it being rough weather, she soon filled with water, and they clung to the boat for safety.

As the ebb tide was setting out strong they drifted out to one of our brigs, who sent her boat to save them; but two of them were gone and lost through exhaustion. Mr Winthorpe was found in the boat quite dead, and Yankee Jack and the other were taken out of the gig nearly so, and when carried alongside the brig, Jack requested to be left in the boat until he recovered and got a little stronger, so the boat was dropped astern, and he in her.

He had not been there long before the rope broke, and being very dark, the boat soon drove out of sight, and the first landfall poor Jack made was on the French shore, where he was soon made a prisoner. We all pitied poor Jack Ellis, a good-tempered fellow, and never expected to see him again. But after the war was over, and Jack released, I met him on the Common Hard at Portsea, and was glad to see poor Jack again: he then belonged to a merchant vessel.

He told me that when he was made a prisoner he was examined strictly to know whether or not he belonged to one of the fire-ships, as by the laws of war they can put any one to death taken in them. But Jack said he belonged to one of the victuallers. They asked him then how he came to have his hand wounded, and he said it was by the boat's gunwale and ship's side as they rolled together, and by sticking to the same story (after being examined thirteen times at Rochefort and other places) he got clear, but remained a prisoner five years. When peace took place in 1814, Jack got released, returned to England, and received the whole of his pay and prize money up to that time.

Lieutenant Jones, who commanded the fire-ship, had likewise a narrow escape. One of the cabin windows had been opened for him to get into the boat, after the fuse was lighted; but the swell was so high, and the sea so rough, they durst not venture near the stern of the vessel for fear of staving the boat against the counter, and – not having a moment to spare – he jumped overboard. The boat took him up, and they all five arrived safe on board.

Lieutenant Davis, with the jolly-boat and four hands, who went in with the explosion vessel, likewise all safely returned on board.

A singular circumstance happened while we lay inside, as follows. The captain of the *Varsovie*, a prisoner, finding we were going to set his ship on fire, got permission to go on board her to get some charts, which he said he set a high value on. He went with Lord Cochrane, and sat alongside of him in the gig, and, strange to say, but actually true, a shot came from the enemy at Aix and killed the French captain on the spot, without either hurting his Lordship or any one in the gig.

Other occurrences happened, but we hardly had time to think of them, being so dangerously situated; for who could ever suppose to see four sail of the line go into Portsmouth Harbour, passing the batteries,

and running up as far as the Hardway and there
anchoring, and destroying part of the enemy's fleet,
and then running the gauntlet out again amidst shot
and shells flying about! Such was the case going into
Aix Harbour. Had a gale come on from the north-west
and blocked us in we should have been in a poor
situation, but kind Providence favoured us in everything.

The killed and wounded in the British fleet are:
Two officers and eight men killed; nine officers and
twenty-six wounded, and one missing (which was
Yankee Jack): total forty-six.

On the evening of April 14th the enemy succeeded
in lightening the three-decker so much that with a
press of sail and a high tide they got her over the bar,
and she went up to Rochefort; the commodore tried
hard to get the *Cassard* over, but failed; the *Etna* bomb
kept throwing shells, but without any effect, as the
swell made her roll so much.

Next day three more of the enemy's line of battle
ships got over the bar and went to Rochefort; three
more remained, but so far up and in the shallow water
that our frigates could [not] get near enough for their
shot to reach them: the *Etna*'s 13-in mortar split, and
all the shells of her 11-in mortar were fired away, and
apparently without doing any execution. Manned all
the launches of the fleet to cover the three remaining
fire-ships that are to be sent in to-night; but a gale
came on with rain, and it was given up.

Next day, the 16th (still stormy weather), the enemy
being afraid of an attack on the *Indiana* frigate, which
lay aground, set her on fire, and she soon blew up.

17TH. – All the enemy's ships this day got over the bar except the *Regulus* (74 guns), which still remained aground near a place called Fouras, about four miles above the Isle of Aix; this day we released several male and female prisoners, gave them a boat, and saw them land safe at Rochelle, and hope they are thankful for their deliverance.

19TH. – By order of the commander in chief public thanks were given to Almighty God through the fleet for our success over the enemy.

28TH. – Orders arrived for the return of Lord Gambier, and we got four months of excellent provisions from the *Caledonia*, and likewise three dozen of Congreve's rockets from the *Cleveland* transport. Next day Lord Gambier sailed for England in the *Caledonia*, leaving the command to Rear-Admiral Stopford in the *Caesar*, with the *Tonnant*, *Revenge*, and *Aigle* and *Medusa* frigates, four gun brigs, a schooner, and two cutters to watch the motions of the enemy.

Arrived the *Naiad* frigate from England, with the *Hound* and *Vesuvius* bombs; but being too late they were ordered to England again. The *Naiad* had some people on board taken out of a sinking galliot which had only left Rochefort yesterday; they informed us that Bonaparte had ordered the chief officers of his ships at Rochefort to be put under arrest, and 'twas thought some would suffer death; and that they were building two hundred gunboats with all haste to protect their coast.

A man named Wall, who called himself an American, ran away from the *Cassard*, stole a boat and got off to our squadron; he informed us that the *Tourville*, *Regulus*, and *Patriot* are so much disabled that they are ordered to be cut down for mortar vessels, and that the *Ocean* is in a bad state; the *Cassard* is to be docked, but the others were not very much damaged; that Captain Lacaille of the *Tourville* is to suffer two years' imprisonment, to be erased from the list of officers and degraded from the Legion of Honour, and that Captain Porteau of the *Indiana* is to be confined to his chamber three months for setting fire to his ship without orders. Captain de la Roncière of the *Tonnère* is acquitted; but John Baptist Lafon, captain of the *Calcutta*, is to be hanged at the yard-arm on board the *Ocean* for shamefully quitting his ship when in presence of the enemy. This is the fellow who had the English colours hung Union down last winter to insult us, and moreover they were hung under the bowsprit and near the privy: they generally who act in this manner are cowards.

30TH. – Divine service performed, and an excellent sermon was preached by the Rev Mr Jones, touching on several remarkable instances of divine favour which happened on several occasions on our behalf, and how the very materials the enemy were collecting to destroy us fell into our hands and acted against themselves; how the winds favoured us in going into Aix Roads, and how they shifted to bring us safe out again; these were such convincing facts that they made a great impression on the ship's company.

Next day a bowsprit with the jibboom spritsail yard and part of the knee of the head hanging to it came floating alongside, and we hoisted them on board, and to our surprise found they had belonged to the *Calcutta* when she blew up, and had come, as it were, to do homage for the insult offered on it two or three months ago, by hanging the English colours under it Union downwards. The rascals little thought at the time it would be so soon in our possession; there surely was something mysterious in this.

MAY 12. – A play was acted on board the *Revenge* called "All the World's a Stage", and several of us went on board to see it, the admiral among the rest, which gave much satisfaction. As for the *Caesar*, we never had diversion of any kind to cheer us up during the many weary dull nights we had passed on this station.

24TH. – Three very long and large boats belonging to the enemy came out from Aix Roads, and in a daring manner lay on their oars for some time nearly within gunshot, staring at us. We sent our boats manned and armed, who soon made them run, and chased them close in to Aix Roads. Five other boats came out and joined their other three; a smart fire commenced, and the shot from their batteries fell around our boats likewise. Our admiral, seeing the enemy were getting too powerful, recalled the boats, and they returned without having a man hurt.

JUNE 5. – This morning a heavy gale of wind and rain came on from the westward, which caused the sea to rise much; struck lower yards and topmasts; at 11 a.m. she drove with two cables out; let go the best bower and veered out another cable, which brought her up.

The *Tonnant* parted from both anchors and nearly drove on shore near Rochelle, but her sheet anchor being let go brought her up; she made a signal of distress, but no assistance could be given in such stormy weather; fortunately she rode the storm out.

10TH. – A cartel came in from Cayenne and anchored near us; three French small craft were sent from Rochelle to take the people out of her. An American and a Maltese who came out in these vessels entered into our service, and would not return to Rochelle again: so much for Bonaparte's popularity! They told us the French ships at Rochefort were getting ready very fast and five of them would soon come down; and sure enough this same afternoon we saw three of the rascals coming down the Charente for Aix Roads. Sent our boats to assist the *Tonnant* in sweeping for her anchors, and found one.

17TH. – This day arrived Rear-Admiral Sotheby in the *Dreadnought* and relieved us in the command; saluted each other with thirteen guns each, distributing our provision (except one month's) to the other ships of the squadron; gave an anchor to the *Tonnant* and in the evening got under way with glad hearts for Old England.

Robert Eastwick

Tempest

1810

Robert Eastwick joined the merchant navy at twelve, rising through the ranks until he secured a master's ticket. He was largely employed on cargo ships in the East Indies, but the following dramatic storm, with its various unhappy conclusions, occurred in the English Channel.

There was an acquaintance of mine, a Mr Hutton, who had formerly been a purser in the East India service, and made a considerable sum of money, and was now owner of a ship called the *Elizabeth*, which was loading in London for Calcutta. Happening to meet him in the city one day we entered into conversation, and it ended in his inducing me to take a one-sixteenth share in the vessel, and also to invest £3,000 in the venture; and I further agreed to accompany him out on the voyage to India.

It being necessary to insure my interest in the *Elizabeth*, I was persuaded by a Mr Allport, who was clerk to my agents, Messrs Porcher and Company, to do so through him, and without acquainting the firm, whereby he declared I should protect myself at a lower rate. I unwisely agreed to this, and nothing could have turned out more unsatisfactory, for in the end it caused me delay, anxiety, and loss, and proved the truth of the old proverb that says, "Penny wise, pound foolish."

We sailed in November with thirty cabin passengers and 300 lascars (of whom we carried 256 as passengers), and a large mixed cargo, making a freight altogether of £13,000. The weather was very unfavourable, and we with difficulty made Portsmouth, where we had to call, and having anchored off Spithead, lay there for some days, windbound, owing to a heavy gale continuing from the west.

Here one of our passengers, a Captain Jackson, had arranged to join us. He had not long been married to a beautiful and accomplished young wife, who, having never before parted from her family, and especially from a favourite sister, became dangerously ill through grief, which brought on a premature confinement. Captain Jackson now wished to give up his passage, although it had cost him four hundred guineas, and remain for another ship. Knowing that he was a poor man I did not like to see him sustain such a loss, and therefore persuaded him to act on the doctor's opinion, which was in favour of the lady proceeding, provided she could be got comfortably on board. It only remained for her embarkation to be suitably arranged, and for this purpose I called personally on Admiral Curtis, who commanded at Portsmouth, and represented the case to him, and he very kindly tendered the loan of his yacht, in which we reached the *Elizabeth* just as she was passing through the Needles. I mention this circumstance because I had afterwards a dreadful reason to regret my successful interference to change Captain Jackson's plans.

Almost immediately after we got into the Channel bad weather again set in, and we were obliged to beat against adverse winds and in a very heavy sea. The ship strained so much, and made such bad weather, that when we were between Scilly and the Land's End she sprung a leak, and began to make water very rapidly. And just about this time the wind shifted to due south, and blew a hard gale, which prevented us from weathering either point. A consultation being called, the captain and officers, on my suggestion, determined to run through; and this was accomplished in safety, despite the thickness of the atmosphere, which quite hid the land from view and made the navigation most difficult. The leak continuing to gain on us, we were obliged to bear up for Cork, and reached the harbour of that place early in December.

Here we stayed some time refitting, and awaiting a favourable wind to sail again. We also shipped twenty more Lascars, a European carpenter, gunner, steward, and baker, and three gentlemen as passengers. The latter were Company's marine officers, one of them being a friend of mine named Calder, who had recently come home from India as chief mate of the *Warren Hastings*, a fine vessel of 1,200 tons burden.

At last the wind shifted round, and under convoy of the *Brisk*, sloop of war, from whom we received our sailing instructions, we started again. For a week we experienced fair weather, and had reached considerably to the west of Scilly, to latitude 49 North and longitude 8 West, when we encountered another gale, and before long the *Elizabeth* again sprung a leak.

To keep her from sinking we were obliged to bear up before the wind, and thus found ourselves once more steering a homeward course. So hard did it blow that, although under double-reefed top-sails only, we ran eastward at the rate of ten knots an hour, the ship plunging in a furious sea, and the pumps constantly at work. Owing to the danger of heaving-to, we dared not enter Falmouth, which we passed about midnight, though we had four and a half feet of water in the hold, and nearly three feet between decks. The cold was intense, and the lascars so benumbed and affected with fright, that they could only be prevented from running below by Europeans standing over the hatch-ways with drawn swords.

Captain Hutton now desired to make Portsmouth, and at 6 p.m. the following evening we hauled close to the wind, head inshore, and with not more than a knot weigh on, and about eleven o'clock sighted the Bill of Portland right ahead. But just at this time it unfortunately happened that the pumps got out of order, and the leak gained so fearfully on us that we were obliged to bear up till morning to get them repaired, and in so doing overshot Portsmouth.

After this it blew a regular hurricane from W.S.W., and we lost our fore and main sails, which were blown to pieces. The lascars had by this time become perfectly useless, and the officers were themselves obliged to go aloft and cut away the pieces of the sails, which were flapping with the report of guns. The night was as dark as pitch, and the ship was tossed about completely at the mercy of the waves, many of which were breaking over her. For two days and nights the passengers had all been assembled in the cuddy, which was half full of water, and where boxes and chests and bedding and miscellaneous articles were being washed about in a manner that added greatly to the noise and general confusion. It was very distressing to see the fear depicted on the faces of these poor people, and observe the different phases in which it was exemplified. Some were praying and lamenting, others moody and silent, and others again wildly excited and delirious in their talk.

When at last daylight came, we bent on another foresail and reefed it; but, owing to the violence of the gale and coldness of the weather, we were unable to get up a fresh mainsail, our strength in Europeans being nothing near sufficient to work the ship properly, and the few lascars we managed to drive aloft refusing to stir out of the tops, and ready from cold, fright, and weakness to surrender life and tumble into the sea when urged out on to the yards. We therefore set the main and mizen staysails, and the weather abating a little towards midday, began to cherish a hope that we might get safe into the Downs.

We succeeded in getting through the Straits, and were approaching the South Foreland, when the main staysail blew to pieces, by which the little weigh the ship had on was so much diminished that the strong tide obliged us to anchor about three miles distant from the shore.

We held for a few hours, but during the night the wind increased, and shifted to north-west, and we began to drift, and by the morning found ourselves

across the Channel and close between Calais and
Gravelines, in a situation which prevented us from
clearing the coast to the westward, or the sands to the
eastward, and with the gale dead on shore. In this
extremity we got out a new Europe sheet cable and
stout anchor, that was part of our cargo, and this was
now let go, and to our intense relief it brought the ship
up; but only till the evening, when with the change of
tide she began to drift again.

And now our position became exceedingly critical.
It was soon apparent that nothing but a cessation of
the tempest would enable us to escape the destruction
that threatened, and which could no longer be disguised or hidden from our passengers. All through the
storm I had endeavoured to cheer and encourage them
whenever I could spare a few moments from the deck –
which was seldom enough, since the navigation of the
ship had been made over to me. The series of misfortunes that had followed the *Elizabeth* since we first
set sail from Portsmouth created a general feeling of
superstitious despondency, not perhaps to be wondered at. Two months ago we had passed Dover
Straits on our outward voyage, and here we were again
at the end of that period, in the same place, and in
much sorrier condition. Landsmen are at the best of
times all adrift at sea, but in gales and foul weather
their ignorance of nautical matters often magnifies the
peril in their eyes, and causes them to exaggerate
danger. I have always endeavoured to affect a cheerful
bearing before my passengers, even when I have
myself felt anxious, finding that a good laugh is the
best physic for such folk. They repose such an implicit
trust in the captain of a ship, and are so guided by his

demeanour, that much depends upon how he conducts himself. Whilst we had plenty of sea room I made it my care to frequently visit the cuddy for a few moments at a time, and cheer all there with the assurance that such blows were common at sea, and that the gale would soon abate, or we be safe in some harbour. But now, with a lee shore under us, and the ship drifting on to it, I did not feel justified in assuming the same confident bearing, although most anxious to avoid creating a sudden panic. I was very deeply concerned about Captain Jackson and his young wife, and being desirous to prepare him for any emergency, I called him into the captain's cabin, and privately pointed out to him on the chart a sand bank, on which I thought it probable we should strike within an hour. But I particularly begged him not to mention this to any one, but only to go to Mrs Jackson, and keep her from being too much alarmed when the shock occurred.

Poor Captain Jackson was himself under such strong apprehensions of alarm on account of that amiable woman, that he seemed unable to grasp my warning, and immediately mentioned what I had confided to him to the third mate, and also to the three officers who were on board as passengers. These at once determined to get the larboard quarter boat ready, and leave the ship privately directly she struck. Being told of this, I at once went and remonstrated with them; but in such hours of danger words are useless, and just as I was speaking the catastrophe I had anticipated occurred, and the *Elizabeth* took ground with great violence.

All was now confusion and alarm. The lascars, who had been huddled below like so many sheep, rushed up on the deck, which soon became crowded, and filled the dark night with their loud foreign cries, as they ran hither and thither in companies, frantic with fright and uncertainty as to what was best to be done. The Europeans, seeing that they were like to be overwhelmed by these natives, gathered together on the poop, and, forming a line, seized cutlasses, belaying-pins, or any weapon they could lay hands on, and kept the lascars from encroaching. Meanwhile minute guns were fired, whose loud reports added to the fright of the poor women clustering on deck, and who appealed with cries and tears to every man they came in contact with to save them.

And now the party who had proposed to leave in the boat began to launch it, and Mrs Jackson and the three officers got into her whilst she hung in the davits. But the lowering was effected so hastily, that when about half-way down a great sea caught it and dashed it to pieces against the side of the ship.

Hearing a shouting and commotion I hurried to the spot, and the first thing I saw was poor Mrs Jackson clinging on by the after-tackle. It was a terrible sight to see a woman so fragile and beautiful thus situated. Her thin white hands clenched the rough ropes with the grasp of despair, whilst her face was turned upwards, and her golden hair becoming uncoiled streamed out into the gale. I at once endeavoured to render what assistance I could to her husband, who was trying to reach down and catch hold of her, but almost immediately another great wave came, and with a pitiable shriek the poor lady fell back into the foaming sea, and was carried away by the resurge into the darkness beyond and never seen again.

Captain Jackson now became frantic, and I was forced to draw him on to the poop with all my strength, as he was preparing to plunge after his wife. I implored him to control his feelings, but he wrestled violently with me and cursed me for keeping him back. Seeing his condition I called four men to my aid, and between us we lifted him up and carried him below to my cabin, where I locked him in until he should again become master of his actions.

Mr Calder, one of the three officers who had been washed out of the boat with Mrs Jackson, managed to catch hold of a small coir rope that hung over the stern of the ship, and the third mate (a great friend of his) seeing this, seized it and tried to haul him on board. But when he had all but succeeded a sea washed him from his grasp. A second and a third attempt – for Calder still clung desperately to the rope – were equally as unfortunate, and at last the poor fellow became exhausted, and losing his hold perished miserably.

I learnt this incident from Laird himself, who came down into the cuddy just as I was returning from confining Captain Jackson in my cabin. Noticing that he was much agitated and also that his hand was bleeding profusely, I asked him how he had hurt it. He seemed surprised at the question, and holding it up close to the lantern, found that he had nearly lost three fingers, which had been sawn to the bone by the friction of the coir rope running through his hand. It was marvellous that he should have remained unconscious of so severe a hurt, but it showed his deep anxiety for the preservation of his friend Calder.

All this time we were bumping on the sandbank,

with the sea around us boiling like a caldron, so that I expected the *Elizabeth* to go to pieces every moment. But the tide falling we presently remained fast, with a heavy list to starboard, and so continued until morning. With the following tide the ship floated again, and began to drift rapidly towards another bank. And now, as a last hope of saving her, we endeavoured to make sail again, with the object of running between the two shoals into deep water, but before we could get sufficient weigh on she struck with such violence as to beat in her bottom, and the water immediately poured in so fast that it was now certain she was past all hope. The wind began, also, to increase again, and the seas to break so furiously over us, that it seemed merely a matter of minutes before the end must come.

At this juncture Captain Hutton came and implored me to try and get ashore in the cutter and obtain assistance, our minute guns and signals of distress having met with no response. The task seemed an impossible one, for the sea was like a whirlpool, and between us and the land there lay a long narrow bank, over which the surf was breaking with such a fury that no boat could hope to cross it. Since the fatality that attended the launching of the quarter-boat, every one seemed to realize that it was impossible to escape by this method, and no further attempt had been made to prepare any other. But the lives of many human beings depending on it, I thought it my duty to respond to the call, and consented to make the attempt. I therefore went down to my cabin to get my watch, which I had left there, and as I came out Captain Jackson followed me.

Having reached the deck I called for volunteers. At

first there was no response, until Captain Jackson
stood by my side, when several others came forward,
and at the last moment a lascar jumping into the boat,
he was at once followed by ten or twelve of his
brethren, until I stopped the inrush by hitting into
the thick of them with an oar, or they would certainly
have swamped us on the spot.

How the cutter drifted clear of the ship I do not
know. For some minutes we seemed to be leaping into
the air, and falling away again on the broken waves
close to the vessel's side, shipping great quantities of
water, and unable to obtain any purchase with the oars
to push off. Every moment I expected to see the boat
either capsize or be dashed into pieces and sink, but by
some great mercy of Providence we gradually drifted
aft until we found ourselves clear of the *Elizabeth*'s
hull. Then our oars went out and we pulled for dear
life.

The cutter proved more seaworthy than any one
would have given her credit for, and with half the
hands bailing and half rowing, we kept her afloat and
headed for the shore. When within a mile of land we
came upon the sand-bank I have mentioned. It ran
parallel with the shore, and over it the breakers dashed
in one continuous turmoil, so that it seemed to us as
though there was not a moment's rest or stay.

I dared not alter our course, as this would have
brought us broadside on, when we would have instantly capsized. All we could do was to lay on our
oars, and watch an opportunity of running through if
such occurred. Standing up in the stern-sheets with
the tiller-ropes in my hands, I kept the cutter's head
up, whilst a man in the bows signalled to me as each

wave came on. At last there was a slight temporary cessation, which every one recognized as by a common instinct, for immediately a great shout went up of, *"Pull! Pull!"* and straining to our utmost endeavour, we rowed direct for the bank.

As we reached it the surf began to make again, and the first wave coiling at least ten feet above our heads, allowed us no hope of saving ourselves. I bent down and prepared for death. It seemed hovering over me. But at this supreme moment, as if from the depths of despair, the great breaker in its curling fall pitched clean beyond the boat, and only buried us in a large body of water, whilst the momentum it gave us hurled us forward and stranded us on the narrow bank as it dispersed. The next surf following broke short behind us, and threw the cutter forward again with such a shock that it sent a great part of the water we had shipped out of her, and so actually helped us across the grim barrier and into smoother water on the other side, and through this we were able to pull to shore with the two oars that were left to us.

The place where we landed was close to Dunkirk. There were hundreds of people on the beach ready to receive us, many of them women, with little pots of hot tea in their aprons ready to revive us, and their kind eyes full of tears at witnessing our distressing situation. Not a soul of us had expected to reach the shore when we put off from the *Elizabeth*, and many times during the passage we had braced ourselves to meet death. And now, by the Divine goodness of God, we were safe on land, and tended by hospitable hands, that snatched us from the waves and assisted us into a place of safety.

Directly I could speak I pointed out the position of the ship, and by means of signs and gesticulations, and the few words of the French language with which I was acquainted, entreated that help should instantly be sent to her. In reply I was informed that several efforts had already been made, from the time our first minute guns were heard, but that all had failed, it being totally impossible for any craft to face the gale blowing in from the sea. This was indeed true, and when I reflected on the terrible danger of the journey we had just made, with the wind abaft us, I was fain to confess that no boat could make way in the teeth of such a storm. I had therefore to content myself with the promise that, were the gale in any way to abate, another attempt to reach the ship and succour the crew should at once be made.

And now an officer with a company of soldiers came marching down to where we stood, and caused us to be mustered, informing us we must go to prison at once, such being the destination awarded us by the law of the land and the fortunes of war. It seemed harsh and undeserved treatment to thus use people who had but just been saved from the jaws of death, and I thought I observed signs of disapprobation amongst the populace. But there was no help for it, and we had to fall in and were conducted to jail between two files of gendarmes.

Shortly after we left the beach, another boat containing two officers and six seamen succeeded in getting ashore from the *Elizabeth*, and they joined us in prison within an hour. They informed us that a little while before they put off from the ship the captain's barge was hoisted out for the ladies, and the two

officers were in it, preparing for its equipment, when it
broke away, without any oars, and getting broadside
on to the sea capsized. A gig that hung over the stern
was then lowered to recover the barge, but the crew of
it, instead of doing so, pulled straight to the shore after
picking up the two officers, who were too exhausted to
remonstrate or do anything. And before they had got
half-way to land the *Elizabeth* went to pieces, and all
the people on board perished.

When she struck on the sands, which occurred on
the 27th of December, 1810, her crew and passengers
numbered 380 souls, including several ladies. Of these
only twenty-two persons were saved, though one other
poor gentleman, Lieutenant Tench, of the 3rd Ceylon
Rifles, managed to reach the shore alone, but only to
meet with a more barbarous fate a few hours afterwards.

And now I was a captive in a French prison, and
without any hope of liberty before me, for our shipwreck occurred during the middle of the war in Spain,
where we were fighting Buonaparte, and there were at
this time no signs of peace. My feelings as I marched
along with my comrades to the town prison were those
of a captive condemned to transportation. I thought of
my wife and family, and tortured myself with a thousand anxieties as to their fate. Life but a few hours
before had seemed very precious; now it appeared
almost worthless. In the reaction of mind and body
following the great exertion and excitement I had just
passed through, a feeling of deep despondency over-
came me, which I found it difficult to contend against.

However, I had to rouse myself and act for my
fellows in misfortune. Having reached the prison,

we were placed in some small, dark, filthy cells, such as were allotted to common felons, three or four of us being crowded into each, with no distinction between black and white. I at once sent for the gaoler, and asked him if he could not accommodate the Europeans of our party better. Whereupon he offered to give us up his own quarters if we would make over to him the whole of the Government allowance we were entitled to receive. This, in default of any other arrangement being then possible, I consented to, and we were removed, to three comfortable rooms that he and his family usually occupied.

The next morning, having finished breakfast, we were discussing our situation, when the gaoler entered and said that a gentleman desired to see me. Following him to a private room, I found a large burly man standing there. I bowed to him and asked him his pleasure.

"Sir," he replied, "my name is Hodges, and I am a countryman of your own, and have come to offer you any assistance that is in my power."

I expressed my appreciation of his kindness but desired him to explain how, being an Englishman, he retained his freedom.

"The nature of my profession protects me," he replied. "In short, I am a smuggler, and have many friends and clients in this port, with whom I do a large trade. I am bound on business to England to-morrow, and if you, or any of your party, desire to have news of your safety carried to your friends, I shall be very happy to convey the same."

I thanked him very heartily, and immediately informed my fellow-prisoners of his offer, of which they

very gratefully availed themselves. Mr Hodges having
followed me into the room, we gave him a list of the
names and addresses of all the people we desired him
to communicate with, and these he wrote down in his
pocket-book, and bidding us good-bye, departed.

Shortly after this, a deputation of townspeople,
representing a committee that had been formed on
our behalf, called upon us. They informed us, that
most of the inhabitants of the town having witnessed
our dreadful shipwreck, had expressed a desire to raise
a public subscription to assist us, and accordingly
arrangements had been made with an innkeeper in
the place to supply us with whatever we required for
our table, whilst another person would attend to
furnish us with any clothes we might want. Furthermore a sum of ready money was placed at our disposal,
to obtain any other necessaries we desired. Nothing
could exceed the liberality and charity of these good
people, whose timely aid and generous sympathy left
us powerless to express our thanks sufficiently.

In addition to this, General O'Mara, who commanded at Dunkirk, directed one of the three Town
Majors to call every morning and see that we did not
want for anything. One of these, on the fourth day
from our landing, asked us if there had not been a
gentleman on board "*who was very tall and an extraordinary dressing man*", and giving such a description
of his appearance that we recognized it at once as
referring to Lieutenant Tench. He then informed us
that the poor gentleman had actually reached the
shore by swimming, but in a most exhausted state,
and had been discovered by one of the *Garda Costa*,
to whom he had offered two guineas to assist him to

some habitation. A soldier coming up whilst he was speaking, and wishing to share the reward, he and the coast-guard began to quarrel, and it ended in the former murdering poor Tench in cold blood, and rifling his pockets, in which were found nearly three hundred guineas in gold. I remembered that Lieutenant Tench had taken charge of this very sum during the storm, for a Mrs Major Midwinter, who was a passenger on board. The horror of the deed so haunted the coast-guard, that he presently came into Dunkirk and confessed the act, whilst the murderer fled to the woods. He was, however, soon captured, and both men were brought and confined in the same prison with us. On the first examination the coast-guard denied all that he had confessed, saying he had spoken out of malice, as he had a private quarrel with the soldier; but my recognition of the murdered man from the description which the coast-guard himself had given, and my knowledge of the money found upon his person, proved that the confession was true. Search parties were then sent out to try and find Lieutenant Tench's corpse, and it was eventually discovered much wounded and hacked about. The inhabitants – particularly the women – were outrageous against these two vile men, who never quitted the prison for the court without being hooted at and pelted on the way; and they both eventually expiated their crime by death.

Nothing could exceed the kindness of every one in the place to us. I daily received invitations to dine out, which by the courtesy of General O'Mara, who granted me parole, I was able to accept. A short while afterwards the deputation paid us a second visit, when they signified their intention of petitioning for our release, and a day or two later brought a letter ready written, and addressed to the Emperor Buonaparte, for my signature, which I appended on behalf of my fellow-prisoners. It was forwarded to the Minister of Marine, but many days elapsed without an answer. Whereupon the commandant of the town, who had great interest, his sister being married to the Minister of War; and his brother being *aide de camp* to Buonaparte, drew up a petition which he sent to his brother, desiring him to present it personally to his Majesty. This was done, and no sooner had the Emperor read it, than he sent for the Minister of Marine, demanding the letter which I had signed. This being presented to him he read it, and immediately with his own hand wrote on the back of it an order for our release, and directed that we should be sent back to England at the expense of the French Government.

This joyful news was soon transmitted to Dunkirk, and the Deputy Commissary of Marine of that place, dressed in full uniform, waited upon us in prison to announce the Emperor's order. Our surprise and joy was unbounded, the reprieve being one quite unheard of in those days. General O'Mara immediately gave us permission to quit the prison, and we received numerous invitations from the townspeople to stay with them so long as we remained in the place. On the following evening I was invited to the theatre to receive the congratulations of several families who had interested themselves on our behalf. It was surprising what an effect our shipwreck had created, the many terrible circumstances connected with it having occurred under public observation, and excited a universal sympathy that found an outlet in all these acts of kindness.

Hearing of our good fortune, the deputation waited upon us again to say that "under our present circumstances they left it to us, as gentlemen, to determine whether we chose to leave Dunkirk under obligations for the expenses we had incurred." Having thanked them for their frankness, we assured them that nothing was farther from our thoughts than to remain indebted to them after we were free, and we forthwith settled to repay them the sum they had expended directly we reached London.

I then asked if there was anything we could do to prove our appreciation of their treatment of us, and in reply they gave me a list of about 150 of their townspeople who were prisoners in England, and the places of their confinement, asking my good offices to procure their release if possible. this I gladly agreed to. I was especially interested in the fate of the son of an old gentleman, who had formerly been a banker, but who was now confined for debt in the same prison as we had been; and also of a fisherman, the husband of a woman who waited upon us at our meals; and for both of whom I promised the exertion of my best endeavour.

I must not omit to relate, as a small tribute to his worth, the noble integrity of the smuggler, Mr Hodges. He had taken my address, and called upon my agents, Messrs Porcher and Company, to acquaint them of my safety, directly he reached London. He further offered, as he was leaving again on business for France, to deliver to me any letter they might entrust to his care. Mr Porcher was so pleased with this man, that he desired to give him a cheque for ten pounds. But this the honest smuggler sturdily refused, protesting that he had come to London on his own business, and not on mine, and that he would accept no reward for such an act of common humanity to a fellow-countryman in distress, as he had been able to render me. He called the next morning for the letter, which he gave to me at Dunkirk three days afterwards. Drawing me on one side to deliver it, he said he had brought me two pounds of coffee and four pounds of sugar for my acceptance, and he capped this act of kindness by offering to supply me with any money I might want.

This, at such a season, and to a person situated as I was, appeared a favour of no ordinary kind. I said I would accept twenty guineas, and further desired him to take charge of a valuable gold time-piece and deliver it to my wife, which he readily consented to do. I then proceeded to write out an order on my agents for thirty pounds, for the money he was lending me, and the balance for the trouble and care of taking my time-piece, which had cost me a hundred guineas, so that I was most anxious to send it to a place of safety. On reading the bill to him, he said I had made it too much, as he had bought the guineas for twenty-three shillings each, which made my debt to him only twenty-three pounds, and that he would not accept of any recompense for the care of the watch. "In that case," I observed, "I will take it back, for the obligation is too much." "You can do as you like," he answered; "I can only say I shall be very sorry if you do." Perceiving he was hurt, I at once said, "Take it, and God bless you for a friend in need." I then wrote out a new order

for the lesser sum, and gave it him, and also three
letters,* all of which, together with my watch, he
safely delivered to my agents.

* One of these letters is before the compiler now, the ink grey and
faded, the paper yellow and stained, and the rude wafer still
adhering to its back, that sealed it eighty years ago. Here are its
contents: –

"DUNKIRK PRISON, *January* 16, 1811.

'MY DEAR LUCY,

"I have left nothing undone to make up as much as possible the
blot I am at present to my family and the world. After, my dear
girl, suffering in danger and horror of mind attending our wreck,
to be led a prisoner and captive, and confined in a jail with felons
full of vermine. This, Lucy, would be nothing, did not keen
reflection come over my mind for the fate of my family. Thank
God, with strict economy, you will be able to live comfortably on
the interest, and spare your poor husband a mite. Fifty guineas a
year shall be the outside. What is against us is the total loss of
cloathes, and being obliged to buy at an enormous price. I have
already laid out £15, which will do but little. I have no business
with much cloathes, they must be put over one's shoulders during
the march, for we are considered as Prisoners of War, and expect to
be marched up-country to Arras immediately. We have been very
kindly treated by some of the inhabitants, particularly by the house
of Richard Faber and Company, to whom all remittances are to be
made. A Mr Hodges, who is going to England, has proved a kind
friend. He takes over my gold timepiece to be delivered to Messrs
Porcher and Company. I have desired it to be sent to you. For
God's sake take care of it, as it is of considerable value through the
correctness of its going. I have written to Messrs Porcher and
Company and Mr Morris to assist you. I hope all the papers are
taken care of. The letters of Captain Hutton for £400 insurance are
of the utmost importance. I hope Mr Allport and some friends will
assist you. God Almighty bless you is the prayer of your unfortunate husband. Write to me by bearer, for God's sake, by this
gentleman to whose kindness I am much indebted. Love to Eliza
and Willie. Your affectionate husband,

"R. W. EASTWICK.

"P.S. – For God's sake write instantly by this good friend."

To return to where I broke off in my narrative. Arrangements were made for our leaving Dunkirk, and on the morning of the 30th of January we embarked on a large French pilot boat, with a post-captain of the French navy to accompany us, and flying the Cartel flag. We had a fair wind, and made the passage across the Straits in six hours. Our sensations as we neared the shore of our own country I will not attempt to describe. We, who had expected a long captivity in French prisons, found ourselves free, and the white Kentish cliffs were a glad sight to eyes that had given up all hope of seeing them for years and years. Our release from captivity seemed almost as wonderful as our escape from the shipwreck.

Having entered Dover harbour, we landed, and were at once surrounded by persons from the different hotels, clamouring recommendations of their several houses. We went to Wright's, and having obtained permission for the French captain to dine with us, I ordered a hasty dinner, so as to leave in an hour, which was all the time he could spare. It was a very plain meal, and we drank but little, yet the charge was exorbitant – four pounds fifteen shillings for a party of seven, I think. I did not say anything, but handed the waiter a five-pound note, telling him to keep the remainder for his trouble. Whereupon the impertinent fellow said he considered it very little. My anger was now aroused, and I desired him to return the note, but as he did not do so I rang for the landlord, and when he appeared mentioned what had occurred, and declared if the man was not discharged, I would publish the treatment I had received in every London newspaper on my arrival. Mr Wright assured me he felt so indignant at the waiter's conduct, that he had already made up his mind to discharge him, even had I not urged it. He made a thousand apologies, and begged me not to injure the reputation of his house by publishing the matter, and he offered to reduce the bill to any amount I considered fair. This, I told him, was not my object; but I recommended him in future to pay more personal attention to the care of his customers, if he would not have comparisons drawn (to his disadvantage) between the treatment at his tavern and that in a French prison.

Saying good-bye to the French officer, Captain Jackson and myself started at six o'clock in the mail coach, and by seven the next morning I was at my home, it being rather more than twenty-four hours since I had left Dunkirk. It is needless to say with what transports of joy my wife received me. She signalized the occasion by presenting me with my second daughter, Anna, five days later.

As for poor Captain Jackson, who had hastened back to comfort an affectionate mother, whom he had left in good health, he found that the shock of hearing of the shipwreck and his subsequent imprisonment had been too much for her, and that she had sunk under it, and was buried two days before his return. So that in one short month the unfortunate young man lost a young and beautiful wife, whose amiability of character attracted all who were brought into contact with her, and a kind and devoted mother to whom he was deeply attached. He was shortly afterwards obliged to set out again for India to rejoin his regiment, and I heard of his death a few months later, a victim to a violent fever.

The day after I arrived I waited on the Marquis of

Wellesley, who was Secretary of State for Foreign Affairs; he was engaged, but I stated the circumstances attending the release of the survivors of the *Elizabeth* to his secretary, Mr Harrison, and expressed a hope that his lordship would view the kindness of the inhabitants of Dunkirk in the way they desired. The next day his lordship sent for me, and informed me that as a matter of policy alone it would be wise to do as I requested, but that the matter did not depend upon him, and he could only promise me his interest, and referred me to the Transport Board, to which I immediately proceeded. The commissioners received me, and heard my story, and Captain Bowen very kindly agreed to all I asked, requesting me to give him the names and also the particulars of the French prisoners whose release was desired. This I immediately did from the list which was in my possession, and he promised me he would at once institute inquiries about them.

About nine days after this, on taking up a newspaper, I read with much gratification that their freedom had been granted to as many French prisoners as there were English captives sent home from Dunkirk. And not long after I received a most handsome letter from the committee of that town, returning me their grateful thanks for what I had done, but begging as a favour that their letter should not be noticed in the public journals, as the known partiality of the inhabitants of Dunkirk for the English might displease the Emperor. There was also an enclosure from the old gentleman the banker, who prayed God to bless me for having restored to him and his family a beloved son, whose freedom had enabled the father to arrange his affairs and procure release from prison; and also a message of thanks from the good woman who had waited on us in prison, and who was made happy by the return of her husband the fisherman.

Before I quit the subject I must once again mention Mr Hodges the smuggler. Finding that he had not cashed the order I had given him on my agents, Messrs Porcher and Company, I desired them, on his coming, to give him a cheque for £40, to repay my loan, and reward him for the safe delivery of my watch. He called on them shortly afterwards, but still adhered to his determination not to accept more than £23, the actual amount of my bill, and when urged to reconsider the matter, he observed that he was sorry that a reward should have been pressed upon him for the second time. My agents, as a last resource, said it was not in their power to deviate from my instructions, and begged he would enable them to carry the same out. But he replied he would rather leave town without getting anything at all than do as they wished, as he could not reconcile it to his conscience to accept payment for what he had done. Such was the noble and disinterested conduct of a smuggler!

We saw him once again, for he called at my house to congratulate me on my freedom, and it was a great pleasure to show him, by the warmth of our welcome and some trifling hospitality, how great an obligation we felt towards him. And I am glad to add that about two years afterwards I had the gratification, through the interest of a friend, of preventing his son (who had been taken in some smuggling transaction) from being sent on board a man-of-war, and securing his free pardon by representing the conduct of his father to us captives at Dunkirk.

Robert Hay

A Pressed Man

1811

Short on pay, long on punishment, the Royal Navy
found itself distinctly underwhelmed with volunteers
for service in the eighteenth and early nineteenth
centuries. Its chief method of recruitment thus be-
came the official Impress Service. Most pressed men
were taken from merchant ships as they sailed into
port, but as 22-year-old seaman Robert Hay dis-
covered, the "Press Gang" also operated on shore.

I was when crossing Towerhill* accosted by a person
in seamen's dress who tapped me on the shoulder
enquiring in a familiar and technical strain "what
ship?" I assumed an air of gravity and surprise and
told him I presumed he was under some mistake as I
was not connected with shipping. The fellow, however, was too well acquainted with his business to be
thus easily put off. He gave a whistle and in a moment

* In London.

I was in the hands of six or eight ruffians who I immediately dreaded and soon found to be a press gang. They dragged me hurriedly along through several streets amid bitter execrations bestowed on them, expressions of sympathy directed towards me and landed me in one of their houses of rendezvous. I was immediately carried into the presence of the Lieutenant of the gang, who questioned me as to my profession, whither I had ever been to sea, and what business had taken me to Towerhill. I made some evasive answers to these interrogations and did not acknowledge having been at sea: but my hands being examined and found hard with work, and perhaps a little discoloured with tar, overset all my hesitating affirmations and I was remanded for further examination.

Some of the gang then offerred me Spirits and attempted to comfort me under my misfortune, but like the friends of Job, miserable comforters were they all. The very scoundrel who first laid hold of me put on a sympathising look and observed what a pity it was to be pressed when almost within sight of the mast of the Scotch Smacks. Such sympathy from such a source was well calculated to exasperate my feelings, but to think of revenge was folly and I had patiently to listen to their mock pity.

I trembled exceedingly in the fear that they would inspect my small bundle, for in it there were a pair of numbered stockings,* which would not only have made them suppose I had been at sea, but would have given them good reason to think I had been in a war

---

* Purser's issue.

ship. I contrived, however, to slip them out unobserved and concealed them behind one of the benches and thus had my fears a little moderated.

In a short time I was reconducted for further examination before the Lieutenant, who told me as I was in his hands and would assuredly be kept I might as well make a frank confession of my circumstances, it would save time and insure me better treatment. What could I do? I might indeed have continued sullen and silent, but whither such procedure might or might not have procured me worse treatment, one thing I knew it would not restore me to liberty. I therefore acknowledged that I had been a voyage to the West Indies and had come home Carpenter of a ship. His eye seemed to brighten at this intelligence. "I am glad of that, my lad," said he, "we are very much in want of Carpenters. Step along with these men and they will give you a passage on board." I was then led back the way I came by the fellow who first seized me, put aboard of a pinnace at Tower Wharf and by midday was securely lodged on board the *Enterprise*.

As soon as the boat reached the ship I was sent down into the great cabin, in various parts of which tables were placed covered with green cloth, loaded with papers and surrounded with men well dressed and powdered. Such silence prevailed and such solemn gravity was displayed in every countenance that I was struck with awe and dread. The tables were so placed as to give the whole of those seated at them a fair opportunity of narrowly scrutinizing every unhappy wretch that was brought in. No sooner did I enter the cabin door than every eye was darted on me. Mine were cast down and fearing there might be some of the

inquisitors who knew me I scarcely dared to raise them
all the time I remained in the cabin.

A short sketch of what had passed between the press
officer and myself had been communicated to the
examining officer, for when I was ushered into his
presence he thus addressed me:

"Well, young man, I understand you are a carpenter
by trade."

"Yes, sir."

"And you have been at sea?"

"One voyage, sir."

"Are you willing to join the King's Service?"

"No, sir."

"Why?"

"Because I get much better wages in the merchant
service and should I be unable to agree with the
Captain I am at Liberty to leave him at the end of
the voyage."

"As to wages," said he, "the chance of prize money
is quite an equivalent and obedience and respect
shown to your officers are all that is necessary to
insure you good treatment. Besides," continued he,
"you may in time be promoted to be carpenter of a line
of Battle ship when your wages will be higher than in
the merchant service, and should any accident happen
to you, you will be provided for."

I argued under great disadvantage. My interogator
was like a judge on the bench; I like a criminal at the
bar, and I had not fortitude to make any reply.

"Take my advice, my lad," continued he, "and
enter the service cheerfully, you will then have a
bounty, and be in a fair way for promotion. If you
continue to refuse, remember you are aboard (cogent

reasoning), you will be kept as a pressed man and treated accordingly."

I falteringly replied that I could not think of engaging in any service voluntarily when I knew of a better situation elsewhere. He said no more, but making a motion with his hand I was seized by two marines, hurried along towards the main hatchway with these words thundered in my ears, "A pressed man to go below." What injustice and mockery, thought I, first to have that best of blessings, liberty, snatched from me and then insulted by a seeming offer of allowing me to act with freedom! But my doom was fixed and I was thrust down among five or six score of miserable beings, who like myself had been kidnapped, and immured in the confined and unwholesome dungeon of a press room.

Here I had full leisure for reflection, but my reflection was very far from being of the agreeable kind. A few hours before I had entered London possessed of Liberty and buoyed up with animating hope. Now, I was a slave immured in a dungeon and surrounded by despair. I had proceeded from Hyde Park Corner in as direct a line as lanes and alleys would admit and had just fallen directly into those merciless hands I so anxiously wished to avoid. Such is the blindness of human nature! We are often on the very brink of a precipice when we think ourselves in the utmost safety and dream not of impending danger.

By some mismanagement on the part of the pursers stewart [d], I was left all that day without food and would have been so the seccond day also, for I had not yet assumed courage to make application, but that two or three of the most humane of the seamen, noticing me, took me into their mess, and applied for my allowance of provisions. With the exception of these few I was generally treated with ridicule and contempt. Seamen who have been pressed together into one ship have usually a great affection for one another. Their trade, their habits, their misfortunes are the same and they become endeared to each other by a similarity of sufferings; but my landward appearance placed me in some measure beyond the pale of sympathy. I was styled by way of distinction and ridicule "the Gentleman", and was considered a priviledged butt for the shafts of nautical witt and banter to be levelled at. I must allow this did not affect me greatly. I knew that I myself had often joined in the same strain of Irony against those who had been brought on board the *Salvador* in landsmans' clothing, and I was now merely getting paid in my own coin. Hence, however, I resolved never again to mock at the sufferings more especially when I had no other reason for such conduct than a difference of occupation or professional habits. I soon became accustomed to the jokes and when any of these nautical punsters brandished their knife and threatened to unbend my ringtail and water sail (the name of the sails set abaft the spanker and below the spanker boom), I calmly tucked up my skirts and tucking them up behind buttoned my coat closely so that they could not accomplish their purpose without coming in front to disengage the button, by which I would have been put upon my guard. I was forced to observe this precaution every night otherwise I would soon have been stumped.

Once or twice a day a limited number were permitted to go on deck to breath the fresh air, but from

the surly manner in which we were treated it was easy
to observe that it was not for our pleasure this indulgence was granted, but to preserve our healths, which
would have soon been greatly endangered had not a
little fresh air been occasionally mixed with the pes-
tiferous breaths and pestilential vapours of the press
room. I remained in this ship something more than a
week, when she became so crowded as to render the
removal of a considerable number a measure of necessity. I, among a considerable number of others, was
put aboard of a cutter when we were very closely
confined, never seeing anything on our passage down
the river but the sky divided into minute squares by
the gratings which covered our dungeon.

We arrived at the Nore shortly after dusk and were
immediately put on board the *Ceres*, guardship. I
rejoiced at its being dark when we were taken aboard
because I thus escaped the prying observation of four
or five hundred gazers among whom I thought it
probable that some one or other would know me.
The following day I got blended with a motley crowd
and was less taken notice of than I would have been at
my first entrance.

Here I considered it folly to dress any longer in my
landsmans habillements. I therefore purchased a sec-
condhand jacket, trowsers and check shirt, in which I
equipped myself and packed up my long coat,
breeches, vest, white neckcloth, etc., lest I should
on some future occasion require their services. What
became of them will be seen in the sequel.

Next morning my acquaintances were greatly surprised to see how completely I had been metamor-
phosed. Not only was my external appearance greatly

changed, but my manners were still more so. Hitherto
I had preserved the greatest taciturnity. I knew that
had I talked much sea phrases would have slipped and
I thought it as well that my behaviour and my dis-
course should correspond with my appearance. Hence
credit was given me for far more wisdom, learning and
politeness than I possessed. How easy then is it to be
thought wise? It is merely to preserve silence and
though we may not thereby give an opportunity of
displaying our wisdom and wit we with great ease can
conceal our ignorance and folly.

I now became somewhat loquacious, probably in
order to make up former lee way, and as I could with
great volubility string together the technical terms of
seamanship, I was soon on a footing with the rest. Next
day my shipmates being in a humorous mood, I flour-
ished my knife over my head, offered a quart of grog to
any one who would point me out the gentleman as I was
determined to close reef him. This was as good to them
as if it had been sterling wit. They all burst out a
laughing, considered me a shrewd fellow and hence-
forth rated my nautical abilities as much too high as they
before had my learning and politeness. Not one of my
shipmates knew my name, except one that was pressed
shortly after myself who called me by name as soon as he
came aboard, and who was no other than one of my
shipmates in the *Edward*. One of those who seized the
boat and pulled ashore in spite of the Captains remon-
strances and threats. Bill, Tom, Dick, Bob, Jack came
all alike familiar to me and when I knew I was spoken to
I answered to all of them promiscuously.

In this ship we had liberty to go on deck at all hours
and were therefore much more comfortable than when

on board the *Enterprise* or cutter. Our distance from
the shore being only about 6 or 8 miles, the land was
seen very clearly and many an anxious, earnest look
did I take of it. Frequently would I feast my eyes for
hours together gazing on it, and my imagination in
forming schemes how to gain it. No hopes or at least
very distant ones could be entertained of success. The
distance from the shore was in itself no small barrier,
but what made the attempt most hazardous, there was
only one point of land where there was any probability
of making a landing at all. This was on a small Island, I
think called Grain. But how was this point to be gained
in the dark? If I went to the right I would be taken up
the Thames and carried to sea at the return of the tide.
If I went to the left I would be carried in amongst the
ships in Sheerness, where I would be sure to be
observed, and either picked up by some of the war
boats, or shot by some of the centinels on duty.

But even suppose the point gained. Still insuperable
difficulties seemed to present themselves. How could I
escape observation in my wet seamans clothes? How
could I pass from that Island to the main? How could I
travel anywhere without being intercepted? But were
even all these obstacles surmountable, how was it
possible to escape from the ship guarded as she was
by Midshipmen, quartermasters, ships corporals and
marines? On a review of all these circumstances any
attempt to escape seemed impracticable, but as the
thoughts of it were easily enough indulged in I was
constantly meditating on the subject.

Amongst those who were pressed about the same time
as myself was a man a few years older than I, a native of

Hartley, by the name of John Patterson. I often observed him casting many a wishfull look to the shore, and often heard him utter a half suppressed sigh as he turned his eyes from it. He doubtless had observed my conduct also, for he frequently looked very earnestly at me as we had occasion to pass each other. We soon came on speaking terms, and from that time forth seemed to enjoy much pleasure in each other's company. Still, however, we abstained from introducing a subject in which it was evident enough both of us had very closely at heart. It was not till after a good many days acquaintanceship had elapsed and many conversations on indifferent topics held that we ventured to open our minds to each other. This was done slowly and with great precaution at first, but soon finding how much our sentiments were in unison we dismissed reserve and became inseperable. From this time almost the whole subject of our thoughts and conversation was the means of escape. All the various ways in which there was the least probability of success were calmly and diliberately discussed, and the arguments for and against them duly weighed. Whatever view we took of the matter, obstacles seemingly insurmountable presented themselves to our view, and had the prize been anything less than the recovery of our liberty, we would have dispaired of success.

"He," says the proverb, "who thinks an object unattainable makes it so." So we resolved to think our escape within the bounds of possibility. Our first consideration was, How were we to get clear of the ship and reach the shore? We at length confined our attention solely to these points, resolved to make the attempt and leave the rest to providence.

Our first step was to procure some bladders which we easily prevailed with one of the men belonging to the ships boats to purchase. We then tore up some old shirts and made them into long narrow bags, large enough to hold a bladder when full blown, and of sufficient length to go round the body below the arm pits. Straps were attached to pass over each shoulder, and one to pass between the legs in order to keep all in a proper position. We had seven bladders in whole, of which Patterson had three large and I four small – our quantity of wind would be about the same, but my four distributing the wind more regularly round the body afterwards proved the most comodious.

At this time the ship was very full of hands insomuch that there were not room for all hands to sleep below. A considerable number therefore slept in the waist hammock nettings. A place on the upper deck projecting a small bit beyond the ships side, where the greater number of beds and hammocks were stowed during the day. As both the sides and top of this place were covered with tarpaulins, we slept in it comfortable enough.

In this station did Patterson and I nightly place ourselves to watch a favourable opportunity of escape. We left our beds to the care of our messmates below, tied our bags of bladders in our coverlets to resemble a bed and free of all suspicion repaired to the hammock netting. Many nights passed away after our resolutions were taken and our preparations made before we were enabled to make the attempt. Some nights the tide did not suit, some it was too light, and some a very strict sentinel was on duty. Still, however, we adhered to our resolutions and our perseverance, as will be seen in the sequel, was crowned with success.

About the tenth or twelfth of October 1811, for I do not remember the precise date, conditions seemed to bid fair for our purpose. The weather was dark and lowering, the wind blew pretty fresh and to all appearance promised a wet night. What was of still greater consequence the tide exactly suited us. As the unfavourable, or I should rather say favourable, state of the weather continued till nightfall we resolved to attempt our project. Before dusk, we purchased and drank two or three glasses of rum each that we might stand the cold, bade adieu to a couple of our bosom confidants and then repaired to our station in the hammock netting.

When the evening drum beat a little before eight o'clock everything seemed favourable. The drum and the storm made noise enough to prevent our movements being heard, and the sentinel who paced the gangway was muffled closely up in his great coat.

When it came to the point my friend Patterson felt strongly inclined to draw back. All the dangers which we had before so amply discussed were again enumerated and amplified. With the same earnestness did I expatiate on the evils of slavery and enumerate the advantages that would result from our success. And how was success to be gained without exertion! My reasoning at last succeeded, and, fearing his resolution might forsake him after I was in the water, I prevailed on him to descend first.

When he gained the water the end of the rope got entangled about his foot and he gave a plunge to clear it. I trembled. The sound, increased as it was by my fears, seemed like the plunging of a grampus, but the noise was drowned by the surrounding storm. As soon as he was clear of the rope I slid softly down and slipped into the water without the smallest noise. I glided smoothly along close by the ship's side not daring to strike out lest my motion should be observed. I kept touching the ship's side with my hands as I floated along, and had thus an idea about how fast the tide carried me along. After I thought myself clear enough of the ship, I struck out and in a minute or two regained my companion. I found him very ill. In his strugle to clear himself of the rope he had swallowed some salt water which made him sick and when I overtook him I found him vomiting. I felt very unhappy on his account and soothed and encouraged him by all the means in my power. After his vomiting had ceased he grew better, and side by side we proceeded cheerily along. I had practised the art of swimming much more than my companion and could therefore proceed with much more ease and expedition. I amused myself with swimming round him relating anecdotes, chaunting in a low voice a verse or two of a song, etc., in encouraging him to put forth his strength. When he became fatigued we took each other by the hand and drifted slowly along untill we recovered strength to put forth farther exertion.

When two or three miles from the ship we were excessively alarmed by the sound of human voices, apparently near at hand and almost immediately observed a boat from the shore standing toward the ship we had quitted. From our relative position we saw she must pass us within a few fathoms. We were overwhelmed with dread and terror. We expected nothing else than to be picked up and taken back where we would have met with the most rigorous punishment and would probably have been put in iron besides as long as we remained in harbour. We dared not to swim out of her way lest the motion should have betrayed us, so that we had no other resource but remain motionless and trust to providence. As she approached our alarm increased. We strove to sink beneath the surface, but were prevented by the buoyancy of our bladders. Fortunately she was rather to windward and the belly of the sail hanging over the lee gunnel in some measure sheltered us from the observation of those on board. What was also in our favour the crew seemed intent on some subject of debate as a continued and indistinct sound proceeded from the boat as long as she was distinguishable. It may here be asked, had we no apprehension of steering a wrong course? We had none. We possessed a most excellent compass. This was no other than the large comet of 1811. We had frequently observed that it lay precisely over the point of land we wished to gain. We therefore shaped our course direct for it and it proved a faithful guide.*

After many a trial to feel ground, Patterson exclaimed with the joy and in the words of Archimedes, "I have found it, I have found it!" I was almost afraid to try lest I should be disappointed, but seeing him at rest I let down my feet and found ground at little more than half a fathom. We found the shore very shelving, for when we first felt the ground we could scarcely observe any traces of the land. I think we had to walk

---

* The comet of 1811 was brilliant for many weeks in the Northern Hemisphere, being specially conspicuous in the autumn of that year.

about three quarters of a mile before we gained the beach and fatiguing walking we found it. On reaching the beach we threw ourselves on our knees to return our united thanks to that being who had brought us deliverance from the mighty waters, and to implore future guidance, strength and fortitude to support us under whatever trials we might still have to endure.

When we had advanced a few paces, we saw a light and by crossing a field or two soon gained it. It proceeded from a pretty large house standing alone. A board resembling a sign was fixed over the door, but we could not see whither it bore any inscription. On knocking at the door a person appeared at the window from which the light proceeded and demanded our business. We dared not tell him our true circumstances, but feigned a story of distress. It however made no impression on him. He told us in a surly tone to be gone, that it was past midnight and that he was determined not to open his door at such an unseasonable hour for any person whatever. We then tried another house whence a light issued, but with no better success. How comfortable would a glass or two of rum have been to us shivering as we were with cold and wetness? but a glass of rum we could not obtain.

We left these houses to retrace our steps to where we landed, but missed our way. We soon however gained the beach at a different and at a much better place. It seemed to be a snug little cove in which a considerable number of small boats were lying. The project on which we mainly depended previous to leaving the ship was to seize a boat and pull over to the Essex shore whence we could go to Maldon by land. Patterson had been at Maldon and knew several of the captains of

coal vessels belonging to the North of England, which
traded there, so that we expected if we could reach that
place in safety it would not be dificult to procure a
passage to the Northward. When we saw so many
boats lying so oportunely, we were overjoyed and
already anticipated the completion of our projects.
After searching through a great number of them we
found one seemingly Dutch built that had a small sail
and a couple of oars aboard. This was just what we
wanted. We slipped her painter and as the wind was
southerly we set sail and stood as near as we could
guess North East. From being so long wet we were
very cold, but getting our oars out and pulling vigorously we soon brought ourselves into a state of agreeable warmth.

About an hour before day break we touched ground
with our oars, on which we hauled a little more to the
eastward resolving to get as far along shore as possible
before dawn. We heard the *Ceres* fire her morning gun
and had the happiness of seeing her hull down. It was
our intention to land before sun rise and we made
several attempts at this, but the shore was so shelving
that we could no where get within half a mile of the
shore. We therefore continued edging along shore as
near as the depth of water would admit. We saw a good
many vessels resembling light colliers bound to the
Northwards, but we could not think of venturing to
pull out to any of them lest they should betray us. We
could easily have coasted it along to Blackwater river
and have got in to Maldon with our boat, but we were
detterred from this by considering that our appearance
would have rendered us suspected, besides when day
broke we saw our sail was merely a man of war's

hammock, and this made our appearance still more suspicious. After a great many attempts during the morning and forenoon made to land, we, about midday, were fortunate enough to discover a small creek just wide enough to receive our boat. The water in it, being pretty deep, she did not ground untill her stern took the land, so that we were enabled to land without wetting our shoes. What became of the boat we never heard, but as we left her in a very snug berth and well moored, and as her owner's name was painted on the inside of her stern, we hoped, and doubted not, that the owner would ultimately recover her.

After passing a small earthen mound erected to keep the sea from breaking into the adjoining fields, we found ourselves on a delightful meadow. The sun was shining in meridian splendour, scarcely a cloud was to be seen in the wide expanse, the mild Zephyrs, as they skimmed along the fragrant meadow or over those fields which showed they had recently richly contributed to the support of man, seemed to whisper congratulations in our ear. We had just escaped from thralldom and were begining to taste the dawning sweets of that blessing so highly valued by Britons. Everything around us tended to exhilerate our spirits and we gave unrestrained scope to our feelings. Had any sober man seen us he would have undoubtedly questioned the soundness of our intellects. We leapt, we run, we rolled, we tumbled, we shouted, we gambolled in all the excess of joy and exultation, and it was not till several minutes elapsed that we could so far restrain the ebulitions of our joy as to permit us to set out on our journey. Observing a farm house at some distance we made up to it and found only one woman

at home. The truth cannot always be told, nor could it
be told here. We were compelled to fabricate a story of
our shipwreck which we did with as few falsehoods as
the case would admit. But sh! how much more difficult
is it to scramble along the mazy paths of falsehood and
prevarication than in the broad plain and open way of
integrity and truth. With whatever care a falsehood
may be fabricated it is supported with the utmost
difficulty. A thousand questions may be put which
the utmost human ingenuity could not have anticipated and a thousand falsehoods have to be uttered in
support and confirmation of the first. The higher we
rear the baseless structure, the more tottering it be-
comes, till at length it falls with a mighty crash and
entombs its shuffling fabricators beneath its massy
ruins.

The woman into whose house we went was of a mild
and kindly disposition, more inclined to pity and
releive than to doubt and question. She herself had
a son who followed the seafaring business and who had
been several times wrecked, so that she felt towards all
those who suffered the same misfortune a kind of
maternal sympathy. She set before us what a well
stored pantry and dairy could afford, pressed us to
partake heartily, which we were both able and willing
to do, and at parting she would accept of no payment.
"Keep your money, my lads," said she, beaming a look
of kindness on us, "you have yet a long way to go (we
had told her we were for the North) and you know not
what you may yet need. May God bless you and
deliver you from all your dangers, as he has from this
last one." The gratitude excited in our breasts by this
genuine treat of English hospitality, blended with the

joy we felt at the recovery of our liberty, excited in us the most delightful emotions. Emotions which the greatest monarch on earth, possessed of unlimited power, abounding in riches, surrounded by flatterers, and wallowing in sensual pleasure, might well envy. We learned at this house that we were about 12 miles from Maldon, for which place, after taking an affectionate leave of our kind hostess, we set out. A luxuriant store of bramble berries by the roadside and a desire to avoid entering Maldon with day light induced us to linger a little by the way so that we did not reach Maldon till after dusk. We readily procured a bed to which after supper we immediately retired and soon made up for last night's lee way.

Isaac Hull

The Defeat of
HMS *Guerriere*

1812

The War of 1812 between Britain and the USA was a inglorious affray, fought for real but obscure reasons of blockades and maritime violations, but at heart a sort of tragic encore to the War of Independence. The Royal Navy, with 584 ships in full commission, was the mightiest maritime power in the world, while the US Navy could muster a mere 8 frigates, 12 sloops and some odd small craft for duties on the Great Lakes. This not withstanding, it managed to give the Royal Navy some nasty surprises, not least because its crews were trained to the highest standard but also because its big 44-gun frigates were superior to any frigate on the sea – as US Navy Captain Isaac Hull found to his pleasure in August 1812.

United State's frigate *Constitution*, off Boston
Light, 30 August 1812

I have the honour to inform you, that on the 19th
instant, at 2 p.m. being in latitude 41, 42, longitude
55, 48, with the *CONSTITUTION* under my command, a sail was discovered from the mast-head
bearing E. by S. or E.S.E. but at such a distance
we could not tell what she was. All sail was instantly
made in chase, and soon found we came up with her.
At 3 p.m. could plainly see that she was a ship on
the starboard tack, under easy sail, close on a wind;
at half past 3 p.m. made her out to be a frigate;
continued the chase until we were within about three
miles, when I ordered the light sails taken in, the
courses hauled up, and the ship cleared for action.
At this time the chase had backed his main top-sail,
waiting for us to come down. As soon as the *CON-
STITUTION* was ready for action, I bore down
with an intention to bring him to close action immediately; but on our coming within gun-shot she
gave us a broadside and filled away, and then were
giving us a broadside on the other tack, but without
effect; her shot falling short. She continued wearing
and manoeuvreing for about three quarters of an
hour, to get a raking position, but finding she could
not, she bore up, and run under top-sails and gib,
with the wind on the quarter. Immediately made sail
to bring the ship up with her, and 5 minutes before
6 p.m. being along side within half pistol shot, we
commenced a heavy fire from all our guns, double
shotted with round and grape, and so well directed
were they, and so warmly kept up, that in 15
minutes his mizen-mast went by the board, and

his main-yard in the slings, and the hull, rigging and sails very much torn to pieces. The fire was kept up with equal warmth for 15 minutes longer, when his main-mast and fore-mast went, taking with them every spar, excepting the bowsprit; on seeing this we ceased firing, so that in 30 minutes after we got fairly along side the enemy she surrendered, and had not a spar standing, and her hull below and above water so shattered, that a few more broadsides must have carried her down.

After informing you that so fine a ship as the *GUER-RIERE*, commanded by an able and experienced officer, had been totally dismasted, and otherwise cut to pieces, so as to make her not worth towing into port, in the short space of 30 minutes, you can have no doubt of the gallantry and good conduct of the officers and ship's company I have the honour to command. It only remains, therefore, for me to assure you, that they all fought with great bravery; and it gives me great pleasure to say, that from the smallest boy in the ship to the oldest seaman, not a look of fear was seen. They all went into action, giving three cheers, and request-ing to be laid close along side the enemy.

Enclosed I have the honour to send you a list of killed and wounded on board the *CONSTITUTION*, and a report of the damages she has sustained; also, a list of the killed and wounded on board the enemy, with his quarter bill, &c.

Killed and wounded on board the United States' frigate *CONSTITUTION*, Isaac Hull, Esqr. Cap-

tain, in the action with his Britannic majesty's frigate
GUERRIERE, James A. Dacres, Esqr. Captain, on
the 20th of August, 1812:

Killed	– W. S. Bush, lieutenant of Marines, and six seamen,	7
Wounded	– lieutenant C. Morris J. C. Aylwin, four seamen, one marine,	7
Total	killed and wounded,	14

Killed and wounded on board the *GUERRIERE*.

Killed	– 3 officers, 12 seamen and marines,	15
Wounded	– J. A. Dacres, captain, 4 officers, 57 seamen and marines,	62
Missing	– lieutenants Pullman and Roberts, and 22 seamen and marines	24
Total	killed, wounded and missing,	101

Samuel Leech

Frigate Engagement: HMS *Macedonian* v. USS *United States*

1812

Unfortunately for the Royal Navy, the bad news about the superiority of the US Navy's big frigates was slow to travel. On 25 October 1812, the hapless 38-gun HMS Macedonian *encountered the 44-gun USS* United States, *a classic case of a minnow trying to bite a piranha, as Samuel Leech, on the fifth gun of the* Macedonian's *deck discovered to many of his messmates' cost.*

At Plymouth we heard some vague rumors of a declaration of war against America. More than this, we could not learn, since the utmost care was taken to prevent our being fully informed. The reason of this secrecy was, probably, because we had several Americans in our crew, most of whom were pressed men, as before stated. These men, had they been certain that war had broken out, would have given themselves up as prisoners of war, and claimed exemption from that unjust service, which compelled them to act with the enemies of their country. This was a privilege which the magnanimity of our officers ought to have offered them. They had already perpetrated a grievous wrong upon them in impressing them; it was adding cruelty to injustice to compel their service in a war against their own nation. But the difficulty with naval officers is, that they do not treat with a sailor as with a *man*. They know what is fitting between each other as officers; but they treat their crews on another principle; they are apt to look at them as pieces of living mechanism, born to serve, to obey their orders, and administer to their wishes without complaint. This is alike a bad morality and a bad philosophy. There is often more real manhood in the forecastle than in the ward-room; and until the common sailor is treated *as a man*, until every feeling of human nature is conceded to him in naval discipline – perfect, rational subordination will never be attained in ships of war, or in merchant vessels. It is needless to tell of the intellectual degradation of the mass of seamen. "A man's a man for a' that", and it is this very system of discipline, this treating them as automatons, which keeps them degraded. When will human nature put more confidence in itself?

Leaving Plymouth, we next anchored, for a brief space, at Torbay, a small port in the British Channel. We were ordered thence to convoy a huge East India merchant vessel, much larger than our frigate and having five hundred troops on board, bound to the

East Indies with money to pay the troops stationed there. We set sail in a tremendous gale of wind. Both ships stopped two days at Madeira to take in wine and a few other articles. After leaving this island, we kept her company two days more; and then, according to orders, having wished her success, we left her to pursue her voyage, while we returned to finish our cruise.

Though without any positive information, we now felt pretty certain that our government was at war with America. Among other things, our captain appeared more anxious than usual; he was on deck almost all the time; the "look-out" aloft was more rigidly observed; and every little while the cry of "Mast-head there!" arrested our attention.

It is customary in men-of-war to keep men at the fore and main mast-heads, whose duty it is to give notice of every new object that may appear. They are stationed in the royal yards, if they are up, but if not, on the topgallant yards: at night a look-out is kept on the fore yard only.

Thus we passed several days; the captain running up and down and constantly hailing the man at the mast-head: early in the morning he began his charge "to keep a good look-out", and continued to repeat it until night. Indeed, he seemed almost crazy with some pressing anxiety. The men felt there was something anticipated, of which they were ignorant; and had the captain heard all their remarks upon his conduct, he would not have felt very highly flattered. Still, everything went on as usual; the day was spent in the ordinary duties of man-of-war life, and the evening in telling stories of things most rare and wonderful; for your genuine old tar is an adept in spinning yarns, and some of them, in respect to variety and length, might safely aspire to a place beside the great magician of the north, Sir Walter Scott, or any of those prolific heads that now bring forth such abundance of fiction to feed a greedy public, who read as eagerly as our men used to listen. To this yarn-spinning was added the most humorous singing, sometimes dashed with a streak of the pathetic, which I assure my readers was most touching; especially one very plaintive melody, with a chorus beginning with,

"Now if our ship should be cast away,
It would be our lot to see old England no more,"

which made rather a melancholy impression on my boyish mind, and gave rise to a sort of presentiment that the *Macedonian* would never return home again; a presentiment which had its fulfilment in a manner totally unexpected to us all. The presence of a shark for several days, with its attendant pilot fish, tended to strengthen this prevalent idea.

The Sabbath came, and it brought with it a stiff breeze. We usually made a sort of holiday of this sacred day. After breakfast it was common to muster the entire crew on the spar deck, dressed as the fancy of the captain might dictate; sometimes in blue jackets and white trowsers, or blue jackets and blue trowsers; at other times in blue jackets, scarlet vests, and blue or white trowsers with our bright anchor buttons glancing in the sun, and our black, glossy hats, ornamented with black ribbons, and with the name of our ship painted on them. After muster, we frequently had church service read by the captain; the rest of the day was devoted to idleness. But we were destined to spend the Sabbath, just introduced to the reader, in a very different manner.

We had scarcely finished breakfast, before the man at the mast-head shouted, "Sail ho!"

The captain rushed upon deck, exclaiming, "Mast-head there!"

"Sir!"

"Where away is the sail?"

The precise answer to this question I do not recollect, but the captain proceeded to ask, "What does she look like?"

"A square-rigged vessel, sir", was the reply of the look-out.

After a few minutes, the captain shouted again, "Mast-head there!"

"Sir!"

"What does she look like?"

"A large ship, sir, standing toward us!"

By this time, most of the crew were on deck, eagerly straining their eyes to obtain a glimpse of the approaching ship and murmuring their opinions to each other on her probable character. Then came the voice of the captain, shouting, "Keep silence, fore and aft!" Silence being secured, he hailed the look-out, who, to his question of "What does she look like?" replied, "A large frigate, bearing down upon us, sir!"

A whisper ran along the crew that the stranger ship was a Yankee frigate. The thought was confirmed by the command of "All hands clear the ship for action, ahoy!" The drum and fife beat to quarters; bulk-heads were knocked away; the guns were released from their confinement; the whole dread paraphernalia of battle was produced; and after the lapse of a few minutes of hurry and confusion, every man and boy was at his post, ready to do his best service for his country, except the band, who, claiming exemption from the affray, safely stowed themselves away in the cable tier. We had only one sick man on the list, and he, at the cry of battle, hurried from his cot, feeble as he was, to take his post of danger. A few of the junior midshipmen were stationed below, on the berth deck, with orders, given in our hearing, to shoot any man who attempted to run from his quarters.

Our men were all in good spirits; though they did not scruple to express the wish that the coming foe was a Frenchman rather than a Yankee. We had been told, by the Americans on board, that frigates in the American service carried more and heavier metal than ours. This, together with our consciousness of superiority over the French at sea, led us to a preference for a French antagonist.

The Americans among our number felt quite disconcerted at the necessity which compelled them to fight against their own countrymen. One of them, named John Card, as brave a seaman as ever trod a plank, ventured to present himself to the captain, as a prisoner, frankly declaring his objections to fight. That officer, very ungenerously, ordered him to his quarters, threatening to shoot him if he made the request again. Poor fellow! He obeyed the unjust command and was killed by a shot from his own countrymen. This fact is more disgraceful to the captain of the *Macedonian* than even the loss of his ship. It was a gross and a palpable violation of the rights of man.

As the approaching ship showed American colors, all doubt of her character was at an end. "We must fight her", was the conviction of every breast. Every possible arrangement that could insure success was accordingly made. The guns were shotted; the matches lighted; for, although our guns were all furnished with first-rate locks they were also provided with matches, attached by lanyards, in case the lock should miss fire. A lieutenant then passed through the ship, directing the marines and boarders, who were furnished with pikes, cutlasses, and pistols, how to proceed if it should be necessary to board the enemy. He was followed by the captain, who exhorted the men to fidelity and courage, urging upon their consideration the well-known motto of the brave Nelson, "England expects every man to do his duty." In addition to all these preparations on deck, some men were stationed in the tops with small-arms, whose duty it was to attend to trimming the sails and to use their muskets, provided we came to close action. There were others also below, called sail trimmers, to assist in working the ship should it be necessary to shift her position during the battle.

My station was at the fifth gun on the main deck. It was my duty to supply my gun with powder, a boy being appointed to each gun in the ship on the side we engaged, for this purpose. A woollen screen was placed before the entrance to the magazine, with a hole in it, through which the cartridges were passed to the boys; we received them there, and covering them with our jackets, hurried to our respective guns. These precautions are observed to prevent the powder taking fire before it reaches the gun.

Thus we all stood, awaiting orders, in motionless suspense. At last we fired three guns from the larboard side of the main deck; this was followed by the command, "Cease firing; you are throwing away your shot!"

Then came the order to "wear ship", and prepare to attack the enemy with our starboard guns. Soon after this I heard a firing from some other quarter, which I at first supposed to be a discharge from our quarter deck guns; though it proved to be the roar of the enemy's cannon.

A strange noise, such as I had never heard before, next arrested my attention; it sounded like the tearing of sails, just over our heads. This I soon ascertained to be the wind of the enemy's shot. The firing, after a few minutes' cessation, recommenced. The roaring of cannon could now be heard from all parts of our trembling ship, and, mingling as it did with that of our foes, it made a most hideous noise. By-and-by I heard the shot strike the sides of our ship; the whole scene grew indescribably confused and horrible; it was like some awfully tremendous thunder-storm, whose deafening roar is attended by incessant streaks of lightning, carrying death in every flash and strewing the ground with the victims of its wrath: only, in our case, the scene was rendered more horrible than that, by the presence of torrents of blood which dyed our decks.

Though the recital may be painful, yet, as it will reveal the horrors of war and show at what a fearful price a victory is won or lost, I will present the reader with things as they met my eye during the progress of this dreadful fight. I was busily supplying my gun with powder, when I saw blood suddenly fly from the arm of a man stationed at our gun. I saw nothing strike him; the effect alone was visible; in an instant, the third lieutenant tied his handkerchief round the wounded arm, and sent the groaning wretch below to the surgeon.

The cries of the wounded now rang through all parts of the ship. These were carried to the cockpit as fast as they fell, while those more fortunate men, who were killed outright, were immediately thrown overboard. As I was stationed but a short distance from the main hatchway, I could catch a glance at all who were carried below. A glance was all I could indulge in, for the boys belonging to the guns next to mine were wounded in the early part of the action, and I had to spring with all my might to keep three or four guns supplied with cartridges. I saw two of these lads fall nearly together. One of them was struck in the leg by a large shot; he had to suffer amputation above the wound. The other had a grape or canister shot sent through his ankle. A stout Yorkshireman lifted him in his arms and hurried him to the cockpit. He had his foot cut off, and was thus made lame for life. Two of the boys stationed on the quarter deck were killed. They were both Portuguese. A man, who saw one of them killed, afterwards told me that his powder caught fire and burnt the flesh almost off his face. In this pitiable situation, the agonized boy lifted up both hands, as if imploring relief, when a passing shot instantly cut him in two.

I was an eye-witness to a sight equally revolting. A

man named Aldrich had one of his hands cut off by a
shot, and almost at the same moment he received
another shot, which tore open his bowels in a terrible
manner. As he fell, two or three men caught him in
their arms, and, as he could not live, threw him
overboard.

One of the officers in my division also fell in my
sight. He was a noble-hearted fellow, named Nan
Kivell. A grape or canister shot struck him near the
heart: exclaiming, "Oh! my God!" he fell, and was
carried below, where he shortly after died.

Mr Hope, our first lieutenant, was also slightly
wounded by a grummet, or small iron ring, probably
torn from a hammock clew by a shot. He went below,
shouting to the men to fight on. Having had his wound
dressed, he came up again, shouting to us at the top of
his voice, and bidding us fight with all our might.
There was not a man in the ship but would have
rejoiced had he been in the place of our master's mate,
the unfortunate Nan Kivell.

The battle went on. Our men kept cheering with all
their might. I cheered with them, though I confess I
scarcely knew for what. Certainly there was nothing
very inspiriting in the aspect of things where I was
stationed. So terrible had been the work of destruction
round us, it was termed the slaughter-house. Not only
had we had several boys and men killed or wounded,
but several of the guns were disabled. The one I
belonged to had a piece of the muzzle knocked out;
and when the ship rolled, it struck a beam of the upper
deck with such force as to become jammed and fixed in
that position. A twenty-four-pound shot had also
passed through the screen of the magazine, immedi-

ately over the orifice through which we passed our
powder. The schoolmaster received a death wound.
The brave boatswain, who came from the sick bay to
the din of battle, was fastening a stopper on a back-stay
which had been shot away, when his head was smashed
to pieces by a cannon-ball; another man, going to
complete the unfinished task, was also struck down.
Another of our midshipmen also received a severe
wound. The unfortunate ward-room steward, who,
the reader will recollect, attempted to cut his throat on
a former occasion, was killed. A fellow named John,
who, for some petty offence, had been sent on board as
a punishment, was carried past me, wounded. I distinctly heard the large blood-drops fall pat, pat, pat, on
the deck; his wounds were mortal. Even a poor goat,
kept by the officers for her milk, did not escape the
general carnage; her hind legs were shot off, and poor
Nan was thrown overboard.

Such was the terrible scene, amid which we kept on
our shouting and firing. Our men fought like tigers.
Some of them pulled off their jackets, others their
jackets and vests; while some, still more determined,
had taken off their shirts, and, with nothing but a
handkerchief tied round the waistbands of their trowsers, fought like heroes. Jack Sadler, whom the reader
will recollect, was one of these. I also observed a boy,
named Cooper, stationed at a gun some distance from
the magazine. He came to and fro on the full run and
appeared to be as "merry as a cricket". The third
lieutenant cheered him along, occasionally, by saying,
"Well done, my boy, you are worth your weight in
gold."

I have often been asked what were my feelings

during this fight. I felt pretty much as I suppose every one does at such a time. That men are without thought when they stand amid the dying and the dead is too absurd an idea to be entertained a moment. We all appeared cheerful, but I know that many a serious thought ran through my mind: still, what could we do but keep up a semblance, at least, of animation? To run from our quarters would have been certain death from the hands of our own officers; to give way to gloom, or to show fear, would do no good, and might brand us with the name of cowards, and ensure certain defeat. Our only true philosophy, therefore, was to make the best of our situation by fighting bravely and cheerfully. I thought a great deal, however, of the other world; every groan, every falling man, told me that the next instant I might be before the Judge of all the earth. For this, I felt unprepared; but being without any particular knowledge of religious truth, I satisfied myself by repeating again and again the Lord's prayer and promising that if spared I would be more attentive to religious duties than ever before. This promise I had no doubt, at the time, of keeping; but I have learned since that it is easier to make promises amidst the roar of the battle's thunder, or in the horrors of shipwreck, than to keep them when danger is absent and safety smiles upon our path.

While these thoughts secretly agitated my bosom, the din of battle continued. Grape and canister shot were pouring through our port-holes like leaden rain, carrying death in their trail. The large shot came against the ship's side like iron hail, shaking her to the very keel, or passing through her timbers and scattering terrific splinters, which did a more appal-

ling work than even their own death-giving blows.
The reader may form an idea of the effect of grape and
canister, when he is told that grape shot is formed by
seven or eight balls confined to an iron and tied in a
cloth. These balls are scattered by the explosion of the
powder. Canister shot is made by filling a powder
canister with balls, each as large as two or three musket
balls; these also scatter with direful effect when discharged. What then with splinters, cannon balls, grape
and canister poured incessantly upon us, the reader
may be assured that the work of death went on in a
manner which must have been satisfactory even to the
King of Terrors himself.

Suddenly, the rattling of the iron hail ceased. We
were ordered to cease firing. A profound silence ensued, broken only by the stifled groans of the brave
sufferers below. It was soon ascertained that the enemy had shot ahead to repair damages, for she was not
so disabled but she could sail without difficulty; while
we were so cut up that we lay utterly helpless. Our
head braces were shot away; the fore and main topmasts were gone; the mizzen mast hung over the stern,
having carried several men over in its fall: we were in
the state of a complete wreck.

A council was now held among the officers on the
quarter deck. Our condition was perilous in the extreme: victory or escape was alike hopeless. Our ship
was disabled; many of our men were killed, and many
more wounded. The enemy would without doubt bear
down upon us in a few moments, and, as she could now
choose her own position, would without doubt rake us
fore and aft. Any further resistance was therefore folly.
So, in spite of the hot-brained lieutenant, Mr Hope,

who advised them not to strike, but to sink alongside, it was determined to strike our bunting. This was done by the hands of a brave fellow named Watson, whose saddened brow told how severely it pained his lion heart to do it. To me it was a pleasing sight, for I had seen fighting enough for one Sabbath; more than I wished to see again on a week day. His Britannic Majesty's frigate *Macedonian* was now the prize of the American frigate *United States*.

Before detailing the subsequent occurrences in my history, I will present the curious reader with a copy of Captain Carden's letter to the government, describing this action. It will serve to show how he excused himself for his defeat, as well as throw some light on those parts of the contest which were invisible to me at my station. My mother presented me with this document on my return to England. She had received it from Lord Churchill and had carefully preserved it for twenty years.

"*ADMIRALTY OFFICE,*
Dec. 29, 1812.

"*Copy of a letter from Captain John Surman Carden, late commander of His Majesty's ship the* Macedonian, *to John Wilson Croker, Esq., dated on board the American ship* United States, *at sea, the 28th October, 1812:*—

"*SIR: It is with the deepest regret, I have to acquaint you, for the information of my Lords Commissioners of the Admiralty, that His Majesty's late ship* Macedonian *was captured on the 25th instant, by the United States ship* United States,

Commodore Decatur commander. The detail is as follows:

"A short time after daylight, steering NW by W, with the wind from the southward, in latitude 29° N, and longitude 29° 30' W, in the execution of their Lordships' orders, a sail was seen on the lee beam, which I immediately stood for, and made her out to be a large frigate, under American colors. At nine o'clock I closed with her, and she commenced the action, which we returned; but from the enemy keeping two points off the wind, I was not enabled to get as close to her as I could have wished. After an hour's action, the enemy backed and came to the wind, and I was then enabled to bring her to close battle. In this situation I soon found the enemy's force too superior to expect success, unless some very fortunate chance occurred in our favor; and with this hope I continued the battle to two hours and ten minutes; when, having the mizzen mast shot away by the board, topmasts shot away by the caps, main yard shot in pieces, lower masts badly wounded, lower rigging all cut to pieces, a small proportion only of the fore-sail left to the foreyard, all the guns on the quarter deck and forecastle disabled but two, and filled with wreck, two also on the main deck disabled, and several shot between wind and water, a very great proportion of the crew killed and wounded, and the enemy comparatively in good order, who had now shot ahead and was about to place himself in a raking position, without our being enabled to return the fire, being a perfect wreck and unmanageable log; I deemed it prudent, though a painful extremity, to surrender His Majesty's ship; nor was this dreadful alternative

resorted to till every hope of success was removed, even beyond the reach of chance; nor till, I trust their Lordships will be aware, every effort had been made against the enemy by myself, and my brave officers and men, nor should she have been surrendered whilst a man lived on board, had she been manageable. I am sorry to say our loss is very severe; I find by this day's muster, thirty-six killed, three of whom lingered a short time after the battle; thirty-six severely wounded, many of whom cannot recover, and thirty-two slightly wounded, who may all do well; total, one hundred and four.

"The truly noble and animating conduct of my officers, and the steady bravery of my crew, to the last moment of the battle, must ever render them dear to their country.

"My first lieutenant, David Hope, was severely wounded in the head, towards the close of the battle, and taken below; but was soon again on deck, displaying that greatness of mind and exertion, which, though it may be equalled, can never be excelled. The third lieutenant, John Bulford, was also wounded, but not obliged to quit his quarters; second lieutenant, Samuel Mottley, and he deserves my highest acknowledgments. The cool and steady conduct of Mr Walker, the master, was very great during the battle, as also that of Lieutenants Wilson and Magill, of the Marines.

"On being taken on board the enemy's ship, I ceased to wonder at the result of the battle. The United States *is built with the scantling* of a 74-*

* Structure.

gun ship, mounting thirty long 24-pounders
(English ship-guns) on her main deck, and
twenty-two 42-pounders, carronades, with two
long 24-pounders, on her quarter deck and forecastle, howitzer guns in her tops, and a travelling
carronade on her upper deck, with a complement
of four hundred and seventy-eight picked men.

"The enemy has suffered much in masts, rigging, and hull, above and below water. Her loss in
killed and wounded I am not aware of; but I know
a lieutenant and six men have been thrown overboard.

JNO. S. CARDEN
"*To J. W. CROKER, Esq., Admiralty.*"

Lord Churchill sent the above letter, with a list of
the killed and wounded annexed, to inform my mother
that the name of her son was not among the number.
The act shows how much he could sympathize with a
mother's feelings.

I now went below, to see how matters appeared there.
The first object I met was a man bearing a limb, which
had just been detached from some suffering wretch.
Pursuing my way to the ward-room, I necessarily
passed through the steerage, which was strewed with
the wounded: it was a sad spectacle, made more
appalling by the groans and cries which rent the air.
Some were groaning, others were swearing most bit-
terly, a few were praying, while those last arrived were
begging most piteously to have their wounds dressed
next. The surgeon and his mate were smeared with

blood from head to foot: they looked more like butchers than doctors. Having so many patients, they had once shifted their quarters from the cockpit to the steerage; they now removed to the ward-room, and the long table, round which the officers had sat over many a merry feast, was soon covered with the bleeding forms of maimed and mutilated seamen.

While looking round the ward-room, I heard a noise above, occasioned by the arrival of the boats from the conquering frigate. Very soon a lieutenant, I think his name was Nicholson, came into the ward-room and said to the busy surgeon, "How do you do, doctor?"

"I have enough to do," replied he, shaking his head thoughtfully; "you have made wretched work for us!" These officers were not strangers to each other, for the reader will recollect that the commanders and officers of these two frigates had exchanged visits when we were lying at Norfolk some months before.

I now set to work to render all the aid in my power to the sufferers. Our carpenter, named Reed, had his leg cut off. I helped to carry him to the after ward-room; but he soon breathed out his life there, and then I assisted in throwing his mangled remains overboard. We got out the cots as fast as possible; for most of them were stretched out on the gory deck. One poor fellow, who lay with a broken thigh, begged me to give him water. I gave him some. He looked unutterable gratitude, drank, and died. It was with exceeding difficulty I moved through the steerage, it was so covered with mangled men and so slippery with streams of blood. There was a poor boy there crying as if his heart would break. He had been servant to the bold boatswain, whose head was dashed to pieces. Poor boy! he felt that he had lost a friend. I tried to comfort him by reminding him that he ought to be thankful for having escaped death himself.

Here, also, I met one of my messmates, who showed the utmost joy at seeing me alive, for, he said, he had heard that I was killed. He was looking up his mess-mates, which he said was always done by sailors. We found two of our mess wounded. One was the Swede, Logholm, who fell overboard, as mentioned in a for-mer chapter, and was nearly lost. We held him while the surgeon cut off his leg above the knee. The task was most painful to behold, the surgeon using his knife and saw on human flesh and bones as freely as the butcher at the shambles does on the carcass of the beast! Our other messmate suffered still more than the Swede; he was sadly mutilated about the legs and thighs with splinters. Such scenes of suffering as I saw in that ward-room, I hope never to witness again. Could the civilized world behold them as they were, and as they often are, infinitely worse than on that occasion, it seems to me they would forever put down the barbarous practices of war, by universal consent.

Most of our officers and men were taken on board the victor ship. I was left, with a few others, to take care of the wounded. My master, the sailing-master, was also among the officers, who continued in their ship. Most of the men who remained were unfit for any service, having broken into the spirit-room and made themselves drunk; some of them broke into the purser's room and helped themselves to clothing; while others, by previous agreement, took possession of their dead messmates' property. For my own part, I was content to help myself to a little of the officer's provisions, which did me more good than could be obtained from rum. What was worse than all, however, was the folly of the sailors in giving spirit to their wounded messmates, since it only served to aggravate their distress.

Among the wounded was a brave fellow named Wells. After the surgeon had amputated and dressed his arm, he walked about in fine spirits, as if he had received only a slight injury. Indeed, while under the operation, he manifested a similar heroism – observing to the surgeon, "I have lost my arm in the service of my country; but I don't mind it, doctor, it's the fortune of war." Cheerful and gay as he was, he soon died. His companions gave him rum; he was attacked by fever and died. Thus his messmates actually killed him with kindness.

We had all sorts of dispositions and temperaments among our crew. To me it was a matter of great interest to watch their various manifestations. Some who had lost their messmates appeared to care nothing about it, while others were grieving with all the tenderness of women. Of these was the survivor of two seamen who had formerly been soldiers in the same regiment; he bemoaned the loss of his comrade with expressions of profoundest grief. There were, also, two boatswain's mates, named Adams and Brown, who had been messmates for several years in the same ship. Brown was killed, or so wounded that he died soon after the battle. It was really a touching spectacle to see the rough, hardy features of the brave old sailor streaming with tears, as he picked out the dead body of his friend from among the wounded and gently carried it to the ship's side, saying to the inanimate form he bore, "O Bill, we have sailed together in a number of ships, we have been in many gales and some battles, but this is the worst day I have seen! We must now part!" Here he dropped the body into the deep, and then, a fresh torrent of tears streaming over his weather-beaten face, he added, "I can do no more for you. Farewell! God be with you!" Here was an instance of genuine friendship, worth more than the heartless professions of thousands, who, in the fancied superiority of their elevated position in the social circle, will deign nothing but a silly sneer at this record of a sailor's grief.

The circumstance was rather a singular one, that in both the contending frigates the second boatswain's mate bore the name of William Brown, and that they both were killed; yet such was the fact.

The great number of the wounded kept our surgeon and his mate busily employed at their horrid work until late at night; and it was a long time before they had much leisure. I remember passing round the ship the day after the battle. Coming to a hammock, I found some one in it apparently asleep. I spoke; he made no answer. I looked into the hammock; he was dead. My messmates coming up, we threw the corpse overboard; that was no time for useless ceremony. The man had probably crawled to his hammock the day before, and, not being perceived in the general distress, bled to death! O War! who can reveal thy miseries!

When the crew of the *United States* first boarded our frigate to take possession of her as their prize, our men, heated with the fury of the battle, exasperated with the sight of their dead and wounded shipmates, and rendered furious by the rum they had obtained

from the spirit-room, felt and exhibited some disposition to fight their captors. But after the confusion had
subsided and part of our men were snugly stowed
away in the American ship, and the remainder found
themselves kindly used in their own, the utmost good
feeling began to prevail. We took hold and cleansed
the ship, using hot vinegar to take out the scent of the
blood that had dyed the white of our planks with
crimson. We also took hold and aided in fitting our
disabled frigate for her voyage. This being accomplished, both ships sailed in company toward the
American coast.

I soon felt myself perfectly at home with the American seamen; so much so that I chose to mess with
them. My shipmates also participated in similar feelings in both ships. All idea that we had been trying to
shoot out each other's brains so shortly before seemed
forgotten. We eat together, drank together, joked,
sung, laughed, told yarns; in short, a perfect union
of ideas, feelings, and purposes seemed to exist among
all hands.

A corresponding state of unanimity existed, I was
told, among the officers. Commodore Decatur showed
himself to be a gentleman as well as a hero in his
treatment of the officers of the *Macedonian*. When
Captain Carden offered his sword to the commodore,
remarking, as he did so, "I am an undone man. I am
the first British naval officer that has struck his flag to
an American": the noble commodore either refused to
receive the sword or immediately returned it, smiling
as he said, "You are mistaken, sir; your *Guerriere* has
been taken by us, and the flag of a frigate was struck
before yours." This somewhat revived the spirits of

the old captain; but, no doubt, he still felt his soul stung with shame and mortification at the loss of his ship. Participating as he did in the haughty spirit of the British aristocracy, it was natural for him to feel galled and wounded to the quick, in the position of a conquered man.

We were now making the best of our way to America. Notwithstanding the patched-up condition of the *Macedonian*, she was far superior, in a sailing capacity, to her conqueror. The *United States* had always been a dull sailer, and had been christened by the name of the Old Wagon. Whenever a boat came alongside of our frigate and the boatswain's mate was ordered to "pipe away" the boat's crew, he used to sound his shrill call on the whistle and bawl out, "Away, *Wagoners*, away", instead of "away, *United States* men, away". This piece of pleasantry used to be rebuked by the officers, but in a manner that showed they enjoyed the joke. They usually replied, "Boatswain's mate, you rascal, pipe away *United States* men, not Wagoners. We have no wagoners on board of a ship." Still, in spite of rebuke, the joke went on, until it grew stale by repetition. One thing was made certain however by the sailing qualities of the *Macedonian*; which was, that if we had been disposed to escape from our foe before the action, we could have done so with all imaginable ease. This however, would have justly exposed us to disgrace, while our capture did not. There was every reason why the *United States* should beat us. She was larger in size, heavier in metal, more numerous in men, and stronger built than the *Macedonian*. Another fact in her favor was that our captain at first mistook her for the *Essex*, which carried short carronades, hence he engaged her at long shot at first; for, as we had the weather gage, we could take what position we pleased. But this maneuver only wasted our shot and gave her the advantage, as she actually carried larger metal than we did. When we came to close action, the shot from the *United States* went "through and through" our ship, while ours struck her sides and fell harmlessly into the water. This is to be accounted for both by the superiority of the metal and of the ship. Her guns were heavier and her sides thicker than ours. Some have said that her sides were stuffed with cork. Of this, however, I am not certain. Her superiority, both in number of men and guns, may easily be seen by the following statistics. We carried forty-nine guns; long eighteen-pounders on the main deck, and thirty-two-pound carronades on the quarter deck and forecastle. Our whole number of hands, including officers, men and boys, was three hundred. The *United States* carried four hundred and fifty men and fifty-four guns: long twenty-four-pounders on the main deck, and forty-two-pound carronades on the quarter deck and forecastle. So that in actual force she was immensely our superior.

To these should be added the consideration that the men in the two ships fought under the influence of different motives. Many of our hands were in the service against their will; some of them were Americans, wrongfully impressed and inwardly hoping for defeat: while nearly every man in our ship sympathized with the great principle for which the American nation so nobly contended in the war of 1812. What that was, I suppose all my readers understand. The British, at war with France, had denied the

Americans the right to trade thither. She had impressed American seamen and forcibly compelled their service in her navy; she had violated the American flag by insolently searching their vessels for her runaway seamen. Free trade and sailors' rights, therefore, were the objects contended for by the Americans. With these objects our *men* could but sympathize, whatever our officers might do.

On the other hand, the crew of our opponent had all shipped *voluntarily* for the term of two years only (most of our men were shipped for life). They understood what they fought for; they were better used in the service. What wonder, then, that victory adorned the brows of the American commander? To have been defeated under such circumstances would have been a source of lasting infamy to any naval officer in the world. In the matter of fighting, I think there is but little difference in either nation. Place them in action under equal circumstances and motives, and who could predict which would be victor? Unite them together, they would subject the whole world. So close are the alliances of blood, however, between England and America, that it is to be earnestly desired, they may never meet in mortal strife again. If either will fight, which is to be deprecated as a crime and a folly, let it choose an enemy less connected by the sacred ties of consanguinity.

Our voyage was one of considerable excitement. The seas swarmed with British cruisers, and it was extremely doubtful whether the *United States* would elude their grasp and reach the protection of an American port with her prize. I hoped most sincerely to avoid them, as did most of my old shipmates; in this we

agreed with our captors, who wisely desired to dispose
of one conquest before they attempted another. Our
former officers, of course, were anxious for the sight of
a British flag. But we saw none, and, after a prosperous
voyage from the scene of conflict, we heard the welcome cry of "Land ho!" The *United States* entered the
port of New London; but, owing to a sudden shift of
the wind, the *Macedonian* had to lay off and on for
several hours. Had an English cruiser found us in this
situation, we should have been easily recovered; and,
as it was extremely probable we should fall in with one,
I felt quite uneasy, until, after several hours, we made
out to run into the pretty harbor of Newport. We fired
a salute as we came to an anchor, which was promptly
returned by the people on shore.

With a few exceptions, our wounded men were in a
fair way to recover by the time we reached Newport.
The last of them, who died of their wounds on board,
was buried just before we got in. His name was
Thomas Whittaker; he had been badly wounded by
splinters. While he lived, he endured excessive tor-
ture. At last his sufferings rendered him crazy, in
which sad state he died. He was sewed up in his
hammock by his messmates and carried on a grating
to the larboard bow port. There Mr Archer, a midshipman of the *Macedonian*, read the beautiful burial
service of the church of England. When he came to
that most touching passage, "we commit the body of
our brother to the deep", the grating was elevated,
and, amid the most profound silence, the body fell
heavily into the waters. As it dropped into the deep, a
sigh escaped from many a friendly bosom, and an air of
passing melancholy shrouded many a face with sad-

ness. Old recollections were busy there, calling up the losses of the battle; but it was only momentary. The men brushed away their tears, muttered "It's no use to fret", and things once more wore their wonted aspect.

Ned Myers

The War of the Lakes

1812–13

Much of the naval War of 1812 was not fought on the oceans, but upon the Great Lakes which lay between the USA and the British colony of Canada. Ned Myers was a volunteer in the US Navy on the Lakes, whose dramatic story was later ghosted by the American adventure writer, James Fenimore Cooper.

The day after I reached the harbour, I was ordered on board the *Scourge*. This vessel was English-built, and had been captured before the war, and condemned for violating the revenue laws, under the name of the *Lord Nelson*, by the *Oneida*, 16, Lt. Com. Woolsey – the only cruiser we then had on the lake. This craft was unfit for her duty, but time pressed, and no better offered. Bulwarks had been raised on her, and she mounted eight sixes, in regular broadside. Her accommodations were bad enough, and she was so tender, that we could do little or nothing with her in a blow. It was often prognosticated that she would prove our coffin. Besides Mr Osgood, who was put in command of this vessel, we had Mr Bogardus and Mr Livingston, as officers. We must have had about forty-five souls on board, all told. We did not get this schooner out that season, however.

The commodore arriving, and an expedition against Kingston being in the wind, a party of us volunteered from the *Scourge* to go on board the *Oneida*. This was in November, rather a latish month for active service on those waters. The brig went out in company with the *Conquest, Hamilton, Governor Tompkins, Pert, Julia,* and *Growler,* schooners. These last craft were all merchantmen, mostly without quarters, and scarcely fit for the duty on which they were employed. The *Oneida* was a warm little brig, of sixteen 24-lb, carronades, but as dull as a transport. She had been built to cross the bars of the American harbours, and would not travel to windward.

We went off the False Ducks, where we made the *Royal George*, a ship the English had built expressly to overlay the *Oneida*, two or three years before, and which was big enough to eat us. Her officers, however, did not belong to the Royal Navy; and we made such a show of schooners, that, though she had herself a vessel or two in company, she did not choose to wait for us. We chased her into the Bay of Quinté, and there we lost her in the darkness. Next morning, however, we saw her at anchor in the channel that leads to Kingston. A general chase now commenced and we ran down into the bay, and engaged the ship and batteries as close as we could well get. The firing was sharp on both sides, and it lasted a great while.

I was stationed at a gun, as her second captain, and was too busy to see much; but I know we kept our pieces speaking as fast as we could for a good bit. We drove the *Royal George* from a second anchorage, quite up to a berth abreast of the town; and it was said that her people actually deserted her, at one time. We gave her nothing but roundshot from our gun, and these we gave her with all our hearts. Whenever we noticed the shore, a stand of grape was added.

I know nothing of the damage done the enemy. We had the best of it, so far as I could see; and I think if the weather had not compelled us to haul off, something serious might have been done. As it was, we beat out with flying colours, and anchored a few miles from the light.

These were the first shot I ever saw fired in anger. Our brig had one man killed and three wounded, and she was somewhat injured aloft. One shot came in not far from my gun, and scattered lots of cat-tails, breaking in the hammock-cloths. This was the nearest chance I ran that day; and on the whole, I think we escaped pretty well. On our return to the harbour, the ten *Scourges* who had volunteered for the cruise, returned to their own schooner. None of us were hurt, though all of us were half-frozen, the water freezing as fast as it fell.

Shortly after both sides went into winter quarters, and both sides commenced building. We launched a ship called the *Madison* about this time, and we laid the keel of another that was named the *Pike*. What John Bull was about is more than I can say, though the next season showed he had not been idle. The navigation did not actually close, notwithstanding, until December.

Our vessels were moored about the harbour, and we were all frozen in, as a matter of course. Around each craft, however, a space was kept cut, to form a sort of ditch, in order to prevent being boarded. Parties were regularly stationed to defend the *Madison*, and in the days we worked at her rigging, and at that of the *Pike*, in gangs. Our larboard guns were landed, and placed in a block-house, while the starboard were kept mounted. My station was that of captain of one of the guns that remained.

The winter lasted more than four months, and we made good times of it. We often went after wood, and occasionally we knocked over a deer. We had a target out on the lake, and this we practised on, making ourselves rather expert cannoneers. Now and then they roused us out on a false alarm, but I know of no serious attempts being made by the enemy to molest us.

The lake was fit to navigate about the middle of April. Somewhere about the 20th the soldiers began to embark, to the number of 1700 men. A company came on board the *Scourge*, and they filled us chock-a-block. It came on to blow, and we were obliged to keep these poor fellows, cramped as we were, most of the time on deck, exposed to rain and storm. On the 25th we got out, rather a showy force altogether, though there was not much service in our small craft. We had a ship, a brig, and twelve schooners, fourteen sail in all. The next morning we were off Little York*, having sailed with a fair wind. All hands anchored about a mile from the beach. I volunteered to go in a boat, to carry

* Toronto.

soldiers ashore. Each of us brought across the lake two of those boats in tow, but we had lost one of ours, dragging her after us in a staggering breeze. I got into the one that was left, and we put half our soldiers in her and shoved off. We had little or no order in landing, each boat pulling as hard as she could. The English blazed away at us concealed in a wood, and our men fired back again from the boat. I never was more disappointed in men, than I was in the soldiers. They were mostly tall, pale-looking Yankees, half-dead with sickness and the bad weather – so mealy, indeed, that half of them could not take their grog, which, by this time, I had got to think a bad sign. As soon as they got near the enemy, however, they became wide-awake, pointed out to each other where to aim, and many of them actually jumped into the water, in order to get the sooner ashore. No men could have behaved better, for I confess frankly I did not like the work at all. It is no fun to pull in under a sharp fire, with one's back to his enemy, and nothing but an oar to amuse himself with. The shot flew pretty thick, and two of our oars were split. This was all done with musketry, no heavy guns being used at this place. I landed twice in this way, but the danger was principally in the first affair. There was fighting up on the bank, but it gave us no trouble. Mr Livingston commanded the boat.

When we got back to the schooner, we found her lifting her anchors. Several of the smaller craft were now ordered up the bay, to open on the batteries nearer to the town. We were the third from the van, and we all anchored within canister range. We heard a magazine blow up, as we stood in, and this brought three cheers from us. We now had some sharp work

with the batteries, keeping up a steady fire. The
schooner ahead of us had to cut, and she shifted her
berth outside of us. The leading schooner, however,
held on. In the midst of it all, we heard cheers down
the line, and presently we saw the commodore pulling
in among us, in his gig. He came on board us, and we
greeted him with three cheers. While he was on the
quarter-deck, a hot shot struck the upper part of the
after-port, cut all the boarding-pikes adrift from the
main-boom, and wounded a man named Lemuel Bryant, who leaped from his quarters and fell at my feet.
His clothes were all on fire when he fell, and after
putting them out, the commodore himself ordered me
to pass him below. The old man spoke encouragingly
to us, and a little thing took place that drew his
attention to my crew. Two of the trucks of the guns
we were fighting had been carried away, and I determined to shift over its opposite. My crew were five
negroes, strapping fellows and as strong as jackasses.
The gun was called the Black Joke. Shoving the
disabled gun out of the way, these chaps crossed the
deck, unhooked the breechings and gun-tackle, raised
the piece from the deck, and placed it in the vacant
port. The commodore commended us, and called out,
"That's quick work, my lads!" In less than three
minutes, I am certain, we were playing on the enemy
with the fresh gun.

As for the old man, he pulled through the fire as
coolly as it were only a snow-balling scrape, though
many a poor fellow lost the number of his mess in the
boats that day. When he left us, we cheered him again.
He had not left us long, before we heard an awful
explosion on shore. Stones as big as my two fists fell on

board of us, though nobody was hurt by them. We cheered, thinking some dire calamity had befallen the enemy. The firing ceased soon after this explosion, though one English gun held on under the bank for some little time.

We did not know the cause of the last explosion until after the firing ceased. I had seen an awful black cloud, and objects in the air that I took for men; but little did we imagine the explosion had cost us so dear. Our schooner lay at no great distance from the common landing, and no sooner were we certain of the success of the day, than Mr Osgood had his boat's crew called away, and he landed. As I belonged to the boat, I had an early opportunity of entering the town.

We found the place deserted. With the exception of our own men, I found but one living being in it. This was an old woman, whom I discovered stowed away in a potato-locker, in the government-house. I saw tables set, and eggs in the cups, but no inhabitant. Our orders were of the most severe kind, not to plunder, and we did not touch a morsel of food even. The liquor, however, was too much for our poor natures, and a parcel of us had broke bulk in a better sort of grocery, when some officers came in and stove the casks. I made sail, and got out of the company. The army had gone in pursuit of the enemy, with the exception of a few riflemen, who, being now at liberty, found their way into the place.

I ought to feel ashamed, and do feel ashamed, of what occurred that night; but I must relate it, lest I feel more ashamed for concealing the truth. We had spliced the mainbrace pretty freely throughout the

day, and the pull I got in the grocery just made me ripe
for mischief. When we got aboard the schooner again,
we found a canoe that had drifted athwart-hawse, and
had been secured. My gun's crew, the Black Jokers,
wished to have some fun in the town, and they proposed to me to take a cruise ashore. We had few
officers on board, and the boatswain, a boatswain's-
mate in fact, consented to let us leave. We all went
ashore in this canoe, then, and were soon alongside of a
wharf. On landing, we were near a large store, and
looking in at a window, we saw a man sitting asleep,
with a gun in the hollow of his arm. His head was on
the counter, and there was a lamp burning. One of the
blacks pitched through the window and was on him in
a moment. The rest followed, and we made him a
prisoner. The poor fellow said he had come to look
after his property, and he was told no one would hurt
him. My blacks now began to look about them, and to
help themselves to such articles as they thought they
wanted. I confess I helped myself to some tea and
sugar, nor will I deny that I was in such a state as to
think the whole good fun. We carried off one good
canoe-load, and even returned for a second. Of course
such an exploit could not have been effected without
letting all in the secret share; and one boat-load of
plunder was not enough. The negroes began to drink,
however, and I was sober enough to see the consequences, if they were left ashore any longer. Some
riflemen came in too, and I succeeded in getting my
Jokers away.

The recklessness of sailors may be seen in our
conduct. All we received for our plunder was some
eight or ten gallons of whisky, when we got back to the

harbour, and this at the risk of being flogged through the fleet! It seemed to us to be a scrape, and that was sufficient excuse for disobeying orders, and for committing a crime. For myself, I was influenced more by the love of mischief, and a weak desire to have it said I was foremost in such an exploit, than from any mercenary motive. Notwithstanding the severity of the orders, and one or two pretty sharp examples of punishment inflicted by the commodore, the Black Jokers were not the only plunderers ashore that night. One master's-mate had the buttons taken off his coat, for stealing a feather-bed, besides being obliged to carry it back again.

I was ashore every day while the squadron remained in the port. Our schooner never shifted her berth from the last one she occupied in the battle, and that was pretty well up the bay. I paid a visit to the gun that had troubled us all so much, and which we could not silence, for it was under a bank, near the landing-place. It was a long French eighteen, and did better service that day than any other piece of John Bull's. I think it hulled us several times.

I walked over the ground where the explosion took place. It was a dreadful sight; the dead being so mutilated that it was scarcely possible to tell their colour. I saw gun-barrels bent nearly double. I think we saw Sir Robert Sheafe, the British general, galloping across the field by himself a few minutes before the explosion. At all events, we saw a mounted officer, and fired at him. He galloped up to the government-house, dismounted, went in, remained a short time, and then galloped out of town. All this I saw; and the old woman in the potato-locker told me the general had been in the house a short time before we landed. Her account agreed with the appearance of the officer I saw, though I will not pretend to be certain it was General Sheafe.

I ought to mention the kindness of the commodore to the poor of York. As most of the inhabitants came back to their habitations the next day, the poor were suffering for food. Our men were ordered to roll barrels of salt meat and barrels of bread to their doors, from the government stores that fell into our hands. We captured an immense amount of these stores, a portion of which we carried away. We sunk many guns in the lake; and as for the powder, *that* had taken care of itself. Among other things we took, was the body of an English officer, preserved in rum, which they said was General Brock's. I saw it hoisted out of the *Duke of Gloucester*, the man-of-war brig we captured, at Sackett's Harbour, and saw the body put in a fresh cask. I am ashamed to say, that some of our men were inclined to drink the old rum.

We burned a large corvette that was nearly ready for launching, and otherwise did the enemy a good deal of harm. The inhabitants that returned were very submissive and thankful for what they received. As for the man of the store, I never saw him after the night he was plundered, nor was anything ever said of the scrape.

Our troops had lost near three hundred men in the attack, the wounded included; and as a great many of these green soldiers were now sick from exposure, the army was much reduced in force. We took the troops on board on the 1st of May, but could not sail, on account of a gale, until the 8th, which made the matter worse. Then we got under weigh, and crossed the lake, landing the soldiers a few miles to the eastward of Fort Niagara. Our schooner now went to the Harbour, along with the commodore, though some of the craft remained near the head of the lake. Here we took in another lot of soldiers, placed two more large batteaux in tow, and sailed for the army again. We had good passages both ways, and this duty was done in a few days. While at the Harbour, I got a message to go and visit Bill Swett, but the poor fellow died without my being able to see him. I heard he was hurt at York, but never could come at the truth.

On the 27th May, the army got into the batteaux, formed in two divisions, and commenced pulling towards the mouth of the Niagara. The morning was foggy, with a light wind, and the vessels getting under weigh, kept company with the boats a little outside of them. The schooners were closest in, and some of them opened on Fort George, while others kept along the coast, scouring the shore with grape and canister as they moved ahead. The *Scourge* came to an anchor a short distance above the place selected for the landing, and sprung her broadside to the shore. We now kept up a steady fire with grape and canister, until the boats had got inshore, and were engaged with the enemy, when we threw round-shot over the heads of our own men upon the English. As soon as Colonel Scott was ashore, we sprung our broadside upon a two-gun battery that had been pretty busy, and we silenced that among us. This affair, for our craft, was nothing like that of York, though I was told the vessels nearer the river had warmer berths of it. We had no one hurt, though we were hulled once or twice. A little rigging was cut; but we set this down as light work compared to what the old Black Joke had seen that day month. There was a little sharp fighting ashore, but our men were too strong for the enemy when they could fairly get their feet on solid ground.

Just after we had anchored, Mr Bogardus was sent aloft to ascertain if any enemy were to be seen. At first he found nobody; but, after a little while, he called out to have my gun fired at a little thicket of brushwood that lay on an inclined plane near the water. Mr Osgood came and elevated the gun and I touched it off. We had been looking out for the blink of muskets, which was one certain guide to find a soldier, and the moment we sent this grist of grape and canister into those bushes, the place lighted up as if a thousand muskets were there. We then gave the chaps the remainder of our broadside. We peppered that wood well, and did a good deal of harm to the troops stationed at the place.

The wind blew on shore, and began to increase; and the commodore now threw out a signal for the boats to land, to take care of the batteaux that were thumping on the beach, and then for their crews to assist in taking care of the wounded. Of course I went in my own boat, Mr Bogardus having charge of her. We left the schooner, just as we quitted our guns, black with powder, in our shirts and trousers, though we took the precaution to carry our boarding-belts, with a brace of pistols each, and a cutlass. On landing we first hauled up the boats, taking some dead and wounded men out of them, and laying them on the beach.

We were now ordered to divide ourselves into groups of three, and go over the ground, pick up

the wounded, and carry them to a large house that had
been selected as a hospital. My party consisted of Bill
Southward, Simeon Grant, and myself, we being
messmates. The first man we fell in with was a young
English soldier, who was seated on the bank quite near
the lake. He was badly hurt, and sat leaning his head
on his hands. He begged for water, and I took his cap
down to the lake and filled it, giving him a drink, then
washing his face. This revived him, and he offered us
his canteen, in which was some excellent Jamaica. To
us chaps, who got nothing better than whisky, this was
a rare treat, and we emptied the remainder of his half-
pint, at a pull a piece. After tapping this rum, we
carried the poor lad up to the house, and turned him
over to the doctors. We found the rooms filled with
wounded already, and the American and English doctors hard at work on them.

As we left the hospital, we agreed to get a canteen a-
piece, and go round among the dead, and fill them
with Jamaica. When our canteens were about a third
full, we came upon a young American rifleman, who
was lying under an apple-tree. He was hit in the head,
and was in a very bad way. We were all three much
struck with the appearance of this young man, and I
now remember him as one of the handsomest youths I
had ever seen. His wound did not bleed, though I
thought the brains were oozing out, and I felt so much
sympathy for him that I washed his hurt with rum. I
fear I did him harm, but my motive was good. Bill
Southard ran to find a surgeon, of whom several were
operating out on the field. The young man kept saying
"no use", and he mentioned "father and mother",
"Vermont". He even gave me the names of his par-

ents, but I was too much in the wind, from the use of rum, to remember them. We might have been half an hour with this young rifleman, busy on him most of the time, when he murmured a few words, gave me one of the sweetest smiles I ever saw on a man's face, and made no more signs of life. I kept at work, notwithstanding, until Bill got back with the doctor. The latter cast an eye on the rifleman, pronounced him dead, and coolly walked away.

There was a bridge, in a sort of a swamp, that we had fired on for some time, and we now moved down to it, just to see what we had done. We found a good many dead, and several horses in the mire, but no wounded. We kept emptying canteens as we went along, until our own would hold no more. On our return from the bridge, we went to a brook in order to mix some grog, and then we got a full view of the offing. Not a craft was to be seen! Everything had weighed and disappeared. This discovery knocked us all aback, and we were quite at a loss how to proceed. We agreed, however, to pass through a bit of woods, and get into the town, it being now quite late in the day. There we knew we should find the army, and might get tidings of the fleet. The battleground was now nearly deserted, and to own the truth, we were, all three, at least two sheets in the wind. Still, I remember everything, for my stomach would never allow me to get beastly drunk; it rejecting any very great quantity of liquor. As we went through the wood, open pine-trees, we came across an officer lying dead, with one leg over his horse, which was dead also. I went up to the body, turned it over, and examined it for a canteen, but found none. We made a few idle remarks, and proceeded.

In quitting the place, I led the party; and as we went through a little thicket, I heard female voices. This startled me a little, and on looking round I saw a white female dress, belonging to a person who was evidently endeavouring to conceal herself from us. I was now alone, and walked up to the women, when I found two; one, a lady, in dress and manner; and the other a person that I have always supposed was her servant. The first was in white; the last was in a dark calico. They were both under thirty, judging from their looks; and the lady was exceedingly well-looking. They were much alarmed; and, as I came up, the lady asked me if I would hurt her. I told her No; and that no person should harm her while she remained with us. This relieved her, and she was able to give an account of her errand on the field of battle. Our looks, half-intoxicated, and begrimed with the smoke of a battle, as we were, certainly were enough to alarm her; but I do not think one of the three would have hesitated about fighting for a female, that they thus found weeping, in this manner, in the open field. The maid was crying also. Simeon Grant and Southard did make use of some improper language, at first; but I brought them up, and they said they were sorry, and would go all lengths with me to protect the women. The fact was, these men supposed we had fallen in with common camp-followers; but I had seen too much of officers' wives in my boyhood, not to know that this was one.

The lady then told her story. She had just come from Kingston, to join her husband; having arrived but a few hours before. She did not see her husband, but she had heard he was left wounded on the field;

and she had come out in the hope of finding him. She then described him, as an officer mounted, with a particular dress, and inquired if we had met with any such person on the field. We told her of the horseman we had just left, and led her back to the spot. The moment the lady saw the body, she threw herself on it, and began to weep and mourn over it, in a very touching manner. The maid, too, was almost as bad as the mistress. We were all so much affected, in spite of the rum, that I believe all three of us shed tears. We said all we could to console her, and swore we would stand by her until she was safe back among her friends.

It was a good bit before we could persuade the lady to quit her husband's body. She took a miniature from his neck, and I drew his purse and watch from him, and handed them to her. She wanted me to keep the purse, but this we all three refused, up and down. We had hauled our manly tacks aboard, and had no thoughts of plunder. Even the maid urged us to keep the money, but we would have nothing to do with it. I shall freely own my faults; I hope I shall be believed when I relate facts that show I am not altogether without proper feelings.

The officer had been hit somewhere about the hip, and the horse must have been killed by another grape-shot, fired from the same gun. We laid the body of the first over in such a manner as to get a good look at him, but we did not draw the leg from under the horse.

When we succeeded in persuading the lady to quit her husband's body, we shaped our course for the lighthouse. Glad were we three tars to see the mast-heads of the shipping in the river, as we came near the banks of the Niagara. The house at the light was empty; but, on my hailing, a woman's voice answered from the cellar. It was an old woman, who had taken shelter from shot down the hold, the rest of the family having slipped and run. We now got some milk for the lady, who continued in tears most of the time. Sometimes she would knock off crying for a bit, when she seemed to have some distrust of us; but, on the whole, we made very good weather in company. After staying about half an hour at the lighthouse, we left it for the town, my advice to the lady being to put herself under the protection of some of our officers. I told her if the news of what had happened reached the commodore, she might depend on her husband's being buried with the honours of war, and said such other things to comfort her as came to the mind of a man who had been sailing so near the wind.

I forgot to relate one part of the adventure. Before we had got fairly clear of the woods, we fell in with four of Forsyth's men, notoriously the wickedest corps in the army. These fellows began to crack their jokes at the expense of the two females, and we came near having a brush with them. When we spoke of our pistols, and of our determination to use them, before we would let our convoy come to harm, these chaps laughed at our pop-guns, and told us they had such things as "rifles". This was true enough; and had we come to broadsides, I make no doubt they would have knocked us over like so many snipes. I began to reason with them on the impropriety of offending respectable females; and one of the fellows, who was a kind of a corporal, or something of that sort, shook my hand, said I was right, and offered to be friends. So we spliced the mainbrace, and parted. Glad enough was the lady to be rid of them so easily. In these squalls she would bring up in her tears, and then when all went smooth again she would break out afresh.

After quitting the light we made the best of our way for the town. Just as we reached it, we fell in with a party of soldier-officers, and we turned the lady and her woman over to their care. These gentlemen said a good word in our favour, and here we parted company with our convoy, I never hearing or seeing anything of either afterwards.

By this time it was near dark, and Bill Southard and I began to look out for the *Scourge*. She was anchored in the river, with the rest of the fleet, and we went down upon a wharf to make a signal for a boat. On the way we saw a woman crying before a watchmaker's shop, and a party of Forsyth's close by. On inquiry we learned these fellows had threatened to rob her shop. We had been such defenders of the sex that we could not think of deserting this woman, and we swore we would stand by her too. We should have had a skirmish here, I do believe, had not one or two rifle officers hove in sight, when the whole party made sail from us. We turned the woman over to these gentlemen, who said, "Ay, there are some of our vagabonds again." One of them said it would be better to call in their parties, and before we reached the water we heard the bugle sounding the recall.

They had given us up on board the schooner. A report of some Indians being out had reached her, and we three were set down as scalped. Thank God, I've got all the hair on my head yet, and, battered as my old hulk has got to be, and shattered as are my timbers, it is black as raven's wing at this moment. This, my old shipmate, who is logging this yarn, says he thinks is a proof my mother was a French Canadian, though such is not the fact, as has been told to me.

Those riflemen were regular scamps. Just before we went down to the wharf, we saw one walking sentinel before the door of a sort of barracks. On drawing near and asking what was going on inside, we were told we had nothing to do with their fun ashore; that we might look in at the window, however, but should not go in. We took him at his word; a merry scene it was inside. The English officers' dunnage had been broken into, and there was a party of the corps strutting about in uniform coats and feathers. We thought it best to give these dare-devils a berth, and so we left them. One was never safe with them on the field of battle, friend or enemy.

We met a large party of marines on the wharf, marching up under Major Smith. They were going to protect the people of the town from further mischief. Mr Osgood was glad enough to see us, and we got plenty of praise for what we had done with the women. As for the canteens, we had to empty them, after treating the crew of the boat that was sent to take us off. I did not enter the town after that night.

We lay some time in the Niagara, the commodore going to the harbour to get the *Pike* ready. Captain Crane took the rest of us off Kingston, where we were join by the commodore, and made sail again for the Niagara. Here Colonel Scott embarked with a body of troops, and we went to Burlington Bay to carry the heights. They were found to be too strong; and the men, after landing, returned to the vessels. We then went to York again, and took possession of the place a second time. Here we destroyed several boats and stores, set fire to the barracks, and did the enemy a good deal of damage otherwise; after which we left the place. Two or three days later we crossed the lake and landed the soldiers again, at Fort Niagara.

Early in August, while we were still in the river, Sir James Yeo hove in sight with two ships, two brigs, and two schooners. We had thirteen sail in all, such as they were, and immediately got under weigh, and man-œuvred for the weather-gauge. All the enemy's vessels had regular quarters, and the ships were stout craft. Our squadron sailed very unequally, some being pret-ty fast, and others as dull as doggers. Nor were we more than half-fitted out. On board the *Scourge*, the only square-sail we had was made out of an English marquée we had laid our hands on at York, the first time we were there. I ought to say, too, that we got two small brass guns at York, four-pounders, I believe, which Mr Osgood clapped into our two spare ports forward. This gave us ten guns in all, sixes and fours. I remember that Jack Mallet laughed at us heartily for the fuss we made with our pop-guns, as he called them, while we were working upon the English bat-teries, saying we might just as well have saved our powder as for any good we did. He belonged to the *Julia*, which had a long thirty-two forward, which they called "Old Sow", and one smart eighteen aft. She had two sixes in her waist, also; but they disdained to use *them*.

While we were up at the harbour, the last time, Mr Mix, who had married a sister of Mr Osgood, took a party of us in a boat, and we went up Black River shooting. The two gentlemen landed, and as we were coming down the river, we saw something swimming, which proved to be a bear. We had no arms, but we pulled over the beast, and had a regular squaw-fight with him. We were an hour at work with this animal, the fellow coming very near mastering us. I struck at his nose with an iron tiller fifty times, but he warded the blow like a boxer. He broke our boat-hook, and once or twice he came near boarding us. At length a wood-boat gave us an axe, and with this we killed him. Mr Osgood had this bear skinned, and said he should send the skin to his family. If he did, it must have been one of the last memorials it ever got from him.

I left the two fleets manœuvring for the wind . . .

About nine o'clock the *Pike* got abeam of the *Wolfe*, Sir James Yeo's own ship, hoisted her ensign, and fired a few guns to try the range of her shot. The distance was too great to engage. At this time our sternmost vessels were two leagues off, and the commodore wore round, and hauled up on the other tack. The enemy did the same; but, perceiving that our leading ships were likely to weather on him, he tacked, and hauled off to the northward. We stood on in pursuit, tacking too; but the wind soon fell, and about sunset it was quite calm.

Throughout the day the *Scourge* had as much as she could do to keep anywhere near her station. As for the old *Oneida*, she could not be kept within a long distance of her proper berth. We were sweeping, at odd times, for hours that day. Towards evening, all the light craft were doing the same to close with the commodore. Our object was to get together, lest the enemy should cut off some of our small vessels during the night.

Before dark the whole line was formed again, with the exception of the *Oneida*, which was still astern, towing. She ought to have been near the commodore, but could not get there. A little before sunset, Mr Osgood ordered us to pull in our sweeps, and to take a spell. It was a lovely evening, not a cloud visible, and the lake being as smooth as a looking-glass. The English fleet were but a short distance to the north-ward of us; so near, indeed, that we could almost count their ports. They were becalmed, like ourselves, and a little scattered.

We took in our sweeps as ordered, laying them athwart the deck, in readiness to be used when wanted. The vessels ahead and astern of us were, generally, within speaking distance. Just as the sun went down below the horizon, George Turnblatt, a Swede, who was our gunner, came to me, and said he thought we ought to secure our guns; for we had been cleared for action all day, and the crew at quarters. We were still at quarters, in name, but the petty officers were allowed to move about, and as much license was given to the people as was wanted. I answered that I would gladly secure mine, if he would get an order for it, but, as we were still at quarters, and there lay John Bull, we might get a slap at him in the night. On this the gunner said he would go aft and speak to Mr Osgood on the subject. He did so, but met the captain (as we always called Mr Osgood) at the break of the quarter-deck. When George had told his errand, the captain looked at the heavens, and remarked that the night was so calm, there could be no great use in securing the guns, and the English were so near we should certainly engage if there came a breeze; that the men would sleep at their quarters, of course, and would be ready to take care of their guns, but that he might catch a turn with the side-tackle-fall round the pommelions of the guns, which would be sufficient. He then ordered the boatswain to call all hands aft to the break of the quarterdeck.

As soon as the people had collected, Mr Osgood said: "You must be pretty well fagged out, men; I think we may have a hard night's work yet, and I wish you to get to your suppers, and then catch as much sleep as you can at your guns." He then ordered the purser's-steward to splice the mainbrace. These were the last words I ever heard from Mr Osgood. As soon as he gave the order, he went below, leaving the deck in charge of Mr Bogardus. All our old crew were on board but Mr Livingston, who had left us, and Simeon Grant, one of my companions in the cruise over the battle-ground at Fort George. Grant had cut his hand off in a saw-mill while we were last at the Harbour, and had been left behind in the hospital. There was a pilot who used to keep a look-out occasionally, and sometimes the boatswain had the watch.

The schooner, at this time, was under her mainsail, jib, and foretopsail. The foresail was brailed, and the foot stopped, and the flying-jib was stowed. None of the halyards were racked, nor sheets stoppered. This was a precaution we always took, on account of the craft being so tender.

We first spliced the mainbrace, and then got our suppers, eating between the guns, where we generally messed, indeed. One of my messmates, Tom Goldsmith, was captain of the gun next to me, and as we sat there finishing our suppers, I says to him, "Tom, bring up that rug that you pinned at Little York, and that will do for both of us to stow ourselves away under." Tom went down and got the rug, which was an article for the camp that he had laid hands on, and it made us a capital bed-quilt. As all hands were pretty well tired, we lay down with our heads on shot-boxes, and soon went to sleep.

In speaking of the canvas that was set, I ought to have said something of the state of our decks. The guns had the side-tackles fastened as I have mentioned. There was a box of canister, and another of grape, at each gun, besides extra stands of both under the shot-racks. There was also one grummet of round-shot at every gun, besides the racks being filled. Each gun's crew slept at the gun and its opposite, thus dividing the people pretty equally on both sides of the deck. Those who were stationed below, slept below. I think it probable that, as the night grew cool, as it always does on the fresh waters, some of the men stole below to get warmer berths. This was easily done in that craft, as we had but two regular acting officers on board, the acting boatswain and gunner being little more than two of ourselves.

I was soon asleep, as sound as if lying in the bed of a king. How long my nap lasted, or what took place in the interval, I cannot say. I awoke, however, in consequence of large drops of rain falling on my face. Tom Goldsmith awoke at the same moment. When I opened my eyes, it was so dark I could not see the length of the deck. I arose and spoke to Tom, telling him it was about to rain, and that I meant to go down and get a nip, out of a little stuff we kept in our messchest; and that I would bring up the bottle if he wanted a taste. Tom answered, "This is nothing; we're neither pepper nor salt." One of the black men spoke, and asked me to bring up the bottle, and give him a nip too. All this took half a minute, perhaps. I now remember to have heard a strange rushing noise to windward as I went towards the forward hatch, though it made no impression on me at the time. We had been lying between the starboard guns, which was the weather side of the vessel, if there were any weather side to it, there not being a breath of air, and no motion to the water; and I passed round to the larboard side, in order to find the ladder, which led up in that direction. The hatch was so small that two men could not pass at a time, and I felt my way to it, in no haste. One hand was on the bitts, and a foot was on the ladder, when a flash of lightning almost blinded me. The thunder came at the next instant, and with it a rushing of winds that fairly smothered the clap.

The instant I was aware there was a squall, I sprang for the jib-sheet. Being captain of the forecastle, I knew where to find it, and threw it loose at a jerk. In doing this, I jumped on a man named Leonard Lewis, and called on him to lend me a hand. I next let fly the larboard, or lee topsail sheet, got hold of the clew-line, and, assisted by Lewis, got the clew half up. All this time I kept shouting to the man at the wheel to put his helm "hard down". The water was now up to my breast, and I knew the schooner must go over: Lewis had not said a word, but I called out to him to shift for himself, and belaying the clew-line, in hauling myself forward of the foremast, I received a blow from the jib-sheet that came near breaking my left arm. I did not feel the effect of this blow at the time, though the arm has since been operated on, to extract a tumour produced by this very injury.

All this occupied less than a minute. The flashes of lightning were incessant, and nearly blinded me. Our decks seemed on fire, and yet I could see nothing. I heard no hail, no order, no call; but the schooner was filled with the shrieks and cries of the men to leeward, who were lying jammed under the guns, shot-boxes, shot, and other heavy things that had gone down as the vessel fell over. The starboard second gun, from forward, had capsized, and come down directly over the forward hatch, and I caught a glimpse of a man struggling to get past it. Apprehension of this gun had induced me to drag myself forward of the mast, where I received the blow mentioned.

I succeeded in hauling myself up to the windward, and in getting into the schooner's fore-channels. Here I met William Deer, the boatswain, and a black boy of the name of Philips, who was the powder-boy of our gun. "Deer, she's gone!" I said. The boatswain made no answer, but walked out on the fore-rigging, towards the mast-head. He probably had some vague notion that the schooner's masts would be out of water if she went down, and took this course as the safest. The boy was in the chains the last I saw of him.

I now crawled aft, on the upper side of the bulwarks, amid a most awful and infernal din of thunder, and shrieks, and dazzling flashes of lightning; the wind blowing all the while like a tornado. When I reached the port of my own gun, I put a foot in it, thinking to step on the muzzle of the piece; but it had gone to leeward with all the rest, and I fell through the port until I brought up with my arms. I struggled up again, and continued working my way aft. As I got abreast of the mainmast, I saw someone had let run the halyards. I soon reached the beckets of the sweeps, and found four in them. I could not swim a stroke, and it crossed my mind to get one of the sweeps to keep me afloat. In striving to get the becket clear, it parted, and the forward ends of the four sweeps rolled down the schooner's side into the water. This caused the other ends to slide, and all the sweeps got away from me. I then crawled quite aft, as far as the fashion-piece. The water was pouring down the cabin companion-way like a sluice; and as I stood, for an instant, on the fashion-piece, I saw Mr Osgood, with his head and part of his shoulders through one of the cabin windows, struggling to get out. He must have been within six feet of me. I saw him but a moment, by means of a flash of lightning, and I think he must have seen me. At the same time, there was a man visible on the end of the main boom, holding on by the clew of the sail. I do not know who it was. This man probably saw me, and that I was about to spring; for he called out, "Don't jump overboard! – don't jump overboard! The schooner is righting."

I was not in a state of mind to reflect much on anything. I do not think more than three or four minutes, if as many, had passed since the squall struck us, and there I was standing on the vessel's quarter, led by Providence more than by any discretion of my own. It now came across me that if the schooner should right, she was filled, and must go down, and that she might carry me with her in the suction. I made a spring, therefore, and fell into the water several feet from the place where I had stood. It is my opinion the schooner sunk as I left her. I went down some distance myself, and when I came up to the surface, I began to swim vigorously for the first time in my life. I think I swam several yards, but of course will not pretend to be certain of such a thing, at such a moment, until I felt my hand hit something hard. I made another stroke, and felt my hand pass down the side of an object that I knew at once was a clincher-built boat. I belonged to this boat, and I now recollected that she had been towing astern. Until that instant I had not thought of her, but thus was I led in the dark to the best possible means of saving my life. I made a grab at the gunwale, and caught it in the stern-sheets. Had I swam another yard, I should have passed the boat, and missed her altogether! I got in without any difficulty, being all alive and much excited.

My first look was for the schooner. She had disappeared, and I supposed she was just settling under water. It rained as if the flood-gates of heaven were opened, and it lightened awfully. It did not seem to me that there was a breath of air, and the water was unruffled, the effect of the rain excepted. All this I saw, as it might be at a glance. But my chief concern was to preserve my own life. I was cockswain of this very boat, and had made it fast to the taffrail that same afternoon, with a round turn and two half hitches, by its best painter. Of course I expected the vessel would drag the boat down with her, for I had no knife to cut the painter. There was a gang-board in the boat, however, which lay fore and aft, and I thought this might keep me afloat until some of the fleet should pick me up. To clear this gang-board, then, and get it into the water, was my first object. I ran forward to throw off the lazy painter that was coiled on its end, and in doing this I caught the boat's painter in my hand, by accident. A pull satisfied me that it was all clear! Someone on board must have cast off this painter, and then lost his chance of getting into the boat by an accident. At all events, I was safe, and I now dared to look about me.

My only chance of seeing, was during the flashes: and these left me almost blind. I had thrown the gang-board into the water, and I now called out to encourage the men, telling them I was in the boat. I could hear many around me, and, occasionally, I saw the heads of men, struggling in the lake. There being no proper place to scull in, I got an oar in the after-rullock, and made out to scull a little, in that fashion. I now saw a man quite near the boat, and, hauling in the oar, made a spring amidships, catching this poor fellow by the collar. He was very near gone; and I had a great deal of difficulty in getting him in over the gunwale. Our joint weight brought the boat down so low that she shipped a good deal of water. This turned out to be Leonard Lewis, the young man who had helped me to clew up the foretopsail. He could not stand, and spoke with difficulty. I asked him to crawl aft, out of the water; which he did, lying down in the stern-sheets.

I now looked about me, and heard another; leaning over the gunwale, I got the glimpse of a man, struggling, quite near the boat. I caught him by the collar too, and had to drag him in very much in the way I had done with Lewis. This proved to be Lemuel Bryant, the man who had been wounded by a hot shot at York, as already mentioned, while the commodore was on board us. His wound had not yet healed, but he was less exhausted than Lewis. He could not help me, however, lying down in the bottom of the boat the instant he was able.

For a few moments I now heard no more in the water, and I began to scull again. By my calculation I moved a few yards, and must have got over the spot where the schooner went down. Here, in the flashes, I saw many heads, the men swimming in confusion, and at random. By this time little was said, the whole scene being one of fearful struggling and frightful silence. It still rained; but the flashes were less frequent, and less fierce. They told me afterwards, in the squadron, that it thundered awfully; but I cannot say I heard a clap after I struck the water. The next man caught the boat himself. It was a mulatto, from Martinique, who was Mr Osgood's steward, and I helped him in. He was much exhausted, though an excellent swimmer; but alarm nearly deprived him of his strength. He kept saying, "Oh! Masser Ned! – Oh! Masser Ned!" and lay down in the bottom of the boat, like the two others; I taking care to shove him over to the larboard side, so as to trim our small craft.

I kept calling out, to encourage the swimmers, and presently I heard a voice saying, "Ned, I'm here, close by you." This was Tom Goldsmith, a mess-mate, and the very man under whose rug I had been sleeping at quarters. He did not want much help, getting in pretty much by himself. I asked him if he were able to help me. "Yes, Ned," he answered, "I'll stand by you to the last; what shall I do?" I told him to take his tarpaulin, and to bail the boat, which by this time was a third full of water. This he did, while I sculled a little ahead. "Ned," says Tom, "she's gone down with her colours flying, for her pennant came near getting a round turn about my body, and carrying me down with her. Davy has made a good haul, and he gave us a close shave; but he didn't get you and me." In this manner did this thoughtless sailor express himself, as soon as rescued from the grasp of death! Seeing something in the water, I asked Tom to take my oar, while I sprang to the gunwale and caught Mr Bogardus, the master's mate, who was clinging to one of the sweeps. I hauled him in, and he told me he thought someone had hold of the other end of the sweep. It was so dark, however, we could not see even that distance. I hauled the sweep along, until I found Ebenezer Duffy, a mulatto, and the ship's cook. He could not swim a stroke, and was nearly gone. I got him in alone, Tom bailing, lest the boat, which was quite small, would swamp with us.

As the boat drifted along, she reached another man, whom I caught also by the collar. I was afraid to haul this person in amidships, the boat being now so deep, and so small, and so I dragged him ahead, and hauled him in over the bows. This was the pilot, whose name I never knew. He was a lakeman, and had been aboard us the whole summer. The poor fellow was almost gone; and, like all the rest, with the exception of Tom, he lay down and said not a word.

We had now as many in the boat as it would carry, and Tom and myself thought it would not do to take in any more. It is true we saw no more, everything around us appearing as still as death, the pattering of the rain excepted. Tom began to bail again, and I commenced hallooing. I sculled about several minutes, thinking of giving others a tow, or of even hauling in one or two more, after we got the water out of the boat; but we found no one else. I think it probable I sculled away from the spot, as there was nothing to guide me. I suppose, however, that by this time all the *Scourge*'s had gone down, for no more were ever heard from.

Tom Goldsmith and myself now put our heads together as to what was best to be done. We were both afraid of falling into the enemy's hands, for they might have bore up in the squall, and run down near us. On the whole, however, we thought the distance between the two squadrons was too great for this; at all events, something must be done at once. So we began to row, in what direction even we did not know. It still rained as hard as it could pour, though there was not a breath of wind. The lightning came now at considerable intervals, and the gust was evidently passing away towards the broader parts of the lake. While we were rowing, and talking about our chance of falling in with the enemy, Tom cried out to me to "Avast pulling". He had seen a vessel, by a flash, and he thought she was English from her size. As he said she was a schooner, however, I thought it must be one of our own craft, and got her direction from him. At the next flash I saw her, and felt satisfied she belonged to us. Before we began to pull, however, we were hailed "Boat ahoy!" I answered.

"If you pull another stroke, I'll fire into you," came back. "What boat's that? Lay on your oars, or I'll fire into you."

It was clear we were mistaken ourselves for an enemy, and I called out to know what schooner it was. No answer was given, though the threat to fire was repeated, if we pulled another stroke. I now turned to Tom and said, "I know that voice; that is old Trant." Tom thought "we were in the wrong shop". I now sang out, "This is the *Scourge*'s boat – our schooner has gone down, and we want to come alongside."

A voice next called out from the schooner, "Is that you, Ned?" This I knew was my old shipmate and schoolfellow, Jack Mallet, who was acting as boat-swain of the *Julia*, the schooner commanded by Sailing-master James Trant, one of the oddities of the service, and a man with whom the blow often came as soon as the word. I had know Mr Trant's voice, and felt more afraid he would fire into us, than I had done of anything which had occurred that fearful night. Mr Trant himself now called out, "Oh-ho! give way, boys, and come alongside." This we did, and a very few strokes took us up to the *Julia*, where we were received with the utmost kindness. The men were passed out of the boat, while I gave Mr Trant an account of all that had happened. This took but a minute or two.

Mr Trant now inquired in what direction the *Scourge* had gone down; and, as soon as I had told him, in the best manner I could, he called out to Jack Mallet, "Oh-ho, Mallet! – take four hands, and go in the boat, and see what you can do; take a lantern, and I will show a light on the water's edge, so you may know me." Mallet did as ordered, and was off in less than three minutes after we got alongside. Mr Trant, who was much humoured, had no officer in the *Julia*, unless Mallet could be called one. He was an Irishman by birth, but had been in the American navy ever since the revolution, dying a lieutenant a few years after this war. Perhaps no man in the navy was more generally known, or excited more amusement by his oddities, or more respect for his courage. He had come on the lake with the commodore, with whom he was a great pet, and had been active in all the fights and affairs that had yet taken place. His religion was to hate an Englishman.

Mr Trant now called the *Scourge*'s aft, and asked more of the particulars. He then gave us a glass of grog all round, and made his own crew splice the mainbrace. The *Julia*'s now offered us dry clothes. I got a change from Jack Reilly, who had been an old messmate, and with whom I had always been on good terms. It knocked off raining, but we shifted ourselves at the galley-fire below. I then went on deck, and presently we heard the boat pulling back. It soon came alongside, bringing in it four men that had been found floating about on sweeps and gratings. On inquiry, it turned out that these men belonged to the *Hamilton*, Lieutenant Winter, a schooner that had gone down in the same squall that carried us over. These men were very much exhausted too, and we all went below, and were told to turn in.

I had been so much excited during the scenes through which I had just passed, and had been so much stimulated by grog, that, as yet, I had not felt much of the depression natural to such events. I even slept soundly that night, nor did I turn out until six the next morning.

When I got on deck, there was a fine breeze; it was a lovely day, and the lake was perfectly smooth. Our fleet was in a good line, in pretty close order, with the exception of the *Governor Tompkins*, Lieutenant Tom Brown, which was a little to leeward, but carrying a press of sail to close with the commodore. Mr Trant, perceiving that the *Tompkins* wished to speak us in passing, brailed his foresail, and let her luff up close under our lee. "Two of the schooners, the *Hamilton* and the *Scourge*, have gone down in the night," called out Mr Brown, "for I have picked up four of the *Hamilton*'s." "Oh-ho!" answered Mr Trant, "that's no news at all! for I have picked up *twelve*: eight of the *Scourge*'s and four of the *Hamilton*'s, aft fore-sheet."

These were all that were ever saved from the two schooners, which must have had near a hundred souls on board of them. The two commanders, Lieutenant Winter and Mr Osgood, were both lost; and with Mr Winter went down, I believe, one or two young gentlemen. The squadron could not have moved much between the time when the accidents happened and that when I came on deck; or we must have come round and gone over the same ground again, for we now passed many relics of the scene, floating about in the water. I saw sponges, gratings, sweeps, hats, &c., scattered about; and, in passing ahead, we saw one of the latter that we tried to catch, Mr Trant ordering it done, as he said it must have been Lieutenant Winter's. We did not succeed, however; nor was any article taken on board. A good look-out was kept for men from aloft, but none were seen from any of the vessels. The lake had swallowed up the rest of the two crews;

and the *Scourge*, as had been often predicted, had literally become a coffin to a large portion of her people.

There was a good deal of manœuvring between the two fleets this day, and some efforts were made to engage; but, to own the truth, I felt so melancholy about the loss of so many shipmates, that I did not take much notice of what passed. All my Black Jokers were drowned, and nothing remained of the craft and people with which and whom I had been associated all summer. Bill Southard, too, was among the lost, as indeed were all my messmates but Tom Goldsmith and Lemuel Bryant. I had very serious and proper impressions for the moment, but my new shipmates, some of whom had been old shipmates in other crafts, managed to cheer me up with grog. The effect was not durable, and in a short time I ceased to think of what had happened. I have probably reflected more on the merciful manner in which my life was spared, amid a scene so terrific, within the last five years, than I did in the twenty-five that immediately followed the accidents.

The fleet went in off the Niagara, and anchored. Mr Trant now mustered the remaining *Scourge*'s, and told us he wanted just our number of hands, and that he meant to get an order to keep us in the *Julia*. In the meantime he should station and quarter us. I was stationed at the braces, and quartered at the long thirty-two as second loader. The *Julia* mounted a long thirty-two and an eighteen on pivots, besides two sixes in the waist. The last were little used, as I have already mentioned. She was a small, but a fast schooner, and had about forty souls on board. She was altogether a better craft than the *Scourge*, though destitute of any quarters, but a low rail with wash-boards, and carrying fewer guns.

I never knew what became of the four *Hamilton*'s that were picked up by the *Julia*'s boat, though I suppose they were put in some other vessel along with their shipmates; nor did I ever learn the particulars of the loss of this schooner, beyond the fact that her topsail sheets were stoppered, and her halyards racked. This much I learned from the men who were brought on board the *Julia*, who said that their craft was ready, in all respects, for action. Some seamen have thought this wrong, and some right; but, in my opinion, it made but little difference in such a gust as that which passed over us. What was remarkable, the *Julia*, which could not have been far from the *Scourge* when we went over, felt no great matter of wind, just luffing up, and shaking her sails to be rid of it.

We lay only one night off the mouth of the Niagara. The next morning the squadron weighed, and stood out in pursuit of the English. The weather was very variable, and we could not get within reach of Sir James all that day. This was the 9th of August. The *Scourge* had gone down on the night of the 7th, or the morning of the 8th, I never knew which. On the morning of the 10th, however, we were under the north shore, and to windward of John Bull. The commodore now took the *Asp*, and the *Madison* the *Fair American*, in tow, and we all kept away, expecting certainly a general action. But the wind shifted, bringing the English to windward. The afternoon was calm, or had variable affairs. Towards sunset, the enemy was

becalmed under the American shore, and we got a
breeze from the southward. We now ceased, and at six
formed our line for engaging. We continued to close
until seven, when the wind came out fresh at S.W.,
putting John again to windward.

I can hardly tell what followed, there was so much
manœuvring and shifting of berths. Both squadrons
were standing across the lake, the enemy being to
windward, and a little astern of us. We now passed
within hail of the commodore, who gave us orders to
form a new line of battle, which we did in the
following manner. One line, composed of the smallest schooners, was formed to windward, while the
ships, brig, and two heaviest schooners, formed
another line to leeward. We had the weathermost
line, having the *Growler*, Lieutenant Deacon, for the
vessel next astern of us. This much I could see,
though I did not understand the object. I now learn
the plan was for the weather line to engage the
enemy, and then, by edging away, draw them down
upon the lee line, which line contained our principal
force. According to the orders, we ought to have
rather edged off, as soon as the English began to
fire, in order to draw them down upon the commodore; but it will be seen that our schooner pursued a
very different course.

It must have been near midnight, when the enemy
began to fire at the *Fair American*, the sternmost
vessel of our weather line. We were a long bit ahead
of her, and did not engage for some time. The firing
became pretty smart astern, but we stood on, without
engaging, the enemy not yet being far enough ahead
for us. After a while, the four sternmost schooners of

our line kept off, according to orders, but the *Julia* and *Growler* still stood on. I suppose the English kept off too, at the same time, as the commodore had expected. At any rate, we found ourselves so well up with the enemy, that instead of bearing up, Mr Trant tacked in the *Julia*, and the *Growler* came round after us. We now began to fire on the headmost ships of the enemy, which were coming on towards us. We were able to lay past the enemy on this tack, and fairly got to windward of them. When we were a little on John Bull's weather-bow, we brailed the foresail, and gave him several rounds, within a pretty fair distance. The enemy answered us, and from that moment he seemed to give up all thoughts of the vessels to leeward of him, turning his whole attention on the *Julia* and *Growler*.

The English fleet stood on the same tack, until it had got between us and our own line, when it went about in chase of us. We now began to make short tacks to windward; the enemy separating so as to spread a wide clew, in order that they might prevent our getting past, by turning their line and running to leeward. As for keeping to windward, we had no difficulty – occasionally brailing our foresail, and even edging off, now and then, to be certain that our shot would tell. In moderate weather, the *Julia* was the fastest vessel in the American squadron, the *Lady of the Lake* excepted; and the *Growler* was far from being dull. Had there been room, I make no doubt we might have kept clear of John Bull, with the greatest ease, touching him up with our long, heavy guns, from time to time as it suited us. I have often thought that Mr Trant forgot we were between the enemy and the land, and that he fancied himself out at sea. It was a hazy moonlight morning, and we did not see anything of the main, though it turned out to be nearer to us than we wished.

All hands were now turning to windward; the two schooners still edging off, occasionally, and firing. The enemy's shot went far beyond us, and did us some mischief, though nothing that was not immediately repaired. The main throat-halyards, on board the *Julia*, were shot away, as was the clew of the mainsail. It is probable the enemy did not keep his luff, towards the last, on account of the land.

Our two schooners kept quite near each other, sometimes one being to windward, sometimes the other. It happened that the *Growler* was a short distance to windward of us, when we first became aware of the nature of our critical situation. She up helm, and, running down within hail, Lieutenant Deacon informed Mr Trant that he had just sounded in two fathoms, and that he could see lights ashore. He thought there must be Indians, in great numbers, in this vicinity, and that we must, at all events, avoid the land. "What do you think we had best do?" asked Lieutenant Deacon. "Run the gauntlet," called out Mr Trant. "Very well, sir; which shall lead?" "I'll lead the van," answered Mr Trant; and then all was settled.

We now up helm, and steered for a vacancy among the British vessels. The enemy seemed to expect us, for they formed in two lines, leaving us room to enter between them. When we bore up, even in these critical circumstances, it was under our mainsail, foretopsail, jib, flying-jib, and foresail. So insufficient were the equipments of these small craft, that we had neither square-sail nor studding-sails aboard us. I never saw a studding-sail in any of the schooners, the *Scourge* excepted.

The *Julia* and *Growler* now ran down, the former leading half a cable's length apart. When we entered between the two lines of the enemy, we were within short canister-range, and got it smartly on both tacks. The two English ships were to leeward, each leading a line; and we had a brig, and three large regular man-of-war schooners, to get past, with the certainty of meeting the *Wolfe* and the *Royal George*, should we succeed in clearing these four craft. Both of us kept up a heavy fire, swivelling our guns round, so as not to neglect any one. As we drew near the ships, however, we paid them the compliment of throwing all the heavy shot at them, as was due to their rank and size.

For a few minutes we fared pretty well; but we were no sooner well entered between the lines, than we got it hot and hard. Our rigging began to come down about our ears, and one shot passed a few feet above our heads, cutting both topsail sheets, and scooping a bit of wood as big as a thirty-two pound shot out of the foremast. I went up on one side myself, to knot one of these sheets, and, while aloft, discovered the injury that had been done to the spar. Soon after, the tack of the mainsail caught fire, from a wad of one of the Englishmen; for, by this time, we were close at it. I think, indeed, that the nearness of the enemy alone prevented our decks from being entirely swept. The grape and canister were passing just above our heads like hail, and the foresail was literally in ribands. The halyards being gone, the mainsail came down by the

run, and the jib settled as low as it could. The topsail-
yard was on the cap, and the schooner now came up
into the wind.

All this time, we kept working the guns. The old
man went up from one gun to the other, pointing each
himself, as it was ready. He was at the eighteen when
things were getting near the worst, and, as he left her,
he called out to her crew to "fill her – fill her to the
muzzle!" He then came to our gun, which was already
loaded with one round, a stand of grape, and a case of
canister shot. This I know, for I put them all in with
my own hands. At this time, the *Melville*, a brig of the
enemy's, was close up with us, firing upon our decks
from her foretop. She was coming up on our larboard
quarter, while a large schooner was nearing us fast on
the starboard. Mr Trant directed our guns to be
elevated, so as to sweep the brig's forecastle, and then
he called out, "Now's the time, lads, – fire away at
'em!" But no match was to be found! Someone had
thrown both overboard. By this time the brig's jib-
boom was over our quarter, and the English were
actually coming on board of us. The enemy were
now all round us. The *Wolfe* herself was within hail,
and still firing. The last I saw of any of our people, was
Mallet passing forward, and I sat down on the slide of
the thirty-two, myself, sullen as a bear. Two or three
of the English passed me without saying anything.
Even at this instant, a volley of bullets came out of the
brig's foretop, and struck all around me; some hitting
the deck, and others the gun itself.

Just then, an English officer came up, and said –
"What are you doing here, you Yankee?" I felt exceedingly savage, and answered, "Looking at your

fools firing on their own men." "Take that for your sauce," he said, giving me a thrust with his sword, as he spoke. The point of the cutlass just passed my hip-bone, and gave me a sharp flesh wound. The hurt was not dangerous, though it bled freely, and was some weeks in healing. I now rose to go below, and heard a hail from one of the ships – the *Wolfe*, as I took her to be. "Have you struck?" demanded someone. The officer who had hurt me, now called out, "Don't fire into us, sir, for I'm on board, and have got posses-sion." The officer from the ship next asked, "Is there anybody alive on board her?" To which the prize-officer answered, "I don't know, sir; I've seen but one man, as yet."

I now went down below. First, I got a bandage on my wound, to stop the bleeding, and then I had an opportunity to look about me. A party of English was below, and some of our men having joined them the heads were knocked out of two barrels of whisky. The kids and bread-bags were procured, and all hands, without distinction of country, sat down to enjoy themselves. Some even began to sing, and as for good fellowship, it was just as marked as it would have been in a jollification ashore.

In a few minutes the officer who had hurt me jumped down among us. The instant he saw what we were at he sang out – "Halloo! here's high life below stairs!" Then he called to another officer to bear a hand down and see the fun. Someone sung out from among ourselves to "douse the glim"! The lights were put out, and then the two officers capsized the whisky. While this was doing, most of the Englishmen ran up the forward hatch. We *Julia*'s all remained below.

In less than an hour we were sent on board the enemy's vessels. I was carried to the *Royal George*, but Mr Trant was taken on board the *Wolfe*. The *Growler* had lost her bowsprit, and was otherwise damaged, and had been forced to strike also. She had a man killed, and, I believe, one or two wounded. On board of us, not a man, besides myself, had been touched! We seemed to have been preserved by a miracle, for every one of the enemy had a slap at us, and for some time we were within pistol-shot. Then we had no quarters at all, being perfectly exposed to grape and canister. The enemy must have fired too high, for nothing else could have saved us.

In July, while I still belonged to the *Scourge*, I had been sent with a boat's crew, under Mr Bogardus, on board an English flag of truce that had come into the harbour. While in this vessel, our boat's crew were "hail-fellows well-met" with the Englishmen, and we had agreed among us to take care of each other, should either side happen to be taken. I had been on board the *Royal George* but a short time, when two of these very men came up to me with some grog and some grub; and next morning they brought me my bitters. I saw no more of them, however, except when they came to shake hands with us at the gangway, as we were leaving the ship.

After breakfast, next morning, we were all called aft to the ward-room, one at a time. I was pumped as to the force of the Americans, the names of the vessels, the numbers of the crews, and the names of the commanders. I answered a little saucily, and was ordered out of the ward-room. As I was quitting the place, I was called back by one of the lieutenants, whose appearance I did not like from the first. Although it was now eight years since I left Halifax, and we had both so much altered, I took this gentleman for Mr Bowen, the very midshipman of the *Cleopatra*, who had been my schoolmate, and whom I had known on board the prize-brig I have mentioned.

This officer asked me where I was born. I told him New York. He said he knew better, and asked my name. I told him it was what he found it on the muster-roll, and that by which I had been called. He said I knew better, and that I should hear more of this hereafter. If this were my old schoolfellow, he knew that I was always called Edward Robert Meyers, whereas I had dropped the middle name, and now called myself Myers. He may not, however, have been the person I took him for, and might have mistaken me for someone else; for I never had an opportunity for ascertaining any more about him.

We got into Little York, and were sent ashore that evening. I can say nothing of our squadron, having been kept below the whole time I was on board the *Royal George*. I could not find out whether we did the enemy any harm or not the night we were taken; though I remember that a sixty-eight pound caronnade, that stood near the gangway of the *Royal George*, was dismounted the night I passed into her. It looked to me as if the trucks were gone. This I know, that the ship was more than usually screened off; though for what reason I will not pretend to say.

At York we were put in the gaol, where we were kept three weeks. Our treatment was every way bad, with the exception that we were not crowded. As to food, we were kept "six upon four" the whole time I was prisoner.* The bread was bad, and the pork little better. While in this gaol, a party of drunken Indians gave us a volley in passing, but luckily it did us no harm.

* By this, Myers means that six men had to subsist on the usual allowance of four men.

George Little

Privateering

1812–13

A merchant seaman from Massachusetts, George Little served the War of 1812 on board privateers, his time engaged in something akin to licensed piracy. And the avoiding of cannibals . . .

A BAND OF RUTHLESS DESPERADOES

I now sailed on my sixth voyage, and arrived safely in Buenos Ayres. After having been there a few days another vessel arrived from Rio, having persons on board with powers to attach my vessel and cargo from under me. I soon learned that the house at Rio, in whose employment I sailed, had failed for a large amount, and that these persons were their creditors.

I was now left without a vessel, and fearing that I should lose the funds placed in their hands, lost no time in getting back to Rio, and when there I found the condition of the house even worse than I had anticipated; for all my two years' hard earnings were gone, with the exception of about five hundred dollars.

With this small sum I took passage in the ship *Scioto*, bound for Baltimore. I was induced to do this because little doubt was then entertained that there would be a war between the United States and England, and I was anxious to get home, if possible, before it was declared. We were fortunate enough to arrive in safety, although the war had been actually declared fifteen days before we got inside of the Capes of Virginia.

When we arrived in Baltimore, I found the most active preparations were in progress to prosecute the war. A number of privateers were fitting out, and everywhere the American flag might be seen flying, denoting the places of rendezvous: in a word, the most intense excitement prevailed throughout the city, and the position of a man was not at all enviable if it were ascertained that he was in any degree favourably disposed towards the British. It happened to fall to my lot to be an eyewitness to the unpleasant affair of tarring and feathering a certain Mr T., and also to the demolishing of the Federal Republican printing office by the mob.

Once more I returned to Boston to see my friends, whom I found pretty much in the same situation as when I left them. Two years had made but little alteration, except that my sister was married, and my father, being aged, had retired from the navy and taken up his residence in Marshfield. Every persuasion was now used to induce me to change my vocation, backed by the strong reasoning that the war would destroy commerce, and that no alternative would be left for seamen but the unhallowed pursuit of privateering.

These arguments had great weight, and I began to think seriously of entering into some business on shore, but then most insuperable difficulties arose in my mind as to the nature of the business I should pursue. My means were limited, quite too much so to enter into the mercantile line, and the only branch of it with which I was acquainted was the "commission"; another obstacle presented itself, which was to fix upon an eligible location. These difficulties, however, soon vanished, for a wealthy relative offered me the use of his credit, and a young friend with whom I was acquainted, having just returned from the south, informed me that there was a fine opening in Richmond, Virginia. Whereupon we immediately entered into a mutual arrangement to establish a commission house in that place. The necessary preparations were made, and we started for the south.

To my great surprise and mortification, however, when we reached Norfolk, I ascertained that my partner was without funds; neither had he the expectation of receiving any. This changed the current of my fortunes altogether. I was deceived by him, consequently all intercourse was broken off between us.

As my prospects were now blasted in reference to establishing myself in business on shore, I resolved once more to embark on my favourite element and try my luck there again. Here too, in Norfolk, all was bustle and excitement, drums beating, colours flying, soldiers enlisting, men shipping in the States' service, and many privateers fitting out, creating such a scene of confusion as I had never before witnessed.

Young and of an ardent temperament, I could not look upon all these stirring movements an unmoved spectator; accordingly I entered on board the *George Washington* privateer, in the capacity of first lieutenant. She mounted one twelve-pounder on a pivot, and two long nines, with a complement of eighty men. She was in all respects a beautiful schooner of the most exact symmetrical proportions, about one hundred and twenty tons burden, and said to be as swift as anything that floated the ocean.

In reference to this enterprise, I must confess, in my cooler moments, that I had some qualms; to be sure here was an opportunity of making a fortune, but then it was counterbalanced by the possibility of getting my head knocked off, or a chance of being thrown into prison for two or three years; however, I had gone too far to recede, and I determined to make the best of it. Accordingly I placed what little funds I had in the hands of Mr G., of Norfolk, and repaired on board the privateer with my dunnage contained in a small trunk and clothes bag. On the morning of July 20th, 1812, the officers and crew being all on board, we weighed anchor, made sail, and stood down the river, with the stars and stripes floating in the breeze, and were saluted with a tremendous cheering from the shore.

I now was on board of a description of craft with which I was entirely unacquainted; I had, therefore, much to learn. The lieutenants and prize-masters, however, were a set of clever fellows, but the captain was a rough, uncouth sort of a chap, and appeared to me to be fit for little else than fighting and plunder. The crew were a motley set indeed, composed of all nations: they appeared to have been scraped together from the lowest dens of wretchedness and vice, and

only wanted a leader to induce them to any act of
daring and desperation.

Our destination, in the first place, was to cruise on
the Spanish main, to intercept the English traders
between the West India islands and the ports on the
main. This cruising ground was chosen because, in
case of need, we might run into Carthagena to refit and
water. When we had run down as far as Lynnhaven
Bay, information was received from a pilot boat that
the British frigate *Belvidere* was cruising off the Capes.
This induced our captain to put to sea with the wind
from the southward, as the privateer's best sailing was
on the wind.

On the morning of the 22nd of July, we got under
way from Lynnhaven Bay, and stood to sea. At 9 a.m.,
when about 10 miles outside of Cape Henry lighthouse, a sail was discovered directly in the wind's eye
of us, bearing down under a press of canvas. Soon
ascertaining she was a frigate, supposed to be the
Belvidere, we stood on upon a wind until she came
within short gunshot. Our foresail was now brailed up
and the topsail lowered on the cap; at the same time the
frigate took in all her light sails and hauled up her
courses. As the privateer lay nearer the wind than the
frigate, the latter soon dropped in our wake, and when
within half-gunshot, we being under cover of her
guns, she furled her topgallant-sails: at the same moment we hauled aft the foresheet, hoisted away the
topsail, and tacked. By this manœuvre the frigate was
under our lee. We took her fire and continued to make
short boards, and in one hour were out of the reach of
her guns without receiving any damage.

This was our first adventure, and we hailed it as a

good omen. The crew were all in high spirits, because
the frigate was considered to be as fast as anything on
our coast at that time. And, furthermore, the captain
had not only gained the confidence of the crew by this
daring manœuvre, but we found we could rely upon
our heels for safety.

Nothing material occurred until we got into the
Mona passage, when we fell in with the *Black Joke*
privateer, of New York, and, being unable to ascertain
her character in consequence of a thick fog, we came
into collision and exchanged a few shots before we
found out we both wore the same national colours.
This vessel was a sloop of not very prepossessing
appearance, but as she had obtained some celebrity
for sailing in smooth water, having previously been an
Albany packet, she was fitted out as a privateer. In a
seaway, however, being very short, she could not make
much more headway than a tub.

It was agreed between the respective captains of the
two vessels to cruise in company, and, in the event of a
separation, to make a rendezvous at Carthagena. We
soon ascertained that our craft would sail nearly two
knots to the *Black Joke*'s one, and it may well be
supposed that our company-keeping was of short
duration.

In two days after parting with her the long wished for
cry of "Sail ho!" was sung out from the mast-head, and
we made all sail in chase. When within short gunshot we
let her have our midship gun, when she immediately
rounded to, took in the sail, hoisted English colours, and
seemed to be preparing to make a gallant defence. In this
we were not mistaken, for, as we ranged up, she opened a
brisk cannonading upon us.

I now witnessed the daring intrepidity of Captain S., for while the brig was pouring a destructive fire into us, with the greatest coolness he observed to the crew, "That vessel, my lads, must be ours in ten minutes after I run this craft under her lee quarter."

By this time we had sheered up under her stern and received the fire of her stern-chasers, which did us no other damage than cutting away some of our ropes and making wind holes through the sails. It was the work of a moment; the schooner luffed up under the lee of the brig, and, with almost the rapidity of thought, we were made fast to her main chains.

"Boarders away!" shouted Captain S. We clambered up the sides of the brig and dropped on board of her like so many locusts, not, however, till two of our lads were run through with boarding-pikes.

The enemy made a brave defence, but were soon over-powered by superior numbers, and the captain of the brig was mortally wounded. In twenty minutes after we got alongside, the stars and stripes were waving triumphantly over the British flag.

In this affair we had two killed and seven slightly wounded, besides having some of our rigging cut away and sails somewhat riddled. The brig was from Jamaica, bound to the Gulf of Maracaibo; her cargo consisted of sugar, fruit, and other produce. She was two hundred tons burden, mounted six six-pounders, with a complement of fifteen men all told. She was manned with a prize master and crew, and ordered to any port in the United States wherever she could get in.

This affair very much disgusted me with privateering, especially when I saw so much loss of life, and beheld a band of ruthless desperadoes, for such I must call our crew, robbing and plundering a few defence-less beings who were pursuing both a lawful and peaceable calling. It induced me to form a resolve that I would relinquish what, to my mind, appeared to be an unjustifiable and outrageous pursuit, for I could not help believing that no conscientious man could be engaged in privateering, and certainly there was no honour to be gained by it. The second lieutenant came to the same determination as myself, and both of us most cordially despised our commander, because it was with his permission that those most outrageous scenes of robbing and plundering were committed on board the brig.

After repairing damages, we steered away for Carthagena to fill up the water casks and provision the privateer, so that we might extend the cruise.

CAUGHT BY CANNIBALS

In a few days we arrived at our destination without falling in with any other vessel, and, on entering the port, we found our comrade, the *Black Joke* privateer, who had arrived a day or two previously. It is well known that, at this time, all the provinces of Spain had shaken off their allegiance to the mother country, and declared themselves independent. Carthagena, the most prominent of the provinces, was a place of con-siderable commerce, and about this time a few men-of-war and a number of privateers were fitted out there.

The Carthagenian flag now presented a chance of gain to the cupidity of the avaricious and desperate, among whom was our commander, Captain S. As soon, therefore, as we had filled up our water, a proposition was made by him to the second lieutenant and myself, to cruise under both flags, the American and Carthagenian, and this to be kept a profound secret from the crew until we had sailed from port. Of course we rejected the proposition with disdain, and told him the consequence of such a measure in the event of being taken by a man-of-war of any nation: that it was a piracy to all intents and purposes, according to the law of nations. We refused to go out in the privateer if he persisted in this most nefarious act, and we heard no more of it while we lay in port.

In a few days we were ready for sea, and sailed in company with our companion, her force being rather more than ours, but the vessel very inferior, as stated before, in point of sailing. While together we captured several small British schooners, the cargoes of which, together with some specie, were divided between the two privateers. Into one of the prizes we put all the prisoners, gave them plenty of water and provisions, and let them pursue their course. The remainder of the prizes were burned. We then parted company, and, being short of water, ran in towards the land in order to ascertain if any could be procured.

In approaching the shore, the wind died away to a perfect calm, and at 4 p.m. a small schooner was seen in shore of us. As we had not steerage-way upon our craft, of course it would be impossible to ascertain her character before dark; it was therefore determined by our commander to board her with the boats under cover of the night. This was a dangerous piece of service, but there was no backing out. Volunteers being called for, I stepped forward, and very soon a sufficient number of men to man two boats offered their services to back me. Every disposition was made for the attack. The men were strongly armed, oars muffled, and a grappling placed in each boat.

The bearings of the strange sail were taken, and night came on perfectly clear and cloudless. I took command of the expedition, the second lieutenant having charge of one boat. The arrangement was to keep close together until we got sight of the vessel; the second lieutenant was to board on the bow and I on the quarter. We proceeded in the most profound silence; nothing was heard save now and then a slight splash of the oars in the water, and before we obtained sight of the vessel I had sufficient time to reflect on this most perilous enterprise.

My reflections were not of the most pleasant description, and I found myself inwardly shrinking, when I was aroused by the voice of the bow-man, saying, "There she is, sir, two points on the starboard bow." There she lay sure enough, with every sail hoisted, and a light was distinctly seen, as we supposed from her deck, it being too high for the cabin windows. We now held a consultation, and saw no good reason to change the disposition of attack, except that we agreed to board simultaneously.

It may be well to observe here, that any number of men on a vessel's deck in the night have double the advantage to repel boarders, because they may secrete themselves in such a position as to fall upon an enemy unawares, and thereby cut them off with little difficulty. Being fully aware of this, I ordered the men, as soon as we gained the deck of the schooner, to proceed with great caution, and keep close together till every hazard of the enterprise was ascertained.

The boats now separated and pulled for their respective stations, observing the most profound silence. When we had reached within a few yards of the schooner, we laid upon our oars for some moments but could neither hear nor see anything. We then pulled away cheerily, and the next minute were under her counter, grappled to her, and every man leaped on deck without opposition.

The other boat boarded nearly at the same moment, and we proceeded in a body, with great caution, to examine the decks. A large fire was in the caboose, and we soon ascertained that her deck was entirely deserted, and that she neither had any boat on deck nor to her stern.

We then proceeded to examine the cabin, leaving an armed force on deck. The cabin, like the deck, being deserted, the mystery was easily unravelled. Probably concluding that we should board them under cover of the night, they, no doubt, as soon as it was dark, took to their boats and deserted the vessel. On the floor of the cabin was a part of an English ensign, and some papers which showed that she belonged to Jamaica. The little cargo on board consisted of Jamaica rum, sugar, and fruit.

The breeze now springing up and the privateer showing lights, we were enabled to get alongside of her in a couple of hours. A prizemaster and crew were put on board, with orders to keep company. During the night we ran ashore, and in the morning took on board the privateer the greater part of the prize's cargo.

Being close in shore in the afternoon, we descried a settlement of huts, and supposing that water might be obtained there, the two vessels were run in and anchored about two miles distant from the beach. A proposition was made to me by Captain S. to get the water casks on board the prize schooner, and, as she drew a light draught of water, I was to run her in and anchor her near the beach, taking with me the two boats and twenty men. I observed to Captain S. that this was probably an Indian settlement, and it was well known that all the Indian tribes on the coast of Rio de la Hache were exceedingly ferocious, and said to be cannibals; and it was also well known that whoever fell into their hands never escaped with their lives; so that it was necessary, before any attempt was made to land, that some of the Indians should be decoyed on board and detained as hostages for our safety.

At the conclusion of this statement a very illiberal allusion was thrown out by Captain S., and some doubts expressed in reference to my courage; he remarking that if I was afraid to undertake the expedition, he would go himself. This was enough for me; I immediately resolved to proceed if I sacrificed my life in the attempt.

The next morning twenty water casks were put on board the prize, together with the two boats and twenty men, well armed with muskets, pistols, and cutlasses, and a supply of ammunition; I repaired on board, got the prize under way, ran in, and anchored about one hundred yards from the beach. The boats were got in readiness, and the men were well armed and the water casks slung ready to proceed on shore. I had examined my pistols narrowly that morning, and had put them in complete order, and, as I believed, had taken every precaution for our future operations so as to prevent surprise.

There were about a dozen of ill-constructed huts or wigwams, but no spot of grass or shrub was visible to the eye, and only here and there the trunk of an old tree. One solitary Indian was seen stalking on the beach, and the whole scene presented the most wild and savage appearance, and to my mind augured very unfavourably.

We pulled in with the casks in tow, seven men being in each boat; when within a short distance of the beach, the boats' heads were put to seaward, and the Indian came abreast of us. Addressing him in Spanish, I inquired if water could be procured, to which he replied in the affirmative. I then displayed to his view some gew-gaws and trinkets, at which he appeared perfectly delighted, and with many signs and gestures invited me on shore. Thrusting my pistols into my belt, and buckling on my cartridge-box, I gave orders to the boat's crew that in case they discovered anything like treachery or surprise after I had gotten on shore, to cut the water casks adrift and make the best of their way on board the prize.

As soon as I had jumped on shore, I enquired if there were any live stock, such as fowls, to be had? Pointing to a hut about thirty yards from the boats, he said that the stock was there, and invited me to go and see it. I hesitated, suspecting some treachery; however, after repeating my order to the boats' crews, I proceeded with the Indian, and when within about a half-dozen yards of the hut, at a pre-concerted signal (as I suppose), as if by magic, at least one hundred Indians rushed out with the rapidity of thought.

I was knocked down, stripped of all my clothing except an inside flannel shirt, tied hand and foot, and then taken and secured to the trunk of a large tree, surrounded by about twenty squaws as a guard, who, with the exception of two or three, bore a most wild and hideous look in their appearance.

The capture of the boats' crews was simultaneous with my own, they being so much surprised and confounded at the stratagem of the Indians, that they had not the power, or presence of mind to pull off.

After they had secured our men, a number of them jumped into the boats, pulled off and captured the prize without meeting with any resistance from those on board, they being only six in number. Her cable was then cut and she was run on the beach, when they proceeded to dismantle her, by cutting the sails from the bolt-ropes, and taking out what little cargo there was, consisting of Jamaica rum and sugar. This being done, they led ropes on shore from the schooner, when about one hundred of them hauled her up nearly high and dry.

By this time the privateer had seen our disaster, stood boldly in and anchored within less than gunshot of the beach; they then very foolishly opened a brisk cannonade, but every shot was spent in vain. This exasperated the Indians, and particularly the one who had taken possession of my pistols. Casting my eye around, I saw him creeping toward me with one pistol presented, and when about five yards off, he pulled the trigger. But as Providence had no doubt ordered it, the pistol snapped; at the same moment a shot from the privateer fell a few yards from us, when the Indian rose upon his feet, cocked the pistol and fired it at the privateer; turning round with a most savage yell, he threw the pistol with great violence, which grazed my head, and then with a large stick beat and cut me until I was perfectly senseless.

This was about 10 o'clock, and I did not recover my consciousness until, as I supposed, about 4 o'clock in the afternoon. I perceived there were four squaws sitting around me, one of whom from her appearance, having on many gew-gaws and trinkets, was the wife of a chief. As soon as she discovered signs of returning consciousness, she presented me with a gourd, the contents of which appeared to be Indian meal mixed with water; she first drank and then gave it to me, and I can safely aver that I never drank any beverage before or since which produced such relief.

Night was now coming on, the privateer had got under way, and was standing off and on, with a flag of truce flying at her mast-head. The treacherous Indian with whom I had first conversed, came and, with a malignant smile, gave me the dreadful intelligence that at 12 o'clock that night we were to be roasted and eaten.

Accordingly at sunset I was unloosed and conducted by a band of about half a dozen savages to the spot where I found the remainder of our men firmly secured by having their hands tied behind them, their legs lashed together, and each man fastened to a stake that had been driven into the ground for that purpose. There was no possibility to elude the vigilance of these miscreants.

As soon as night shut in, a large quantity of brush

wood was piled around us, and nothing now was wanting but the fire to complete this horrible tragedy. The same malicious savage approached us once more, and with the deepest malignity taunted us with our coming fate. Having some knowledge of the Indian character, I summoned up all the fortitude of which I was capable, and in terms of defiance told him that twenty Indians would be sacrificed for each one of us sacrificed by him. I knew very well that it would not do to exhibit any signs of fear or cowardice, and having heard much of the cupidity of the Indian character, I offered the savage a large ransom if he would use his influence to procure our release.

Here the conversation was abruptly broken off by a most hideous yell from the whole tribe, occasioned by their having taken large draughts of the rum, which now began to operate very sensibly upon them; and as it will be seen operated very much to our advantage. This thirst for rum caused them to relax their vigilance, and we were left alone to pursue our reflections, which were not of the most enviable or pleasant character. A thousand melancholy thoughts rushed over my mind. Here I was, and in all probability in a few hours I should be in eternity, and my death one of the most horrible description. Oh! thought I, how many were the entreaties and arguments used by my friends to deter me from pursuing an avocation so full of hazard and peril. If I had taken their advice, and acceded to their solicitations, in all probability I should at this time have been in the enjoyment of much happiness.

I was aroused from this reverie by the most direful screams from the united voices of the whole tribe, they having drunk largely of the rum, and become so much intoxicated that a general fight ensued. Many of them lay stretched on the ground with tomahawks deeply implanted in their skulls, and many others, as the common phrase is, were dead drunk. This was an exceedingly fortunate circumstance for us. With their senses benumbed, of course they had forgotten their avowal to roast us, or, it may be, the Indian to whom I proposed ransom had conferred with the others, and they no doubt agreed to spare our lives until the morning.

It was a night however of pain and terror, as well as of the most anxious suspense, and when the morning dawn broke upon my vision, I felt an indescribable emotion of gratitude, as I had fully made up my mind the night previous that long before this time I should have been sleeping the sleep of death.

It was a pitiable sight, when the morning light broke forth, to see twenty human beings stripped naked, with their bodies cut and lacerated, and the blood issuing from their wounds, with their hands and feet tied, and their bodies fastened to stakes with brush wood piled around them, expecting every moment to be their last. My feelings on this occasion can be better imagined than described; suffice it to say, that I had given up all hopes of escape, and gloomily resigned myself to death.

When the fumes of the liquor had in some degree worn off from the benumbed senses of the savages, they arose and approached us, and for the first time the wily Indian informed me that the tribe had agreed to ransom us. They then cast off the lashings from our bodies and feet, and with our hands still secured drove us before them to the beach.

Then another difficulty arose: the privateer was out of sight, and the Indians became furious. To satiate their hellish malice they obliged us to run on the beach while they let fly their poisoned arrows after us. For my own part my limbs were so benumbed that I could scarcely walk, and I firmly resolved to stand still and take the worst of it, which was the best plan I could have adopted, for when they perceived that I exhibited no signs of fear, not a single arrow was discharged at me. Fortunately before they grew weary of this sport, to my great joy the privateer hove in sight. She stood boldly in with the flag of truce flying, and the savages consented to let one man of their own choosing go off in the boat to procure the stipulated ransom.

The boat returned loaded with articles of various descriptions, and two of our men were released. The boat kept plying to and from the privateer bringing with them such articles as they demanded, until all were released except myself.

Here it may be proper to observe, that the mulatto man who had been selected by the Indians performed all this duty himself, not one of the privateer's crew daring to hazard his life with him in the boat. I, then, was left alone, and for my release they required a double ransom. I began now seriously to think that they intended to detain me altogether. My mulatto friend, however, pledged himself that he would never leave me.

Again, for the last time, he sculled the boat off. She quickly returned with a larger amount of articles than previously. It was a moment of the deepest anxiety, for there had now arrived from the interior another tribe, apparently superior in point of numbers, and elated with the booty which had been obtained. They demanded a share, and expressed a determination to detain me for a larger ransom. These demands were refused, and a conflict ensued of the most frightful and terrific character. Tomahawks, knives, and arrows, were used indiscriminately, and many an Indian fell in that bloody contest. The tomahawks were thrown with the swiftness of arrows, and were generally buried in the skull or the breast; and whenever two came in contact with the famous "Indian hug", the strife was soon over with either one or the other, by one plunging the deadly knife up to the hilt in the body of his opponent; nor were the poisoned arrows of less swift execution, for wherever they struck, the wretched victim was quickly in eternity.

I shall never forget the frightful barbarity of that hour; although years have elapsed since its occurrence still the whole scene in imagination is before me – the savage yell of the war whoop, and the direful screams of the squaws still ring afresh in my ears.

In the height of this conflict, a tall Indian chief, who I knew belonged to the same tribe with the young squaw who gave me the drink, came down to the beach where I was. The boat had been discharged and was lying with her head off. At a signal given by the squaw to the chief, he caught me up in his arms with as much ease as if I had been a child, waded to the boat, threw me in, and then with a most expressive gesture, urged us off. Fortunately, there were two oars in the boat, and feeble as I was I threw all the remaining strength I had to the oar. It was the last effort, as life or death hung upon the next fifteen minutes.

Disappointed of a share of the booty, the savages

were frantic with rage, especially when they saw I had eluded their grasp. Rushing to the beach, about a dozen threw themselves into the other boat which had been captured and pulled after us; but fortunately, in their hurry, they had forgotten their muskets, and being unacquainted with the method of rowing, of course they made but little progress, which enabled us to increase our distance.

The privateer having narrowly watched all these movements, and seeing our imminent danger, stood boldly on toward the beach, and in the next five minutes she lay between us and the Indians, discharging a heavy fire of musketry among them. Such was the high excitement of my feelings that I scarcely recollected how I gained the privateer's deck. But I was saved, nevertheless, though I was weak with the loss of blood and savage treatment, my limbs benumbed, and body scorched with the piercing rays of the sun: the whole scene rushing through my mind with the celerity of electricity, it unmanned and quite overpowered me; I fainted and fell senseless on the deck.

The usual restoratives and care were administered and I soon recovered from the effects of my capture. Some of the others were not so fortunate; two of them especially were cut in a shocking manner, and the others were so dreadfully beaten and mangled by clubs, that the greatest care was necessary to save their lives.

My dislike for the captain had been very much increased since that unhappy, disastrous affair; it never would have occurred if he had taken my advice, as his illiberality, and the hints he threw out in reference to my want of courage, were the causes of my suffering, and the sad result of the enterprise. I determined, therefore, in conjunction with the second lieutenant, to leave the privateer as soon as we arrived in Carthagena, to which port we were bound.

David Porter

A Frigate in the
South Pacific

1812–14

Built at Salem in 1799, the Essex *was a small but highly armed frigate of 40 carronades, and 6 long 12 pounders. In 1812 the* Essex *under the command of David Porter USN, was sent to the South Pacific to wreck British whaling and shipping endeavours. On receiving this intelligence, the Admiralty sent in pursuit the frigate* Phoebe *(36) and sloop* Cherub *(18). The two sides eventually met for action off Valparaiso.*

To the Secretary of the Navy, Washington
Essex Junior, July 3d, 1814– at sea.
SIR,
I sailed from the Delaware on 27 October 1812 and repaired with all diligence (agreeable to the instructions of Commodore Bainbridge) to Porto Praya, Fernando de NoroNho and Cape Frio,

and arrived at each place on the day appointed to meet him. On my passage from Porto Praya to Fernando I captured his Britannic majesty's packet *Nocton*; and after taking out about £11,000 sterling in specie, sent her under command of lieutenant Finch, for America. I cruized off Rio de Janeiro and about Cape frio, until the 12 January 1813, hearing frequently of the commodore, by vessels from Bahia. I here captured one schooner, with hides and tallow. I sent her into Rio. The Montague, the admiral's ship, being in pursuit of me, my provisions getting short, and finding it necessary to look out for a supply, to enable me to meet the commodore by the 1st April off St. Helena, I proceeded to the Island of St. Catharine's (the last place of rendezvous on the coast of Brazil) as the most likely to supply my wants, and at the same time, afford me that intelligence necessary to enable me to elude the British ships of war on the coast, and expected there.

I here procured only wood, water and rum, and a few bags of flour; and hearing of the commodore's action with the *Java*, the capture of the *Hornet* by the *Montague*, and of considerable augmentation of the British force on the coast, several being in pursuit of me, I found it necessary to get to sea as soon as possible. I know, agreeable to the commodore's plan, stretched to the southward, scouring the coast as far as Rio de la Plata. I heard that Buenos Ayres was in a state of starvation, and could not supply our wants, and that the government of Montevideo was inimical to us. The commodore's instructions now left it completely discretionary with me what course to pursue, and I determined on following that which had not only met his approbation, but the approbation of the then Secretary of the Navy.

I accordingly shaped my course for the Pacific; and after suffering greatly from short allowance of provisions, and heavy gales off the Horn, (for which my ship and men were ill provided). I arrived off Valparaiso on 14 March 1813. I here took in as much jerked beef and other provisions as my ship would conveniently stow, and ran down the coast of Chili and Peru. In this track I fell in with a Peruvian corsair, which had on board 24 Americans, as prisoners, the crews of two whale ships, which she had taken on the coast of Chile. The captain informed me that, as allies of Great Britain, they would capture all they should meet with, in expectation of a war between Spain and the United States. I consequently threw all his guns and ammunition into the sea, liberated the Americans, wrote a respectful letter to the viceroy, explaining the cause of my proceedings, which I delivered to her captain. I then proceeded for Lima, and recaptured one of the vessels as she was entering the port. From thence I shaped my course for the Gallapagos Islands, where I cruized from the 17th April until 3rd October 1813; during this time I touched only once on the coast of America, which was for the purpose of procuring a supply of fresh water, as none is to be found among these islands, which are, perhaps, the most barren and desolate of any known. While among this group I captured the following British ships, employed chiefly in the spermaceti whale fishery, viz.

	Tons	Men	Letters of Marque Gun	Pierced for
Montezuma	270	21	2	
Policy	273	25	10	18
Georgiana	280	25	6	18
Greenwich	338	25	10	20
Atlantie	355	2	8	20
Rose	220	21	8	20
Hector	270	25	11	20
Catharine	270	29	8	18
Seringapatam	350	31	14	26
Charlton	274	21	10	18
New Zealander	259	23	8	18
Sir A. Hammond	301	31	12	18
Total	3460	279	107	

As some of these ships were captured by boats and others by prizes, my officers and men had several opportunities of showing their gallantry.

The *Rose* and the *Charlton,* were given up to the prisoners; the *Hector, Catharine* and the *Montezuma* I sent to Valparaiso, where they were laid up; the Policy Georgiana and New Zealand I sent for America; the *Greenwich* I kept as a storeship to contain the stores of my other prizes, necessary for us and the *Atlantic*, now called the *Essex Junior*, I equipped with 20 guns and gave the command of her to Lieutenant Downes.

Lieutenant Downes had conveyed the prizes to Valparaiso, and on his return brought me letters informing me that a squadron under Commodore James Hillyard, consisting of the frigate *Phoebe*, of 36 guns had sailed on 6 July for this sea. The *Racoon* and *Cherub* had been seeking me for some time on the coast of Brazil, and, on the return from their cruize joined the squadron sent in search of me in the Pacific. My ship, as it may be supposed, after being near a year at sea, required some repairs to put her in a state to meet them; which I determined to do, and bring them to action, if I could meet them on near equal terms. I proceeded now, in company with the remainder of my prizes to the island of Nooa-heevah or Madison's Island, lying on the Washington group, discovered by a Captain Ingraham of Boston. Here I caulked and completely overhauled my ship, made for her a new set of water casks, her old ones being nearly decayed, and took on board from my prizes, provisions and stores for upwards of four months, and sailed for the coast of Chile on 12 December 1813. Previous to sailing I secured the *Seringapatam*, *Greenwich* and *Sir A. Hammond* under the guns of a battery which I erected for their protection; after taking possession of this fine island for the United States, and establishing the most friendly intercourse with the natives, I left them under charge of Lietenant Gamble, of the marines, with 21 men, with orders to repair to Valparaiso, after a certain period.

I arrived on the coast of Chile, on the 12th January 1814; looked into Conception and Valparaiso, found at both places only three English vessels, and learnt that the squadron which sailed from Rio de Janeiro had not been heard of since their departure, and was supposed to be lost in eneavouring to double Cape Horn.

I had completely broken up the British navigation in the Pacific; the vessels which had not been captured by me, were laid up and dare not venture out. I had afforded the most ample protection to our own vessels, which were, on my arrival, very numerous and unprotected. The valuable whale industry there is entirely destroyed, and the actual injury we have done them may be estimated at two and a half millions of dollars, independent of the vessels in search of me. They have supplied me amply with sails, cordage, cables, anchors, provisions, medicines, and stores of every description; and the slops on board them have furnished clothing for the seamen. We had, in fact, lived on the enemy since I had been in that sea, every prize having proved a well found store ship for me. I had not yet been under the necessity of drawing bills on the department for any object, and had been able to make considerable advances to my officers and men on account of pay. For the unexampled time we had kept the sea, my crew had continued remarkably healthy. I had but one case of the scurvy, and had lost only the following men by death, viz.: John S. Cowan, lieutenant; Robert Miller, surgeon; Levi Holmes, O.S; Edward Sweeny, do; Samuel Groce, seaman; James Spafford, gunner's mate; Bejamin Geers, John Rodgers, quarter gunners; Andrew Mahan, corporal of marines; Lewis price, private Marine . . .

I had now done all the injury that could be done the British commerce in the Pacific, and still hoped to signalize my cruize by something more splendid, before leaving that sea. I thought it not improbable that commodore Hillyar might have kept his arrival secret, and believing he would seek me at Valparaiso, as the most likely place to meet me. I determined to cruize about that place, hoping to be compensated by the capture of some merchant ships, said to be expected from England.

The *Phoebe*, agreeable to my exectations, came to seek me at Valparaiso, where I was anchored with the *Essex;* my armed prize, the *Essex Junior*, on the look out off the harbour. But, contrary to the course I thought he would pursue, Hillyar brought with him the *Cherub* sloop of war.

On getting their provisions on board they went off the port for the purpose of blockading me, where they cruized for near six weeks; during which I endeavoured to provoke a challenge and frequently, but ineffectually to bring *Phoebe* alone to action. Commodore Hillyar seemed determined to avoid a contest with me on nearly equal terms, and from his extreme prudence in keeping both his ships ever after constantly within hail of each other, there were no hopes of any advantages to my country from a longer stay in port. I therefore decided to put to sea the first opportunity which should offer; and I was the more strongly induced to do so, as I had gained certain intelligence, that the *Tagus*, 58, and two other frigates had sailed for that sea in pursuit of me. I had reason to expect the arrival of the *Raccoon*, from the north-west coast of America. A rendezvous was appointed for the *Essex Junior* and every arrangement made for sailing, and I intended to let them chase me off, to give the *Essex Junior* a chance of escaping, On the 28 March, the day after this determination was formed, the wind came to blow fresh from the southward, when I parted my larboard cable and dragged my starboard anchor directly out to sea. Not a moment was to be lost in getting sail on the ship. The enemy were close in with the point forming the west side of the bay; but on opening them, I saw the prospect of passing to windward, when I took in my top-gallant-sails, which were set over single-reefed-topsails, and braced up for this purpose; but on rounding the point, a heavy squall struck the ship, and carried away her main top-mast, precipitating the men who were aloft into the sea, who were drowned.

Both ships now gave chase to me, and I endeavoured, in my disabled state, to regain the port; but finding that I could not recover the common anchorage, I ran close into a small bay, about three quarters of a mile to leeward of the battery, on the east side of the harbour, and let go my anchor within pistol-shot of the shore, where I intended to repair my damages as soon as possible. The enemy continued to approach, shewed an evident intention of attacking us, regardless of the neutrality of the place where I was anchored; and the caution observed in in their approach to the attack of the crippled *Essex*, was truly ridiculous, as was their display of their motto flags and the number of jacks at all their mast heads. I, with as much expedition as circumstances would admit of, got my ship ready for action, and endeavoured to get a spring on my cable, but had not succeeded when the enemy, at 54 minutes past 3 p.m. made his attack, *Phoebe* placing herself under my stern, and the *Cherub* on my starboard bow; but the *Cherub* soon finding her situation a hot one, bore up and ran down under the stern also, where both ships kept up a hot raking fire . . . I had got 5 long twelve pounders out of the stern ports, which were worked with so much bravery and skill, that in half an hour we so disabled both as to compel them to haul off to repair damages. In the course of this firing I had, by the great exertions of Mr Edward Barnwell, the acting sailing master, assisted by Mr Limscott, the boatswain, succeeded in getting springs on our cable three different times; but the fire of the enemy was so excessive, that before we could get our broadside to bear, they were shot away, and thus rendered useless to us.

My ship had received many injuries and several had been killed and wounded; but my brave officers and men, notwithstanding the unfavourable circumstances under which we were brought to action, and the powerful force opposed to us, were no ways discouraged; all appeared determined to defend their ship to the last extremity, and to die in preference to shameful surrender. Our gaff with the ensign had been shot away but FREE TRADE AND SAILOR'S RIGHTS, continued to fly at the fore. Our ensign was replaced by another and one was made fast in the mizen rigging. The enemy soon repaired his damages for a fresh attack. He now placed himself with both his ships on my starboard quarter, out of reach of my carronades, and where my stern guns could not be brought to bear. He there kept up a most galling fire, which was out of my power to return, when I saw no prospect of injuring him without getting under weigh and becoming the assailant.

My top-sail sheets and haul-yards were all shot away as well as the jib and fore-top-mast stay sail haul-yards, and that being the only sail I could set, I caused it to be hoisted, my cable to be cut and ran down on both ships, with the intention of laying the *Phoebe* on board. The firing on both sides was now tremendous. I had let fall my fore-topsail and foresail, but the want of tacks and sheets had rendered them almost useless to us; yet we were enabled, for a short time to close with the enemy; and although our decks were now strewn with dead, and our cockpit filled with wounded – although our ship had been several times on fire, and was rendered a perfect wreck, we were still encouraged to a hope to save her, from the circumstance of the *Cherub* being compelled to haul off. She did not return to close action, though she apparently had it in her power to do so, but kept up a distant firing with her long guns.

The *Phoebe*, from our disabled state, was enabled, however, by edging off, to choose the distance which best suited her long guns, and kept up a tremendous fire on us, which mowed down my brave companions by the dozen. Many of my guns had been rendered useless by the enemy's shot, and many of them had their whole crews destroyed. We manned them again from those which were disabled, and one gun in particular was three times manned; 15 men were slain at it in the action! but strange as it may appear, the captain of it escaped with only a slight wound. Finding that the enemy could now choose his distance, and, as the wind for the moment seemed to favour the design, I determined to endeavour to run her on shore, land my men and destroy her. We had approached within musket shot of the shore when the wind shifted from the land and payed our head down on the *Phoebe*. My ship was now totally unmanageable yet, as her head was towards the enemy I still hoped to be able to board him.

At this moment Lieut. Cdr. Downes came aboard (from *Essex Junior*), to receive my orders, under the impression that I should soon be a prisoner. Finding that my last attempt at boarding would not succeed I directed him to return to his own ship. The slaughter on my ship had now become horrible; the enemy continued to to rake us, and we unable to bring a gun to bear. I therefore directed a hawser to be bent to the sheet anchor, and the anchor to be cut from the bows to bring her head round. This succeeded. We again got our broadside to bear, and as the enemy was much crippled and unable to hold his own, I have no doubt he would soon have drifted out of gun-shot before he discovered we had anchored, had not the hawser unfortunately parted. My ship had taken fire several times during the action, but alarmingly so forward and aft at this moment; the flames were bursting up each hatchway, and no hopes were entertained of saving her; our distance from the shore did not exceed three-quarters of a mile, and I hoped many of my brave crew would be able to save themselves, should the ship blow up, as I was informed the fire was near the magazine, the explosion of a large quantity of powder below, served to increase the horrors of our situation. Our boats were destroyed by the enemy's shot; I therefore directed those who could swim to jump overboard, and endeavour to gain the shore. Some reached it, some were taken by the enemy, and some perished in the attempt; but most preferred sharing with me the fate of the ship.

We who remained, now turned our attention wholly to extinguishing the flames; and when

we succeeded, went again to our guns, where the
firing was kept up for some minutes, but the crew
had by this time become so weakened, and they all
declared to me the impossibility of making further
resistance, and entreated me to surrender my ship
to save the wounded, as all attempts at opposition
must prove ineffectual, almost every gun being
disabled by the destruction of their crews. I now
sent for the officers of divisions to consult them;
but what was my surprise to find only acting
lieutenant Stephen Decator M'knight remaining,
who confirmed the report respecting the condition
of the guns on the quarter deck – those on the spar-
deck were not in a better state. Lieut. Wilmer, after
fighting most gallantly throughout the action, had
been knocked overboard by a splinter, while getting the sheet anchor from the bows and was
drowned. Acting Lieutenant John G. Cowell
had lost a leg, Mr Edward Barnwell, acting sailing
master, had been carried below, after receiving
two severe wounds, one in the breast and one in the
face, and acting lieutenant William Odenheimer
had been knocked overboard from the quarter, an
instant before, and did not regain the ship until
after the surrender.

I was informed that the cockpit, the steerage, the
wardroom and the birth deck, could contain no
more wounded; and that the wounded were killed
while the surgeons were dressing them. The enemy, from the smoothness of the water, and the
impossibility of our reaching him with our carronades, and the little apprehension that was excited

by our fire, which had now become much slackened, was now able to take aim at us as a target. In
fine I saw no hopes of saving her, and at twenty
minutes after 6 p.m. gave the painful order to
strike the colours. Seventy-five men, including
officers, were all that remained of my whole crew,
after the action, capable of doing duty, and many of
them severely wounded, some of whom have since
died. The enemy still continued his fire and my
brave, though unfortunate companions were still
falling about me. I directed an opposite gun to be
fired, to show them we intended no further resistance; but they did not desist; four men were killed
at my side, and others in different parts of the ship.
I now believed he intended to show us no quarter,
and that it would be as well to to die with my flag
flying as struck, and was on the point of again
hoisting it, when, about ten minutes after hauling
the colours down, he ceased firing.

We have been unfortunate, but not disgraced; the
defence of the *Essex* has not been less honourable
to her officers and crew, than the capture of an
equal force, and I now consider my situation less
pleasant than that of commodore Hillyar, who in
violation of every principle of honour and gener-
osity, and regardless of the rights of nations, attacked the *Essex* in her crippled state within pistol
shot of a neutral shore; when for six weeks I had
daily offered him fair and honourable combat, on
terms greatly to his advantage: the blood of the
slain must be on his head and he has yet to reconcile
his conduct to Heaven, to his conscience and the

world. The annexed extract of a letter from commodore Hillyar, which was written previously to
his returning me my sword, will show his opinion
of our conduct.

My loss has been dreadfully severe; 58 killed or
have since died of their wounds, and among them
is lieutenant Cowell; 39 were severely wounded,
27 slightly, and 31 are missing; making in all 154
killed wounded and missing.

The loss in killed and wounded has been great with
the enemy; among the former is the first lieutenant
of the *Phoebe* and of the latter Captain Tucker of
the *Cherub*, whose wounds are severe. Both the
Essex and the *Phoebe* were in a sinking state, and it
was with difficulty they could be kept afloat until
anchored in Valparaiso next morning. The shattered state of the *Essex* will, I believe, prevent her
ever reaching England, and I also think it will be
out of their power to repair the damages of the
Phoebe, so as to enable her to double Cape Horn.
All the masts and yards of *Phoebe* and *Cherub* are
badly crippled and their hulls much cut up; the
former had eighteen 12-pounder shot through her
below her water line, some three feet under water.
Nothing but the smoothness of the water saved
both the *Phoebe* and *Essex*.

Soon after my capture, I entered into an agreement
with commodore Hillyar to disarm my prize, the
Essex Junior, and proceed with the survivors of my
officers and crew in her to the United States,

taking with me her officers and crew. He consented to grant me a passport to secure her from further capture.

In justice to commodore Hillyar, I must observe that (although I can never be reconciled to the manner of his attack on the *Essex*, or his conduct before the action) he has, since our capture, shown the greatest humanity to my wounded, (whom he permitted me to land, on condition that the United States should bear the expenses,) and has endeavoured, as much as lay in his power, to alleviate the distresses of war by the most generous and delicate deportment towards my officers and crew; he gave orders that the property of every person should be respected; which orders, however, were not as strictly attended to as might be expected; beside being deprived of books, charts etc. both myself and officers lost many articles of our clothing, some to considerable account. I should not have considered this last circumstance of sufficient importance to notice, did it not mark a striking difference between the navy of Great Britain and that of the United States, highly credible to the latter.

By the arrival of the *Tagus*, a few days after my capture, I was informed that besides the ships which had arrived in the Pacific in pursuit of me, and those still expected, that others were sent to cruize for me in the China Seas, off New Zealand, Timor and New Holland, and that another frigate was sent to the river la Plate. To possess the *Essex* it

has cost the British government near six millions of
dollars, and yet, sir, her capture was owing entirely
to accident; and if we consider the expedition with
which navy contests are now decided, the action is a
dishonour to them. Had they brought their ships
boldly into action, with a force so very superior, and
having the choice of position, they should either
have captured or destroyed us in one fourth the
time they took about it.

During the action our consul general, Mr Poinsett,
called upon the governor of Valparaiso, and requested him to use the batteries to protect the *Essex*.
This request was refused, but he promised that if
she should succeed in reaching the common anchorage, that he would send an officer to the British
commander and request him to cease firing, but
declined using force under any circumstances, and
there is no doubt that there is perfect understanding
between them. This conduct, added to other assistance to the British, and their friendly reception
after the action, and the strong bias of the faction
which govern Chile in favor of the English, as well
as their inhospitality to the Americans, induced Mr
Poinsett to leave the country. Finding some difficulty in the sale of my prizes, I have taken the *Hector*
and the *Catharine* to sea and burnt them with their
cargoes.

I exchanged lieutenant M'Knight, Mr Adams and
Mr Lyman and eleven seamen, for part of the crew
of the *Sir Andrew Hammond*; and sailed from
Valparaiso on 27 April, where the enemy were still

patching up their ships to put them in a state for proceeding to Rio de Janeiro. I have the honour to be etc.

D PORTER

The Escape of the *Hornet*

1815

The USS Hornet *was a 16-gun sloop dispatched to the South Pacific, a sea almost unknown to American warships.*

US Ship *Hornet*, St. Salvadore, 10 June 1815
I have the honour to report, that the PEACOCK and this ship, having continued off Christian d'Acunha, the number of days directed by you, in your letter of instructions, proceeded in company to the eastward on the 12th of April, bound to the second place of rendezvous. Nothing of any importance occurred to us until the 27th of April, when at 7 a.m. in latitude 38 30 south and longitude 33 east, we made a strange sail to the south east to which we gave chase. The wind was from the north east by north and light throughout the day, and by sun-down we had neared the chase considerably. It was calm during the night, and at daylight on the 28th he was still in sight. A breeze springing up from the north west, we crowded sail with

steering sails on both sides; the chase standing to the northward upon a wind. At 2.45 p.m. the *PEACOCK* was about six miles ahead of this ship; and observing that she appeared to be suspicious of the chase, I took in starboard steering sails, and hauled up for the *PEACOCK*. I was still, however, of opinion that the chase was an Indiaman, though indeed the atmosphere was quite smoky and indistinct, and I concluded, as she was very large, that captain Warrington was waiting for me to join him, that we might together go along side of her. At 3.22 p.m. the *PEACOCK* made the signal that the chase was a ship of the line and an enemy. I immediately took in all steering sails, and hauled upon a wind; the enemy then upon our lee quarter, distant about eight miles. By sun-down I had perceived the enemy sailed remarkably fast, and was very weatherly. At 9 p.m. as the enemy was gaining upon us, and as there was every appearance that he would be enabled to keep sight of us during the night, I considered it necessary to lighten this ship. I therefore threw overboard 12 tons of kentledge, part of our shot, some of our heavy spars, cut away the sheet anchor and cable, and started the wedges of the masts. At 2 a.m. the enemy being rather before our lee-beam, I tacked to the westward; the enemy also tacked and continued in chase of us. At day-light, on the 29th, he was within gun shot upon our lee quarter. At 7 a.m. having hoisted English colours, and a rear admiral's flag, he commenced firing from his bow guns. As his shot went over us, I cut away the remaining anchor and cable, threw overboard the launch, six of our guns, more of our shot, and every heavy article that was at hand; the enemy fired about thirty shot, not one of which took effect, though most of them passed over us. While he was firing, I had the satisfaction to perceive that we slowly dropt him, and at 9 a.m. he ceased his fire.

At 11 a.m. the enemy was again coming up with us. I now therefore threw overboard all our remaining guns but one long gun, nearly all our shot, all our spare spars, cut away the top-gallant forecastle, and cleared every thing off deck, as well as from below, to lighten us as much as possible. At noon the enemy again commenced firing. He fired many shot, only three of which came on board; two striking the hull and one passing through the jib. It is, however, extraordinary, that every shot did not take effect, for the enemy, the second time he commenced firing, was certainly with-in three quarters of a mile of this ship, and the sea quite smooth.

I perceived from his sails that the effect of his fire was to deaden his wind, and at 2 p.m. he again ceased firing. At 2.30 p.m. the wind which had previously, and greatly to our disadvantage, backed to the south east, hauled to the westward, and freshed up. At sun-down the enemy was about four miles astern. The wind was fresh, and we went at the rate of nine knots throughout the night. We saw the enemy at intervals through the squalls during the night, and at day-light on the 30th he was about 12 miles astern, still in chase of us. At 9.30 a.m. he took in steering sails, reefed his top-sails and hauled to the eastward, and at 11 a.m. he was entirely out of sight. During the chase the enemy appeared to be very crank, and I therefore conclude he must have lightened while in chase of us. I did not at any time fire our stern chasers, because it was manifest the enemy injured his sailing by his firing.

As we had now no anchor, no cable, no boat, and but one gun, there was of course an absolute necessity for relinquishing our intended cruize; and as in our then condition, it would have been extremely hazardous on account of the enemy's cruizers, to approach our own coast, I considered it most advantageous to proceed for this port. I arrived here yesterday, and on my arrival received information of the peace between the United States and Great Britain. Permit me to state that it was with the most painful reluctance, and upon the fullest conviction that it was indispensable in order to prevent a greater misfortune, that I could bring my mind to consent to part with my guns; and I beg leave to request, that you will be pleased to move the honourable the Secretary of the Navy, to call a court of inquiry to investigate the loss of the armament of this ship. It will be very satisfactory to me to have such an investigation.

A Ship's Officer

During this tedious and anxious chace, the wind was variable, so as to oblige us to make a perfect circle round the enemy. Between 2 and 3 o'clock yesterday, not a person on board had the most distant idea that there was a possibility of escape. We all packed up our things, and waited until the enemy's shot would compel us to heave to and surrender, which appeared certain. Never has there been so evident an interposi-

tion of the goodness of a Divine Father; my heart with
gratitude acknowledges his supreme power and goodness. On the morning of the 28th it was very calm, and
nothing but murmurs were heard throughout the ship,
as it was feared we should lose our anticipated prize;
many plans had been formed by us for the disposal of
our plunder. The seamen declared they would have
the birth deck carpeted with East India silk, supposing
her an Indiaman from India; while the officers, under
the impression that she was from England, were making arrangements how we should dispose of the
money, porter, cheese, &c. &c. Nothing perplexed
us more than the idea that we should not be able to
take out all the good things, before we should be
obliged to destroy her. We were regretting our ship
did not sail faster, as the PEACOCK would certainly
capture her first, and would take out many of the best
and most valuable articles before we should get up.
(This very circumstance of our not sailing as fast as the
PEACOCK, saved us in the first instance from inevitable
capture; for when captain Warrington made the signal
for the sail to be an enemy of superior force, we were
four leagues to windward.) We all calculated our
fortunes were made, but alas! "we caught a Tartar."

During the latter part of the chase, when the shot and
shells were whistling about our ears, it was an interesting sight to behold the varied countenances of our
crew. They had kept the deck during all the preceding
night, employed continually in lighting the ship, were
excessively fatigued, and under momentary expectation of falling into the hands of a barbarous and
enraged enemy. The shot that fell on the main deck,

struck immediately over the head of one of our gallant fellows, who had been wounded in our glorious action with the *penguin*, where he was lying in his cot very ill with his wounds; the shot was near coming through the deck, and it threw innumerable splinters all around this poor fellow, and struck down a small paper American ensign, which he had hoisted over his bed. Destruction apparently stared us in the face, if we did not soon surrender, yet no officer, no man, in the ship showed any disposition to let the enemy have the poor little *HORNET*. Many of our men had been impressed and imprisoned for years in their horrible service, and hated them and their nation with the most deadly animosity; while the rest of the crew, horror struck by the relation of the sufferings of their shipmates, who had been in the power of the English, and now equally flushed with rage, joined heartily in execrating the present authors of our misfortune.

Captain Biddle mustered the crew and told them he was pleased with their conduct during the chase, and hoped still to perceive that propriety of conduct which had always marked their character, and that of the American tar generally, that we might soon expect to be captured, &c. Not a dry eye was to be seen at the mention of capture. The rugged hearts of the sailors, like ice before the sun, warmed by the divine power of sympathy, wept in unison with their brave commander. About 2 o'clock, the wind which had crossed us, and put to the test all our nautical skill to steer clear of the enemy, now veered in our favour and we left him. This was truly a glorious victory over the horrors of banishment and the terrors of a British floating dungeon. Quick as thought every face was changed from the gloom of despair to the highest smile of delight, and we began once more to breathe the sweets of liberty. The bitter sighs of regret were now changed, and I put forth my expression of everlasting gratitude to him, the supreme Author of our being, who has thus signally delivered us from the power of a cruel and vindictive enemy.

Sources

William Beatty, *The Death of Lord Nelson, 21 October 1805*, Edward Arber, 1807.

Captain Biddle, *Official Letters of the Military and Naval Officers of the United States During the War with Great Britain in the Years 1812, 13, 14, 15*, ed John Brannan, Washington, 1823.

John Brown, *Maritime History* website, transcribed by Michael Philips, nd.

Thomas Cochrane (Tenth Earl of Dundonald), *Adventures Afloat*, Thomas Nelson & Sons, 1907.

William Henry Dillon, *A Narrative of My Professional Adventures, 1790–1839*, Vol. I, ed Michael A Lewis, Navy Records Society, 1953.

James Durand, *An Able Seaman of 1812*, ed George S Brooks, Yale University Press, 1926.

Robert Eastwick, *A Master Mariner: Being the Life and Adventures of Captain Robert Eastwick*, ed Herbert Compton, T Fisher Unwin, 1891.

James Gardner, *Recollections of James Anthony Gardner, Commander RN*, ed Sir R Vesey Hamilton, Navy Records Society, 1906.

Isaac Hull, *Official Letters of the Military and Naval Officers of the United States During the War with Great Britain in the Years 1812, 13, 14, 15*, ed John Brannan, Washington, 1823.

Thomas Graves, *Logs of the Great Sea Fights*, ed ST Jackson, 1899–1900.

Robert Hay, *Landsman Hay: The Memoirs of Robert Hay 1785–1847*, ed MD Hay, Rupert Hart-Davis, 1952.

George Vernon Jackson, *The Perilous Adventures and Vicissitudes of a Naval Officer, 1801–1812: Being the Memoirs of Admiral George Vernon Jackson 1787–1876*, ed Harold Burrows, William Blackwood and Sons Ltd, 1927.

Samuel Leech, *Thirty Years from Home or, A Voice from the Main Deck*, Tappen, Whittemore and Mason, 1843.

George Little, *Life on the Ocean: or, Twenty Years at Sea: Being the Personal Adventures of the Author*, Waite, Pierce, 1845.

Horatio Nelson, *Nelson's Letters*, ed Geoffrey Rawson, JM Dent & Son, 1960.

Ned Myers, *A Life Before the Mast*, as told to J. Fenimore Cooper, 1909.

William Parker, *The Life of Admiral of the Fleet Sir W Parker*, Augustus Philimore, 1876.

David Porter, *Journal of a Cruise Made to the Pacific Ocean by Captain David Porter in the United States Frigate Essex, in the years, 1812, 1813, and 1814*, Wiley and Halstead, 1822.

William Richardson, *A Mariner of England: An Account of William Richardson from Cabin Boy in the Merchant Service to Warrant Officer in the Royal Navy, as told by himself*, ed Colonel Spencer Childers, John Murray, 1908.

RF Roberts, *Letters of the English Seamen*, ed EH Moorhouse, Chapman & Hall, 1910.

Sam, Letters of the English Seaman, ed EH Moorhouse, Chapman & Hall, 1910.

Acknowledgements

As ever, my thanks are due to all at Constable & Robinson, in particular Krystyna Green and Nick Robinson, not least for their patience and inspiration. I also wish to acknowledge the help of Hugh Lamb, not just on this book but on previous titles. Hugh Lamb is simply the best proofreader in the business.

Bibliography

Bennett, G., *Nelson the Commander*, London, 1972

Brodie, B., A *Guide to Naval Strategy*, New York, 1965

Brodie, B., A *Sea Warfare in the Machine Age*, Princetown, 1941

Callender, G., *The Naval Side of British History*, London, 1924

Clowes, William Laird, *The Royal Navy*, London, 1889–1890

Corbett, J., *Fighting Instructions, 1530–1816*, London, 1905

Corbett, J., *The Campaign of Trafalgar*, London, 1910

Dugan, James, *The Great Mutiny*, New York, 1965

Fitchett, W.H., *Nelson and his Captains*, London, 1902

Gardiner, Leslie, *The British Admiralty*, London, 1968

Hattendorf, JB et al, *British Naval Documents, 1204–1960*, London, 1993

Henderson, James, *The Frigates*, London, 1970

Hickey, D.R., *The War of 1812: A Forgotten Conflict*, Urbana Ill, 1989

Hill, Richard, *The Oxford Illustrated History of the Royal Navy*, Oxford, 1965

Kennedy, Ludovic, *Nelson's Captain*, NY, 1951

Kennedy, Paul, *The Rise and Fall of British Naval Mastery*, London, 1976

Landstrom, B., *The Ship*, New York, 1961

Lavery, Brian, *Nelson and the Nile*, Annapolis, 1998

Lavery, Brian, *The Ship of the Line*, London, 1983

Lavery, Brian, *Nelson's Navy*, London, *1989*

Lewis, M., *A Social History of the Navy, 1793–1815*, London, 1960

Lloyd, Christopher, *Lord Cochrane*, London, 1947

Lloyd, Christopher, *St Vincent and Camperdown*, London, 1963

Longridge, N., *The Anatomy of Nelson's Ships*, London, 1965

Mallalieu, J.P.W., *Extraordinary Seamen*, NY, 1958

Marder, A.J., *The Anatomy of Sea Power*, Hamden, 1964

McKee, C., *A Gentlemanly and Honourable Profession: The Creation of the US Naval officer corps, 1787–1815*, Annapolis, 1991

McKenzie, R.H., *The Trafalgar Roll: The Ships and the Officers*, Annapolis, 1989

Northcote Parkinson, C., *Britannia Rules*, London, 1977

Oman, C., *Nelson*, London, 1947

Pivka, Otto von, *Navies of the Napoleonic Era*, Newton Abbott, 1980

Pope, D., *England Expects*, London, 1960

Pratt, Fletcher, *Prebel's Boys: Commodore Prebel and the Birth of American Sea Power*, NY, 1950

Rodger, N.A.M., *The Wooden World*, London, 1986

Southey, Robert, *The Life of Nelson*, Annapolis, 1990 ed

Swanson, C., *Predators and Prizes, American Privateering*, Columbia SC, 1991

Uden, Grant and Cooper, Richard, *A Dictionary of British Ships and Seamen*, NY 1980

Warner, O., *Nelson's Battles*, London, 1965

Appendix I

Life & Death in the Royal Navy, 1794–1805

Some statistics, tables and regulations

Allowance of Provisions
from Regulations and Instructions, 1808

Day	Bisket lbs.	Beer gals.	Beef lbs.	Pork lbs.	Pease pints	Oat-meal pints	Sugar ozs.	Butter ozs.	Cheese ozs.
Sunday	1	1	–	1	0.5	–	–	–	–
Monday	1	1	–	–	–	0.5	2	2	4
Tuesday	1	1	2	–	–	–	–	–	–
Wednes-day	1	1	–	–	0.5	0.5	2	2	4
Thursday	1	1	–	1	0.5	–	–	–	–
Friday	1	1	–	–	–	0.5	2	2	4
Saturday	1	1	2	–	–	–	–	–	–
Weekly Total	7	7	4	2	2	1.5	6	6	12

The men ate in messes, usually consisting of eight men.

Causes of Death
Fatal Casualties in the Royal Navy in 1810

CAUSE OF DEATH	NUMBER	PERCENTAGE
By Disease	2592	50.0
By Individual Accident	1630	31.5
By Foundering, Wreck, Fire, Explosion	530	10.2
By the Enemy, killed in action	281	5.4
By the Enemy, died of wounds	150	2.9
All Causes	5183	100

British and Enemy Casualties
In the Six Major Victories

Battle	British			Enemy estimated			
	killed	wou-nded	total	killed	wou-nded	total	pris-oners
First of June 1794	287	811	1098	1500	2000	3500	3500
Cape St. Vincent 1797	73	227	300	430	570	1000	3157
Camperdown 1797	203	622	825	540	620	1160	3775
The Nile 1798	218	677	895	1400	600	2000	3225
Copenhagen 1801	253	688	941	540	620	1160	3775
Trafalgar 1805	449	1241	1690	4408	2545	6953	7000
Total	1438	4266	5749	9068	7245	16313	22657

Table from Lewis, *A Social History of the Navy 1793–1815*

Gratuities to the Relations of Officers and Others Killed in Action

1. To a widow, her husband's full pay for a year.
2. Orphans, each the one-third proportion of a widow; posthumous children are esteemed orphans.
3. Orphans married are not entitled to any bounty.
4. If there is no widow, a mother, if a widow and above fifty years of age, is entitled to a widow's share.
5. The relations of officers of fire-ships are entitled to the same bounty as those of officers of like rank in fourth rates.
6. Captains are to set down the names of the killed at the end of the muster book, and on what occasion.
7. This bounty extends to those who are killed in tenders, in boats, or on shore, as well as to those on board the ships; also to those who are killed in action with pirates, or in engaging British ships through mistake. They who die of their wounds after battle are all equally entitled with those killed in action.

– *The Naval Chronicle*, 1799

Appendix II

"This naval life"

Some selections from the 1798–9 journal of Aaron Thomas, a Royal Navy sailor serving aboard HMS *Lapwing* in the West Indies during the French Revolutionary War. Thomas was born in Wigmore, Herefordshire, England, in 1762 and died of disease at St Kitts in 1799. The material is reprinted from the University of Miami Library website, www.library.miami.edu/archives/thomas/introduction

Religion:

"There is no Clergyman there. no canonical man to bury their dead, or Christian their Children. No man to Join together in holy Wedlock. or Church weomen. and yet most of the islander are good people. They are a fine set of looking persons. Very Tractable, and all might be easly made true followers of God. The men & weomen are hale looking but generally very lank in their bodies, they live on Yams, Sweet Potatoes, and the roots which their Island produceth, their wants are few & their supplies are many. On Sundays they have nothing to do, but visit each other, had they a Holy man amongst them *His House* would be the general redevoze for all of the Island on Sunday."

"Ashore at St. Kitts this day, the Captain waited an hour for *all the* Boats Crew. – He swore he would flog the Coxwain and all of them, when they were found; pray where have you all been, says the Captain; We have *all been to Church* says the Coxwain, – I will Church you all says the Captain when you get aboard. – But the Captain took no notice of it, further than remarking to Capt Brown that he was very angry with them, but the extreme novelty of a Boats Crew, being absent from the Boat, and found *in a Church*; instead of a Grog Shop; was so *new*. so *singular*, and so uncommon a *thing*; – That their answer melted his rath, into complete forgiveness."

Slavery:

"At 5 Captain Charles Mais of Ship Nevis of Bristol, from Nevis for Bristol with this Convoy came aboard, to beg us to take a Negro and Mulatto, who had secreted themselves in his Ship, and wanted to run away from their owners in Nevis. at 6 Both of them came aboard and were put in Irons. The Negro was a youth of about 17. said his father and mother were *Salt Water Negros*, which mens people who crossed the Sea, in coming from Africa. I asked him is reasons for runing away. Sir says he, tell me one thing, will you runaway from good. – My owner only gave four pints of India Corn a week, he does not import provisions, therefore he cannot give us so much to eat, as those great Gentleman that do, as he must pay a higher price for it. – Bad usage Sir, made me run away, as some Gentleman gave their Negros 9 pints of Corn a week, but my owner only gives his Negros 4 pints a week. – my name is Robin, I belong to Mr Henry Dickson of Indian Castle in Nevis. Last Sunday being Negroes Holyday, I went aboard the Ship to sell Sweetmeate, And finding she was going away a sudden resolution came into my head to get off, as it is better to be free, than to be a Slave; So while they were geting the ship under weigh, yesterday morning; I hid myself in the Hold, and this evening being very hungry I came on Deck, but I did not think the Ship was to Anchor again, untill she got to England. but they stoped here & I am taken & c."

"Sunday 21 October. At 15 minutes past 12 AM a Sail passed us, were ship and gave chace, at 2 spoke the chace. She was a Sloop her name [*blank*] from the Coast of Africa, bound to Tortola with 90 slaves on board, in great destress, as every Soul on board, had been 2 days without anything to eat, and that on this day, (Sunday) they intended to cast Lotts amongst the Blacks, and eat one. – They left the coast on the Sixth of June, and had made no land since, we sent them on board, one Barrel of Beefe, and one Bag of Buiscuts, as they might make Tortola this evening, if the Breaze continued. – They had no Candles in the Sloop for 3 weeks back."

"The lands are tilled by the Black people, brought from Africa who do the work here, which Horses do in England. – When a Cargo of these Black people arrive from Africa, they are chained and exposed for Sale, in the same manner as you expose Sheep & Pigs at Shrewsbury Fairs. – I have seen them on these occasions, primed with Ginger, exactly in the same manner, as you prime a Horse, before you lead him into the fair to be sold. And if any of these poor creatures are so old, as to have grey hairs in their heads; the Slave Dealer on the morning of Sale, will rub his head over, with an Ointment, that will hide his grey hairs for several days." (p. 141)

"I asked Parson Masset the reason why Slaves are not permited to marry, his answer was in these words! "Why should other people take my property away, if you, as being a free man should take a fancy to one of my Slaves, and carry her away & marry her, I hold it as our Law that you, by so doing; have Stolen my property, – if a Slave was allowed to Marry: the contentions that would flow from it, would be endless, take it all togather allowing such a thing, would in the course of 15 or Twenty years make property in Slave a dubious and uncertain matter." (p. 247)

Corporal punishment:

"Saturday 13 October. Captain Harvey paid much attention to the circumstances of the Robery last night. The theife Thomson accused many people, of Robing Mr Taylor before, – In Thompsons Pillow was found a Bag, containing 6 Joes, secreted there; being the produce of his former plundering, With money of Thomsons in other people hands, and the money in the Bag, it was proved that he had about 15 Joes, and all except Three; was plunder. a poor french Boy about Twenty days Back, lost 8 Dollars in little Bag from under his head, as he laid asleep, and the money which was found in Thomsons Pillow Case, was enclosed in this Identical Bag, which the Boy owned, as soon as he saw it.

At 10 AM Thomsons arms was lashed; the Ships Company formed a Lane all around the Waiste of the Ship, every man being provided with a Nettle, 2 Marines faced him with each a Bayonet pointed at the Theifc, a Cord was thrown over the prisoners body, the ends of which were held behind by Two Quartermasters, Things being thus ordered he run the Gauntlet, every man striking him as he passed; the noise of which I thought at the time, resembled Reapers at work, when cuting Corn. After passing once round, he fainted and & droped down. – The Surgeon threw some Hartshorn in his face, and he was ordered into Irons, to receive more punishment when his back recovers."

Disease:

"At half past Seven PM. Peter Bird a Seaman Aged Twenty Three departed this life. He had been ill of a Flux about nine days. – About three months ago this young man showed me a Letter which he had from his Mother. he also told me, that his mind was fixed upon young weoman in London: who he *intended to Marry*, when the war was over adding I am but a young man, and she will forgive me for leaving her as I did. – So I see this poor youth, was boasting in his strength, but the Lord has told us of this folly, by taking one away from amongst us, who has been in the Ship more than 4 years, and during all that period, has never been in the Sick List untill nine days before his death."

"I am sorry to inform you, quella our Bastimento is

very sickly. several of our hale, healthy looking Lads, have died suddenly of fevers, within these 9 days. We have sent a number to the Hospital, where some have died also. – My old Ship the Concord, is now refiting in English Harbor Antigua, She has been there about 4 weeks, since which time she has buryed 27 men, and has 98 sick in the Hospital at this time."

"Took another live Gigger from out of the under part of my second Toe, of my left foot. – It is a foolish thing to be to proud. – We all know that grubs & worms destroy our Carcases when dead, but in this climate the Gigger worm eats its way under our Skin, lays his Eggs there, without our knowledge, until its young ones, by it motions give us uneasyness. – we then look at the place and see a loathsome wound in which is 90, or 130 live Insects. the wound must be cut open, and all the insects taken clean out, or else its effects will be fatal. – from this Insects creeping alive, under the Skin of my two feat, I have not them both laped up in rags. – The Giggers by getting into the feet of Soldiers, have stoped the military progress of many good General in the West Indies. – It is said that a Gigger, at a certain period of his age will fly: it must be so, or how do they get about ones breasts & c. – One of our men a few days ago, had one taken out of his private parts in the Cockput. in which were 85 eggs."

"The Black Negro Girls have the Pox amongst them, as well as our white Ladies in England. There is at this time Eleven Venerals in the List. Silvia the Spaniard. Farthing & Hassels cases are uncommonly virulent and malignant. The only good, the unhappy Captain Cook did in visiting the North & South

Pacific Ocean; was to *give the Pox*; to the Inhabitants of *every Island* where the Adventure & Resolution watered at as when these 2 Ships left Maderia in August 1772. Each had several veneral patients on board. which arose from the amours which the English Sailors had; with the Portuguese Puttani, in Funchal."

Alcohol consumption:

"Punished the Boy Skipper on his Backside with 12 Lashes for giving yesterday half a Gill of Rum to Gater the Marine for washing his Cloaths. – There is something particular in this case. The Boys are allowed their Rum. and if they drink it, they often get drunk with it, therefore it is understood, they may give it to persons who wash & mind for them: And many Boys in some Ships sell their Liquior. But this particular Boy was floged for giving his Liquior away to a Marine who had done work for him. So that by floging this Lad, it is the same as giving out orders, for all the Boys to drink their own allowance, and thereby get drunk with it. The best that can be said of it is; that it will encourage intoxication."

"William Woodcock had half a Dozen Lashes, for being the person, who requested Elder to bring off the Quart of Gin;

NB at the Gangway the Captain declared to Elder, that he would flog him, untill he confessed who the Bladder of Gin belonged to, – Elder took 2 Dozen, and then he confessed it was Woodcock, who the Gin was for.

CONTRAST. The Captain got drunk. – so drunk; – that he fell three times off his Horse – I myself at

Breakfast heard him say – "I drank too much wine yesterday: I would give Sixpence had I not drank so much." – Yet this man who got so drunk as to fall 3 times off his Horse; gave 30 lashes on the bare backs of 2 men, for attempting to obtain the possession of one Quart of Gin."

Morals:

"What a Desolute life does man lead in the West Indias. The Blacks never marry. But have intercourse one with another promiscuously. All the white men; Planters as well as merchants: have connection with their female Negros. As to the black Girls themselves, any white or Creole man may have commerce with them, so very little difficulty is there on this head, that it is as easy to lye with them, as it is to convey a glass of wine to your mouth, when you have it in your hand. – A white Sailor may go amongst the Hutts upon an Esstate, where there is 70 female Negros and he will not find the smallest opposition to his will, but will be courted to stop amongst them."

"Capt Renolds of the Etrusco was ordered to carry home a Lady, who was going from England to the East Indias to see her Husband. At St Helens she heard of her Husbands death. She took a passage from Spence back to England again, & in the Passage back was captured by french Privateer, & carried to Guadulupe, she got her Liberty was ordered to go home in the Etrusco. but Renolds said he would not take her unless she slept with him all the passage."

Prize-taking:

"Sunday 26th. off Fort Royal Bay. at daylight saw a small strange Sail, which bore down towards us, but when she came near enough to reconoitre, she hauled her wind, & made sail from us; at 6 AM we made sail in Chace, at 7 she hoisted french Colours, worked her Sweeps, and made every effort to escape. We fired – Grape, and round shot at her until 30 minutes past Eight; when she struck her colours, and shortened Sail. She proved to be La Fortune french Schooner of 6 swivels (4 of which she threw overboard in Chace) and 22 men, from Guadulupe, but last from Descada. – Got the Prisonors aboard, gave the Prize a Tow Rope, and made sale for fort Royal Bay. – This small Schooner in her last Cruizc took, a prize when each man shared 2500 Dollars each. – This Schooner will not fetch more than 40 Joes at Martinico, but the French Prisonors say, was she at Basseterre in Guadulupe, she would sell for 150 Joes, because they are just the size Vessels which the French want to anoy our commerce with. The Captain of the Schooner says, that this little Schooner will fetch more money in Guadulupe then a Ship of 300 Ton. – so much do they run on Privateering."

"There is more Prize money made in the West Indias than there is at home, but to counterbalance this advantage one Guinea in England, will go as far as two Guineas in the West Indias."

"Monday the 18th of March 1799 At 8 A M gave Chace to a Strange Sail. at 2 P M came up with the Chace, she proved to be a Sweedish Schooner from Cyane to St. Batholomew, laden with Cotton, Drugs &

live Turtles. She had four french Passengers aboard, and a small part of the Cargo, no doubt was french property, but the trouble of taking her in, Condemnation, Admiralty & Expences, would a made it a poor Prize, so the Captains thought it best to let her go on, on her voyage."

Social hierarchy:

"In my present situation, I can speak and walke with whom I like, but had I laid hold of the public situation which you hint at; I could not a done so, for had I spoken to persons in an inferior rank to myself, my Brother officers, would have said, that I acted deregoratory to my Character. Saint James, in his Epistle to his Bretheren says, Chapter 2 Verse 9. "If he have respects to persons, ye commit sin; and are convinced of the Law, as transgressors. – Now was I a Purser, the moment I became one, I must bid advice, to ever *saying* a civil word, or ever giving a *civil* look, to any one of the men before the Mast, in presence of a superior Officer, for it is held in the Navy, to be a proof, of something shocking & bad, to speake to the men with civillity, and if you do, do it: your promotion is damed. now for my own part, I never am more happier, than when conversing with my inferiors, for from them I learn more of life, than I do by conversing with Officers, whose general talke is to abuse high & low, or every body whom they know. – besides let my Ideas be what they will, I can never give, but on general sentiment at the Wardroom, or Gunroom table, and at the Captains Table, I must set 3 hours, to hear him talke of *himself*, and must *never* contradict a word he utters, but nod *yes* to everything he says, and do not you think this forced tacitity, is paying very dear, for a plate of Mutton, a Tumbler of Porter & Six glasses of wine."

His own character:

"For my own part, I never had had any illness; but most of the hair on my head, is turned white; – and I call this circumstance now a happy thing. – It has done me more good, than all the Sermons, I ever heard in my life. It has buryed my pride. – Drowned all the envy which I had within me. taught me to be humble. To look with charitable eyes on all things, and in earthly matters, to have no greatter hope, than to sequester myself in the lonely shade of spreading trees, and out of the sight and hearing of pertinant man."

Appendix III

Tables of battlefleet tonnages and strength, 1790–1815

and the complete list of ships in the Royal Navy in April 1794

BATTLEFLEET TONNAGES OF THE MAJOR POWERS 1790–1815

The figures represent effective useable tonnage (in thousands of tons)

	Britain	France	Holland	Spain	Denmark	Sweden	Russia (Baltic)	Russia (Black Sea)	USA
1790	334	231	87	188	71	31	114	14	
1795	312	180	51	203	70	26	114	24	
1800	330	136	35	176	67	29	114	31	
1805	360	129	33	104	49	25	123	32	
1810	413	148	31	77	4	27	85	30	
1815	358	179	52	47	4	27	92	47	11

Taken from J.Glete, *Navies and Nations: Warships, Navies and State Building in Europe and America, 1500–1850*, Stockholm, 1993.

Strength of the Royal Navy, 1794
compared with 1814

Rate	Guns	Average tonnage	1794			1814		
			In full commission	Reserve or repair	Relegated	In full commission	Reserve or repair	Relegated
First 3 decks	100/120	2,500	5	1	none	7	none	2
Second 3 decks	98	2,200	9	7	3	5	3	4
Third 2 decks	64/80	1,750	71	24	22	87	16	80
Fourth 2 decks	50	1,100	8	4	7	8	2	9
Fifth 2 decks	44	900	12	3	3	2	none	1
Fifth Frigates	32/44	900	66	3	4	121	11	45
Sixth Frigates	28	600	22	2	4	none	none	4
Sixth Post-ship	20/24	500	10	2	2	25	4	11
Unrated vessels	4/18	70/450	76	3	7	360	6	46

Reprinted from *The Frigates*, James Henderson, Adlard Coles, 1970

Below is an approximately alphabetical list of ships in the Royal as of April 1794, derived from 'Steel's original and Correct List of the Royal Navy'.

Understanding the list:

Status:
O-Ordinary
C-In commission
B-Building

Ship:
*means captured from, with 'B' = Batavian, 'F' = France, 'E' = Spain.

Other abbreviations:

ASSp – Armed Storeship   Lug – Lugger
AT – Armed Transport   PS – Prison Ship
Bp – Bomb   Sch – Schooner
Bg – Brig   Sp – Sloop
Corv – Corvette   SS – Storeship
Cut – Cutter   Sur Sp –
                                   Surveying Ship
FS – Fireship   Ten – Tender
GS – Guardship   Yt – Yacht
Gy – Galley   ˜ – Hired
HS – Hospital Ship (& rigged as brig)

Locations:

Ch = Chatham   N = Nore
Cnl = Channel   Po = Portsmouth
Cv = on convoy to   Py = Plymouth
Df = Deptford   Sh = Sheerness
EI = East Indies   Spit = Spithead
G = Gibraltar   WI = West Indies
J = Jamaica   Wo = Woolwich
M = Mediterranean

Status	Ship	Guns	Locations	Year Built
O	Atlas	98	Py repairing	1782
C	Albion	74	Ch	1763
C	Alcide	74	M	1779
C	Alexander	74	Cnl	1773
C	Alfred	74	With Admiral Bowyer	1778
C	Arrogant	74	N	1761
C	Audacious	74	Spit	1785
C	Africa	64	Spit	1781
C	Agememnon	64	M	1781
C	America	64	Spit	1777
O	Anson	64	Ch serviceable	1743
O	Ardent	64	M	1783
C	Argonaut*F	64	Py refitting	1782
C	Asia	64	Cv to WI	1764

Status	Ship	Guns	Locations	Year Built
C	Adamant	50	Cv to WI	1779
B	Antelope	50	Sh	–
C	Assistance	50	Cv to M	1781
O	Acteon	44	Po	1779
C	Adventure	44	Spit	1784
C	Argo	44	Cv to St Helena	1781
C	Assurance	44	M	1780
O	Apollo	38	Df fitting	1794
C	Arethusa	38	With Admiral Macbride	1781
C	Artois	38	Df fitting	1794
C	L'Aigle *F	36	M	1782
C	Active	32	Ireland	1780
O	Aeolus	32	Ch repairing	1758
C	L'Aimable *F	32	M	1782
C	Alarm	32	WI	1758
O	Amazon	32	Py repairing	1773
C	Amphion	32	Spit	1780
C	Andromache	32	Ireland	1781
O	Andromeda	32	Py fitting	1784
C	Aquilon	32	G	1786
C	Astrea	32	Cv to M	1781
C	Alligator	28	WI	1786
C	Aurora	28	Bristol Channel	1777
C	Ariadne	20	M	1776
O	Albicore, Sp	16	N	1793
O	Alert, Sp	16	Cnl	1793
O	Ariel, Sp	16	Po	1779
O	Atlanta,Sp	14	Po	1776
O	Alecto, FS	12	Po	1779
O	Aetna,Bb	8	Wo repairing	1781
C	Assistant, Ten	8	Df	1791
C	Britannia	100	M	1762
C	Barfleur	98	Cnl	1768
C	Boyne	98	WI	1790
O	Blenheim	90	Py	1761
C	Bedford	74	M	1775
C	Bellerophon	74	Spit	1786
C	Bellona	74	Spit	1760
C	Berwick	74	M	1779
O	Bombay Castle	74	Py repairing	1782
C	Brunswick	74	With Admiral Bowyer	1790
C	Belliqueux	64	Cv to WI	1780
O	Bienfaisant	64	Py repairing	1759
O	Bristol	50	Ch Church ship	1775
C	Beaulieu	40	WI	1791
O	Belle Poule *F	36	Ch repairing	1779
C	Blanche	32	WI	1786
C	Blonde	32	WI	1787

Status	Ship	Guns	Locations	Year Built
C	Boston	32	Cv to Newfoundland	1762
O	Boreas, SS	28	Sh	1774
C	Brilliant	28	Cnl	1779
C	Bien Aimé, ASSp	20	EI	1793
C	Bonetta, Sp	16	Po	1779
O	Brisk, Sp	16	Po	1784
C	Bulldog, Sp	14	Africa	1782
O	Brazen, Cut	14	Py	1781
C	Birbice, Sch	?	WI	?
C	Black Joke, Lug	10	Spit	1793
C	Cambridge, GS	80	Py	1750
C	Caesar	80	Cnl	1793
C	Canada	74	Po	1766
C	Captain	74	M	1787
O	Carnatic	74	Py repairing	1783
B	Centaur	74	Wo	?
C	Colossus	74	Po	1787
O	Conqueror	74	Ch repairing	1775
C	Courageux	74	M	1761
C	Culloden	74	Py	1783
O	Cumberland	74	Ch	1774
O	Chichester, R	74	Py	1753
C	Le Caton, HS, *F	64	Py	1782
O	Crown	64	Po	1782
C	Centurion	50	EI	1774
C	Chatham	50	Py Convalescent ship	1758
C	Charon	44	Spit	1783
C	Chichester, SS	44	Po fitting	1785
C	Concorde, *F	36	Po	1783
C	Crescent	36	With Admiral Macbride	1784
C	Castor	32	Ostend	1785
C	Ceres	32	WI	1781
C	Cleopatra	32	Po	1780
C	Carysfort	28	St George's Channel	1767
C	Circe	28	Cnl	1785
C	Cyclops	28	M	1779
O	Champion	24	Wo serviceable	1779
O	Camel, ASSp	24	Wo	1782
C	Camilla	20	Py fitting	1776
B	Cerberus	?	Southampton	?
O	Cygnet, Sp	18	Po	1776
O	Calypso, Sp	16	Po	1783
C	Cormorant, Sp	16	Cnl	1794
C+	Childers, Sp	14	Df	1778
C	Comet, FS	14	Spit	1783
C	Conflagration, FS	14	M	1783
O	Cockatrice, Cut	14	Po	1782
C	Catherine, Yt	8	Df	1720

Status	Ship	Guns	Locations	Year Built
O	Chatham, Yt	8	Ch	1741
C	Chatham, Ten	?	EI	1790
B	Dreadnought	98	Po	–
O	Duke	98	Py repairing	1777
C	Defence	74	With Admiral Macbride	1763
O	Defiance	74	Ch refitting	1783
C	Diadem	64	M	1782
C	Dictator	64	to Africa	1783
O	Director	64	Ch	1784
C	Diomede	44	EI	1781
C	Dolphin, HS	44	M	1781
O	Dover	44	Po	1784
O	Diamond	38	Df fitting	1791
O	Diana	38	Df fitting	1794
C	Daedalas	32	Virginia	1780
C	Druid	32	Cruising	1783
C	Dido	28	M	1784
C	Daphne	20	Cv to Downs from Py	1776
C	Dorset, Yt	10	Dublin	1753
C	Dromedary, SS	24	WI	1779
C+	Drake, Sp	14	Sh	1779
C	Discovery, Sp	10	Nootka Sound	1790
C+	Daedalus, SS	?	Botany Bay	–
C	Deptford, Ten	8	On impress service	1788
O	Edgar	74	Ch	1773
C	Egmont	74	M	1766
O	Elephant	74	Po	1789
O	Elizabeth	74	Po	1768
C	Excellent	74	Po	1786
O	Eagle	64	Ch reparing	1777
O	Essex, R	64	Po	1763
O	Europe	64	Py repairing	1769
C	Europa	50	J	1782
C	Expedition	44	On ordnance service	1781
C	Experiment	44	WI	1780
C	Enterprise	28	Tower to receive men	1774
C	Eurydice	24	Spit	1784
C	La Eclair *F	20	M	1793
C	Echo, Sp	16	Coasting convoy	1784
C	L'Espion, Sp *F	16	Py	1793
C	Expedition, Cut	10	Cnl	1775
C	Experiment, Lug	10	Cruising	–
O	Formidable	98	Py repairing	1777
B	Foudroyant	80	Py	–
O	Fame	74	Py	1759
C	Fortitude	74	M	1780
O	Fortunée, PS *F	40	Langstone	1779
C	Flora	36	With Admiral Macbride	1780

Status	Ship	Guns	Locations	Year Built
C	Fox	32	G	1780
C	Fairy, Sp	16	Africa	1778
C	Favourite, Sp	16	Df fitting	1794
C	Fly, Sp	16	Cruising	1776
C+	Fortune, Sp	16	Cruising	1778
C	Fury, Sp	16	Cruising	1790
C+	Falcon, Sp	14	Cnl	1782
C	Ferret, Sp	14	Cnl	1784
O	Flirt, Sp	14	Df	–
C	Flying Fifth, Sch	?	J	–
C	Glory	98	With Admiral Bowyer	1788
C	Gibraltar *E	80	Spit	1780
C	Ganges	74	Py refitting	1782
O	Goliath	74	Po repairing	1781
O	Grafton	74	Po serviceable	1771
O	Grampus	50	Df repairing	1782
C	Gladiator, HS	44	Po	1783
C	Gorgon	44	M	1784
O	Greyhound	32	Limehouse repairing	1783
C	Grana, HS *E	28	Ch	1781
C	Le Goelan, *F	14	J	1793
B	Hibernia	110	PY	–
C	Hannibal	74	Py refitting	1786
C	Hector	74	With Admiral Macbride	1779
C	Hero, PS	74	R.Medway	1753
C	Hebe, *F	38	Cnl	1782
C	Hermione	32	J	1782
C	Heroine	32	EI	1783
C	Hind	28	G	1785
C	Hussar	28	Halifax	1784
C	Hawke, Sp	16	Cnl	1793
O	Hazard, Sp	16	Ch	1794
C	Hornet, Sp	16	Df fitting	1794
C	Hound, Sp	16	J	1790
C+	Helena, Sp	14	Spit	1778
C	Impregnable	90	Spit	1786
C	Illustrious	74	M	1789
C	Invincible	74	Cruising	1765
C	Irresistable	74	WI	1782
O	Indefatigable	64	Po serviceable	1784
C	Inflexible, SS	64	Spit	1780
C	Intrepid	64	Py for J	1770
O	Isis	50	Sh	1774
C	L'Imperieuse *F	40	G	1793
C	Inconstant	36	M	1783
C	Iphigenia	32	J	1780
C	Iris	32	N	1783
C	Inspector, Sp	16	WI	1782

Status	Ship	Guns	Locations	Year Built
C	Incendiary, FS	14	Py refitting	1782
O	Jupiter	50	Sh repairing	1778
B	Jason	38	Df	–
C	Juno	32	M	1780
C	King's Fisher, Sp	18	Cruising	1782
O	Kite, Cut	14	Po	1778
O	London	98	Po	1766
C	Leviathan	74	Spit	1790
C	Lion	64	To China Sept 1792	1777
O	Leander	50	Po	1780
C	Leopard, GS	50	Downs	1790
C	Latona	38	Cnl	1781
C	Leda	36	M	1783
C	Lowestoffe	32	M	1762
B	Lively	32	Northam	–
C	Lapwing	28	Wo fitting	1785
C	Lizard	28	Lisbon	1757
C	Lark, Sp	16	Wo fitting	1794
O	Lynx, Sp	16	Wo serviceable	1794
C	Liberty, Cut	16	Cruising	1779
C	Lutin *F	16	Newfoundland	1793
C	Lutine, Bb	?	M	–
O	Magnificent	74	Po serviceable	1766
C	Majestic	74	With Admiral Rowley	1785
C	Marlborough	74	Spit	1767
B	Mars	74	Df	–
C	Minotaur	74	Cnl	1793
C	Monarch	74	Cnl	1765
C	Montague	74	With Admiral Bowyer	1779
C	Magnanime	64	Py repairing	1780
O	Modeste, R *F	64	Po	1759
O	Monmouth	64	Po repairing	1773
O	Medway, R	60	Py	1755
O	Medusa, GS	50	Cork	1785
C	La Modeste *F	40	M	1793
C	Minerva	38	EI	1780
C	Melampus	36	With Admiral Macbride	1785
C	Magiciene *F	32	WI	1781
C	Meleager	32	M	1785
C	Mermaid	32	Sh	1785
O	Maidstone	28	Sh repairing	1758
O	Medea	28	Po reparing	1778
O	Mercury	28	Po	1780
C	Myrmidon, Slopship	20	Py	1780
O	Merlin, Sp	20	Sh repairing	1777
C	Martin, Sp	14	Cruising	1789
C	Megaera, FS	14	spit	1782
C	Mutine, Cut *F	14	Cnl	1778

Status	Ship	Guns	Locations	Year Built
C	Mary, Yt	10	Df repairing	1723
C	Medina, Yt	10	Isle of Wight	1771
C	Marie Antoinette, Sch *F	10	J	1793
B	Neptune	98	Df	–
O	Namur	90	Py	1756
O	Nassau	64	Py repairing	1785
C	Nonsuch	64	Ch	1774
C	La Nymphe *F	36	With Admiral Macbride	1780
C	Niger	32	Spit	1759
C	Nemesis	28	M	1780
C	Narcisus	20	Df fitting	1781
C	Nautilus, Sp	16	WI	1784
C	Nimble, Cut	14	North Sea	1781
B	Ocean	98	Wo	–
C	Orion	74	Cnl	1787
C	L'Orseau *F	36	spit	1793
C	Orpheus	32	EI	1780
C+	Orestes, Sp *Bat	18	Spit	1781
C+	Otter, Sp	14	Sh	1782
O	Prince George	98	Ch serviceable	1772
C	Princess Royal	98	M	1773
B	Prince of Wales	98	Po	–
O	Prince	98	Po	1788
C	Le Pegase, HS *F	74	Po	1782
C	Powerful	74	J	1783
O	Polyphemus	64	Ch serviceable	1782
O	Prothee *F	64	Po repairing	1780
O	Prudent	64	Py repairing	1768
O	Prince Edward, R *Bat	60	Ch	1781
O	Portland	50	Po repairing	1770
O	Princess Caroline, R *Bat	50	Sh	1781
C	Phaeton	38	Cnl	1782
O	La Prudente *F	38	Po serviceable	1779
O	Perserverence	36	Po	1781
O	Phoenix	36	Wo	1783
C	Pallas	32	Cnl	1794
C	Pearl	32	Milford	1762
C	Penelope	32	J	1783
C	Pegasus	28	Spit	1779
C	Pomona	28	Spit	1778
C	La Prompte *F	28	Po	1793
C	Proserpine	28	Spit	1777
C	Porcupine	24	Py	1779
O	Prosperity, ASSp, R	22	Sh	1782
C	Perseus	20	Py refitting	1776
O	Peterell, Sp	16	Ch fitting	1794

Status	Ship	Guns	Locations	Year Built
C	Providence, Sp	16	Wo	1791
B	Pylades, Sp	16	Rotherhithe	–
C	Pluto	14	Newfoundland	1782
C	Pilote, Cut *F	14	Cruising	1778
O	Portsmouth, Yt	8	Po serviceable	1755
O	Princess Augusta, Yt	8	Df	1710
C	Placentia, Sp	?	Newfoundland	1790
C	Queen Charlotte	100	Spit	1790
C	Queen	98	Spit	1769
C	Quebec	32	Madeira	1781
C	Royal George	100	Cnl	1788
C	Royal Sovereign	100	Spit	1786
C	Royal William	84	Spit	1719
C	Ramillies	74	With Admiral Bowyer	1785
C	Resolution	74	With Admiral Macbride	1770
C	Robust	74	Po refitting	1764
O	Royal Oak	74	Po repairing	1769
C	Russell	74	Cnl	1764
C	Raisonable	64	Po	1768
O	Repulse	64	Po serviceable	1780
C	Ruby	64	Spit	1775
O	Rippon, R	60	Py	1758
O	Renown	50	Ch repairing	1774
C	Romney	50	M	1762
O	Rainbow, R	44	Wo	1761
C	Regulus	44	Spit	1785
C	Resistance	44	EI	1782
C	Roebuck	44	WI	1774
O	La Reunion *F	38	Po	1793
C	Romulus	36	G	1785
C	Resource	28	WI	1778
C	Rose	28	WI	1783
C	Redoubt, Floating battery	20	Ostend	1793
O	Le Robert *F	20	Py refitting	1794
O	Racehorse, Sp	16	Sh	1783
O	Ranger, Sp	16	Df	1794
B	Rattler, Sp	16	Northam	–
C	Rattlesnake, Sp	16	WI	1791
C	Ranger, Cut	14	Cnl	1787
C	Rattler, Cut	14	Py	–
C	Resolution, Cut	14	Cnl	1779
O	Royal Charlotte, Yt	10	Df	1749
C	St George	98	M	1785
C	Sandwich, GS	98	N	1759
C	Saturn	74	Po refitting	1786
C	Suffolk	74	Spit	1765
O	Sultan	74	Po repairinng	1775

Status	Ship	Guns	Locations	Year Built
C	Swiftsure, GS	74	Cork	1787
C	St Albans	64	Cv to WI	1764
C	Sampson	64	Cv to St Helena	1781
C	Sceptre	64	WI	1781
O	Scipio	64	Ch fitting for a HS	1782
O	Standard	64	Py repairing	1782
C	Stately	64	Po refitting	1784
O	Salisbury	50	Po	1769
O	Serapis	44	Ch serviceable	1781
C	Severn	44	Py refitting	1786
C	Sheerness	44	North Sea	1787
B	Sea Horse	38	Rotherhithe	–
O	Santa Leocadia *E	36	Wo repairing	1781
C	Santa Margarita *E	36	WI	1779
C	Sole Bay	32	WI	1785
C	Southampton	32	Cnl	1757
B	Stag	32	Ch	–
C	Success	32	WI	1781
C	Syren	32	Py refitting	1782
C	Sybil	28	Df fitting	1779
C	Squirrel	24	St George's Channel	1785
C	Sphynx	20	Sh	1775
C	Savage, Sp	16	Cruising	1778
C	Scorpion, Sp	16	Cv to WI	1785
C+	Scourge,Sp	16	N	1779
C	Serpent, Sp	16	Cnl	1789
C	Shark, Sp	16	Po	1780
O+	Swallow, Sp	16	Po	1781
C	Swift, Sp	16	Po for EI	1793
C	Sea Flower, Cut	16	WI	1782
C+	Scour, Sp	14	G	1781
C+	Speedy, Sp	14	G	1782
C	Swan, Sp	14	Cv to WI	1767
C	Spitfire, Sp	14	Cruising	1782
C	Speedwell,Cut	14	Spit	1780
C	Sprightly, Cut	14	Cnl	1778
O	Sultana,Cut	14	Py	1780
C	Spider, Cut *F	12	Cnl	1782
C	Spitfire, Sch	8	J	1793
B	Téméraire	98	Ch	–
C	Terrible	74	M	1785
C	Theseus	74	Ch	1786
C	Thunderer	74	Ch fitting	1783
C	Tremendous	74	With Admiral Bowyer	1784
O	Triumph	74	Po repairing	1764
O	Trident	64	Po serviceable	1768
B	Tiger	50	Po	–
C	Trusty	50	Cork	1782

Status	Ship	Guns	Locations	Year Built
C	Thetis	38	Cnl	1782
C	Thalis	36	Po	1782
C	Terpsichore	32	WI	1786
C	Tartar	28	M	1756
C	Thisbe	28	Spit	1783
C	Triton	28	Po fitting	1773
O	Termagent, Sp	18	Sh	1781
O	La Trompeuse *F	18	Py	1794
C	Thorn, Sp	16	NN	1779
C	Trespassy, SS	?	Newfoundland	1790
O	Trimmer, Sp *F	16	Sh	1782
C	Tisiphone, Sp	12	M	1781
O	Tyral, Cut	12	Cnl	1781
C	Terror, Bb	8	Spit	1779
C	Union, HS	90	Sh	1756
C	Ulysses	44	WI	1779
B	Unicorn	32	Ch	–
B	Ville de Paris	110	Ch	–
C	Victory	100	M	1765
C	Valiant	74	Cnl	1759
C	Vanguard	74	WI	1787
O	Venerable	74	Ch serviceable	1784
C	Vengeance	74	WI	1774
C	Victorious	74	Ch fitting	1785
C	Veteran	64	WI	1787
O	Vigilant	64	Po serviceable	1774
C	Venus	32	With Admiral Rowley	1758
C	Vestal	28	North Sea	1779
O	Viper * F	18	?	1794
C	Vulture,Sp (Slopship)	14	Po	1776
C	Viper,Cut	12	Cnl	1780
C	Vesuvius, Bb	8	WI	1776
C	Windsor Castle	98	M	1790
O	Warrior	74	Po serviceable	1781
O	Warspite, R	74	Po	1758
C	Warwick, R	50	Ch	1767
C	Woolwich	44	WI	1785
C	Winchelsea	32	WI	1764
O+	Wasp, Sp	16	Sh	1782
C+	Weazle,Sp	12	Cnl	1783
C	Woolwich, Ten	10	On impress service	1788
O	William & Mary, Yt	8	Df	1694
O	Yarmouth, R	64	Py	1754
O	Zealous	74	CH serviceable	1786
C	Zebra, Sp	16	WI	1780

Reprinted from:
Navies of the Napoleonic Era, Pivka, Otta von, David and Charles Ltd, 1980

Naval Strategy and Tactics at the time of Trafalgar

by
Admiral Sir Cyprian Bridge G.C.B.

Read to the Institution of Naval Architects, July 19th 1905

In taking account of the conditions of the Trafalgar epoch we have to note two distinct but, of course, closely related matters. These are the strategic plan of the enemy and the strategic plan adopted to meet it by the British. The former of these was described in the House of Commons by William Pitt at the beginning of the war in words which may be used without change at the present time. On May 16, 1803, the war, which had been interrupted by the unstable Peace of Amiens, was definitely resumed. The struggle was now to be a war, not so much between the United Kingdom and the French nation as between the United Kingdom and the great Napoleon wielding more than the resources of France alone. Speaking a week after the declaration of war, Pitt said that any expectation of success which the enemy might have must be based on the supposition that he could break the spirit or weaken the determination of the country by harassing us with the perpetual apprehension of descents on our coasts; or else that our resources could be impaired and our credit undermined by the effects of an expensive and protracted war. More briefly stated, the hostile plan was to invade the United Kingdom, ruin our maritime trade, and expel us from our over-sea possessions, especially in the East, from which it was supposed our wealth was chiefly derived. The plan was comprehensive, but not easily concealed. What we had to do was to prevent the invasion of the United Kingdom and defend our trade and our outlying territories. As not one of the hostile objects could be attained except by making a maritime expedition of some kind, that is to say, by an expedition which had to cross restricted or extensive areas of *water*, it necessarily followed that our most effective method of defence was the keeping open of our sea communications. It became necessary for us to make such arrangements that the maritime paths by which a hostile expedition could approach our home-coasts, or hostile cruisers molest our sea-borne trade, or hostile squadrons move to the attack of our trans-marine dependencies – that all these paths should be so defended by our Navy that either the enemy would not venture to traverse them or, if he did, that he could be driven off.

Short as it is, time at my disposal permits me to give a few details. It was fully recognized that defence of the United Kingdom against invasion could not be secured by naval means alone. As in the times of Queen Elizabeth, so in those of George III, no seaman of reputation contended that a sufficient land force could be dispensed with. Our ablest seamen always held that small hostile expeditions could be prepared in secret and might be able to slip through the most complete lines of defence that we could hope to maintain. It was not discovered or alleged till the twentieth century that the crew of a dinghy could not land in this country in the face of the Navy. Therefore an essential feature of our defensive strategy was the provision of land forces in such numbers that an invader would have no chance of succeeding except he came in strength so great that his preparations could not be concealed and his expedition could not cross the water unseen.

As our Mercantile Marine was to be found in nearly every sea, though in greater accumulation in some areas than in others, its defence against the assaults of an enemy could only be ensured by the virtual ubiquity of our cruising force. This, of course, involved the necessity of employing a large number of cruisers, and of arranging the distribution of them in accordance with the relative amount and value of the traffic to be protected from molestation in different parts of the ocean. It may be mentioned here that the term "cruiser," at the time with which we are dealing, was not limited to frigates and smaller classes of vessel. It included also ships of the line, it being the old belief of the British Navy, justified by the experience of the many campaigns and consecrated by the approval of our greatest admirals, that the value of a ship of war was directly proportionate to her capacity for cruising and keeping the sea. If the ocean paths used by our merchant ships – the trade routes or sea communications of the United Kingdom with friendly or neutral markets and areas of production – could be kept open by our Navy, that is, made so secure that our trade could traverse them with so little risk of molestation that it could continue to be carried on, it resulted as a matter of course that no sustained attack could be made on our outlying territory. Where this was possible it was where we had failed to keep open the route or line of communications, in which case the particular trade following it was, at least temporarily, destroyed, and the territory to which the route led was either cut off or seized. Naturally, when this was perceived, efforts were made to re-open and keep open the endangered or interrupted communication line.

Napoleon, notwithstanding his super-eminent genius, made some extraordinary mistakes about warfare on the sea. The explanation of this has been given by a highly distinguished French admiral. The Great Emperor, he says, was wanting in exact appreciation of the difficulties of naval operations. He never understood that the naval officer – alone of all men in the world – must be master of two distinct professions. The naval officer must be as completely a seaman as an officer in any mercantile marine; and, in addition to this, he must be as accomplished in the use of the material of war entrusted to his charge as the members of any armed force in the world. The Emperor's plan for the invasion of the United Kingdom was conceived on a grand scale. A great army, eventually 130,000 strong, was collected on the coast of North-Eastern France, with its headquarters at Boulogne. The numerical strength of this army is worth attention. By far the larger part of it was to have made the first descent on our territory; the remainder was to be a reserve to follow as quickly as possible. It has been doubted if Napoleon really meant to invade this country, the suggestion being that his collection of an army on the shores of the Straits of Dover and the English Channel was merely a "blind" to cover another intended movement. The overwhelming weight of authoritative opinion is in favour of the view that the project of invasion was real. It is highly significant that he considered so large a number of troops necessary. It could not have been governed by any estimate of the naval obstruction to be encountered during the sea passage of the expedition, but only by the amount of the land force likely to be met if the disembarkation on our shores could be effected. The numerical strength in troops which Napoleon thought necessary compelled him to make preparations on so great a scale that concealment became quite impossible. Consequently an important part of his plan was disclosed to us betimes, and the threatened locality indicated to us within comparatively narrow limits of precision.

Notwithstanding his failure to appreciate all the difficulties of naval warfare, the Great Emperor had grasped one of its leading principles. Before the Peace of Amiens, indeed before his campaign in Egypt, and even his imposing triumphs in Italy, he had seen that the invasion of the United Kingdom was impracticable without first obtaining the command of the sea. His strategic plan, therefore, included arrangements to secure this. The details of the plan were changed from time to time as conditions altered; but the main object was adhered to until the final abandonment of the whole scheme under pressure of circumstances as embodied in Nelson and his victorious brothers-in-arms. The gunboats, transport boats, and other small craft, which to the number of many hundreds filled the ports of North-Eastern France and the Netherlands, were not the only naval components of the expedition. Fleets of line-of-battle ships were essential parts of it, and on their effective action the success of the scheme was largely made to depend. This feature remained unaltered in principle when, less than twelve months before Trafalgar, Spain took part in the war as Napoleon's ally, and brought him a great reinforcement of ships and important assistance in money.

We should not fail to notice that, before he considered himself strong enough to undertake the invasion of the United Kingdom, Napoleon found it necessary to have at his disposal the resources of other countries besides France, notwithstanding that by herself France had a population more than 60 per cent greater than that of England. By the alliance with Spain he had added largely to the resources on which he could draw. Moreover, his strategic position was geographically much improved. With the exception of that of Portugal, the coast of Western Continental Europe, from the Texel to Leghorn, and somewhat later to Taranto also, was united in hostility to us. This complicated the strategic problem which the British Navy had to solve, as it increased the number of points to be watched; and it facilitated the junction of Napoleon's Mediterranean naval forces with those assembled in his Atlantic ports by supplying him with allied ports of refuge and refit on Spanish territory; such as Cartagena or Cadiz; between Toulon and the Bay of Biscay. Napoleon, therefore, enforced upon us by the most convincing of all arguments the necessity of maintaining the British Navy at the "two-power standard" at least. The lesson had been taught us long before by Philip II, who did not venture on an attempt at invading this country till he was master of the resources of the whole Iberian peninsula as well as of those of the Spanish dominions in Italy, in the Burgundian heritage, and in the distant regions across the Atlantic Ocean.

At several ports on the long stretch of coast of which he was now the master, Napoleon equipped fleets that were to unite and win for him the command of the sea during a period long enough to permit the unob-structed passage of his invading army across the water which separated the starting points of his expedition from the United Kingdom. Command of the sea to be won by a powerful naval combination was thus an essential element in Napoleon's strategy in the time of Trafalgar. It was not in deciding what was essential that this soldier of stupendous ability erred: it was in choosing the method of gaining the essential that he went wrong. The British strategy adopted in opposi-tion to that of Napoleon was based on the acquisition and preservation of the command of the sea. Formu-lated and carried into effect by seamen, it differed in some important features from his. We may leave out of sight for the moment the special arrangements made in the English Channel to oppose the movements of Napoleon's flotillas of gunboats, transport boats, amid other small craft. The British strategy at the time of Trafalgar, as far as it was concerned with opposition to Napoleon's sea-going fleets, may be succinctly de-scribed as stationing off each of the ports in which the enemy's forces were lying a fleet or squadron of suitable strength. Though some of our admirals, notably Nelson himself, objected to the application of the term "blockade" to their plans, the hostile ships were to this extent blockaded, that if they should come out they would find outside their port a British force sufficient to drive them in again or even to defeat them thoroughly and destroy them, Beating them and thus having done with them, and not simply shutting them up in harbour, was what was desired by our admirals. This necessitated a close watch on the hostile ports; and how consistently that was maintained let the history of Cornwallis' command off Brest and of Nelson's off Toulon suffice to tell us.

The junction of two or more of Napoleon's fleets would have ensured over almost any single British fleet a numerical superiority that would have rendered the defeat or retirement of the latter almost certain. To meet this condition the British strategy contemplated the falling back, if necessary, of one of our detachments on another, which might be carried further, and junction with a third detachment be effected. By this step we should preserve, if not a numerical superiority over the enemy, at least so near an equality of force as to render his defeat probable and his serious maltreatment, even if undefeated, a certainty. The strategic problem before our Navy was, however, not quite so easy as this might make it seem. The enemy's concentration might be attempted either towards Brest or towards Toulon. In the latter case, a superior force might fall upon our Mediterranean fleet before our watching ships in the Atlantic could discover the escape of the enemy's ships from the Atlantic port or could follow and come up with them. Against the probability of this was to be set the reluctance of Napoleon to carry out an eccentric operation which a concentration off Toulon would necessitate, when the essence of his scheme was to concentrate in a position from which he could obtain naval control of the English Channel.

After the addition of the Spanish Navy to his own, Napoleon to some extent modified his strategic arrangements. The essential feature of the scheme remained unaltered. It was to effect the junction of the different parts of his naval force and thereupon to dominate the situation, by evading the several British fleets or detachments which were watching his. Before Spain joined him in the war his intention was that his escaping fleets should go out into the Atlantic, behind the backs, as it were, of the British ships, and then make for the English Channel. When he had the aid of Spain the point of junction was to be in the West Indies.

The remarkable thing about this was the evident belief that the command of the sea might be won without fighting for it; won, too, from the British Navy which was ready, and indeed wished to fight. We now see that Napoleon's naval strategy in the time of Trafalgar, whilst it aimed at gaining command of the sea, was based on what has been called evasion. The fundamental principle of the British naval strategy of that time was quite different. So far from thinking that the contest could be settled without one or more battles, the British admirals, though nominally blockading his ports, gave the enemy every facility for coming out in order that they might be able to bring him to action. Napoleon, on the contrary, declared that a battle would be useless, and distinctly ordered his officers not to fight one. Could it be that, when pitted against admirals whose accurate conception of the conditions of naval warfare had been over and over again tested during the hostilities ended by the Peace of Amiens, Napoleon still trusted to the efficacy of methods which had proved so successful when he was out-maneuvering and intimidating the generals who opposed him in North Italy? We can only explain his attitude in the campaign of Trafalgar by attributing to him an expectation that the British seamen of his day, tried as they had been in the fire of many years of war, would succumb to his methods as readily as the military formalists of Central Europe. Napoleon had at his disposal between 70 and 80 French, Dutch, and Spanish ships of the line, of which some 67 were available at the beginning of the Trafalgar campaign. In January, 1805, besides other ships of the class in distant waters or specially employed, we – on our side – had 80 ships of the line in commission. A knowledge of this will enable us to form some idea of the chances of success that would have attended Napoleon's concentration if it had been effected. To protect the passage of his invading expedition across the English Channel he did not depend only on concentrating his more distant fleets. In the Texel there were, besides smaller vessels, 9 sail of the line. Thus the Emperor did what we may be sure any future intending invader will not fail to do, viz., he provided his expedition with a respectable naval escort. The British naval officers of the day, who knew what war was, made arrangements to deal with this escort. Lord Keith, who commanded in the Downs, had under him 6 sail of the line in addition to many frigates and sloops; and there were 5 more line-of-battle ships ready at Spithead if required.

There had been a demand in the country that the defence of our shores against an invading expedition should be entrusted to gunboats, and what may be called coastal small craft and boats. This was resisted by the naval officers. Nelson had already said, "Our first defence is close to the enemy's ports," thus agreeing with a long line of eminent British seamen in their view of our strategy. Lord St. Vincent said that "Our great reliance is on the vigilance and activity of our cruisers at sea, any reduction in the number of which by applying them to guard our ports, inlets, and beaches would, in my judgment, tend to our destruction." These are memorable words, which we should do well to ponder in these days. The Government of the day insisted on having the coastal boats; but St. Vincent succeeded in postponing the preparation of them till the cruising ships had been manned. His plan of defence has been described by his biographer as "a triple line of barricade; 50-gun ships, frigates, sloops of war, and gun-vessels upon the coast of the enemy; in the Downs opposite France another squadron, but of powerful ships of the line, continually disposable, to support the former or attack any force of the enemy which, it might be imagined possible, might slip through the squadron hanging over the coast; and a force on the beach on all the shores of the English ports, to render assurance doubly sure." This last item was the one that St. Vincent had been compelled to adopt, and he was careful that it should be, in addition to those measures of defence in the efficacy of which he and his brother seamen believed. Concerning it his biographer makes the following remark "It is to be noted that Lord St. Vincent did not contemplate repelling an invasion of gunboats by gunboats," etc. He objected to the force of sea-fencibles, or "long-shore organization", because he considered it more useful to have the sea-going ships manned. Speaking of this coastal defence scheme, he said: "It would be a good bone for the officers to pick, but a very dear one for the country."

The defence of our ocean trade entered largely into the strategy of the time. An important part was played by our fleets and groups of line-of-battle ships which gave usually indirect, but sometimes direct, protection to our own merchant vessels, and also to neutral vessels carrying commodities to or from British ports. The strategy of the time, the correctness of which was confirmed by long belligerent experience, rejected the employment of a restricted number of powerful cruisers, and relied upon the practical ubiquity of the defending ships, which ubiquity was rendered possible by the employment of very numerous craft of moderate size. This can be seen in the lists of successive years. In January, 1803, the number of cruising frigates in commission was 107, and of sloops and smaller vessels 139, the total being 246. In 1805 the numbers were – Frigates, 108; sloops, etc., 181; with a total of 289. In 1805 the figures had grown to 129 frigates, 416 sloops, &c., the total being 545. Most of these were employed in defending commerce. We all know how completely Napoleon's project of invading the United Kingdom was frustrated. It is less well known that the measures for defending our sea-borne trade, indicated by the figures, just given, were triumphantly successful. Our Mercantile Marine increased during the war, a sure proof that it had been effectually defended. Consequently we may accept it as established beyond the possibility of refutation that branch of our naval strategy at the time of Trafalgar which was concerned with the defence of our trade was rightly conceived and properly carried into effect.

As has been stated already, the defence of our sea-borne trade, being in practice the keeping open of our ocean lines of communication, carried with it the protection, in part at any rate, of our transmarine territories. Napoleon held pertinaciously to the belief that British prosperity was chiefly due to our position in India. We owe it to Captain Mahan that we now know that the eminent American Fulton – a name of interest to the members of this Institution – told Pitt of the belief held abroad that "the fountains of British wealth are in India and China." In the great scheme of naval concentration, which the Emperor devised, seizure of British Colonies in the West Indies had a definite place. We kept in that quarter, and varied as necessary a force capable of dealing with a naval raid as well as guarding the neighbouring lines of communication. In 1803 we had 4 ships of the line in the West Indian area. In 1804 we had 6 of the same class; and in 1805, while the line-of-battle-ships were reduced to 4, the number of frigates was increased from 9 to 25. Whether our Government divined Napoleon's designs on India or not, it took measures to protect our interests there. In January, 1804, we had on the Cape of Good Hope and the East Indies Stations, both together, 6 sail of the line, 3 smaller two-deckers, 6 frigates, and 6 sloops, or 21 ships of war in all. This would have been sufficient to repel a raiding attack made in some strength. By the beginning of 1805 our East Indies force had been increased; and in the year 1805 itself we raised it to a strength of 41 ships in all, of which 9 were of the line and 17 were frigates. Had, therefore, any of the hostile ships managed to get to the East Indies from the Atlantic or the Mediterranean ports, in which they were being watched by our navy, their chances of succeeding in their object would have been small indeed.

When we enter the domain of tactics strictly so called, that is to say, when we discuss the proceedings of naval forces whether single ships, squadrons, or fleets, in hostile contact with one another, we find the time of Trafalgar full of instructive episodes. Even with the most recent experience of naval warfare vividly present to our minds, we can still regard Nelson as the greatest of tacticians. Naval tactics may be roughly divided into two great classes or sections, viz., the tactics of groups of ships, that is to say, fleet actions; and the tactics of what the historian James calls "single ship actions," that is to say, fights between two individual ships. In the former the achievements of Nelson stand out with incomparable brilliancy. It would be impossible to describe his method fully except in a rather lengthy treatise. We may, however, say that Nelson was an innovator, and that his tactical principles and methods have been generally misunderstood down to this very day. If

ever there was an admiral who was opposed to an
unthinking, headlong rush at an enemy it was he. Yet
this is the character that he still bears in the conception
of many. He was, in truth, an industrious and patient
student of tactics, having studied them in what in these
days we should call a scientific spirit, at an early
period, when there was but little reason to expect that
he would ever be in a position to put to a practical test
the knowledge that he had acquired and the ideas that
he had formed. He saw that the old battle formation in
single line ahead was insufficient if you wanted as he
himself always did – to gain an overwhelming victory.
He also saw that, though an improvement on the old
formation, Lord Howe's innovation of the single line
abreast was still a good deal short of tactical perfection.
Therefore, he devised what he called, with pardonable
elation, the "Nelson touch", the attack in successive
lines so directed as to overwhelm one part of the
enemy's fleet, whilst the other part was prevented
from coming to the assistance of the first, and was
in its turn overwhelmed or broken up. His object was
to bring a larger number of his own ships against a
smaller number of the enemy's. He would by this
method destroy the part attacked, suffering in the
process so little damage himself that with his whole
force he would be able to deal effectively with the
hostile remnant if it ventured to try conclusions with
him. It is of the utmost importance that we should
thoroughly understand Nelson's fundamental tactical
principle, viz., the bringing of a larger number of ships
to fight against a smaller number of the enemy's.
There is not, I believe, in the whole of the records
of Nelson's opinions and actions a single expression

tending to show that tactical efficiency was considered by him to be due to superiority in size of individual ships of the same class or – as far as *materiel* was concerned – to anything but superior numbers, of course at the critical point. He did not require, and did not have, more ships in his own fleet than the whole of those in the fleet of the enemy. What he wanted was to bring to the point of impact, when the fight began, a larger number of ships than were to be found in that part of the enemy's line.

I believe that I am right in saying that, from the date of Salamis downwards, history records no decisive naval victory in which the victorious fleet has not succeeded in concentrating against a relatively weak point in its enemy's formation a greater number of its own ships. I know of nothing to show that this has not been the rule throughout the ages of, which detailed history furnishes us with any memorial no matter what the class of ship, what the type of weapon, what the mode of propulsion. The rule certainly prevailed in the battle of August 10 last off Port Arthur, though it was not so overwhelmingly decisive as some others. We do not yet know enough of the recent sea fight in the Straits of Tsushima to be able to describe it in detail; but we do know that at least some of the Russian ships were defeated or destroyed by a combination of Japanese ships against them.

Looking back at the tactics in the time of Trafalgar, we may see that the history of them confirms the experience of earlier wars, viz., that victory does not necessarily fall to the side which has the biggest ships. It is a well-known fact of naval history that generally the French ships were larger and the Spanish much larger than the British ships of corresponding classes. This superiority in size certainly did not carry with it victory in action. On the other hand, British ships were generally bigger than the Dutch ships with which they fought; and it is of great significance that at Camperdown the victory was due not to superiority in the size of individual ships, but, as shown by the different lists of killed and wounded, to the act of bringing a larger number against a smaller. It remains to be seen how far the occurrences in the battle of the Japan Sea will support or be opposed to this conclusion; but it may be said that there is nothing tending to upset it in the previous history of the present war in the Far East.

I do not know how far I am justified in expatiating on this point; but, as it may help to bring the strategy and tactics of the Trafalgar epoch into practical relation with the stately science of which in our day this Institution is, as it were, the mother-shrine and metropolitical temple, you may allow me to dwell upon it a little longer. The object aimed at by those who favour great size of individual ships is not, of course, magnitude alone. It is to turn out a ship which shall be more powerful than an individual antagonist. All recent development of man-of-war construction has taken the form of producing, or at any rate trying to produce, a more powerful ship than those of earlier date, or belonging to a rival navy. I know the issues that such statements are likely to raise; and I ask you, as naval architects, to bear with me patiently when I say what I am going to say. It is this: If you devise for the ship so produced the tactical system for which she is specially adapted you must, in order to be logical,

base your system on her power of defeating her particular antagonist. Consequently, you must abandon the
principle of concentration of superior numbers against
your enemy; and, what is more, must be prepared to
maintain that such concentration on his part against
yourself would be ineffectual. This will compel a
reversion to tactical methods, which made a fleet
action a series of duels between pairs of combatants,
and – a thing to be pondered on seriously – never
enabled anyone to win a decisive victory on the sea.
The position will not be made more logical if you
demand both superior size and also superior numbers,
because if you adopt the tactical system appropriate to
one of the things demanded, you will rule out the
other. You cannot employ two different and opposed
tactical systems.

It is not necessary to the line of argument above
indicated to ignore the merits of the battleship class.
Like their predecessors, the ships of the line, it is really
battleships which in a naval war dominate the situation. We saw that it was so at the time of Trafalgar, and
we see that it has been so in the war at present in
progress, at all events throughout the 1904 campaign.
The experience of naval war, down to the close of that
in which Trafalgar was the most impressive event, led
to the virtual abandonment of ships of the line above
and below a certain class. The 64-gun ships and
smaller two-deckers had greatly diminished in number, and repetitions of them grew more and more rare.
It was the same with the three deckers, which, as the
late Admiral Colomb pointed out, continued to be
built, though in reduced numbers, not so much for
their tactical efficiency as for the convenient manner in

which they met the demands for the accommodation required in flag-ships.

The tactical condition which the naval architects of the Trafalgar period had to meet was the employment of an increased number of two-deckers of the medium classes.

A fleet of ships of the line as long as it could keep the sea, that is until it had to retreat into port before a stronger fleet, controlled a certain area of water. Within that area smaller men-of-war as well as friendly merchant ships were secure from attack. As the fleet moved about, so the area moved with it. Skilful disposition and mancrnivring added largely to the extent of sea within which the maritime interests that the fleet was meant to protect would be safe. It seems reasonable to expect that it will be the same with modern fleets of suitable battleships.

The tactics of "single ship actions" at the time of Trafalgar were based upon pure seamanship backed up by good gunnery. The better a captain handled his ship the more likely he was to beat his antagonist. Superior speed, where it existed, was used to "gain the weather gage," not in order to get a suitable range for the faster ship's guns, but to compel her enemy to fight. Superior speed was also used to run away, capacity to do which was not then, and ought not to be now, reckoned a merit in a ship expressly constructed for fighting, not fleeing. It is sometimes claimed in these days that superior speed will enable a modern ship to keep at a distance from her opponent which will be the best range for her own guns. It has not been explained why a range which best suits her guns should not be equally favourable for the guns of her opponent; unless, indeed, the latter is assumed to be weakly armed, in which case the distance at which the faster ship might engage her would be a matter of comparative indifference. There is nothing in the tactics of the time of Trafalgar to make it appear that – when a fight had once begun – superior speed, of course within moderate limits, conferred any considerable tactical advantage in "single ship actions," and still less in general or fleet actions.

Taking up a position ahead or astern of a hostile ship so as to be able to rake her was not facilitated by originally superior speed so much as by the more damaged state of the ship to be raked. Raking, as a rule, occurring rather late in an action.

A remarkable result of long experience of war made itself clearly apparent in the era of Trafalgar. I have already alluded to the tendency to restrict the construction of line-of-battle ships to those of the medium classes. The same thing may be noticed in the case of the frigates. Those of 44, 40, and 28 guns relatively or absolutely diminished in number; whilst the number of the 38-gun, 36-gun, and 32-gun frigates increased. The officers who had personal experience of many campaigns were able to impress on the naval architects of the day the necessity of recognising the sharp distinction that really exists between what we should now call the "battleship" and what we should now call the "cruiser." In the earlier time there were ships which were intermediate between the ship of the line and the frigate. These were the two deckers of 56, 54, 50, 44, and even 40 guns. They had long been regarded as not "fit to lie in a line," and they were never counted in the frigate classes. They seemed to have held a nondescript position, for no one knew exactly how to employ them in war any more than we now know exactly how to employ our armoured cruisers, as to which it is not settled whether they are fit for general actions or should be confined to commerce defending or other cruiser service. The two-deckers just mentioned were looked upon by the date of Trafalgar as forming an unnecessary class of fighting ships. Some were employed, chiefly because they existed, on special service; but they were being replaced by true battleships on one side and true frigates on the other.

In conclusion, I would venture to say that the strategical and tactical lessons taught by a long series of naval campaigns had been mastered by our Navy by the time of the Trafalgar campaign. The effect of those lessons showed itself in our ship building policy, and has been placed on permanent record in the history of maritime achievement and of the adaptation of material means to belligerent ends.

Reprinted from *Royal Navy During the Napoleonic Era* website, http://home.gci.net

Operating Procedures, USS *Constellation*, 27 June 1798

From Captain Thomas Truxton, USN, to his Sea Lieutenants and Master:

Gentlemen, the watch lists being subdivided in the mode I prescribed, you are to observe that when all hands are employed otherwise than at Quarters, the division of work should be made under the various officers of each watch according to the nature of the work; as for instance, when at the rigging the Master will direct the Boatswain to employ his first mate in performing what is to be done at the foremast, and bowsprit, and his second mate, the main, and mizen mast, and these take in every thing that is wanting to be done or repaired, from the top-gallant mast's heads down, as well as the jib boom, gaff and what relates to the cables, sails, anchors, boats etc., etc., etc., etc.

In cleaning the ships, and performing the various work below, the Boatswain's mates, under direction of the midshipmen, and Master's mates, are to have that business performed; the carpenter, and his crew, is to have everything in order respecting the pumps, and what relates to his duty in stopping leaks, and preserving the hull etc., etc., etc.,

The gunner, and his crew are to see the guns kept dry, well puttied, and everything belonging to the cannon, or connected with the cannon, in good order, and in readiness at a moment's warning.

The Purser, Steward, and Cooper's duty has been so clearly defined, as well as the other officers, that it is unnecessary to mention it here.

Whenever a sail is in sight, I must be immediately informed, night or day, a good look-out must always be kept, and in daylight a man at each masthead. The printed, and other instructions, if attended to, must make everything appear plain and clear.

The general superintendence of the duty is by the commissioned officers; the lieutenants are particularly answerable for what relates to the guns in their respective divisions.

The Master and Boatswain the rigging etc. – the people as well as officers must repair to their stations, whenever all hands or the watch is called, and they are not to leave their post under any pretence whatever without leave.

We have an infant navy to foster, and to organize, and it must be done.

From: Office of Naval Records. *Naval Documents Related to the Quasi-War Between the United States and France. Naval Operations from February 1797 to October 1798.* (Washington, DC: 1935)